Routledge Revivals

Imperialism Intervention and Development

Originally published in 1979 *Imperialism, Intervention and Development* provides an introduction to key issues in international politics in the post-World War II era. The emphasis is on conflict – particularly the confrontation between East and West and the contention between rich industrialised nations and the poor 'developing' nations. The book debates the causes of Western intervention, expansion and counter-revolution in the Third World and the consequences of that intervention for economic development. The spectrum and depth of the articles is both comprehensive and varied, including examples of 'mainstream' academic perspectives on the issues examined, incorporating many of the radical critiques of these mainstream approaches. Other more basic material, presupposing little prior knowledge in the field is concerned is also included.

Imperialism Intervention and Development

Andrew Mack, David Plant, Ursula Doyle

First published in 1979
by Croom Helm Ltd

This edition first published in 2018 by Routledge
2 Park Square, Milton Park, Abingdon, Oxon, OX14 4RN

and by Routledge
711 Third Avenue, New York, NY 10017

Routledge is an imprint of the Taylor & Francis Group, an informa business

© 1979 Andrew Mack, David Plant, Ursula Doyle

All rights reserved. No part of this book may be reprinted or reproduced or utilised in any form or by any electronic, mechanical, or other means, now known or hereafter invented, including photocopying and recording, or in any information storage or retrieval system, without permission in writing from the publishers.

Publisher's Note
The publisher has gone to great lengths to ensure the quality of this reprint but points out that some imperfections in the original copies may be apparent.

Disclaimer
The publisher has made every effort to trace copyright holders and welcomes correspondence from those they have been unable to contact.

A Library of Congress record exists under LCCN: 79315101

ISBN 13: 978-1-138-32887-7 (hbk)
ISBN 13: 978-0-429-42739-8 (ebk)
ISBN 13: 978-1-138-38489-7 (pbk)

IMPERIALISM, INTERVENTION AND DEVELOPMENT

EDITED BY: Andrew Mack, David Plant and Ursula Doyle

CROOM HELM LONDON

©Copyright 1979 Croom Helm Ltd

Croom Helm Ltd
2-10 St John's Road, London SW11

ISBN 0-7099-0141-0

Printed in Great Britain by
Biddles Ltd, Guildford, Surrey

TABLE OF CONTENTS

PART I: IMPERIALISM AND INTERVENTION

1 Introduction

SECTION ONE: DECOLONISATION

20 Introduction

24 Anticolonial Nationalism and Western Response   T. Smith

40 Decolonisation   D. K. Fieldhouse

SECTION TWO: THE COLD WAR AND IMPERIALISM

54 Introduction

58 The Cold War and the Korean War   D. W. Ziegler

73 Did Anyone Start the Cold War?   Ronald Steel

SECTION THREE: COUNTERREVOLUTION AND REVOLT IN THE THIRD WORLD

91 Introduction

95 Patterns of Intervention   Richard Barnet

114 Counterinsurgency in the Third World: Theory and Practice   Andrew Mack

SECTION FOUR: INTERVENTION AND THE ECONOMIC IMPERATIVES OF CAPITALISM

139 Introduction

143 Scarce Resources: The Dynamic of American Imperialism   Heather Dean

160 Foreign Expansion as an 'Institutional Necessity' for U.S. Corporate Capitalism   T. H. Moran

179 Does the U.S. Require Imperialism?   S. M. Miller Roy Bennett and Cyril Alapatt

PART II: IMPERIALISM AND DEVELOPMENT

194 Introduction

SECTION FIVE: INSIDE THE THIRD WORLD

199 Introduction

203 Social Perspectives   Peter Marris

222 The Causes of Poverty: A Classification
                                         J. K. Galbraith

233 The Rational Choice   Julius Nyerere

SECTION SIX: THIRD WORLD POVERTY AND THE WEST

244 Introduction

246 The Radical Theory of Development   S. Rosen and W. Jones

257 Radical Theories of Development: An Assessment
                                       A. Mack and R. Leaver

286 Outwitting the 'Developed' Countries   Ivan Illich

SECTION SEVEN: THE WORLD POPULATION/FOOD CRISIS

298 Introduction

301 How Poverty Breeds Overpopulation
                                       Barry Commoner

315 The Reproduction Function   The Economist

323 Era of Agricultural Scarcity Looms   Survey of International Development

340 Patriarchy is Alive and Well   E. Skjønsberg

SECTION EIGHT: CHINA'S DEVELOPMENTAL APPROACH

345 Introduction

348 The Chinese Approach to Development
                                Dennis Woodward

373 China's Relevance for Third World Development
                                Bill Brugger

ACKNOWLEDGEMENTS

Barnet, R. — "Patterns of Intervention" — chapter II (abridged) of *Intervention and Revolution*. MacGibbon and Kee Ltd., London, Reprinted with permission from the author.

Brugger, W. — "China's Relevance for Third World Development". Printed with permission from the author.

Commoner, B. — "How Poverty Breeds Overpopulation" in *Ramparts*, August/September, 1975. Reprinted with permission from the author.

Dean, H. — "Scarce Resources: the Dynamics of American Imperialism" in K. Fann and D. C. Hodges, *Readings in U.S. Imperialism*, Porter Sargent, Boston 1971. Permission applied for.

The Economist — "The Reproduction Function". *The Economist*, 8th January, 1977. Reprinted with permission from *The Economist*, London.

Fieldhouse, D. K. — "Decolonisation" — chapter 17 of *The Colonial Empires*, 1966. Reprinted with permission from publisher, Weidenfeld and Nicolson Ltd., London.

Galbraith, J. K. — "The Causes of Poverty: A Classification", chapter 14 of *Economics, Peace and Laughter*. Andre Deutsch, 1971. Reprinted by permission of Andre Deutsch Ltd., London.

Illich, I. — "Outwitting the 'Developed' Countries." Reprinted with permission from *The New York Review of Books*, Copyright © 1969-71, Nyrev. Inc.

Mack, A.	"Counterinsurgency in the Third World: Theory and Practice" (abridged) *British Journal of International Studies*, No. 1, 1975. Reprinted with permission from Longman Group Ltd., London.
Marris, P.	"Social Perspectives" in Dudley Seers and Leonard Joy (eds.). *Development in a Divided World* 1971, pp. 84-105. Copyright © Penguin Books, 1970. Reprinted with permission from Penguin Books Ltd.
Miller, S.M./ Bennett, R./ Alapatt, C.	"Does the U.S. Economy Require Imperialism?" in *Social Policy*, September/October, 1970. Reprinted with permission from *Social Policy*.
Moran, T.	"Foreign Expansion as an 'Institutional Necessity' for U.S. Corporate Capitalism—The Search for a Radical Model"—in *World Politics*, April 1973. Reprinted with permission from Princeton University Press.
Nyerere, J.	"The Rational Choice" in *Freedom and Development*, Oxford University Press, 1973. Copyright Julius K. Nyerere. Reprinted with permission from the author.
Rosen, S./ Jones, W.	"The Radical Theory of Development"—extract from *The Logic of International Relations*, 1976. Reprinted with permission from Winthrop Publishers Inc.
Skjønsberg. E.	"Partriarchy is Alive and Well" in CERES, No. 44, 1975.
Smith, T.	"Anticolonial Nationalism and Western response"—extract from *The End of the European Empire: Decolonization after World War II*. Reprinted with permission from D. C. Heath and Co., Lexington, 1975.

Steel, R.	"Did Anyone Start the Cold War?" Reprinted with permission from *The New York Review of Books*. Copyright © 1969-71. Nyrev, Inc.
Survey of International Development	"Era of Agricultural Scarcity Looms" in *Survey of International Development* (November/December) 1975. Reprinted by permission of the Editor, William P. J. Boichel.
Woodward, D.	"The Chinese Approach to Development". Printed with permission from the author.
Ziegler, D. W.	"The Cold War and the Korean War"—extract from chapter 3 of *War, Peace and International Politics*. Reprinted with permission from Little Brown and Co., Boston, 1977.

Preface

A first edition of this reader was published at Flinders University under the title *East/West North/South: Intervention, Development and Imperialism.* Our decision to put the reader together followed a fruitless search for a low-cost introductory text to post-war international politics which counterposed orthodox and radical theoretical analyses of a number of key issues associated with the East/West and North/South conflict syndromes.

Five articles from the first edition have been removed and four new articles have been introduced—those of Smith, Ziegler, Brugger and the Mack article in Section Six.

The various editorial introductions and some of the locally produced contributions were typed, and after editorial mutilation, frequently re-typed, by Marie Baker, Anne Gabb and Linda Kelly of the Flinders University Politics Department.

Colin Ames, Angela Fletcher and other members of the Flinders University Relations Unit did the typesetting and layout and managed to meet deadlines despite often adverse circumstances.

Finally we would like to thank the first year Politics students at Flinders University whose enthusiasm for many of the papers included determined their selection in the first place.

PART I

IMPERIALISM AND INTERVENTION

Introduction

The selection of articles in this reader is intended to provide an introduction to some of the key issues in international politics in the post-World War II era. As the title implies, our concern is with conflict and in particular with the various manifestations of the confrontation between East and West on the one hand; and the growing conflict between North and South, the rich industrialised nations and the poor 'developing' nations, on the other.

In our choice of papers, we have tried to avoid both the behavioural social science predilection for producing ahistorical theory and the international historian's tendency to create atheoretical history. We have attempted to provide examples both of 'mainstream' academic perspectives on the various issues examined, and some of the radical critiques of these 'mainstream' approaches. We have also tried to select material which assumes no previous knowledge of the subject and which eschews unnecessary jargon.

Given the enormous range of conflict issues which this period encompasses, it has been necessary to be brutally selective. At the risk of oversimplification, we may note that the readings in Part I concentrate on the debates over the causes of various forms of Western (primarily American) counterrevolutionary intervention in the Third World since World War II. Part II consists of a series of papers which examine some of the causes of 'underdevelopment' in the Third World. Whereas Part I is concerned more with the *causes* of various forms of Western expansion into the Third World, Part II examines some of the *consequences* of that expansion for development. Both Parts I and II have been subdivided into four sections, each of which contains two or more papers which concentrate on fairly specific issues raised by the general debate.

Overview of Part I

The first section of Part I examines the origins and evolution of the decolonisation struggle in the Third World in the post war period. This essentially North/South conflict was deeply affected by the contemporaneous development of the conflict between East and West, which is the focus of the second section of Part I. In the third and fourth sections, we present a series of papers which examine some patterns and techniques of counter-revolutionary interventions in the Third World and the ongoing debate about the causes of these interventions.

In 1945, Europe's vast colonial empires were still virtually intact. By 1965, more than forty countries had rebelled successfully against alien rule, and only vestiges of direct colonial rule remained. Yet, despite formal political independence the new nations of the Third World (with a few significant exceptions) remained bound by close political, ideological and, above all, economic ties to the West. Radical critics argued that 'independence' had meant little more than a change of flag and national anthem. While formal political control had been abandoned by the metropolis, the more subtle forms of domination, which had created the 'dependency syndrome' and were now labelled 'neo-colonialism', had been strengthened.

There is no doubt that colonial rule - and the parallel penetration of Western institutions and values in areas not under direct European political domination (e.g. Latin America) - had created wrenching social change in the Third World. In Asia, Africa and Latin America, new social and economic gulfs opened between the indigenous 'modernising élites', whose members aspired to European lifestyles, and the mass of the population, which lived either in the countryside or in the swelling slums which were growing up around the major cities. Self-sufficient subsistence economies had been largely destroyed and replaced by production systems oriented towards the export of primary commodities and minerals to the West.

The stresses wrought by this western-induced 'modernisation process' also provided the social impetus for revolutionary change. The radical movements which emerged in Asia, Africa and Latin America in the 1950s, and throughout the 1960s and 1970s, were occasionally inspired and sometimes aided by the Soviet Union or China. But whether or not there was any direct link between indigenous radical revolt and the international communist movement, Third World revolution was perceived in Washington as being inspired by Moscow or Peking. The American response was consistently hostile. In fact, there is no doubt that a major thrust of US foreign policy since World War II has been to contain, and where possible, suppress revolution. The key question, one to which all the articles in Part I of this reader relate either directly or indirectly is, "why"?. Why should the world's richest, most powerful and most secure nation go to such lengths to repress radical revolts in weak underdeveloped countries thousands of miles from its frontiers? At this point, a word of explanation is perhaps necessary. Our concentration on United States policies throughout much of Part I (and some of Part II) does not arise from any particular sympathy for, or animus against, the US or American foreign policy, but simply because the United States has been the dominant global superpower in post-war international politics.

Of all the major combatants in World War II, only the United States emerged richer and more powerful in 1945 than in 1941. Only the United States had the material capability and political inclination to assume a truly global role in 1945. And in the years which followed, it was American economic power which flooded Europe with Marshall Aid to help successfully rebuild a vigorous anti-communist Europe to confront a resurgent Soviet Union. It was American economic power which created a new, post-war international economic order, following the Bretton Woods conference, held in 1944, even before the war was over. The core institutions of this new Western economic order, the International Monetary Fund and the World Bank, were American-dominated.

United States' military power was also unsurpassed. On every continent, America's military presence was felt directly, in the form of US garrisons, or indirectly via a vast global network of military aid and assistance programmes. And with the progressive weakening and final demise of European colonialism, America's self-imposed responsibility for what was euphemistically described as 'world order' was broadened even further. Thus the United States, with its global commitments to counter-revolution in a revolutionary world, forms the central reference point for most of the key issues under discussion in this reader.

It is our contention that the relationship between revolt and counterrevolution in the Third World cannot be understood without reference to the East/West confrontation in Europe at the close of the Second World War. This confrontation, now known as the Cold War, was rooted in the struggle over the carve-up of post-war Europe between Russia and the West. In Section II, we move back in history from the end of the Third World decolonisation period in the mid 1960s, to the Europe of the 1940s, when the long simmering conflict between bourgeois democracy and the Soviet revision of Marxism first became deeply polarised.

Understanding, or attempting to understand, the origins of the Cold War is important for at least two reasons. Firstly, because the assumptions underlying the US doctrine of containing communism were accorded such wide assent in US foreign policy circles that they became a virtually unassailable conventional wisdom. Providing the ground rules for the conduct of US foreign policy for two decades, these assumptions remained unchallenged even though the configuration of world politics was to change dramatically during this period. The second reason for examining the outbreak of the Cold War is that the controversies over its causes foreshadow the later debates surrounding the motivations of US counter-revolutionary policies in the Third World. We turn to these policies and the debates over *their* motives in Sections III and IV.

Section III contains two papers which examine in some detail both the patterns of US intervention in the Third World and the evolution of American counterinsurgency methods. Both papers also discuss the motivations which underly these policies, but neither does so in any great detail. In Section IV, we turn to the question of cause or motive - "*why* has the US foreign policy been counterrevolutionary?". We examine in particular the debate surrounding the radical thesis that US foreign policy is primarily a response to the economic imperatives of American capitalism and that without secure access to expanding markets and to raw material and investment outlets, the US corporate system cannot survive. Since revolution in Third World countries is seen as threatening secure US access to Third World economic resources, revolution must be suppressed. This thesis is vigorously opposed by those (both critics and supporters of US foreign policy) who argue that economic interests rarely have more than peripheral salience in determining American opposition to radical revolt in the Third World. As we hope to show later, a number of interesting and important problems are raised when attempting to weigh up the rival claims of the protagonists of 'power politics', 'ideology' or 'economic imperialism' interpretations of the roots of American foreign policy.

The Concept of Imperialism

Throughout this reader the term 'imperialism' occurs frequently. Various concepts of imperialism and their associated theories are the source of considerable current controversy; many of these theories are central to the debates which occur in both parts of this reader. For this reason we have felt that a brief - and necessarily crude - introduction to the concept of imperialism, the different meanings assigned it and some of the debates which surround it would be of value.

The marked upsurge of interest in Marxist theories of imperialism during the past decade has been stimulated in part by the traumas of the Vietnam War, and in part by the increased awareness of the growing North/South development gap and the failure of the First UN Development Decade. These theories of imperialism have sought to explain counterrevolution and underdevelopment in the Third World from a radical perspective, and, in attempting this, they have frequently stood established and Establishment theories on their heads. Thus instead of seeing US foreign policy as oriented defensively towards a hostile and expansionist Soviet Union, theories of imperialism have argued that the reverse was true: that the US was the aggressor. US counter-revolutionism, it was argued, was a characteristic and indeed necessary response to the economic and political imperatives of the US capitalist system. The conventional wisdoms of development theory have come under a parallel attack. Whereas the liberal theories of underdevelopment in the 1950s and early 1960s argued that the causes of Third World poverty were to be found within the Third World itself, the imperialism theories argued that Third World poverty arose from rich country exploitation.

The term 'imperialism' is problematic: many different and sometimes incompatible meanings have been assigned it. *Theories* of imperialism often seek to explain quite different phenomena, or the same phenomena from different perspectives, and this complexity has led some social scientists to argue that the term ought to be banished from the vocabulary of serious scholarship. This argument has alarming implications since, if the same logic were applied to political science, we should be forced to jettison many of the discipline's core concepts - 'power', 'legitimacy', 'structure' and 'democracy' to name but a few. It must be admitted, however, that the coexistence of many different theories of imperialism - sometimes complementary, sometimes contradictory and sometimes dealing with completely different events, does pose problems.

The 'New Imperialism'

The literal meaning of the term 'imperialism' is 'rule by emperor'; no theories of imperialism use the term in this sense today. The first modern theories of imperialism are those which sought to explain the competitive scramble for overseas colonies between the major European powers in the last quarter of the 19th century and the beginning of the 20th. Known as the 'New Imperialism', this dramatic episode in world history is important for our purpose for at least three reasons. Firstly, and most obviously, the expansion overseas of European capital and institutions transformed the world. Secondly, the debate about the causes of this expansion introduces the Leninist theories and the work of J.A. Hobson, which still provide the central reference point for contemporary Marxist imperialism theories. Thirdly, this debate - between theories emphasising economic determination and others which deny it - foreshadows the later controversies over the origins of the Cold War and the causes of American interventionism in the Third World in the post World War II period.

a)   *The Leninist Theories*

Of all the theories of imperialism, that of V.I. Lenin is still the best known. Produced as a political pamphlet rather than a scholarly study, Lenin's polemic still retains a powerful political and intellectual resonance sixty years after it was published.

The core proposition of Lenin's theory is that the pressure to expand overseas which led to 'the grab for colonies' was an expression of the economic imperatives of mature capitalism; imperialism was quite simply the 'highest stage of capitalism'. Lenin and his Marxist contemporaries argued with considerable force that once a capitalist mode of production reaches a certain stage of development it confronts a series of inevitable crises. Crudely expressed, these arise out of the tendency for the productive capacity of industrial capital to outstrip the capacity for consumption of the mass of the population - this being limited by their low wages. (Note: this 'underconsumptionist' interpretation of Lenin's theory is an oversimplification of a very complex argument.) The Marxists further argued that, since any redistribution of income to augment the buying power of the masses was impossible under capitalism, an *external* solution to the crisis was necessary. The problem of 'excess capacity' or 'surplus capital' could be and was, resolved by exporting it to the so-called backward countries. Here, as Lenin had observed, profits were high; capital scarce; and land and raw materials cheap. Without this expansion overseas, capitalism would collapse from its own internal contradictions. Imperialism thus became an *institutional necessity* for the survival of capitalism at the highest stage of its development. Since each of the capitalist states of Europe confronted similar internal economic crises, all felt compelled to expand overseas. Expansion overseas necessitated political protection for the new foreign markets, investments and raw material sources, and colonial annexation served this purpose while keeping rivals out.

Lenin's study of imperialism did not deny that political motives for European colonial expansion might be important, but the theoretical basis for his analysis of imperialist expansion was the 'laws of motion' of the capitalist system. A few liberal economists like J.A. Hobson (whose research Lenin had drawn on to produce his own theory) also argued that imperialism was economically motivated. But, Hobson had argued against the Leninist thesis that imperial expansion was *necessary* for the survival of capitalism. He believed that the 'under-consumption' problem could be resolved by socio-economic reforms which would have the effect of increasing aggregate consumption levels and thus avoiding the crisis which Lenin and Marx had predicted.

Ever since Lenin's pamphlet 'Imperialism the Highest Stage of Capitalism' first appeared in 1917, the theory it espoused has been subjected to intense criticism. Most has come from liberal historians and economists who were antipathetic to Lenin's revolutionary politics, but some influential neo-Marxist theorists like Michael Barratt Brown and Harry Magdoff have also taken issue with some of Lenin's core theoretical precepts. Today, there can be little doubt that Lenin's theory is seriously, perhaps irreparably, flawed in a number of its central arguments. But the general thesis (which many liberal historians of the era rejected) of a clear, though not necessarily direct, relationship between the evolution of the capitalism in Europe and its expansion overseas seems incontestable.

b) Non-Marxist Approaches

The non-Marxist, non-economistic explanations of the 'New Imperialism' emphasised political, strategic and (to a lesser degree) ideological factors. The scramble for overseas possessions was seen by some analysts as an extension of the competitive politics of the European 'balance of power' to the world 'periphery'. From this perspective, imperialist expansion was a wholly political phenomenon; indeed, many statesmen believed that empire was desirable for its own sake, arguing not without reason, that it increased national prestige. The non-Marxists also maintained that overseas expansion had a strong *strategic* motivation. Territorial annexation abroad was sometimes necessary to protect areas of key strategic importance and trade routes or simply to prevent annexation by other powers. However, the notion of a purely 'strategic' motivation for annexation is not as clear as it appears at first sight. One of the most frequently cited examples of 'strategic' annexation is the British occupation of Egypt in 1882. Egypt's strategic importance lay in the Suez Canal, but the importance of the canal was in large part economic, since it formed the vital link between Britain and India where British economic interests were enormous. Thus, the distinction which the anti-Marxists laboured to drive between politics and economics turns out to be a false and unnecessary dichotomy. However, this example does illustrate the so-called *level of analysis* problem which occurs constantly in literature on imperialism. We are confronted with a political phenomenon (British annexations in the 1860s, or US military intervention in the 1960s) the immediate causes of which appear wholly political or strategic. But, at another, 'deeper', level of analysis the salience of economic factors cannot be ignored.

In addition to geo-political and strategic explanations of the 'New Imperialism', some historians and many statesmen of the era laid considerable stress on *ideology*, arguing that Europe had a civilising mission to fulfill in the subjugated colonies. From this perspective, Europe's role in Africa and elsewhere was to promote the betterment of Africans rather than that of Europeans. This type of explanation is most obviously applicable to the various Christian missions which streamed into the Third World in the 19th century, intending to impose their alien religious ideologies on the indigenous peoples. However, it also proved useful for self-serving statesmen who made sententious speeches about 'imperial responsibilities' and the 'white man's burden' without revealing that the latter was carried on black backs.

Contemporary Imperialism

When we turn from Europe's expansionism in the late 19th century to the debate over the origins of the Cold War, and the causes of revolution and counter-revolution in the Third World, we again find economic, strategic and ideological explanations being invoked and similar level of analysis problems occurring. Between the debates of the 19th century and those of today there are, however, two important differences.

Firstly, ideological explanations are taken more seriously today than they were previously for fairly obvious reasons. These include the 1917 Russian revolution; the creation of a communist state, ideologically committed (in theory at least) to the overthrow of capitalism; and the subsequent evolution of the Soviet Union into a global superpower. Declarations that European colonialism was motivated by an ideological crusade to bring civilisation and Christianity to heathen savages overseas were rarely taken seriously, except perhaps by missionaries themselves. At most they served as justificatory rationalisations for annexationist policies designed to benefit the colonisers rather than the colonised. However, ideology cannot be so lightly dismissed as an explanatory factor when examining the origins of the Cold War or the causes of US involvement in Vietnam. The 'crusade against communism' was very real.

The second difference lies with the political connotations of the term 'imperialism' itself. Among students of the 'New Imperialism', there was no doubt that the expansionism which they sought to explain was indeed imperialism. Today, assigning precise meanings to the concept of imperialism is extremely difficult. This is largely because the term now has connotations which are wholly pejorative and critical. This was not always the case. Although Hobson and Lenin were critical of imperialism, many 19th century statesmen could describe themselves with evident pride as 'imperialists'; today, the term would never be used for self-description. To label a nation's foreign policy 'imperialist' today is not merely to describe but also to criticise it. The potential for confusion is obvious when we note that left wing radicals use the term 'imperialist' to describe US foreign policy, while right-wing conservatives use the same term to characterise Soviet foreign policy. The Chinese depict *both* US and USSR as imperialist powers.

In common usage, the term 'imperialism' suggests the domination, or attempted domination, by one nation of other nations. This domination does not have to be direct, as is the case with colonialism or military occupation, it may be effected by less obtrusive economic and political means. When the latter is the case, the term 'neo-colonialism' or neo-imperialism is often used. Imperialism may even take the form of cultural dominance or hegemony - in this case the term 'cultural imperialism' may be employed.

However, Marxist and neo-Marxist theorists argue, with some force, that the term 'imperialism' should be limited to those theories which locate the *causes* of the impetus to foreign domination within the economic imperatives of the capitalist system. And the common emphasis on economic imperatives, on the *institutional necessity* for overseas expansionism, unites the Leninist theories of 19th century imperialism with contemporary neo-Marxist theories. However other non-Marxist critics of American foreign policy also describe American interventionism in the Third World as 'imperialist' without claiming (indeed sometimes denying) that it is motivated primarily by economic necessity. None of these usages is 'correct' or 'incorrect', but again we must warn that differences exist and recognise that different usages are important.

The Cold War and Intervention

A major difficulty in analysing the origins of the Cold War or the causes of interventionism in the Third World is not that we have no explanations for these events, but that we have too many. A situation in which we have more than one adequate explanation for the phenomena to be explained is said to be 'over-determined'. In such a situation, it is difficult to know what criteria we should use to choose between the competing explanations. It may also be the case that the different explanatory foci are not contradictory but complementary, and that no choice is necessary. Both the level of analysis problem, noted earlier, and that of 'over determination' are prevalent in the controversies over the origins of the Cold War and the causes of US counter-revolutionary policies in the Third World.

As in the case of the debates over the causes of 19th century imperialism, we can discern three *analytically* separable explanatory approaches to the origins of the Cold War and America's subsequent counter-revolutionary foreign policy orientation. These approaches stress the primacy of 'ideological', 'strategic' and 'economic' causation respectively. The first two sets of factors are frequently conjoined, while theories emphasising the economic determination of foreign policy tend to stand apart. The latter are associated with Marxist approaches and are rarely propounded by conservative or 'mainstream' scholars. It should be noted that the following descriptions of each approach are *purely analytic* - that is to say they represent an *artificial* isolation of the different factors for the purpose of analysis. Such isolation would never occur in reality. The 'ideology'/'strategy' distinction is particularly difficult to maintain when attempting to explain anti-communist foreign policies.

a) The Ideological Approach

Here the primary assumption is that foreign policy is motivated by ideological imperatives. 'Ideology' is loosely defined for our purposes as the set of core political values which infuse the world view of the foreign policy élite. These core values are said to determine foreign policy, and conflict between nations derives from conflicting national ideologies. In the case of the Cold War and interventionism, the absolute incompatibility of capitalist and communist ideologies is claimed to cause conflict between the Soviet and American states. On the western side, the conflict is seen in terms of 'freedom versus tyranny', or 'democracy versus totalitarianism' and so forth. The communist states naturally see things differently. For pro-Western ideologues, communism is to be opposed because it is *evil*. In its pure form, the ideological approach predicts conflict between capitalist and communist states, *even where there are no strategic or economic interests at stake*. Alliances are made between nations on the basis of political affinity. Thus the NATO alliance and the Warsaw Pact link nations with similar ideologies, and in opposition to others with antipathetic ideologies. Ideology serves to cement the link between countries within each alliance, while also defining the antagonism between the alliances.

b) The Strategic or Power Politics Approach

Here the argument is somewhat different. The strategic or 'power politics' approach in its purest form appears completely amoral. It is based on the simple, and not implausible, assumption that international politics is essentially anarchic and resembles a Darwinian struggle for survival between nations. In the absence of a supra-national world government able to create a framework of law analagous to that which exists within the frontiers of a nation state, *all* nations will try to maximise their power. Indeed the 'struggle for power' is held to be the very essence of international political activity. Alliances are formed *not* on the basis of political affinity but on the criterion of 'national interest'. Alliances are marriages of convenience and may be made with nation states of *any* ideological persuasion. Thus, from this perspective, the hostility between the United States and the Soviet Union would exist *regardless* of their different ideologies.

If foreign policy were motivated purely by ideological factors, the 1970s US rapprochement with China - the most obviously communist of the socialist states - would not have made sense. In terms of the strategic approach, it makes perfect sense. Since conflict between states is the very essence of international politics, the more powerful a state is the greater the threat it poses to other states, irrespective of its ideological persuasion. In reality, it is extremely difficult to disentangle these different motivations - yet the distinctions may be important. For the ideologues, communism must be opposed because it is evil, even if it poses no obvious threat. But the 'realpolitik' rationality of a pure 'power politics' or 'strategic' approach would define the ideologues' position as both naive and dangerous. For the latter, the morality of communism is beside the point - the Soviet Union should be vigorously opposed if and when its actions are seen as intruding on Western spheres of influence, otherwise it can be left alone. In a great many cases the two approaches prescribe exactly the same policy. From the American point of view, for example, both ideological imperatives and those of power politics would *seem* to require that communism be contained and revolution repressed. But this is not always the case.

During the 1960s there was a growing realisation within the US foreign policy élite that communism was not (as had been previously assumed) a Moscow-controlled monolith. The Sino-Soviet split made it quite clear that communist states could be just as nationalistic and antipathetic towards each other as capitalist states. From a 'power politics' perspective, this in turn meant that communist revolutions were a far less serious cause for alarm than had previously been believed. But for the anti-communist ideologue, the problem with communism was not simply that it posed a threat to US security, but that it was *evil* and should be opposed for this reason.

c) *The Economic or 'Imperialism' Approach*

In their most specific formulations, economic explanations of expansionism and intervention argue that such policies derive from the economic imperatives of advanced capitalism. The US opposes communism not because of any moral commitment to freedom or ideological antipathy to totalitarianism, nor for reasons of security, but because communism (and other non-communist revolutions) threaten vital US global *economic* interests. If Third World or even advanced capitalist countries such as Italy or France, succumb to communism, then US access to important markets and vital strategic raw materials (such as oil and rare minerals) will be blocked; the flow of profits from US investments overseas will dry up, and the vast assets of US multinational corporations will be lost as the victorious revolutionaries nationalise foreign firms. Denied these outlets and resources, the US corporate capitalist economy will succumb to crisis. (The parallels with Lenin's theory here are quite obvious). Hence, the prime function of US foreign policy must be to protect these economic interests by crushing any political movements which attempt to threaten them. Communism and other forms of radical left-wing nationalism pose the most obvious threats in this context, but threats from other capitalist powers must also be resisted. From this perspective, the US is seen as having supported independence movements against colonial rule in Africa in the 1950s largely because American corporations wanted access to the market and investment opportunities which that continent offered. Capitalist Europe's colonial system denied the US access to these market and investment opportunities, so the US supported (albeit sometimes ambiguously) African independence movements in their struggle against European domination. A second motive for supporting 'moderate' independence movements is the obvious one of keeping the communists out. In fact, ultimately, the US was even prepared to support liberation movements which espoused radical ideologies in Portuguese Africa in an abortive attempt to keep other radical movements closely aligned with Moscow out of power.

Since the US has frequently intervened in conflicts in which no direct US economic interests of any consequence are at stake, many liberal theorists claim that these cases invalidate the imperialism theories of intervention. Vietnam is the most obvious case, since here was an example of a huge US military investment in an area with virtually no American economic interests. There are a number of responses to this critique.

First, it is claimed that the US had to 'defend' Vietnam because the demonstration effect of a communist victory there could have triggered insurgencies in areas where the US *did have vital economic interests*. And since the US *was* worried about the demonstration effect - this being the sophisticated version of the Domino Theory of communist expansionism - this argument has a certain plausibility. But it also, of course, makes the imperialism thesis more difficult to falsify. However, there is a more serious objection. The *Pentagon Papers* revealed that an ideological obsession with the dangers of communism led the United States into the Vietnam war and that, in the decisions leading to intervention, US global economic interests were virtually ignored. Remembering that the *Pentagon Papers* were based on secret and confidential policy papers and memoranda, this seems to be a powerful indictment of the economic imperatives approach. The sophisticated Marxist response to this critique is to agree with the facts but immediately to raise the question of the *origins* of the anti-communist ideology which did determine the decision to intervene. Here, we have another example of the *level of analysis problem*. In terms of immediate causation, we can see from *The Pentagon Papers* that ideology was clearly critical in the decision to intervene, whereas economic imperatives were of negligible *direct* importance. But now the key question becomes: "whence the ideology?". In fact, there can be no doubt that the origins of the western ideological antipathy to communism are intimately related to the perceived imperatives of the capitalist system: anti-communist and pro-capitalist imperatives are but two sides of the same coin. Without pressing the point too far, we can see that, whereas the US involvement in Vietnam appears at first to invalidate the economic imperatives approach, this is not necessarily the case. The first radical counter-argument derived from alleged US concern with the demonstration effect. This made the economic imperatives thesis difficult to falsify. The second counter-argument renders this imperialism theory quite unfalsifiable. This is sufficient reason for behavioural social scientists to reject the thesis in its entirety. However students of international politics are under no obligation to accept the methodological canons of behaviouralism, and we should not forget that arguments which cannot be falsified may still be true.

Imperialism and Underdevelopment

The theories of imperialism discussed above sought to explain the *causes* of capitalist expansion into the Third World. The imperialism theories dealing with underdevelopment, to which we now turn, examine the *consequences* of this expansion for economic development *in* the Third World.

Insofar as Lenin paid any attention to the problem of development, it was to argue that imperialism would ultimately *promote* capitalist development in the colonies. Capitalists might be motivated by greed - and capitalism was certainly exploitative, but it was nevertheless ultimately a progressive force. Destroying the bonds of 'traditional society', and liberating people from what Marx called the 'idiocy of rural life', the capitalist mode of production revolutionised the productive capacities of human labour. Capitalism held the potential assurance that the material needs of society could be more than satisfied. To turn the potential into reality required socialism, and, since capitalism bore within itself the seeds of its own destruction, that potential would be realised.

a) Liberal Democratic Theories

In the 1950's and early 1960's, most non-radical development theorists also believed that capitalism was a progressive force - though not because it led to revolution. For these theorists, the underdevelopment of the Third World is to be understood in terms of the persistence of pre-capitalist values and institutions. Pre-capitalist modes of production such as subsistence farming were grossly inefficient, and without scientific knowledge or mechanical aids agricultural productivity was extremely low. Any surpluses generated were so small that they were immediately consumed rather than being used for productive investment. Promoting development in such a context requires the penetration of capitalist values, technology and institutions. According to this view, those societies most deeply penetrated by capitalist production relations will be the wealthiest and most developed; those least penetrated will be the poorest and least developed. In the former category, we would find Singapore, Mexico, the Ivory Coast and Brazil; in the latter, countries like Afghanistan, Mali, Paraguay and Burma.

For the liberal development theorist, the track record of capitalism in the rich countries provided proof enough that, *in principle*, the poor nations could break out of the poverty trap. The real barriers to progress are argued to arise within these nations, and particularly from the persistence of traditional values and institutions, and from the difficulties of adapting to new values and new forms of social and economic organisation. 'Traditional' values might differ enormously across different Third World countries, but whatever the differences, this 'traditionalism' was held to be incongruent (to a greater or lesser degree) with 'modern'values. Traditional societal values were said to lack 'achievement orientation'; to engender minimal interest in material gain; and to have little interest in, or understanding of, the virtues of saving, investment and the need to defer gratification when working for long term goals. Liberal development theories had, and still have, bastardised analogues in popular and racist European notions that Africans and Asians are poor because they are innately stupid and inferior. However, it should be immediately said that *no* liberal development theories have made such racist claims.

The liberal argument stressed that non-European *cultural* relations and values were inimical to successful capitalist development. Variations in value systems in different Third World societies meant that some adapted more easily than others to the requirement of capitalist production relations. However, values were only a part of the problem. Third World countries also lacked the *infrastructure* (roads, railways, harbours, communication systems), the technology and the capital for successful development. To the problem (incongruent values and inadequate infrastructure) thus diagnosed, the solution was the *diffusion* of values, technology and capital from the rich countries to the poor. The diffusion process has been ongoing now for more than a hundred years - colonialism, foreign trade, aid and investment have all played a part. Persisting underdevelopment may arise from insufficient diffusion and/or continued resistance to diffusion by 'traditional' elements.

b) Marxist Theories of Imperialism and Underdevelopment

Modern Marxists reject the sanguine view of the progressive character of western capitalism articulated by the liberal democratic theorists and, somewhat differently, by Marx himself and by Lenin. The neo-Marxists argue a very different case. Third World countries are locked into a 'dependency' syndrome which locates them at the bottom end of the international division of labour (see below). They are burdened by mushrooming debts and huge balance of payments deficits, and their consumption patterns are tied to the manufactured products of the West. Marxists (with a few exceptions) today argue that the opportunities for *relatively independent industrial growth* - such as existed for Europe, America and Japan previously - no longer exist for Third World countries under capitalist relations of production. Third World poverty, the impossibility of independent capitalist development, and the growing gap between the rich nations and the poor are all functions of *imperialism* according to the new Marxist theories.

The theories of imperialism discussed previously sought to explain colonialism and counterrevolution as responses to the alleged imperatives of advanced capitalist nations which required access to Third World raw materials, markets and cheap labour. Since socialist revolutions threatened this access, any moves towards socialist development had to be blocked. Thus the imperialism/intervention theories, which derived originally from Lenin, provide plausible (not necessarily correct) explanations for the absence of socialist development in the Third World. But they do not provide any satisfactory explanations for the problems associated with *capitalist* development in the Third World.

As already noted the theories which concentrate on underdevelopment rather than intervention, are concerned essentially with the consequences of capitalist expansion in the Third World rather than its causes. These theories return to the 'technical' Leninist conception of imperialism as a *system* - 'the highest stage of capitalism'. The global capitalist economy *is* imperialism in this sense. Underdevelopment can only be understood within the context of this total system, and thus it is a fundamental mistake to claim that the causes of underdevelopment are located *within* the political boundaries of Third World nation states. Marxist theorists argue that underdevelopment can only be explained by examining the relationships of dominance and subordination, and the mechanisms of exploitation and blockage, which transcend national boundaries. Imperialism is conceived by most Marxist scholars as a global system of metropoles and satellites, a key characteristic of which is the transfer of 'surplus' (wealth in various forms) from the latter to the former. Thus wealth is transferred from the Third World countryside (local satellite), to Third World city (local metropole), then from Third World city (which now becomes a global satellite), to Europe or the United States (global metropole).

How does the incorporation of Third World nations as satellites in the orbit of the international capitalist system contribute to their underdevelopment? Very crudely we can say that the imperialism theories locate two mechanisms by means of which *un*developed Third World countries (those outside the world market) become 'underdeveloping' countries. The first is 'exploitation'. The term 'exploitation' is not used here in the technical Marxist sense, but to mean an exchange relationship in which one party benefits disproportionately. Applied to North/South relationships, 'exploitation', entails a net transfer of wealth from poor to rich countries. The most obvious case is the 'sucking out of wealth' from Third World economies by multinational corporations - and the surplus thus extracted is not inconsiderable. Currently, American multinationals put US$1.0 billion into the so-called less developed countries each year, while repatriating US$2.5 billion in profits. Of far greater importance according to some theorists is the unequal exchange which arises from trading relationships between rich and poor countries. The *international division of labour*, in which poor countries produce primary commodities, while rich nations monopolise the growth-generating processing industries, is frequently argued to be the major cause of underdevelopment. Here one should perhaps point out that for most of the Marxist theorists, underdevelopment does *not* derive from the conscious desire of wicked capitalists in the West to impoverish Third World nations. Exploitation will occur as long as the international division of labour exists *regardless of the intentions of capitalists*. If, to take another example, we ask why multinationals repatriate their profits from, say, Zaire, the answer is not because multinationals wish to impoverish Zaire, but because Zaire lacks profitable outlets for re-investment while these abound in Europe and America. The 'wicked capitalist' thesis, in these views, is naive since it implies that the wickedness of the capitalists rather than the nature of capitalism creates underdevelopment.

The second mechanism which theories of imperialism identify as causing underdevelopment can be labelled 'blockage'. 'Exploitation' and 'blockage' usually, but not necessarily, co-exist. However, it is quite possible to be 'exploited' in the sense employed above without capitalist development being 'blocked'. Take, for example, the contentious case of multinational corporation profit remittances. Measuring the difference between investment capital flowing *into* a Third World economy and repatriated profits flowing *out* tells us nothing about what happened to the investment within that economy. Suppose a multinational corporation (MNC) invests one million dollars in a Third World country over a period of five years. Once the enterprise is established and successful, the multinational begins to repatriate profits. At the end of five years of successful business, the MNC has repatriated a total of one and a half million dollars. There has been a *net* outflow of half a million dollars. We may certainly define this as exploitation if we wish, but we must also ask what has happened to this investment during the five years. Measuring net capital outflows suggests that such investment is pure loss to the Third World economy, but it could well be the case that the MNC has generated five million dollars worth of economic activity during its five years of operation. If this were so, then, despite the net outflow of capital, the investment would, on balance, have been a productive one for the Third World country.

If this example shows that it is possible for 'exploitation' to exist without blocking productive forces, then the reverse is also true: we can have 'blockage' without 'exploitation'. Rich countries erecting quota barriers against manufactured goods from Third World countries block the development of Third World manufacturing industries without any exploitation (i.e. unequal exchange) being involved. To give another example, the United States might provide lavish aid to prop up regimes which had no interest in promoting *any* type of development. Here again we could say that development has been 'blocked' without any exploitation. 'Exploitation' and 'blockage' are *the only possible mechanisms* via which the rich capitalist states can 'underdevelop' the Third World.

Conclusion

We have outlined two clusters of theories of imperialism. The first dealt with the causes of capitalist expansion overseas, with counter-revolution and with intervention, the second with the consequences of this expansionism for economic development in the Third World. We suggested that the relationship between the two clusters of theories was rather tenuous. To explain successfully *both* counter-revolution *and* underdevelopment would require a *metatheory* which would embrace both clusters of imperialism theories thus far examined. No such theory exists at the present time.

SECTION I: DECOLONISATION

Introduction

As we noted in the general introduction, a recurring theme throughout this reader is the so-called North/South conflict. Today this conflict is concerned mainly with economic issues—the growing gap between rich nations and poor; the Third World debt crisis; the inequities of international trade relations, and so forth. Such was not always the case. In the two decades following World War II, the conflict between North and South centred on the issue of colonial independence.

D. K. Fieldhouse, in the following article argues that, "Nothing in the history of modern colonial empires was more remarkable than the speed with which they disappeared." Yet it is far from clear that decolonisation *has* meant the disappearance of imperialism. Many radical theorists, as Tony Smith points out in the second article in this section, maintain that imperialism still exists. These theorists claim that the direct European political control which characterised colonialism has been replaced by the indirect economic control which they have labelled "neo-colonialism".

The neo-colonialism thesis, which forms the central focus of much of the second part of this volume, can be stated fairly simply. During the period of colonial rule, many Third World economies were transformed from production for domestic consumption, to production for export. Third World exports provided the foreign exchange to buy the manufactured imports on which colonial (and post-colonial) societies came increasingly to depend. Post-colonial 'dependency' extended beyond the economic sphere. Western models of politics, western life styles, western scientific and military practice, were all adopted by the new post-colonial regimes. Only in a few countries, where the struggle against imperialism had entailed protracted warfare and the creation of an independent, cohesive and highly motivated resistance organization, was the dependency syndrome avoided. When the indigenous élite simply, and without protracted struggle, inherited both the colonial governing institutions and relationships with the metropole, independence brought few changes. Indeed, critics sometimes claimed that all that had changed was the color of the ruling élite's skin. To describe the new order they coined the term 'neo-colonialism'. It meant, to paraphrase Clausewitz, the continuation of colonialism by other means. In place of direct political controls were the more subtle and pervasive mechanisms of economic and ideological control. Thus both the changes wrought by colonial rule, *and* the nature and duration of the independence struggle, which Fieldhouse analyses, have important consequences for post-colonial development.

Anti-colonial nationalism was, as Fieldhouse demonstrates, a creation of colonial rule. The deeper the penetration of western values and institutions, the greater was the social and economic change in the colony, and the more widespread and intense the eventual nationalist response. But it was not until the end of the Second World War that the struggle against colonialism intensified. The disintegration of empire had, in Fieldhouse's words, '...two components—a demand by the subject people for independence and the inability or unwillingness of the imperial power to resist it.' By the end of World War II, the imperial powers had, in general, accepted the inevitable, and much of the conflict was over the *timing* rather than the principle of independence. In some cases, most notably where there were large white settler populations (Algeria, Rhodesia, Portuguese Africa), the *principle* of independence was bitterly resisted by the settlers. However the colonisers and colonised were by no means the only actors in this drama.

The culmination of World War II had led not only to the great upsurge in anti-colonial nationalism, but also to the hostile confrontation between East and West which became known as the Cold War. The origins of the Cold War are the subject of the section which follows; here we simply wish to indicate that the parallel processes of decolonisation and East/West confrontation were often linked—sometimes intimately. Whichever of the explanatory frameworks (ideology, power politics, or economic imperatives) which we described in the general introduction, is employed, there is no doubt that the political allegiances of the emergent new nations of the Third World were of great interest to the two new superpowers. Both the United States and the Soviet Union posed as champions of decolonisation, but, while anti-colonial sentiments were often genuine, it is clear that considerations of Cold War rivalry weighed heavily in the decision-making process on both sides. Each side sought to maximise its own political influence and minimise that of the other.

At the end of the Second World War, America—true to a genuine anti-colonial tradition—strongly opposed the re-imposition of French colonial rule in Indo-China. But, when it became clear that Vietnamese anti-colonialism was revolutionary, the United States switched its support to the French colonialists. By 1954, when the French were forced to withdraw, the United States was paying 80% of France's war costs.

But if the US opposition to communism overrode its support for anti-colonial independence movements on occasions, the Soviet Union was in no position to criticise. Faced with movements for independence on their own doorstep—Hungary in 1956 and Czechoslovakia in 1968—the Russians responded with savage repression.

Portugal's long and bitter struggle in Africa was the last of the European colonial wars. Each of the factors to which Fieldhouse's analysis of the evolution of anti-colonial nationalism refers may be found in the history of the liberation movements in Angola, Mozambique and Guinea Bissau. Yet while the struggle between coloniser and colonised is the *central* feature of Portugal's Africa wars, these wars are also superpower proxy conflicts. Take the case of Angola. On the one hand, the United States backed both colonial Portugal *and* an anti-communist, anti-colonial liberation movement known as the FNLA (the latter was covertly aided by the CIA). On the other hand, the Soviet Union backed the ultimately victorious MPLA.

At the risk of stating the obvious it may be useful at this point to re-emphasise the fact that the United States has generally intervened in the Third World to support anti-communist and pro-capitalist regimes and political movements. The Soviet

Union's support for various Third World countries has similarly tended to follow ideological lines. However, both powers seem also to follow the maxim: 'my enemy's enemy is my friend'. Here the criterion for support is not so much ideological affinity as the potential recipient country's degree of antipathy towards the rival superpower. Superpower alignments with Third World nations have obvious political implications; they also have important consequences for the economic development of the countries concerned. To give one obvious, and important, example—the possibilities for autonomous socialist economic development are blocked where right wing regimes in the Third World are maintained in power by external aid and—when necessary—intervention.

Since war between the superpowers themselves has been rendered suicidal by the possession of mutual nuclear 'overkill' capabilities, the conflict between East and West has frequently taken the form of proxy wars (or near wars) on the world 'periphery'. Superpower interference in colonial conflicts—sometimes overt, as in the above cases, but more often covert—is one example of such conflict waging by proxy. In the conflicts we have described, the North/South dimension—the struggle between European colonisers and Third World colonised—was always central. But, as we have indicated, few of these struggles were unaffected, while many were intensified and transformed, by the bitter East/West antagonisms to which we turn in the following section.

Anticolonial Nationalism and Western Response

Tony Smith

During the two decades following World War II, the maps of overseas empire which had established their place in so many classrooms of Europe were drained of their traditional colors of rose and blue: one-third of the people of the earth were freed from colonial rule. At the same time millions of others who had been subject to European power without falling under formal colonial jurisdiction reestablished their national identities. With the entry of the Communist Chinese into Peking in January 1949, the outlines of a new period of world history, one that signaled the end of a long era of unquestioned European hegemony over the technologically backward areas of the globe, seemed to be emerging from the ruins of World War II. Through Asia, the Middle East, North Africa and Africa south of the Sahara, a tidal wave of local nationalism was gathering to cast out the European rulers.

Many commentators on this period characterize the process of decolonization most highly by its speed. Yet this is to neglect the history of nationalist agitation and organization that began in modern form with the success of the Young Turks in overthrowing the Sultan in 1908, and with the hesitant emergence of republican government in China under Sun Yat-sen following the collapse of the Manchu dynasty in 1911. The contact of these two bureaucratic empires with European power in the nineteenth century had contributed to setting into motion forces that spelled the eventual disintegration of their traditional orders. But in the very process, groups that were dedicated to reworking the character of their countries had begun to mobilize so that they might meet the threats of the international system. Only in Japan had a modernizing elite emerged to save the country from European sway, but the significance of this example was also appreciated by other nationalists, from China to the Middle East, who were opposed to Western rule.

European rivalries also undermined colonial regimes. The impact of World War I prompted a liberalization of imperial rule in an effort to secure more wholehearted colonial support in the provision of men and material. So in 1916 France moved fully to assimilate the Four Communes of Senegal into the French Republic, and offered a series of overdue reforms to the Muslim elite in Algeria, including an end to special native taxes, a relaxation of the provisions of the native penal code, and a token increase in the political voice of the Muslim community at the local level. Similarly Great Britain found herself obliged to declare that the eventual goal in India was self-government (the Montagu-Chelmsford Commission leading to the reforms of 1919), and entered into negotiations with the local political leadership in Egypt, which led to a form of semi-independent status for this country in 1922. (But it was not until the Anglo-Egyptian Treaty of 1936 that the Egyptians themselves recognized a relaxation of London's grip.) Such examples could easily be multiplied.

In the years following World War II, the pace of colonial nationalism quickened. The slow spread of Western education, the increasing economic development of areas related to European capitalism, and the accumulating wisdom acquired from political discussion and agitation by colonized subjects of many different social and economic categories were serving to create the necessary basis for strong nationalist movements after 1945. During this period a hallmark of modernity—political parties—began to form for the first time in many of these areas. The National Congress Party of India had been founded in 1885, substantially earlier than an organized Western local elite arose in most of the imperial domains, but its functional equivalent could clearly be discerned throughout the lands of European rule by the early thirties (with the exception of certain parts of black Africa), while the Congress Party's own stance became substantially more antagonistic to continued British rule.

Outside the colonial order, other challenges to the international supremacy of Western Europe were beginning to be sounded in the interwar years. The most striking initial defiance was that of the Turkish nationalist Mustafa Kemal, or Ataturk. Reacting to the wartime designs of France, Britain, Greece, Italy and Russia to reduce his nation to an area of some 20,000 square miles, Ataturk in 1919 stirred his countrymen to a resistance effort that by 1923 had established the boundaries of a modern state of 300,000 square miles. So, too, in China, first the Kuomintang and—by 1921—an indigenous Communist Party, were beginning their organizational efforts to re-establish the sovereignty and international autonomy of the Chinese state.

It was the Russian Revolution of 1917, however, that presented the most fundamental challenge to the imperial order. Not only was Lenin capable of formulating a theoretical attack on Western colonialism that was ideological dynamite, but he was able to back it up with an organizational method and the resources of the Soviet state. His new socialist government immediately renounced Czarist designs on Constantinople, the northern part of Persia and Manchuria. Instead Lenin offered material aid to Ataturk, Reza Khan Pahlevi in Teheran, the emir of Afghanistan, the Wafd Party in Egypt, and the Kuomintang in China in their respective efforts to diminish Western influence in their national affairs. The subsequent growth of local Communist parties, the action of Comintern, and the conduct of other national Communist parties—most notably the French—played an undeniably important role in the groundswell of opposition to Western rule (although Communist influence fell far short of being the "international menace" that Western statesmen immediately after 1921 began to use as a scapegoat in their explanations of colonial discontent).

The challenge of the Russian Revolution and the growth of anti-Western nationalist sentiment in Asia, the Middle East and Africa did not go unnoticed in Paris and London. Nor did these capitals fail to recognize how gravely the terrible toll of World War I—the millions dead, the material destruction, the pretentions of cultural superiority debunked—crippled their own ability to maintain their international rank. They could, however, look to the map, where substantial gains had been registered. Not only had these countries claimed Germany's African colonies (leaving to Japan Berlin's Pacific holdings north of the Equator, while Australia and New Zealand took those to the south), but they had proceeded to the final dismemberment of the Ottoman Empire (after the occupation of

Algiers in 1830, Egypt in 1882, and machinations in the Balkans over the preceding several decades). The League of Nations duly sanctioned these arrangements, and the evident powerlessness of the Arabs—the most politically advanced group of people under colonial rule—suggested that European might had no serious challengers.

More, World War I had amply demonstrated to public opinion and to the leadership of both France and Great Britain the practical advantages of empire, for there was general agreement that the hundreds of thousands of workers, the vast stores of supplies, and the million and a half fighting men furnished by the two empires had given these countries a decisive edge in the struggle against Germany. At the same time, the increasing participation of socialist parties in their respective national governments meant that except for the nascent Communist parties and a scattering of intellectuals, fundamental opposition to imperial possessions ceased in the Western democracies. Leftist critics no longer directed their attacks against colonialism as a system, but instead called for remedies to specific abuses, and this in the interests of the mother country as well as the foreign subjects. In short, just at the moment when powerful forces were beginning to assemble to put an end to European rule overseas, many Europeans were for the first time coming to the conclusion that their national survival might depend on the preservation of empire. Faced with the growing power of the United States, Japan and the Soviet Union, the proposition that local nationalisms would be the wave of the future appeared a bit absurd. It was easy, then, to predict the international role of a European nation bereft of empire. The example of Spain was there for all to ponder.

Whatever the European will, the increasing strength of nationalist organization in most areas of European domination proceeded apace in the 1930s. Here the impact of World War II proved decisive. The fall of Singapore in February 1942, and the surrender of Rangoon a month later, climaxed the expansion of Japan's Greater Asian Co-Prosperity Sphere and encouraged (as in the case of the Dutch East Indies), or permitted by default (as in the case of French Indochina), the mobilization of such strong nationalist forces that it seemed highly improbable that the old colonial regimes could reinstate themselves without being severely contested. Similarly, World War II exacerbated tensions in the most important of imperial possessions—India—sharply intensifying the demands for independence at the same time that it placed the British in a more unfavorable position either to refuse or to stall. In Africa, although its influence was less direct, the war strained colonial relations as well, since the northern part of the continent was an important theater of military action (with the conspicuous absence of the dominant colonial authority, France, noted by all), while southern Africa suffered harsh requisitions in order to further the Allied war effort.

Despite the established pedigree of local nationalism in most imperial domains by 1945, and despite the apparent decline of European power internationally, virtually no one foresaw the scope of the decolonization process—much less its speed—in the immediate aftermath of the war. Part of the reason is undoubtedly that changes of such magnitude are very seldom predicted. More specifically, however, the Europeans professed pride in the solidarity of their empires during the conflict, while interpreting the character of the emerging postwar international order as one to be marked by the increasing interdependence of nations—not by their fragmentation at the hands of local nationalists. National independence seemed a vain, anachronistic goal. Better, then, to refurbish the imperial system, the British by the addition to the Commonwealth of non-European members (first of all India), while the French energetically began debating the structure of the projected French Union.

The forecast of the character of the new international order was to turn out to be correct; the forecast of which units would join in association proved mistaken. For in the decade and a half after the end of World War II, London and Paris came to realize that their best safeguards lay not in revitalized empire but in a united Europe. In the meantime, especially on the Continent, the imperial reflex held sway, motivated by established myths about colonial rule. Except now the first victims of the web of postponed good intentions, half-truths, and paternalistic stances were not the colonized but the colonizers. How else can we understand declarations such as that by Vincent Auriol, a Socialist and the first President of the French Fourth Republic, who found on his visit to Algeria in the summer of 1949 "unforgettable signs of affection, loyalty and confidence"? More than a year after a series of rigged elections had begun to ensure that nationalist agitators did not obtain a public forum, Auriol could report that everywhere "the people cried their love for France."

A further reason for discounting the significance of colonial unrest after 1945 was that the major menace to the West seemed to come from Soviet Russia. Outright opposition over the fate of

Poland began in 1945 and the Cold War was officially inaugurated in the West with the announcement of "containment" in the Truman Doctrine of March 1947. Western strategic thinking at this time was preoccupied with such problems as calculating the damage a nuclear attack would inflict on the Soviets as against the number of hours it would take Russian divisions to occupy Western Europe. It remained unanticipated that the major theater of conflict in the postwar period would be the so-called Third World.

Yet in short order the first violence to wrack these politically unstable areas of the world made its appearance. On May 8, 1945, the very day Paris was celebrating the defeat of Germany, Muslim riots around the town of Setif in Western Algeria claimed over a hundred European lives. Reaction was swift. French planes strafed forty-four Muslim hamlets, a cruiser offshore bombarded more, and groups of settler vigilantes summarily executed hundreds of natives. As testimony to the ferocity of the repression, how many Muslims died in these events has never been determined, though estimates range from 6,000 to 45,000. The following year war broke out in Indo-china, in a struggle that would eventually kill 100,000 French (including mercenary auxiliaries) and cost the lives of untold thousands of Vietnamese. Again, in 1947, an uprising in Madagascar killed some 100 Europeans, provoking a French repression that by official estimates took 80,000 native lives. By the time the Algerian conflict ended in 1962, another 750,000 deaths had been added to the rolls of decolonization.

"Police action" that mushroomed into armed repression occurred in the British Empire as well, most notably in Malaya (1948-1954) and in Kenya (1952-1955). But the British possessions came more to be noted—as the Conservatives especially had warned—for the violence the subject masses inflicted on each other rather than for nationalist confrontations between London and the various local leaders. Thus it was Greek against Turk on the island of Cyprus, Jew against Arab in Palestine, and most tragic of all, Hindu against Muslim on the Indian subcontinent. Struggles between blacks and Asians in East Africa, between Africans and Arabs in the Sudan and Zanzibar, between Nigeria and Biafra and within Northern Ireland have been later indirect consequences of this same decolonization process.

After the books on imperialism come the studies on decolonization. Yet in addition to emphasizing that decolonization was not so speedy a movement as it is sometimes described, it is also important to point out that the imperialist phase of the relations between industrial and technologically backward countries is far from concluded. Surely some skepticism is warranted toward the statement of the noted historian of imperialism, William F. Langer, when he writes in "Farewell to Empire" (*Foreign Affairs*, October 1962) that "thoughtful people, particularly in the Western world, are bound to reflect on this epochal upheaval and to realize that one of the very great revolutions in human affairs has taken place." One may similarly doubt that Rupert Emerson, another dean of colonial studies is justified in writing in *The Journal of Contemporary History* (January 1969) of the "spectacular demise" of the old imperial order, while asking, "Is there any other occasion on which so global and commanding a scheme of things was swept away in so brief a time?" For although Portugal has at long last agreed to independence for Angola and Mozambique, white-settler regimes remain strongly ensconced in Rhodesia and the Union of South Africa, and a multitude of cultural, economic and political ties still bind many of the former imperial possessions to the capitals of Europe. France, for example, continues to control the education, currency and armies of a number of her former African colonies. Indeed, it is common to hear it observed that through her teachers, fiscal controls and army personnel, France is more influential today at all levels of African society than in the heyday of direct political control from Paris.

Today the argument that imperialism has not ended goes under the heading of "dependency theory" or "neo-colonialism." While it is obviously oversimplifying to reduce a complex and variously interpreted position to a few propositions, a summary presentation of the argument is basic to efforts to conceptualize accurately the character of present-day decolonization. According to the theory of neo-colonialism, most Third World nations have become dependent on the international economic system dominated by the Western capitalist powers and Japan for markets, technology, financing and even basic foodstuffs to such a point that these less-developed countries may be called "hooked": they cannot do with their dependence, but, just as well, they cannot do without it.

They cannot do with dependence because their form of incorporation into the international system has tended to preclude their industrialization, relegating them instead to the less dynamic forms of growth associated with agriculture or the extractive industries. Where manufacturing occurs it is generally under the auspices of multinational corporations with their headquarters in the West which, for whatever benefits they may bring in the form of managerial know-how, marketing and the like, take far more than they bring and—what is more important—make it virtually impossible for local, self-sustaining industrialization to develop. At the same time, however, so this theory runs, the necessary remedy to the problem—a break with the international system—is not available to most of these countries. In some cases the economies of the less-developed countries have become so dependent on exports to the international system that the requirements of their single-crop economies dictate continued participation in the very process that is victimizing them.

In other instances adjustments might be made, but not without cutting the base from under the present dominant classes that rely on the international system for the trade, investment and military aid, which secure the power and privileges of these elites. In short, dependence grows from and serves to perpetuate an asymmetrical power relation internationally, from which the less-developed countries can only escape with great difficulty. A few, like Algeria, may have the sort of natural resources, population base and national leadership that make this break possible. For the rest, only war or a serious depression afflicting the industrial West will weaken the international system sufficiently to allow local autonomous development. Thus the direct political control through colonization is replaced by the indirect economic control of decolonization. The result is the same: imperial domination. From this point of view, the national anthems and flag ceremonies of decolonization were nothing more than ideological smokescreens covering a more rationalized economic exploitation of the world.

In order to determine the validity of this thesis, the student must look to the series of accords signed since 1958 between the European Economic Community (EEC) and those areas of the world over which these countries once exercised direct or informal control. In such an analysis the year 1975 serves as an appropriate watermark date. For in the winter of 1975, the EEC, enlarged by the entry of Great Britain, concluded a convention at Lomé, Togo, associating forty-six less-developed states with the EEC in a form of international economic bloc. The convention thereby marks clearly the emergence of a new order restructuring relations between Europe and many of the less-developed countries that had previously gravitated toward Western capitals, but which in the aftermath of World War II had moved to establish their own political identities.

Thus the rapid distintegration of the imperial order politically in the first two decades following the war has seemingly given way to a decade of economic reintegration. The easy dislocation of the new system is difficult to imagine. To be sure, the outlines of such an order are still sketchy and remain fragile; the reintegration of Europe with these areas of its former dominance is by no means devoid of problems. Preeminent among these are: (1) the rivalries among the European capitals— and particularly Paris and London— however much they may recognize overriding common interests in their association; (2) the rivalries among states of the less-developed countries as they seek a common front in their negotiations with the EEC; and (3) the rivalries between the Europeans to one side and the members of the Associated States to the other—or the question of neo-colonialism.

It is, of course, by no means self-evident that such an arrangement will fail to serve the interests of all parties involved in it (albeit some more than others). Certainly relations may be "imperial" without being "exploitive." So long as an imperial center is not threatened by the growth in power of a dependent to it, it may actually see its own interests served. (One thinks, for example, of the relation between Britain and Portugal in the nineteenth century, or that between the United States and Iran today.) To be able to establish theoretically that an imperial relation is exploitive—as the present-day interpreters of neo-colonialism and dependency would have it—is by no means to establish that such a relation actually exists. The distinction between the logic of a theory and the logic of history appears too often to be forgotten.

Whatever the merits of the debate, the term neo-colonialism seems a misnomer for this phenomenon, however, since Britain established a somewhat similar arrangement in the nineteenth century with Latin America after Spain's prostration during the Napoleonic Wars. From the perspective of the past, then, the satellite states of "informal empire" are certainly not unique to the contemporary period. Nor are economic motives the only impetus to domination. Imperialism of the strong against the weak is as old as human history, and there is little reason to be confident that the period described as one of decolonization will guarantee the undisturbed sovereignty of the new nations of the world. Like a chameleon changing colors, imperialism may be expected to appear in different form but with similar consequences. We would be naive indeed not to anticipate that among its chief practitioners may well be some of its former victims and most outspoken critics.

The debate over the causes of the "new imperialism," which began in the final quarter of the nineteenth century, exhibits far more unity and erudition than does contemporary discussion of the decolonization process. There simply are no works today that attempt to be as comprehensive in accounting for the loss of empire as Hobson, for one, was comprehensive in his explanation of its acquisition. This is the case because, in part, economic interpretations of the root motivations of imperial policy (still the pacesetters in discussions of four centuries of European overseas expansion) fail to elucidate at all well the vicissitudes of decolonization. So Great Britain, whose security for three centuries had depended closely on foreign trade, investment and domination, decolonized with relative ease, while France, with far less material interest in her possessions, dug in to stay. More fundamentally, perhaps, the exponents of an economic interpretation of history have tended to doubt how genuinely revolutionary a development decolonization actually has been, and have stressed instead the continued cultural, social and political weight of neo-colonialism based on the character of the contemporary economic international order. Whatever the reasons, the present debate lacks the hard analytical edge of the earlier (and still continuing) controversy over the origins of European expansion.

The problem, then, is to attempt to establish, by a more systematic approach than case studies alone permit, the primary factors at work in ·creating the various patterns of decolonization. Here, as I have suggested, economic considerations do not now appear to be of much significance, although one line to take might be that the more advanced economy of the British was able to adjust more easily to control without political domination than was the case for the French. Instead, commentators make reference to a host of causative forces behind political policies—such as the influence of past imperial ideology, of past experience in colonial matters, of national psychology, or contemporary domestic politics and of international strategic calculations—without, however, expending much effort on refining the guiding concepts invoked, assigning them relative weights as motivating factors behind the various imperial policies, framing them as disprovable interpretations of political behavior, or putting them within a broadly historical and comparative framework.

Suppose, then, that we attempt briefly to account for the more signal differences in the British and French responses to the challenge of decolonization. Surely an important part of the answer must be the historical experiences that had come to establish a characteristically national attitude and method for handling colonial affairs. Thus, unlike the French, who had aspirations for making fellow citizens out of their colonial subjects and so creating "the Greater France of 100 million Frenchmen," the British had typically spoken of eventual self-government. It could be that this goes back to a fundamental difference in philosophic temperament: when the French were declaring the universal Rights of Man, Burke was moved to say that he knew only of the Rights of Englishmen. In other words, leaving aside such important exceptions as Lyautey and Jules Harmand, who championed "association" rather than "assimilation" as goals for national policy, the French claimed a general relevance for their national values that the British never assumed, believing instead in the basic distinctness of different social patterns.

In each case, of course, the dominant culture was asserting its superiority over the natives, but the British version of this common claim proved more amenable to fulfillment in the light of the course of history (however much it, like the French policy of assimilation had attached its promise in practice to an infinitely receding historical horizon).

Nor should we forget that the nineteenth century had given the British long acquaintance with the practice of what today would be called neo-colonialism. That is, the British came early to appreciate the advantages of "informal empire," of supporting a dependable local elite in order to assure a stable environment for trade and investment. Such an arrangement worked well with Latin America after the Napoleonic Wars and was contemplated for China, Persia, the Ottoman Empire and Africa thereafter. Only the inability of native regimes to maintain themselves in the face of mounting domestic and foreign pressures prompted Britain's direct (and generally begrudging) intervention. Although London finally had undertaken to experiment with a protectionist empire during the interwar period, this style had never suited the Free Trade Imperialists anything like it had the French.

Still more importantly, the British, unlike the French, had developed a successful method for dealing with colonial discontent long before 1945. In a sense, one may mark the first phase of British decolonization as stretching from the Durham Report of 1839 relative to Canada, to the Statute of Westminster of 1931. By this series of measures, Britain created the Dominion system and institutionalized a procedure for gradually loosening control over her possessions. For a time, to be sure, the final character of the Commonwealth, as it came to be called, was in doubt. During the interwar years (if not earlier), however, it became clear that the sometime dream of Imperial Federation, whereby London would control the economic, defense and foreign policies of the several allied Anglo-Saxon peoples, would never come to fruition. Instead the measured progress within the colonies from representative to responsible government and from there to Commonwealth status would culminate in the establishment of fully sovereign states.

Of course there is the mistake encountered frequently in the works of Britishers especially;, of seeing in retrospect a grand design for decolonization that in fact did not exist. Closer inspection commonly reveals the British to have been following Burke's sage counsel to "reform in order to preserve": London made concessions more usually to subvert opposition to British rule than to prepare for its demise. So, for example, to see Indian independence in 1947 as necessarily following from the Government of India Act of 1935, which in turn unerringly confirmed the intentions of the Government of India Act of 1919 (itself the natural product of the Morley-Minto reforms of 1909), assumes a British gift for prophecy that a closer examination of the historical record fails to sustain. What is lacking in these accounts is a sense of the conflicts, hesitations and uncertainties of the past and of the attempts to reinterpret or renege on the promise of eventual independence for India.

Nonetheless, the British *did* establish a tradition of meeting colonial discontent by reforms that associated the subject peoples more closely with their own governing. The prior evolution of the Dominion system *did* exert an important influence on the style of British policy toward India. And the ultimate decision to grant India independence and to permit her to withdraw if she wished from the Commonwealth *did* constitute a momentous precedent for British policy toward the rest of her empire. Seen from this perspective, there is something a bit pathetic about the French, whose naiveté and relative paucity of experience found expression in resolutions voted from the Brazzaville Conference of January 1944 through the debates establishing the ill-fated French Union in 1946.

Prewar theory and practice did not alone decide postwar

imperial policy, however. The international situation after 1945, as well as past precedent, was crucial in determining British and French responses to the pressures of decolonization. Here the character of relations with the United States was central. Thus although Great Britain had been a greater international power than France before 1939, she adjusted more easily to her postwar decline in part, certainly, because of her greater confidence in the United States. Wartime experience had been important in laying the ground for this trust, as one can see in comparing the quite different relationships Roosevelt had with Winston Churchill and Charles de Gaulle. For de Gaulle, Roosevelt had little but distrust; for Churchill, the American leader had unstinted admiration. In turn, the French sought an international role after the war as little dependent as possible on the United States (although to their continual annoyment this proved to be no easy task), while Britain looked forward eagerly to what Churchill in his Fulton, Missouri speech of March 1946 called "the fraternal association of the English-speaking peoples ... a special relationship between the British Commonwealth and Empire and the United States."

When should the beginning of this alliance between the English-speaking peoples be dated? Is 1823 too early, when the British celebrated the Monroe Doctrine as a policy well suited to support Pax Britannica? Or the Open Door Notes of the late nineteenth century when the United States lent its support to the British scheme of things in China? Perhaps the decisive moments would be better put after World War I, when the British had to reckon with America's coming international paramountcy. So at the Washington Naval Conference in 1921, Britain finally accepted parity with the United States in sea power and moved away from her alliance with Japan—clear indications that her most important international alliance would henceforth be with her former North American colony. The Anglo-American Trade Agreement of 1938 only confirmed this orientation, when the British agreed partly to dismantle their imperial preference system, both in response to American pressures and in the hope of securing greater assistance from Washington to counter the growing menace of Hitler. Subsequently the Americans exacted imperial concessions in return for Lend Lease and in the name of the Atlantic Alliance. Not that London gave in willingly during these negotiations. To the contrary, British leaders sought to preserve as many advantages for their country as possible and greatly resented many of the demands made by the Americans. But there was nothing like the French feeling—born of decades of lack of national confidence—that others were waiting like vultures for her to show weakness in order to redivide her empire. One need only consider the ease with which the United States replaced Britain in Greece and Turkey in 1947 to appreciate the gap between French and British attitudes in regard to the expansion of American power. In an important sense, then, one can mark the beginning of British decolonization in the interwar period, both in the style of her imperial policy and in the character of her international alliances. The same simply cannot be said of France.

Domestic politics and institutions also account for the difference in French and British reactions to nationalist agitation. Britain had a "loyal opposition," a stable two-party system and a strong executive. France, to the contrary, was plagued by disloyal opposition from both the Right and Left, by a multiparty system and by a weak executive. Hence the French were not so able as the British to process a problem of the magnitude of decolonization. In my opinion, commentators have tended to exaggerate the shortcomings of what was pejoratively referred to as *le système,* since a stubborn colonial consensus from the Socialists to the Right contributed as much to the ineffectiveness of the political system as this in turn, made a far-sighted policy impossible to determine and implement.

Analyses of the vicissitudes of French decolonization typically present a view of the Republic's governments as "divided," "indecisive" and "immobile," and so rally to de Gaulle's earliest warnings against the deficiencies of the Fourth Republic. But as a review of both the Indochinese policy of the Blum and Ramadier governments in 1946-1947 and the Algerian policy of the Mollet Government of 1956-1957 demonstrates, it was unity, resolution and action that at these critical junctures of Socialist national leadership were the hallmarks of the regime. What typified these decisive periods of Socialist leadership was not so much the fatal logic of a political system as the fatal logic of a colonial perspective. Time and again throughout the history of the Fourth Republic, beneath the invective of political division, one finds a shared anguish at the passing of national greatness, a shared humiliation at three generations of defeat, a shared nationalistic determination that France retain her independence in a hostile world—all brought to rest on the conviction that the colonies, and especially Algeria, would remain French.

Studies that obscure this common commitment, through a gentlemen's agreement to focus strictly on the shortcomings of the system as a system, foster a sort of collective amnesia that will no doubt remain until the actors of the period have left the political scene (perhaps another decade). Where, for example, can one find in the annals of French leaders anything equivalent to the entry in the journal of Hugh Dalton, assistant to Mountbatten in negotiating the independence of India, dated February 24, 1947?

> If you are in a place where you are not wanted and where you have not got the force, or perhaps the will, to squash those who don't want you, the only thing to do is to come out. This very simple truth will have to be applied other places too, e.g., Palestine.

Dalton's realism and lucidity were quite characteristic of the British. Certainly the same cannot be said for the French (as the sections from French and British parliamentary debates illustrate). It was not so much the French political system that was responsible, then, for the problems of decolonization, as it was the misperceptions of the collective mind of the political elite. This is not to deny, however, that the greater stability of the British political system made for less trouble in decolonizing, if for no other reason than that there was no particular reason to believe the loss of empire was the logical outcome of inefficient government. After the traumas of the thirties and the humiliation of the Occupation, the charges of being a *bradeur d'empire* raised much more profound self-doubt in the National Assembly than did charges of "scuttle" at Westminster.

The natural home for decolonization sentiment was the political Left. Here a comparison of the French Socialist Party with Labour in Britain reveals another important difference. To be sure, Labour hesitated, stalled and cast about on occasion for ways of granting independence that would favor future British interests. But the French socialists could not boast a study group to bear comparison with the Fabian Colonial Bureau. Nor does the French Overseas Minister from January 1946 until November 1947, Marious Moutet, measure up terribly well to the British Colonial Secretary from late 1946 until 1950, Arthur Creech-Jones. It should be recalled that Socialists were in power in both France and England in 1947, but as parliamentary speeches attest, while French Prime Minister Ramadier was calling for votes of war credits to pursue the struggle in Indochina and staging emotional calls for support of the French army, British Prime Minister Attlee was extracting his country even more quickly from India than initial plans had projected.

These brief remarks only suggest the sort of work that still needs to be done on decolonization: the separation of different categories of analysis from national psychology to the capacities of domestic political institutions; the assignment to them of weights of relative importance based on their influence on political behavior; their co-ordination in an historical and comparative fashion. Case studies will of course point up idiosyncrasies in the general movement, but it should be possible to create a more dynamic and synthetic overview of the period than is now available. One thing is certain: the enterprise promises to be a fertile field for scholarly debate.

Decolonisation

D.K. Fieldhouse

Nothing in the history of the modern colonial empires was more remarkable than the speed with which they disappeared. In 1939 they were at their peak: by 1965 they had practically ceased to exist. This was the more surprising because none of the classical explanations seemed to apply. When the original American colonies demanded independence they had had from one and a half to three centuries in which to evolve as mature societies, conscious of their separate identity. Most colonies in Africa, Asia and the Pacific which achieved independence after 1945 were annexed only in the last decades of the nineteenth century, and few looked like proto-nation states in 1939. Nor were the great imperial powers deprived of their colonies by victorious enemies, as Germany was in 1919. Italy lost some of her colonies during and after the Second World War, and Japan lost all her possessions. But Britain, France, the United States, Belgium, and Holland were victors in 1945, and Spain and Portugal had been neutrals. Most significant of all, the end of empire cannot be explained in terms of the decadence of the imperial powers. Europe and America were relatively richer and more powerful in the mid-twentieth century than ever before, and decolonization was not evidence of decline in the west. Why, then, did it take place?

It is impossible as yet to give a satisfactory answer, for the events are too recent and have not been fully studied. Moreover no one explanation fits all cases, for decolonization had roots as various as the colonial territories. It is possible only to indicate factors which appear to have been generally influential, and which at the same time throw most light on the character of European colonialism in its last phase.

The disintegration of an empire always has two components — a demand by the subject people for independence and the inability or unwillingness of the imperial power to resist it. Which of these was more important in the period after 1945?

There is no doubt that colonial demands for independence were in many places very strong: the difficulty is to discover their roots. They were certainly not the same in the modern tropical dependencies as they had been in the old settlement colonies of America and Australasia, for these had a natural affinity with their parent states derived from common race, language, religion, and culture. Though habitually disobedient, European settlers were also instinctively loyal. The greed, incompetence or arrogance of the metropolis might strain this loyalty; in course of time awareness that colonial interests were diverging from those of the parent state led to demands for greater devolution of authority within the imperial system. But colonies were likely to demand full independence only if such grievances were not remedied, or if some extraordinary strain, such as isolation from Europe during the Napoleonic wars, was placed on the imperial relationship. Conversely, if an imperial power admitted the reasonableness of colonial demands, it was often possible to avoid total separation. Thus the British self-governing colonies of the nineteenth century became Dominions — sovereign states, yet closely linked to Britain and each other in the Commonwealth. Alternatively, France, Portugal, Spain and the United States were able fully to incorporate some at least of their colonies into their metropolitan constitutional systems, evading the problem of colonial independence altogether. In short, the 'nationalism' of a settler colony was not necessarily incompatible with empire. Association implied no indignity or tyranny: in the mid-twentieth century Canada was no less a nation than the United States because part of the Commonwealth and still subject in certain respects to the British parliament.

Little of this applied to the non-European tropical dependencies which formed the bulk of the modern empires.

Unless they had substantial settler minorities they had no necessary community of interest with their masters. Centuries of alien rule might naturalize certain European institutions, implant Christianity, influence habits of mind; but only rarely did they transmute subjects into quasi-Europeans. Tropical empire was based on power. It might be beneficial; it certainly depended for its continuance on at least tacit approval and support from the majority of the subject people. But it could never take colonial loyalty for granted, for it remained alien and its roots were shallow.

It should therefore have caused Europe no surprise that the tropical dependencies ultimately became conscious of having little in common with their masters and demanded independence as nation states. Yet colonial nationalism did in fact surprise the imperial powers in the twentieth century. They were familiar with nationalism in Europe; but they associated it only with relatively small and ethnically homogeneous countries like Italy, Greece, the Balkan states, Poland and Czechoslovakia, and they regarded it as a specifically European phenomenon. Few colonies had any natural unity: most were artifacts created by European statesmen or colonial administrators, without common histories, religions, languages or cultures. For these reasons, and also because they were reluctant to recognize their existence, European states for long minimized the importance of nationalist movements in their colonies. The British had to admit that nationalism was a significant force in India and Ceylon by the 1920s, but in most other places they and other European powers did not take it seriously until after 1945. Thereafter they were surprised by the speed of developments only because they had previously turned blind eyes to what was clearly evident.

Colonial nationalism undoubtedly existed as a growing protest against alien rule; but what were its roots? There are three broad alternative explanations. It may have existed continuously from the moment of occupation; it may have been artificially injected by the infusion of European ideas and practices; or it may have been the product of fundamental changes in colonial society during the period of occupation.

Evidence can be found to support each interpretation. In many places nationalism, in the sense of hostility to alien rule, certainly existed from the beginning, and was expressed in strong initial resistance to effective occupation by Europeans and later in major rebellions. Such resistance was common wherever there were advanced non-Christian religions and non-

European cultures - in Islamic North and West Africa, in India, Indo-China and China; but it occurred also in 'pagan' Africa, usually where indigenous states were strong - in Dahomey, Ashanti, Zululand and Matabeleland, or where religious leaders stirred up resistance over an area transcending tribal boundaries, as in the Maji-Maji rebellion in German East Africa. In some colonies this initial hostility survived crushing military defeat, erupting into major rebellions and possibly providing a nucleus for later nationalist movements. But elsewhere initial defeat seemed entirely to eradicate it; and this makes it impossible to generalize. All that seems certain is that resentment against European rule was most enduring in societies with advanced religions and cultures, because there the destruction of indigenous political authorities and institutions did not destroy the main focus of common interest. Yet even where it survived, such indigenous nationalism was never strong enough to unseat colonial rulers so long as it was expressed in traditional forms. The Indian Mutiny of 1857 demonstrated conclusively that hereditary *élites*, once subordinated to alien rule, could not provide the spearhead of successful rebellion, and other colonial dependencies had the same experience. If, therefore, colonial nationalism was as old as colonial occupation, in the modern period it could be effective only by adopting totally new forms of expression.

There is a strong case, also, for seeing the roots of nationalism in the impact of alien ideas and practices which, by infecting dependencies with European ideals of liberty and equality, made them resent subordination. There is no doubt that the easiest dependency to rule was one whose hereditary rulers became willing collaborators, acting as middlemen between their subjects and the alien power. One advantage of indirect rule was that it preserved such hierarchical systems and thus obstructed the growth of liberal and democratic concepts among the masses. Conversely the need for every imperial power to train an indigenous *élite* to serve in the administration was a solvent of stability, for few Europeans could envisage advanced education other than in their own language and using their own concepts; so that the educated *élite* were necessarily imbued with European ideas. Some they rejected; but those they adopted were often incompatible with alien rule: for example, equality before the law in colonies with different legal systems for Europeans and others; the principle of parliamentary elections, where there was no representative legislature; and the right of national self-determination. Once such ideas were fairly grafted they invariably stimulated nationalist movements, normally led by the minority of *evolués* - indigenous peoples who had left their own traditional social groups but found themselves excluded from the preserves of the white man. Personal ambition and idealism combined to give urgency to their demands; although they were seldom able to persuade an area as vast as Nigeria or India that it was a united nation, they found a substitute in the argument that subject peoples were at least united in common subjection and in racial difference from their masters. On this basis they were able to create mass parties in most colonies which were pledged first to greater self-government and ultimately to independence.

Yet, in many ways, this is an unsatisfactory explanation of the strength of colonial nationalism, at least in countries like India which pioneered the demand for independence. Because they were seldom traditional leaders and because their political concepts were alien, many colonial politicians found it difficult to arouse general support: where they could do so effectively a further explanation may be necessary. It is, in fact, possible that modern nationalism became powerful because fundamental changes had taken place in certain dependencies since they were first occupied, destroying the conditions which had made alien rule practicable. European occupation eventually affected most aspects of colonial life. Large-scale manufactures and mining produced urban agglomerations and therefore a new rootless proletariat. Changes in the class structure created a new balance of interests, often unfavourable to indigenous agents of imperial rule. Growing populations often led to land-hunger and resentment. Better communications broke down the isolation of tribal communities. Religious revivals strengthened awareness of the difference between Europeans and subjects. In short, social changes of these and other kinds may, in many if not most places, have generated increasing resentment at many aspects of alien rule, not necessarily because it was alien, but because the imperial power was associated with conditions which the masses now wanted to change. Ultimately it was shrugged off as part of a rejected *ancien régime*.

None of these explanations is completely or generally satisfactory. It is seldom possible to trace continuous hostility to alien rule throughout the colonial period. Few colonies acquired in the later nineteenth century had undergone fundamental social changes by 1939; most seemed all too static. In the years after 1950 many colonial politicians were clearly copying other nationalist leaders and adopting their ideas rather than creating their own or expressing deep-seated national desires. Yet, where two or more of these influences coincided, as they did in India, Indonesia, Indo-China and parts of Islamic Africa, strong movements for independence grew first and became most powerful. India, with a large class of men educated in European principles, with strong religious and cultural traditions and social changes reflecting a century and a half of British rule, played the same role as pioneer and pace-setter for the modern tropical empires as the United States did for the first American colonies and Canada for the nineteenth-century British settlement colonies. India might succeed where other weaker dependencies could not: but the concessions she extracted before 1939 and the independence she gained in 1947 were proof that colonial nationalism was a force which could no longer be ignored.

Colonial demands for self-government or full independence were a challenge to Europe: but it is wrong to assume that the imperial powers were necessarily unable to meet and reject the challenge. Empire would be destroyed only if the forces of nationalism proved too strong to resist, or if the imperial powers changed their attitudes and refused to struggle. Was decolonization the result of Europe's inability to maintain its power or of her declining will to do so?

It is unlikely that any European state could indefinitely have controlled its larger dependencies, once hostility became general, unless it had the support of a strong settler community, as in Algeria, Kenya, Rhodesia and South Africa. But the question is largely academic: no dependency was ever entirely hostile; no European state every employed all its resources in repressing a colony. The important question was how much a dependency was worth to the metropolis, and so what effort it was prepared to make to retain it. In fact, Europe emancipated most of her colonies long before she was forced to do so; and this can be explained only by considering the purposes for which colonies were occupied and held and the changing moral climate of the west after about 1930.

The essential feature of many tropical colonies was that full occupation and government were an unwelcome concomitant of strictly limited interests — strategic, diplomatic, commercial or moral. Process of time often made even these original functions irrelevant: for example, Britain no longer had a substantial interest in East Africa once there was no German or French threat to her power in the Indian Ocean or in Egypt.

Sometimes, of course, new functions replaced the old: some colonies which were acquired for strategic purposes blossomed into producers of oil, minerals or tropical raw materials. But even these did not necessarily make full imperial control essential, for a stable successor state might provide an effective political framework for economic activity, and decolonization would relieve the metropolis of administrative burdens.

It was therefore by no means certain that, in the last resort, European states would resist nationalist demands for self-government: if they considered the question rationally they might even encourage them. At the same time concessions were likely to be made slowly. The habit of power, the assumption that Europeans could supply better government than their subjects, concern for minority interests, fear that colonies could not maintain the complex political and economic systems created by the west; all tended to breed distrust of nationalist demands and encouraged delaying action. Yet, by 1939 cooperation in government was far advanced in India and Ceylon; it was developing, though more slowly, in Indonesia, and concessions were being made in other places whose nationalist movements were still embryonic. The British were the most ready to admit that a dependency was entitled to self-government once it had proved its fitness, for the evolution of the Dominions since the 1840s provided a model for constitutional advance: others were slower to accept evidence of political capacity in their dependencies and slower still to foster it. In any case Europe still felt confident that it could control the timetable of transferring power. Even to liberals there seemed to be an infinity of time and a multitude of intermediate stages before colonies were likely to become autonomous.

Why, then, did the empires fall like a pack of cards after 1945? The explanation lies in two closely related influences. The first was the Second World War, which had an effect on many tropical colonies comparable with that of the Napoleonic wars on the Spanish and Portuguese colonies in America. From 1940 to 1945 France, Belgium and Holland were cut off from their dependencies: coincidentally Japan occupied all European possessions in the east to the borders of India and northern New Guinea. Had these been settler colonies they would have looked forward to reunion with their parent states: since they were not, many nationalists welcomed the Japanese as liberators; and even when reaction against them developed it was focussed on the desire for full independence after Japan was defeated rather than a return to empire. When allied forces reoccupied these dependencies in 1945 France and Holland found it impossible to reconstitute full colonial rule: even in Burma the British found the desire for independence so strong that they conceded it in 1948. Thus the Japanese occupation finally destroyed the already weakened foundations of European power in South-East Asia.

Other parts of the colonial world were less catastrophically affected by the war, for even in French and Belgian territories colonial government continued in isolation from the metropolis. Yet everywhere the war changed the climate of opinion. In India Congress opposed co-operation with Britain and extracted a firm promise of independence once the war was over. Ceylon also was promised internal self-government. Allied defeats and then the Anglo-American occupation stimulated nationalists throughout Islamic North Africa; and in tropical Africa greatly increased contacts with the outside world and knowledge of European defeats encouraged criticism of colonial regimes. Thus, while Europe retained political control over all dependencies outside South-East Asia in 1945 and could still decide whether or not to make concessions, the task was now considerably harder. The question was whether the imperial powers had sufficient determination to face the moral and physical cost of fighting a rearguard action against colonial nationalists.

The second and more important consequence of the war was that it brought about a fundamental change in European attitudes to empire and weakened the will to rule. In the 1930s believers in empire were already on the defensive against denunciations of 'imperialism' by Marxists and the left; they reacted by liberalizing administrative practices and taking a stand on the doctrine of trusteeship. But empire still seemed morally justifiable, provided its methods conformed to advancing standards. The war changed this self-confidence. Italian and Japanese conquests before 1939 had seemed immoral; German imperialism within Europe aroused horror. Wartime idealism, typified by United States interpretation of the Atlantic Charter, and recognition that many colonies were contributing to the allied war effort generated criticism of colonial regimes and readiness to make major changes after the war. The rise to world dominance of the United States and Russia - the two professedly anti-colonial powers, the creation of the United Nations as a forum for international opinion on colonial matters and the active investigations undertaken by its Trusteeship Council (replacing the far less critical Mandates

Commission of the League) combined to put all imperial powers on the defensive.

For these and other reasons the attitude of Europe to its tropical colonies changed rapidly after 1945. There was no sudden determination to liberate them; but it began to be admitted that most would ultimately have to be given self-government. The question was how complete this would be and how soon it would come. The problem was largely confined to Africa, the West Indies, Malaya and the Pacific islands, for the British were committed to full independence for India, Ceylon and Burma, and neither France nor Holland succeeded in re-imposing full control over their eastern dependencies. Caribbean colonies were certain to be given political concessions because of their relative sophistication; Tunisia and Morocco as protected states were clearly destined for full self-government; but it seemed very unlikely that the tropical colonies in Africa, the Indian Ocean or the Pacific would gain independence or even full autonomy in the foreseeable future. In most of them nationalist parties were weak and few possessed sufficient men of political or administrative experience to run government on western lines. European policy in the decade after 1945 was therefore to concede power rapidly in the more advanced dependencies, but to prepare the rest for self-government during a long period of apprenticeship. Had this timetable been maintained few if any colonies in tropical Africa or the Pacific would have achieved more than self-government under restraint, such as the British settlement colonies had before 1914, by the middle 1960s.

In fact this timetable was torn up: during the 1950s the retreat from empire changed from a measured crawl to an uncontrolled gallop. Dogmatism is impossible, but it seems likely that the reason lay in two interacting developments. On the one hand an increasing number in Britain, France and other western countries (Portugal and Spain only excepted) gradually adopted the view that 'colonialism' was morally undesirable and should be ended as soon as possible. They even rejected the traditional claim of white minorities in 'mixed' colonies to predominate by virtue of superior capacity. On the other hand the rapid growth of mass nationalist parties in many colonies made colonial government an ever-increasing nuisance to the powers. Liberals were appalled at the measures taken to suppress sedition, and even those who believed that a long period of political apprenticeship was necessary in the interests of the colonial peoples themselves began to think that the price of retaining power in the interim was becoming too high. Moreover decolonization was a cumulative process: the liberation of one territory stimulated demands in others and at the same time often made it pointless for the imperial powers to hold them. Thus the independence of India in 1947 and the evacuation of the Suez Canal military base in 1956 automatically destroyed most of the interest Britain had previously had both in East Africa and South-East Asia. Empires had to some extent formed interlocking systems: when some parts were removed many others lost their imperial functions.

These were the roots of decolonization after 1945. It is not always possible to give a precise date at which a colonial territory became 'independent' because there were many intermediate steps between full subjection and total sovereignty. In the following chronological survey the criterion used is the acquisition of full internal self-government by a dependency coupled with freedom to sever any remaining links with the metropolis - as in foreign relations and defence - at its own choice.

The twenty years after 1945 divide into two parts. Before 1950 Europe released only those dependencies which had been on the verge of independence in 1939 or were able to demand it as a direct result of the Second World War. During the second phase, which began in about 1956, the majority of the remaining dependencies were released, although in 1945 most of these had seemed unlikely to be fitted for independence within a generation or more. During the first period most of the new states were in the Islamic Middle East or in the east; thereafter the majority were in Africa.

For four years after 1945 the speed of decolonization was breathtaking. In 1946 the Philippines became a sovereign state and Jordan and Syria ceased to be British or French mandates. In 1947 India and Pakistan became independent as members of the Commonwealth. Ceylon followed their example in 1948; but Burma, who became independent in the same year, did not accept membership and Israel, throwing off the British mandate, was not offered it. In 1949 the Netherlands recognized the sovereign independence of Indonesia, but continued until 1956 to hope for close political relations with her. In 1949 France conceded sovereignty to Laos, Cambodia and Vietnam (Annam and Tongking); but these remained within the French Union until France finally lost power in Indo-China in 1954.

Apart from the liberation of Libya in 1951, which had been under British and French military control since its conquest from Italy during the war, there now followed a pause. Europe was not yet convinced that empire was morally objectionable and the problems of multi-racial societies in Algeria, Central Africa and Kenya complicated matters. Most powers therefore tried to temper nationalist demands with judicious concessions. The second phase began tentatively in 1956, when Morocco and Tunisia denounced their relationships with France and left the Union. In the same year Britain evacuated the Egyptian Sudan, and in 1957 Malaya became a sovereign state within the Commonwealth, though Singapore, North Borneo and Sarawak did not join it until 1963 as part of the new Federation of Malaysia. None of these concessions was really surprising, since all were Islamic states which had retained varying degrees of autonomy as French or British protectorates. The crucial event which marked the beginning of the last phase of decolonization and showed that Europe's will to rule was cracking was the independence of the Gold Coast - renamed Ghana - in 1957. This was the first 'pagan' dependency to become entirely free: a tropical African colony which lacked natural unity and had possessed no sort of autonomy in 1945. It owed is primacy partly to its economic wealth but even more to the political skill of Kwame Nkrumah, leader of the main nationalist party, who made it intolerable for Britain to retain power. His appointment as prime minister in 1951 was an epoch-making event, for it stimulated nationalist movements throughout Africa; and Ghana's independence in 1957 pointed to general decolonization. The next major step was taken by France, who abolished the 1946 Union in 1958 and gave all dependencies the option of full independence or sovereignty within the new French Community. French Guinea alone opted for the first and became independent in 1958. The remainder achieved independence in 1960 when the Community was dissolved.

1960 proved the most important year in the period of decolonization, for the greater part of the French empire then became independent. The federations of West and Equatorial Africa split up into a multiplicity of sovereign states, though many retained special links with France and each other: Ivory Coast, Dahomey, Upper Volta, Senegal, Mauritania, Niger, Mali, Gabon, Central African Republic and Chad. Togo and Cameroun, both trust territories, also became independent, the latter including the area previously administered by Britain. Madagascar became independent as the Malagasy Republic. In 1960 also Britain liberated Nigeria; British and Italian Somaliland were fused in the Somali Republic; and the Belgian

Congo became independent. Thereafter the 'wind of change' continued to blow strongly. In 1961 Britain ended her control over Cyprus, Sierra Leone, Tanganyika and Kuwait; in 1962 she freed Jamaica, Trinidad and Tobago (following the collapse of the non-independent West Indian Federation set up in 1957), and Uganda. In the same year France ended her long war in Algeria and granted full independence. In 1963 Britain liberated Zanzibar and Kenya: significantly Kenya became an African state in which the once influential British settler community was merely a tolerated minority. The same rejection of the claims of Europeans to rule African majorities was shown by the dissolution of the Federation of Rhodesia and Nyasaland at the end of 1963, and this was followed by independence for Nyasaland (Malawi) and Northern Rhodesia (Zambia) in 1964. Rhodesia remained a British dependency, and was not likely to be given independence until her constitution satisfied the African majority that they would ultimately gain political power. In 1964 also Britain made Malta independent. Since this was against the will of many Maltese it showed that the British were now anxious to wind up the remnants of their empire as quickly as possible.

By 1965 the process of decolonization was almost complete: all that remained of the old empires were either territories which had been fully incorporated within the parent states (or which it was still hoped to incorporate), or places which were apparently too small or poor to be able to stand alone. France retained Martinique, Guadeloupe, Reunion, and Guiana as incorporated Overseas Departments, and Polynesia, New Caledonia, French Somaliland, the Comoro Islands, St Pierre-et-Miquelon and a few other islands as dependent Overseas Territories. Portugal, now the main exponent of the principle of incorporation as the alternative to decolonization, still held most of her empire: the Madeira Islands and the Azores, long incorporated with the metropolis, the Cape Verde Islands, Guinea, Sao Tome, Angola, Mozambique, Macao and part of Timor. The Netherlands retained Surinam and the Netherlands Antilles, also in close association with the parent state. Spain had fully incorporated the Canary Islands and kept her small west African territories - Ifni, Spanish Sahara, Rio Muni and Fernando Po. Russia retained all her colonial territories in Central Asia and the Far East, but treated them as integral parts of the USSR. The United States fully incorporated Hawaii as a state of the Union in 1959. She kept Porto Rico as a fully self-governing dependency, but acknowledged her right to secede.

The Virgin Islands, Guam, American Samoa and smaller Trust Territories in the Pacific also survived as United States dependencies. Britain, which had possessed the largest empire, also retained the longest list of dependencies, of which the more important were Aden, the Bahamas, Bermuda, Barbados, the Leeward and Windward Islands, and other small Caribbean islands, British Guiana and British Honduras; the Falkland and other small Atlantic islands; Fiji, Gambia (due for independence in 1965), Gibraltar, the High Commission Territories in South Africa, Hong Kong, the Maldive Islands, Mauritius, Tonga and the Western Pacific High Commission Territories. Several of these were expected to receive independence in the near future. But Britain, like other imperial powers, was faced with the apparently insoluble problem of deciding the future of many small territories which had no evident capacity to act as sovereign states.

It is too early to pass judgement on the consequences of colonialism or decolonization. Neither was wholly good or bad; but the end of empire exposed many of its defects as the winding up of a business concern demonstrates previously concealed weakness. The virtue of European empire was to provide a framework of political stability in Africa, South-East Asia and the Pacific at a time when European power and intervention were seriously eroding indigenous states and social forms and when international competition might have led to constant friction. Imperial rule was also a medium through which the technical and intellectual achievements of the west were transmitted to other parts of the world. Its defect was that alien rule destroyed as much as it created. Indigenous social and political institutions had to be modified or destroyed to make imperial government possible: thereafter they could not be revived in their old form, and the end of empire was bound to leave a dangerous vacuum. Given a sufficiency of time and clarity of aim Europe might have grafted her own political, economic and cultural values on to indigenous stock, not assimilating it but cultivating a new and virile hybrid. In some places this was done: in India, Ceylon and perhaps Java, where alien rule lasted for more than a century and a half. But most other dependencies were still standing between two worlds at the moment of independence, unable to return to their past, but inexperienced in European modes. Morally the west was right to give them freedom when it was strongly demanded: politically it was necessary to do so, for the price of refusal was too high. Yet the aftermath was fraught with danger. The stability of a few great inter-continental empires was replaced by the instability of a multitude of small sovereign states, many of them lacking unity, economic resources or political skill. The end of empire meant the Balkanization of Africa and South-East Asia.

The future of the one-time dependencies therefore remained unpredictable. To the new states the end of subordination seemed the threshold of a brave new world: they would become powerful industrialized states, as China and Japan had already done, and would hold the political balance between the great power blocs of the east and west. But to the historian evidence from the past offered less cause for optimism. The United States and the British Dominions were examples of colonies which flourished as sovereign states. But the end of Spanish power in America, the dissolution of Turkish power in the Balkans, and the chaos which often succeeded empires in the more distant past suggested that decolonization might also generate confusion and economic decline. In 1964 the end of empire in Africa and South-East Asia seemed more likely to lead to political dictatorship, economic decay and even endemic minor wars than to brilliant new civilizations.

The conclusion was obvious. The western powers had failed to prepare their dependencies for freedom before the demand became morally irresistible: they could not shrug off responsibility by conceding sovereignty. The need was not to expiate past 'exploitation' - which was not a significant feature of European imperialism - but to compensate for failure to act more positively. In the post-colonial era duty and self-interest alike impelled them to help one-time subjects to build prosperous and self-sufficient nations from the rubble of the colonial empires.

SECTION II: THE COLD WAR AND IMPERIALISM

Introduction

Neither decolonisation, nor the subsequent confrontations in the Third World between revolution and counterrevolution, can be fully understood without reference to the East/West conflict which rapidly polarised in the years immediately following World War II. In this section we move back in time, from the culmination of the decolonisation process, to the debates over the causes of the conflict between the United States and the Soviet Union, which became known as the Cold War.

The Cold War was a state of intense antagonistic competition - ideological, political, and economic, which fell short of direct armed conflict. While its temporal limits are subject to debate, it certainly continued from early in 1946 until the aftermath of the Cuban Missile Crisis in 1962, and the full revelation of the Sino-Soviet split - also in the early 60's. Some see it as continuing until the American defeat in Vietnam.

Orthodox, conservative historians, such as John Spanier, see the origins of the Cold War predominantly in power political and ideological terms. These writers blame the Soviet Union for starting the Cold War, pointing to what they see as the USSR's duplicity in Poland; the occupation and control of Eastern Europe; and the events in Northern Iran in 1946; as examples of communist expansion which had to be countered with a firm containment policy by the United States. For the conservatives, the American military involvement in Greece in 1947; in the Berlin Crisis of 1948-9; and the creation of NATO in 1949; are examples of the defensive containment of communist aggression.

Radical historians take a very different stance. Emphasising the role of economic factors in the origins of the Cold War, and seeing these factors in the context of theories of imperialism, they tend to see the US as initially aggressive and the Soviet Union as defensively reactive. The radicals argue that the war-ravaged Soviet Union was fully occupied in domestic reconstruction and in consolidating its influence in Eastern Europe in the immediate post-war years. The Russians, according to this view, had neither the inclination, nor the capability, for fulfilling the aggressive and expansionist role assigned them by conservative historians. The United States, on the other hand, was more outward looking and had both the capability and will to effect changes at the international level. With opportunities for trade and investment in Eastern Europe thwarted by Communist takeovers, the United States concentrated on Western Europe. An American aided economic recovery of Europe was seen as providing trade and investment outlets for American industry and capital—offsetting the danger of depression at home, and enabling U.S. corporate capitalism to expand abroad.

However, European recovery required massive American aid which was to be provided by the Marshall Plan. To get Congressional approval for this plan in 1947, a deliberate campaign of intense anti-Soviet propaganda, which reflected the Truman Doctrine (of containment), was mounted. Thus Marshall Aid, according to the radical view, was a response to the perceived needs of *American* capitalism, but it was sold to the public as a programme for buying off an alleged threat of communism in Western Europe.

The radical historians (often Marxist), who emphasise economic factors form a sub-group among those students of the Cold War who have become known as 'Revisionists'. The 'Revisionist' theories of the origins of the Cold War have only been widely discussed during the past decade. These new theories are so called because they have revised the fundamental assumptions of the orthodox Cold War historians. Whereas the latter tended to assign almost total responsibility for starting the Cold War to the Soviet Union, the Revisionists have tended to blame the U.S. However, many revisionists reject the Marxian emphasis on the economic determination of U.S. foreign policy which characterises the writings of the radical historians. Among the liberal revisionists, some emphasise the personality of U.S. political leaders, contrasting Truman's anti-communism with Roosevelt's more pro-Soviet line. Others, as Ronald Steel points out, argue that America's stance was *imperial* rather than imperia*list*. An imperial or 'globalist' foreign policy seeks global dominance, but it is motivated by ideology, by a sense of historic mission, or by a sense of immense power; and economic factors play a subordinate role in its determination. America's historic mission, as the world's first democracy, was seen, mistakenly in the eyes of these historians, as requiring the promotion and preservation of democracy everywhere. Since the major threat to democracy was held to be communism - preserving democracy necessitated policies of containment and counterrevolution.

The predominant view, particularly of recent historians, is that the United States played the major role in the traumatic transition from what might otherwise have been mildly competitive co-existence, to the state of intensely antagonistic competition which characterised the Cold War. However, it should be remembered when evaluating the differing explanations, that it is not necessary to accept the single factor accounts which tend to be favoured by radical or conservative historians. U.S. Secretary of State, Cordell Hull, for example, may have seen that the U.S. would gain economically from an international policy of free trade, but he seems also to have been convinced that such a policy would help to avoid war.

Neither should it be forgotten when considering these explanations, that a new international order was emerging in 1945. In the 19th century and the first forty years of the 20th, the 'balance of power' had been centred in Europe and usually involved four or five substantial powers. Now, at the end of the war, there were two superpowers; a trans-Atlantic balance; and a mutual lack of experience of being at the centre of the world stage. Add to this the psychological impact of the use of the atomic bomb by the United States, combined with the knowledge that the Soviet Union was also developing this weapon, and it is not surprising that each side viewed the other with insecurity, suspicion and unease. In this situation mistakes were made; misperception and over-reaction were not infrequent. New rules of international co-existence had to emerge and a new *modus vivendi* to be established.

Thus it may be argued that the new configuration of post-war international politics, in itself, meant that the Cold War was, to some extent, inevitable. But the structure of world politics is a factor which would, of course, have affected both sides. Although strongly influenced by the new environment, the intense antagonism of the Cold War seems to have been rooted in other sources; in particular the ideological rivalry between West and East which had been temporarily submerged in the wartime alliance against Germany.

Once the Cold War had begun, however, and particularly after the Korean War, it was difficult for the United States foreign policy elite to escape from the McCarthyite world view it had, in more than one sense, created. Real change did not come until, as Andrew Mack points out in Section III, the emergence of the Sino-Soviet split had undermined the concept of a communist monolith, and defeat in Vietnam finally made possible, and necessary, the toleration of independent communist movements and states. If Cold War had given way to *detente* in the North Atlantic area by the early 60's, by the mid 70's its demise was world wide.

The Cold War and The Korean War

D. W. Ziegler

Today Cold War is a term of disapproval, contrasted unfavorably with "relaxation of tensions" or "detente." Even those who question the wisdom of Secretary Kissinger's policy of detente are careful to say they don't want a "return to the Cold War." Yet when the term was first used, the emphasis was on the adjective "cold," not the noun "war." Cold War was contrasted with "hot war" or "shooting war" and its most vocal opponents were those who wanted to "get it over with" by launching a preventive war against the Soviet Union.

Despite the intense rivalry between the United States and the USSR in the late 1940's and early 1950's, the struggle never did turn into all-out war between them. But the Cold War period did include a highly destructive war in Korea (two million battle deaths) which was widely viewed at the time as a war between the United States and the USSR (with the North Koreans and the Chinese acting as Soviet proxies). We will look first at the Cold War to see how a local dispute in the Korean peninsula became a conflict involving major powers.

Origins of United States-Soviet Rivalry:
Iran, Greece, Turkey

The search for the origins of the Cold War is a major scholarly industry. There are vast numbers of books and articles on the subject to choose from. Some trace the origins of the war back to 1917 and the Bolshevik victory in Russia. Others see the origin in the policies of one country or another during World War II. In our introduction to the subject, we will concentrate only on the more immediate causes.[1]

During World War II the United States pursued a single goal—to remove the threat to United States interests posed by German and Japanese power. All other goals were subordinated to this one. As a result, the Americans consistently rejected Winston Churchill's suggestions to fight with more attention to political goals. He wanted to invade the Balkans in order to cut off a Russian advance into that region. The Americans replied that this area would be too costly to invade and that such an invasion would not lead to the defeat of Germany any more speedily than an invasion in Italy or France.

The Soviet Union, on the other hand, had a number of foreign policy goals that could be fulfilled by the war. The Russians worried just as much about German power as the Western democracies did. They were less concerned about Japan because they had been able to pursue a successful appeasement policy toward Japan on their own far eastern border from 1930 to 1945. They had also tried an appeasement policy toward Germany in 1939, signing a Non-Aggression Pact a few weeks before Germany invaded Poland and then taking control over a portion of Poland (as provided for in a secret portion of the Pact) as their reward. But Hitler doublecrossed Stalin in 1941 and invaded Russia so that by the time the United States entered the war Russia was lined up with Britain in opposition to Germany. But the Soviet desire for expansion, illustrated in Poland by the secret deal with the Germans, extended to other areas as well. The old empire of the Russian tsar had extended much farther than the boundaries of the Soviet Union in 1939. Some areas under tsarist control had been able to achieve national independence when the Russian empire collapsed; other parts had been claimed by Russia's neighbors and annexed by them while the new Bolshevik regime was too weak to do anything about it. But the Soviet government had never given up its claims to areas once ruled by the tsar and saw an opportunity in the war to regain this territory.

As a result of World War II, Russia acquired (or reacquired) large amounts of territory in Europe along its eastern borders— parts of Finland; the entire countries of Estonia, Latvia, and Lithuania; parts of Poland, Germany, and Rumania. this acquisition of territory was passively accepted by the Western democracies, in part because they felt Russia deserved something in return for its losses in fighting the Germans and also because the Red Army was firmly in control of these areas and nothing could be done to remove them short of starting World War III. Along its southern border, however, the USSR encountered resistance. One area into which it wished to expand was the northern province of Iran called Azerbaijan. An "Azerbaijani Soviet Republic" had existed briefly at the time of the Russian revolution. It was subsequently divided, with part incorporated into Iran and part into the Soviet Union. In 1941, acting out of fear of losing Iran's oil resources to the Germans because of the pro-German sympathies of the Shah of Iran, Russia and Britain together occupied Iran, removed the Shah, and established their own troops in the country, the Russians in the north, the British in the south. They agreed to remove the troops as soon as the war ended.

The British did remove their troops, the Russians did not, Instead they sponsored an autonomous Azerbaijani Republic, ruled by the local communist party. By 1946, the situation was tense. If the pattern of Europe were to be repeated, then the Red Army would not withdraw but stay to support a puppet regime. After a period of diplomatic maneuvering, in April 1946 the Russians agreed to withdraw, in return for promises of reform in Azerbaijan and the establishment of a Soviet-Iranian oil company. In May 1946, the Soviet troops did withdraw. The Iranian army promptly occupied the province, executed the leaders of the autonomous republic, and suppressed the communist party. Furthermore, the Iranian parliament refused to ratify the Soviet-Iranian Oil Company, so that the Russians gained nothing at all.

Like so many other incidents in the Cold War, the Azerbaijan incident can be cited to prove different contentions. It could be used as evidence that Stalin was not committed to expansion. Or it could be evidence that Stalin's expansionist desires could be checked only by vigorous resistance. Credit for bringing about the Russian withdrawal has been given to the United Nations (then just getting started and still meeting in London), to the British who sent a note of protest, to the Americans who talked about extending the draft, to the British and Americans together who showed their solidarity through Churchill's "Iron Curtain" speech at Fulton, Missouri, or to the skillful diplomacy of the premier of Iran. What is significant is that Soviet policy in Azerbaijan was perceived at the time as an attempt at Soviet expansion that was repulsed by Western policy. It was taken as a model of how to deal with the Russians.[2]

The Truman Doctrine and
The Marshall Plan

A seemingly parallel situation appeared in two other countries to the south of Russia, Turkey and Greece. Turkey, like many of the other countries bordering on Russia, had taken advantage of Russian weakness during the Bolshevik revolution and the civil war that followed it in the 1920's to reclaim some disputed territory, in particular the province of Khars. Following the end of the war in Europe in 1945, the Soviet Foreign Minister requested that the Turks hand this territory over to the Soviet Union. The diplomatic note was backed up by "routine military maneuvers" in the bordering areas of the Soviet Union. The Turks rejected the Soviet request but were uneasy about how far Russian pressure would go.

In the case of Greece, there was no claim to territory by the Soviet Union or actual occupation of territory by the Red army; rather the Greek government was fighting a civil war against communist guerillas who, it was assumed, were controlled by Stalin. Both Greece and Turkey had traditionally looked to Britain as the great power that supported them against their powerful northern neighbor. But Britain, weakened by the burden of fighting the Germans during the war, was suffering a financial crisis that made it impossible for it to continue to play the role of a great power in this part of the world. The British approached the Americans and asked them if they would consider abandoning their traditional policy of isolation and provide aid to Turkey and Greece.

This British request was followed by weeks of feverish activity in Washington as government officials debated whether the United States should assume the role traditionally played by great powers and whether the American people would accept this departure from traditional policy. This second question was much more important in the minds of the officials. Everyone remembered how Woodrow Wilson had failed to win the support of the Congress for his plan for a League of Nations, with the result that the United States made no contribution to world politics in the two decades that led up to World War II. In an effort to avoid repeating Wilson's error, it was decided that President Truman should address both houses of Congress, outlining the new American policy of involvement abroad and giving the broadest possible justification for it. On March 12, 1947, President Truman made the address that became known as the "Truman Doctrine." This was a United States pledge to "support free peoples who are resisting attempted subjugation by armed minorities or by outside pressures."³ The Truman Doctrine was clearly a turning point in American foreign policy and as disenchantment has grown in recent years with American involvement abroad, critics have concentrated on it as a source of much of our trouble. Even some who agreed at the time with the policy of extending aid to Greece and Turkey objected to the universal language in which the policy was couched. Why "free peoples"? they asked. Why not just say "Greece and Turkey" and reserve the right to decide whether other countries will get aid at some time in the future.

The ease with which the Truman Doctrine gained acceptance by Congress and the support it got from leaders of both parties in subsequent years make it easy to forget the genuine fears that troubled the planners in 1947. It seemed a realistic possibility that such a departure from traditional policies might be rejected, on the one hand by traditional isolationists, on the other by a new group of idealists who wanted to rely totally on the United Nations. The Truman Doctrine was widely thought at the time to be a step toward a more mature and responsible foreign policy than the one that America had followed in the years between the two world wars.

The Truman Doctrine, seen by Americans as a program to prevent Soviet interference in Greece and Turkey, was immediately interpreted by the Soviet Union as a "fresh intrusion of the USA into the affairs of other states." This became the typical pattern of Cold War exchanges. Each side interpreted its own moves as defensive and those of its rival as aggressive.

Convinced of Soviet aggressive intentions, the West reacted with defensive measures, first in Azerbaijan, then in Greece and Turkey. The weak condition of the European economies became a cause for concern, not only for humanitarian reasons but also because it was believed that weak economies would make these countries more susceptible to communist takeovers. A few months after President Truman had announced that the United States would give military assistance to Greece and Turkey, his Secretary of State, George Marshall, announced that the United States would make available economic assistance to all the countries of Europe. This offer of aid was open to all but it seemed likely to the planners in Washington that the Russians would find such aid incompatible with the rigid control and secrecy they were accustomed to exercising over their own economy. The Washington planners were correct, Marshall Plan aid was rejected both by the USSR and by countries under its control.

Whatever suspicions Stalin had could only be confirmed by these policies. Measures that the West interpreted as defensive were, from the Russian perspective, preparations for aggression. Whatever Stalin's original intentions for the countries of Eastern Europe, there was no longer any possibility of independent development. Perhaps it had been his intention all along, perhaps Western policy had only speeded up his schedule, perhaps Western policy provoked him into it. Whatever the origin, Stalin now proceeded to eliminate anyone with pro-Western leanings in countries liberated from the Nazis by the Red Army—Bulgaria, Rumania, and Hungary.

The Cold War in Europe: Poland, Berlin

It was in Poland that relations with the West became most strained. Poland was different from the other countries of East Europe—it was the country for which Britain and France had originally gone to war against the Germans, it had fought against the Nazis instead of collaborating with them, and enough Poles had immigrated to the United States to make events in Poland a matter of some national concern. Poland had been one of the main topics at the conferences held at Yalta (February 1945) and Potsdam (July 1945) by the three major victors to decide the political fate of Europe after the German defeat. The West had asked in general for the guarantee of fundamental rights and freedoms in East Europe; specifically it asked that the communist government installed in Poland by the Red Army be broadened to include Poles who had spent the war either in exile in London or fighting the Germans in the underground inside Poland. Although the Russians had promised this at Yalta and reaffirmed it at Potsdam the promises were not kept. Perhaps the Russians did not believe that the United States was sincere in its solicitude for the Poles. They were aware that concentrations of Poles in cities such as Chicago and Milwaukee gave them some importance in domestic politics in America. Perhaps they thought that these voters would be satisifed if Presidents Roosevelt and Truman obtained promises on paper.

In fact, the Americans made their demands on idealistic grounds. The war against the Nazis had been fought to guarantee democratic freedoms to the people of Europe and the Americans wanted to see this principle applied. This idea contrasted with the British approach under Churchill. He had agreed in a realistic way in 1944 to a rough division of Europe into spheres of influence, reflecting the relative power of each side. Under this division, the West was to have predominant influence in Greece, while Russia would predominate in Rumania and Bulgaria. In fact, in 1944 when the British had harshly repressed the Greek communists on behalf of an autocratic Greek regime, the Russians made no move to aid the communists. The Churchill-Soviet agreement did not cover northern Europe, but when the British and Americans complained about what was happening inside Poland, Stalin replied, in effect, "Did we say anything to you about Greece?"[5]

The Americans' professed dislike of "spheres of influence" must have seemed like hypocrisy to the Russians as long as the Americans professed the Monroe Doctrine, for that doctrine certainly appeared to reserve a sphere of influence for the United States in Latin America. But words did not speak as loud as actions. In July 1945, the United States Army withdrew 100 miles from the westernmost point it had reached in Germany, to allow the Russians to move up to a line arranged long in advance of the German defeat. Throughout 1945 the strength of the United States Army in Europe was rapidly running down, as the American government tried to meet the popular demand for as rapid a demobilization as possible. On V-E day (Victory in Europe, May 7, 1945) the United States Army in Europe numbered 3,100,000. A year later 391,000.[6] Anyone interested in power (and as good Leninists the Soviet leaders were obliged to be) could see that whatever the United States might say about events in Poland, it was in no position to do anything about them. Pulling troops back 100 miles was more eloquent than any diplomatic protest.

By 1947 it was clear that Poland would be ruled by the Polish Communist Party in a way acceptable to Russia. In February 1948, the government of Czechoslovakia was expunged of its pro-Western parties. In June 1946 the city of Berlin, itself under four-power administration but totally within the Soviet Zone of Occupation, was cut off from contact with the rest of Germany by a Soviet blockade.

The United States wished to react strongly to the Berlin Blockade, because it believed that its legal right to be in Berlin was unassailable, but it lacked the military means to do much. Only one combat-ready division in the entire United States Army was not committed to occupation duty. General Marshall said, "We did not have enough to defend the airstrip at Fairbanks." President Truman decided to airlift supplies into Berlin, but it took all the available transport aircraft in the air force to accomplish that. As a gesture to show United States firmness, President Truman made one of the few moves available to him and sent a number of B-29 bombers to Britain. This was the first time since the end of the war that bombers (ones capable of carrying the atomic bomb) were stationed outside the United States. It was followed by discussion within the government of assistance to a rearmed Europe, eventually including Germany. In June 1948 the United States Senate passed a bipartisan resolution supporting collective defense in Western Europe and in April 1949 the North Atlantic Treaty was signed, by which "the Parties agree that an armed attack against one or more of them in Europe or North America shall be considered an attack against them all." From this treaty developed the North Atlantic Treaty Organization, or NATO.

Bipolarity

Whatever one considers to be the beginning of the Cold War, by 1949, when the North Atlantic Treaty was signed, we were clearly deeply involved in it. A number of features set this period off from times of peace. One was a high level of hostility between East and West, as manifested in public statements and propaganda. Another was recurring international crises provoked by incidents of violence, such as the shooting down of United States airplanes flying near the border of the Soviet Union. Still another feature was the spread of East-West rivalry into nearly every area of life. Anything that hurt our side helped them and vice versa. Richard Nixon, then Vice President, welcomed the Supreme Court decision of 1954 outlawing school segregation as our greatest victory in the Cold War.[8]

As more and more areas of life were affected by the rivalry between the United States and the USSR, a new form of international politics took shape, unlike the system of the nineteenth or first half of the twentieth centuries. Instead of a number of major states, there were only two, and these so exceeded in power all the others that they were known as superpowers. Each acted as a pole around which all the other countries in the world aligned themselves, giving this form of international politics its name, bipolarity. Each superpower and its surrounding client states were known as a bloc—the Soviet bloc or the Western bloc. These blocs were held together by military alliances (NATO in the West, the Warsaw Pact organization in the East), by economic organizations (the Organization for European Economic Cooperation in the West, the Council for Mutual Economic Assistance in the East), and by political values shared by the political leaders. Countries not part of either bloc were of two types—those explicitly neutral by choice or imposition (Sweden, Switzerland and Austria, for example), and the "nonaligned" states of Africa, Asia, and Latin America that became known as the Third World. In the early days of the Cold War, both superpowers looked on nonalignment as immoral. The Soviet Union saw no difference in India after the British departed in 1947. If a country was not with them, it was against them. The Soviet attitude toward the Third World began to shift around the time of the death of Stalin in 1953. From then on, Third World countries were wooed by the communists. But the United States persisted for several years more in condemning neutralism. John Foster Dulles, Secretary of State under President Eisenhower, called nonalignment "an immoral and short-sighted conception."[9] Only under President Kennedy did the United States adopt the same policy as the Soviet Union, arguing now that if they weren't against us, they were for us.

The Cold War was a period of intense rivalry stopping short of all-out war. Preparations for war were made and the enemy in a potential war was clearly identified, but the weapons were not used. Each side engaged in propaganda warfare, in such forums as the United Nations and radio broadcasts. Each side practiced subversion, that is, contracts with citizens of other countries without the approval of their government. Each side maintained sizable armed forces; the United States for the first time continued the draft into peacetime. But United States troops never went into combat against Soviet troops.

Hot War in Korea

One characteristic of the Cold War was that all areas of the world were drawn into the United States-USSR rivalry. When fighting broke out in Korea in June 1950, it was automatically seen as an episode in the Cold War. True, the Russians themselves were not fighting, but they were supplying materiel and even advisers to the North Koreans. Americans often referred to it as a "war by proxy." For its part, the United States did not leave the fighting to its proxy, South Korea, but sent troops, ultimately committing about 250,000 men. Yet despite this outbreak of an actual shooting war, the conflict remained limited and did not escalate into the third world war everyone feared.

Korea had been a virtual protectorate of Japan ever since the Russo-Japanese War of 1905. With the defeat of Japan by Russia and the United States in 1945, Korea was divided in the middle, at the 38th parallel, to facilitate the Japanese surrender; the Russians, who had been fighting the Japanese north of Korea in

Manchuria, occupied the northern half, the Americans occupied the southern. Along with the Russians came members of the Korean Communist Party who had spent the war years in exile in Russia. The United States allowed the formation of political parties in the South. Koreans in both parts of the country stated that they wanted reunification but an American-Soviet commission was unable to agree on means for achieving it. In 1947 a United Nations resolution called for elections in both zones of occupation for a single Korean parliament, which would then set up a provisional government. The Russians refused entry to the UN commission that was to supervise these elections and in May 1948 elections were held by the UN in the South alone. Three months later elections were conducted by the Russians in the North.

With the communist party firmly in control in the North, the Russians announced withdrawal of their occupation forces, completed by January 1949. This move increased pressure on the Americans to withdraw from the South, a move that was being considered already for other reasons. One of these was the hostility of the Koreans to foreign occupation; Americans anticipated demonstrations, riots, and other acts of violence that would make continued occupation difficult. Also, there was budgetary pressure from domestic sources to cut back military forces. The military did not see any great need for retaining troops in Korea—they considered it would be a liability in any future war, which would undoubtedly be fought globally with nuclear weapons. Therefore, in June 1949, the United States withdrew its troops, leaving behind (as the Russians had in the North) military advisers— a total of 500 for the 60,000 man South Korean army. But to keep the South from going to war and reunifying the country by force, the United States took with its departing forces all weapons that could be used offensively—airplanes, tanks, and heavy artillery.

Theories on the Cause of the Korean War

A year after the United States withdrawal, on June 25, 1950, the North Koreans launched a massive attack on the South. It was not the low-level violence that had become typical of the Cold War, like the guerrillas in Greece or communist party violence in Czechoslovakia, but conventional warfare—armed troops riding in tanks crossing a well demarcated frontier. The attack was obviously well planned and because there were Russian advisers throughout the North Korean Army (and because supplies such as gasoline were coming from Russia), it was assumed that the Russians were responsible for the attack.[10]

But the precise reason for the attack was a subject for debate in Washington. A number of interpretations were offered at the time.[11] The most popular was the belief that the Korean attack was a feint, a diversionary move to weaken the defense of Europe. The rearmament of Europe was just getting under way and American attention was concentrated there. Even General Charles de Gaulle, who was not noted for being pro-American or anti-Russian, expected at any time a Russian attack in Europe. The analogy between divided Korea and divided Germany was too compelling. In each case the section of the country occupied by the Russians had built up military forces and was issuing belligerent statements, but the section occupied by the West was still weak, underarmed, and inadequately protected by occupying forces.

Another popular view about the causes of the war was that this was Soviet probing for soft spots. After all, Secretary of State Dean Acheson, just six months before, had declared that the United States would not defend Korea. He had defined a 'defensive perimeter" for the United States in the Pacific, running from the Aleutians to Japan and then the Ryukyu Islands (Okinawa) and the Philippines. Outside the perimeter were the island of Formosa where the Nationalist Chinese were holding out against the Communists, and Korea. 'It must be clear," Acheson said, "that no person can guarantee these areas against attack."[12] One could say that the North Koreans were simply taking Acheson at his word. When you draw a line in the dirt and warn the other guy not to cross it, his move is at least to step up to the line.

But although some Americans interpreted the attack in this way, others held the contradictory view that the Russians were testing the West's resolve, just as Hitler had done in Munich. President Truman said we had been tough in Iran, Berlin, and Greece and we must show the same toughness in Asia. Chairman of the Joint Chiefs of Staff Omar Bradley said, "We have to draw the line somewhere."[13] Evidently Bradley and Truman forgot that Acheson had drawn a line only six months before.

Some of the President's advisers saw this attack as more serious, the opening of a Soviet move for world conquest. General Douglas MacArthur, head of United States Occupation Forces in Japan, wrote that "here in Asia is where the Communist conspirators have elected to make their play for global conquest."[14] John Foster Dulles, a Republican working for the Truman administration to prepare a peace treaty with Japan, saw the Korean attack as a move to head off a Pacific version of NATO. Russia already owned Sakhalin Island and the Kurile Islands to the north of Japan. Korea, Dulles believed, threatened Japan from the south, so Russia's strategic move would place Japan "between the upper and lower jaws of the Russian bear."[15] From such a dominating position Russia could exert diplomatic pressure to keep Japan at the very least neutral between East and West.

No one in 1950 seems to have considered a theory for the start of the war that has come to seem at least equally plausible: the simple desire by the North Koreans for reunification. Stalin's personality makes it seem unlikely that the North Koreans could have started the war without his permission, but it is possible that the North Korean leader Kim Il Sung was able to convince Stalin that he could win a quick easy victory and Stalin agreed to go along with him. In this interpretation, responsibility for beginning the war would rest primarily with the North Koreans.

Despite Acheson's speech putting Korea outside our defensive perimeter, the United States did go to the aid of South Korea, first with air and naval units, then with ground troops brought over from Japan.[16] As the decision to aid Korea was being made, it was also decided to go to the UN and request Security Council action on behalf of South Korea. The Council supported the United States because Russia was then boycotting the Security Council as a protest against its failure to seat the new Communist Chinese regime in place of Nationalist China. Thus Russia was not there to use its veto. The United States military action in Korea became the United Nations military action, although the United States provided by far the largest contingent of UN forces and all UN forces were under United States command.

Further actions taken by the United States at this time show the importance attributed to the interpretation that the war was part of an overall communist strategy. One thing the United States did was to reverse itslf on the issue of Formosa, now putting it inside our defensive perimeter by sending the Seventh Fleet to patrol the Straits of Taiwan. The United States also tempered its opposition to colonial regimes enough to give aid to the French, who were fighting Vietnamese Communists and nationalists in Indo-China.

The Course of the Korean War: Expansion and Chinese Intervention

Lacking substantial weapons, the South Koreans were unable to resist the North Korean army and fell back to the south, almost more quickly than United States troops could arrive. But the

United States was able to maintain a toehold on the Korean peninsula inside a small perimeter around the port of Pusan. Then on September 15, 1950, in a bold and risky move, General MacArthur staged an amphibious landing in the center of the east coast of Korea at Inchon. The invasion was a success and United States forces were able to drive in from Inchon toward the South Korean capital of Seoul, trapping North Korean forces as reinforced United States troops broke out of the Pusan perimeter. The success of this move reversed the fortunes of the war and encouraged United States leaders to consider a more ambitious aim than the one with which they had started (merely expelling the North Koreans from the South). The United States now decided to push on across the 38th parallel and reunite the entire country.

The major objection to this move among government officials was the possibility that China might then intervene in the war. China was known to be concerned about events in Korea and the United States gave serious consideration to the possibility of Chinese intervention. In November 1950, the Chinese did intervene massively, inflicting a grave defeat on the United States forces, reversing once again the fortunes of war and prolonging it for almost three more years. Whatever the reasons for the attack by the North Koreans in June, the escalation of the war in November can be blamed on two factors—the failure of United States intelligence and the failure of Chinese diplomacy. United States intelligence agencies knew that the Chinese Communists were Marxists and that Karl Marx had stressed material interests. In a rather simple-minded way, they looked for material interests that China might have in Korea. They came up with only one: hydroelectric stations along the Yalu River (which formed the border between much of Korea and China). Acting on this assessment, the United States took great pains to assure the Chinese that these stations would not be harmed (as indeed they were not, until long after the Chinese intervention). But that assessment of Chinese interests was wrong. What the Chinese cared most about, we now believe, was the continued existence on Korean soil of a communist regime. Perhaps some change in borders would have been tolerated, but not the extinction of the North Korean state.[17]

The Chinese for their part were not successful in communicating their intentions to the United States. After all, General MacArthur had been told at the time military operations north of the 38th parallel were approved, that he was allowed to conduct operations in North Korea only so long as there had been "No entry into North Korea by major Soviet or Chinese Communist forces, no announcement of an intended entry, and no threat by Russian or Chinese Communists to counter our military operations militarily in North Korea."[18] The Chinese did issue a warning on October 3 through the Indian ambassador to China, K. M. Panikkar, but this warning was not seen as an unambiguous signal by the Americans. Panikkar and other Indians had favored the Chinese Communists in the past, and this made their judgment suspect in the eyes of the Americans.[19] The Chinese warning did not come until the eve of the UN vote on a resolution to approve the expansion of the war, and once the United States was publicly committed in this way, a warning had much less force than it would have even a few days earlier.[20]

An earlier and more direct warning would have kept the United States out of North Korea, but the Chinese failed to give it. They were in fact preparing for military entry into the war with great secrecy, moving large numbers of men into Korea at night, keeping them carefully hidden from United States reconnaissance aircraft during the day. The result was a spectacular tactical victory for Chinese military forces. But to get it they risked strategic defeat. That is, if the Chinese had crossed the Yalu River into Korea openly and massively when the United States was still hesitating south of the 38th parallel, the United States would not have pursued the war further. The orders to MacArthur indicate that. But then there would have been no glorious victory for the Chinese military forces. The Chinese kept their intervention secret and achieved the military victory at the price of a diplomatic defeat.[21]

But the worst did not come to pass. The war remained limited. The Chinese entry into the war resulted in a United States retreat to the south, then a counterattack north again that resulted in a stabilized line in about the middle of the peninsula. Armistice talks began in 1951; they were completed in July 1953, when an armistice line very similar to the one achieved in 1951 was agreed on.

Professor Ziegler no longer agrees with all the views expressed above and wishes to refer readers to an essay by E. Friedman entitled 'Problems in Dealing with an Irrational Power: America Declares War on China' in E. Friedman and M. Seldon (eds.) *America's Asia: Dissenting Essays on Asian-American Relations* (New York: Pantheon Books, 1971).

NOTES

1. A staggering number of books have been published on the Cold War. Among the most readable of the traditional interpretations is Adam Ulam, *The Rivals* (New York: Viking Press, 1971). A brief and readable version of the radical reinterpretation is by Carl Oglesby and Richard Shaull. *Containment and Change* (New York: Macmillan, 1967). A very literate moderate view is Louis Halle, *The Cold War as History* (New York: Harper and Row, 1967).
2. One account ov events in Azerbaijan is Joseph Marion Jones, *The Fifteen Weeks* (New York: Viking Press, 1955), pp. 48-58.
3. The entire speech is printed as an appendix in Jones's book, pp. 269-274.
4. *Izvestia* (13 March 1947), quoted in Alvin Z. Rubinstein, ed., *The Foreign Policy of the Soviet Union*, 2nd ed. (New York: Random House, 1966), p. 231.
5. Harry S. Truman, *Memoirs*, Volume I *Year of Decisions* (Garden City, N.Y.: Doubleday, 1955), pp. 85-86.
6. Robert W. Coakley and Richard M. Leighton, *The United States Army in World War II. The War Department. Global Logistics and Strategy 1943-1945* (Washington, D.C.: Office of the Chief of Military History, Department of the Army, 1968), p. 836.
7. Quoted in John C. Sparrow. *History of Personnel Demobilization in the United States Army* (Washington, D.C.: Office of the Chief of Military History, Department of the Army, 1951), p. 380.
8. Cited by Kenneth Waltz, "The Stability of a Bipolar World," *Daedalus* Vol. 93, No. 3 (Summer 1964), p. 883.
9. Commencement address at Iowa State College, Ames, Iowa, June 9, 1956, in *Department of State Bulletin*, Vol. 34, No. 886 (June 18, 1956), pp. 99-100.
10. David Rees, *Korea: The Limited War* (New York: St. Martin's Press, 1964), pp. 19-20.
11. Contemporary interpretations are described by Alexander L. George in "American Policy-Making and the North Korean Aggression," *World Politics*, Vol. 7, No. 2 (January 1955), pp. 209-232.
12. The speech was published in *Department of State Bulletin*, Vol. 22, No. 551 (January 23, 1950), pp. 111-118. For Acheson's justification of his speech, see his *Present at the Creation* (New York: Signet Books, 2969z0, p. 567.
13. Harry Truman, *Memoirs*, Volume II: *Years of Trial and Hope* (Garden City, N.Y.: Doubleday, 1956d), p. 335.
14. Ibid., p. 445.
15. John Spanier, *The Truman-MacArthur Controversy and the Korean War* (Cambridge: Harvard University Press, 1959). p. 25.
16. For an explanation of why the United States responded in spite of its declared policy not to, see Ernest May. *The Nature of Foreign Policy: The Calculated versus the Axiomatic*," *Daedalus*, Vol. 91, No. 4 (:Fall 1962), pp. 633-667.
17. Allen S. Whiting, *China Crosses the Yalu* (Stanford: Stanford University Press, 1960), p. 155.
18. Truman, *Memoirs* II, p. 360.
19. Truman, *Memoirs* II, p. 362.
20. Richard Neustadt, *Presidential Power* (New York: Signet, 1964), especially p. 131.
21. Thomas C. Schelling, *Arms and Influence* (New Haven: Yale University Press, 1966), p. 55 fn.
22. Frank E. Armbruster, "China's Conventional Military Capability," in Frank E. Armbruster and others, *China Briefing* (Chicago: University of Chicago Center for Policy Study, 1968), pp. 59-60.

Did Anyone Start the Cold War?[1]

Ronald Steel

I

Vietnam, as we have learned from the Pentagon Papers, was no aberration. It resulted logically from the decisions made and the attitudes assumed throughout the cold war. It was Harry Truman who in 1950 provided aid to the French to put down Ho Chi Minh's independence movement. It was Dwight Eisenhower and John Foster Dulles who continued paying for France's colonial war and who threatened to intervene with American troops and atomic weapons. After that war was lost, they installed Ngo Dinh Diem and defied the Geneva accords calling for elections to unify Vietnam. Later it was John F. Kennedy, a true believer in the domino theory, who got rid of Diem when he ceased to be malleable and who dispatched American combat troops to ensure an anti-communist South Vietnam. The expansion of the war by Lyndon Johnson and the current efforts of Richard Nixon to achieve with air power and South Vietnamese mercenaries the victory denied American troops are all outgrowths of the same decisions about communism and America's role in the world

To reject the war in Vietnam is to question the basic assumptions on which American foreign policy rests. It is to ask not only whether the prevalent conception of the cold war might now be wrong, but whether it was ever right. It means re-examining a set of attitudes, the decisions that flowed from them, and the perceptions on which they were based. This reexamination has been going on for some time in the work of younger historians, many of them disciples of William Appleman Williams and rediscoverers of Charles Beard. While their works are contentious and often heavily slanted toward Marxist economics, they have thrown new light on the cold war and its origins.

They differ from liberal historians in that they condemn not only American behavior, but the motives that lie behind it. For them there is no such thing as accident, inadvertence, or error. American policy is deliberate, single-minded, and determined by the larger economic forces that motivate the society. Whereas liberals and "political realists" criticize American post-war diplomacy for being too ideological or for displaying a faulty concept of the national interest, these radical revisionists see that diplomacy as the necessary instrument of the capitalist order.

Liberal critics such as Morgenthau, Lippmann, and Kennan see the nation swaying between the twin poles of isolationism and globalism, unable to balance its great power with an enlightened concept of its vital interests. They believe American statesmen are "unrealistic" in trying to impose moral judgments on the amoral behavior of nations. They believe like William Pfaff in his eloquently argued new book, *Condemned to Freedom*, that while Vietnam "has constituted the calamitous triumph of American hypocrisy and cant over American seriousness," nonetheless, "the regrettable truth is that the foreign policy of the United States in the postwar period has, for the most part, been a popular policy pursued out of Wilsonian motivations and for reformist, even utopian goals."

To be a liberal critic is not, of course, the same thing as being a liberal policy maker, and nobody is harsher on the politicians than these critics. As Pfaff, whose book is a blistering account of the failure of liberal governments to preserve liberal values, has written,

> It took a visionary liberal administration fully to translate the globalism of American rhetoric, which the Republican party wholly shared, into a program of national action. Vietnam was consciously made into a test of liberal international reform by the Kennedy and Johnson administrations — of liberal "nation building," carried on behind a shield of Green Beret counterinsurgent warfare — against the Asian communist "model" of radical national transformation.

Damning though it is, this is essentially a liberal critique resting on assumptions that radicals do not share. It is not American "seriousness" that radicals question, for they believe that those who are responsible for American foreign policy are both serious and determined. Rather it is that American diplomacy is based upon the demands of the world capitalist system, of which the United States is the chief beneficiary and defender. This, and not a condemnation of the Vietnam war or of militarism or of a national security bureaucracy, is what separates them from the liberals. In fact, they deny that the military exerts a heavy weight on foreign policy or that the bureaucracy has a momentum of its own. To their minds American policy is not marked by mistakes and shortsightedness: it has, for the most part, been remarkably successful in imposing an American order upon the world.

Radical historians see American policy as inherently, indeed inexorably, counterrevolutionary. They trace this policy at least as far back as the era of imperial expansion at the turn of the century — marked by the acquisition of the Philippines and Puerto Rico, and the suzerainty over Cuba — and view the Open Door as the rationale for imperial expansionism. Thus, following the analysis used by Williams in *The Tragedy of American Diplomacy*, N. Gordon Levin has written that Wilsonianism "defined the American national interest in liberal-internationalist terms in response to war and social revolution, the two dominant political factors of our time."[2] Similarly, the struggle over the League of Nations was not, as a conventional historiography would have it, one pitting blind isolationism against enlightened involvement, but rather one over whether or not American economic interests could be better protected by a free-hands policy, that is, by unilateralism.

In their analysis of the more recent cold war period, radicals reject the theory that the United States responded defensively to Soviet intransigence, or that, as Kennan and Lippmann would argue, a necessary aid program under the Marshall Plan became unduly militarized in NATO and its sibling alliances. Rather they maintain that the United States challenged Moscow directly by refusing to accept a Soviet sphere of influence in Eastern Europe, by raising the specter of a rearmed Germany, and by rattling the atomic bomb. Committed to the triumph of capitalism and suppression of revolution, the United States, in the words of Gabriel Kolko, one of the most impassioned of the radicals, was committed to intervene "against the Soviet Union, against the tide of the left, and against Britain as a coequal guardian of world capitalism — in fact, against history as it had been and had yet to become."[3]

According to this view, the Russians were not threatening Western Europe and, initially at least, did not intend to dominate Eastern Europe by imposing a system of satellites. All the Russians wanted was a sphere of influence along their borders, similar to the one that the United States enjoyed in the Western Hemisphere, and a guarantee against German militarism. However, when the United States refused to accept this — and instead openly showed its hostility to the Soviet Union by abruptly cancelling lend-lease, ignoring Moscow's request for a $6 billion loan, and refusing to honor the German reparations plan tentatively agreed to at Yalta — the Russians had no choice but to exert full control over the satellites and build their defenses behind the Iron Curtain. (The brutality and terror used to exert this control have mostly been ignored by the revisionists, just as conventional historians have ignored the brutality of our own client states in Latin America and Asia.)

While the cold war began in Europe, it could not be confined there, since it involved far more than a struggle with Russia over access to Eastern Europe. Its true meaning, according to the radicals, has been the attempt by the United States to achieve a world order congenial to capitalist penetration and to consolidate a non-territorial empire ("the free world") whose preservation is considered essential to American security. For a country like the United States, a diplomacy of counter-revolution is not a choice, but a matter of necessity. The empire stands or falls as a whole; it must always be defended at its weakest link. Thus the importance of Vietnam as a test case ("stand by our commitments") to preserve American hegemony and the capitalist order on which it feeds.

Radicals lean heavily on an economic interpretation of history to back up their analysis. But even liberals who reject this Marxist approach have nonetheless been influenced by elements of the radical argument and have had to revise some of their own theories. Thus Arthur Schlesinger, who in 1966 in a letter to *The New York Review* declared it was time to "blow the whistle" on revisionism, a year later wrote that "revisionism is an essential part of the process by which history, through the posing of new problems and the investigation of new possibilities, enlarges its perspectives and enriches its insights."[4]

Even the designation of the United States as an imperial power, which was once considered absurd, has been accepted by historians on the center and the right. Some, like George Liska, have extolled it,[5] while others, like Robert Osgood, have simply taken note of it by defining an imperial power as one whose "vital interests extend far beyond the protection of the homeland [to] embrace all the outlying areas of commitment . . . [these] become equivalent to the preservation of an international order and a distribution of power upon which order must depend."[6] By this liberal historian's definition the United States is clearly an imperial, if not necessarily an imperialist, power.

Robert Tucker, a colleague of Liska and Osgood at the Washington Centre of Foreign Policy Research, takes the argument further by viewing American policy as maintaining a world imperial structure. For those determined to preserve that structure, he states, the war in Vietnam is an integral part of the containment policy that was originally applied to Europe in the late Forties, "and both are found to serve the same vital interests and to further the same over-all purpose of achieving and maintaining a desirable world order."[7] If the containment argument is accepted, then it is irrelevant to insist that the circumstances are different in Asia today from what they were in Europe — for obviously they are. The question is whether the reasons for following a containment policy remain valid.

Tucker comes close to the radicals' argument when he says that America became a counterrevolutionary power not because nationalistic revolutions dominated by the left would necessarily contribute to Russian or Chinese power, but because leftist regimes would resist American control. Thus Kennedy's well-known remark that he saw in "descending order of preference" three possibilities in the Dominican Republic following the assassination of Trujillo: "a decent democratic regime, a continuation of the Trujillo regime, or a Castro regime. We ought to aim at the first, but we really can't renounce the second until we are sure that we can avoid the third." Lyndon Johnson was simply following suit when he sent the Marines to suppress a popular insurrection in the Dominican Republic against a US-supported military regime in 1965.

Vietnam was part of the same pattern. The American intervention was based on the belief that the failure to contain communism in Southeast Asia would threaten the entire imperial system on which American economic and political hegemony rests. In official speeches, this was usually described as the "preservation of world order", but its meaning was the same. W.W. Rostow, one of the most vocal advocates of the aggression in Vietnam, was particularly outspoken when he explained: "It is on this spot that we have to break the liberation war — Chinese type. If we don't break it here, we shall have to face it again in Thailand, Venezuela, elsewhere. Vietnam is a clear testing ground for our policy in the world."

The question of interventionism, therefore, is not one of undifferentiated "globalism", but of ensuring political control wherever it is threatened. Interventions can, of course, be stimulated by domestic politics, as in the Cuban missile crisis, or by the effort to compensate for foreign policy setbacks in other areas. Thus, Kennedy's decision to send a man to the moon followed on the heels of the Bay of Pigs fiasco, and his expansion of the Vietnam war was stimulated by his disastrous encounter with Khrushchev at Vienna. As Chester Bowles has suggested in his recent autobiography, *Promises to Keep*, Kennedy, uncertain and eager to assert himself, "subconsciously at least, was searching for some issue on which he could prove at relatively low cost that he was, in fact, a tough President who could not be pushed around by the Soviets, the Chinese, or anyone else". Bowles vocally dissented from Kennedy's adventure in Vietnam and the militarized liberals who supported and encouraged it. This was one of the reasons he was eased out of the higher councils of the Administration.

Bowles, of course, is no radical, and like many other liberal critics of the war, sees Vietnam as illustrating how a nation, "with the very best of intentions, once it loses touch with political realities, can delude itself and its people." Radical critics would deny both the good intentions and the self-delusion. But even if one does not accept all their promises, particularly the economic determinants, their argument is a powerful one which explains a good deal more about American foreign policy than the conventional liberal critique of "inadvertence" and excessive "moralism".

To be sure, ideology, idealism, and even domestic politics played a part in the decision to go into Vietnam. There were people who believed, or convinced themselves, that what we were doing in Southeast Asia was not only necessary for our own security, but good for the people who lived there. Moreover, no President has ever been willing to be responsible for the "loss" of any country anywhere to communism. According to Kenneth O'Donnell, John F. Kennedy said he would get us out of Vietnam

— just as soon as the 1964 elections were safely over. As Daniel Ellsberg observed in these pages a few months ago,[8] "For twenty years, — since the 'fall of China' and the rise of McCarthy — Rule 1 of Indochina policy for an American President has been: Do not lose the rest of Vietnam to communism before the next election." In invoking the specters of Wallace or Reagan and a right-wing reaction to "bugging out" in Vietnam, Nixon, like Kennedy, has clearly shown that at least part of his policy of defending the "free world" is influenced by the next elections.

In addition to domestic political pressures, there is pressure, both public and private, from high-ranking generals and admirals who believe that wars of "containment", like other wars, are meant to be won — however reluctant they may be to get involved in them in the first place. While it is hardly fair to blame the military for getting us into Vietnam or for an imperial foreign policy that has been designed by civilian lawyers, academicians, and businessmen, the Pentagon nonetheless has a vested interest in an American empire that has to be defended with bases, fleets, and supply lines. In evolving less bellicose policies, any President has to reckon with the joint Chiefs of Staff and with their powerful allies on Congressional committees.

Like a good many other liberal historians, Tucker has been persuaded by the radicals to see calculation rather than inadvertence in American interventionism, but has remained skeptical about the economic determinants of foreign policy. In his provocative new book, *The Radical Left and American Foreign Policy*, he gives the radicals their due on political grounds, but criticizes their "archaic" arguments of dependency on foreign markets and Third World raw materials. His refutation of the Marxist arguments used, for example, by Harry Magdoff in *The Age of Imperialism* seems convincing. In spite of his skepticism on these grounds, Tucker accepts the radicals' central thesis of the imperialist nature of America's counterrevolutionary diplomacy. "America's interventionist and counter-revolutionary policy," he writes, "is the expected response of an imperial power with a vital interest in maintaining an order that, apart from the material benefits this order confers has become synonymous with the nation's vision of its role in history."

Adopting key elements of the radical critique, Tucker affirms that the post war policy of universalism was simply a cover for a spheres of influence policy that the United States pursued for itself, but sought to deny the Soviet Union, that the United Nations was manipulated to consolidate America's leadership, and that in the post war period, we have defined our interests in such a way that "the only policy the Russians could have pursued which would not have incurred American hostility was one that placed Russian security and not only security — largely at the mercy of the good intentions of others, above all, America." By this, he means that the Russians could not realistically have been expected to accept such programs as the Baruch plan for the control of atomic energy, with its built-in American monopoly, or the restoration of anti-communist governments in Eastern Europe.

In arguing that American imperialism rests on the needs of capitalism for expanding markets and access to raw materials, radicals quote Dean Acheson's 1944 statement before a Congressional committee that the United States required foreign markets to absorb its "unlimited creative energy" if it were not to slide back into a depression, or Harry Truman's March, 1947, speech, in which he said, clearing the ground for the forthcoming aid program to Greece and Turkey, that "the American system could survive in America only if it became a world system." Although Tucker agrees that such statements are revealing of the attitude of American corporate leaders, he denies that they reveal the root of American policy, and suggests that "their purpose is largely to elicit support for a policy that is pursued primarily for quite different reasons."

Those reasons, he would argue, are rooted in the fear that the United States cannot be secure in a world hostile to its example. To American leaders, "the prospect of the growing irrelevance of the American example must raise the issue of American security in the greater than physical sense." Thus, he takes to task radicals who "cannot consistently accept the view that an interventionist and counter-revolutionary America has been motivated more by the prospect that the American example, and, in consequence, American influence, might otherwise become irrelevant than by the prospect that in a hostile world, America would no longer enjoy the material benefits her hegemonial position has conferred."

For Tucker, it is not the compulsions of capitalism, "it is power itself, more than a particular form of power, which prompts expansion." America behaves imperialistically because it has the power to do so. In this sense, it is like any other imperial power of the past — regardless of its economic structure. Thus,

Tucker asks whether a socialist America would pursue a significantly different foreign policy, or whether it would also identify its security with a pro-American world equilibrium. This is a basic question which radicals have not satisfactorily answered, but which is central to any serious criticism of the use of American power.

II

Whatever their approach to Marxian economics, critics of American interventionism put special emphasis on the early postwar period, which set the pattern for the policies that followed. Radical historians see the United States as largely responsible for the onset of the cold war. Whether one accepts this argument — I do not see how a postwar conflict of interests between America and Russia could easily have been avoided, since both were superpowers with imperial ambitions, and other potential rivals had been eliminated — the way the cold war developed was neither accidental nor predetermined. It resulted from decisions consciously made and deliberately applied, from judgments tenaciously held, and from a series of actions which triggered understandable counter-reactions from the other side.

Among revisionists, there is general agreement on the origins of the cold war: that American policy after the death of Roosevelt caused the Soviet Union to tighten its hold on Eastern Europe, and that there was no objective Soviet threat to American security to account for the uncompromising anti-Soviet attitude of the Truman Administration. In *Architects of Illusion*, Lloyd Gardner, for example, summarizes his thoughtful study of American policy makers in the 1940s with the judgment that "responsibility for the *way* in which the cold war developed, at least, belongs more to the United States," since at the end of the war, "it had much greater opportunity and far more options to influence the course of events than the Soviet Union." The United States stimulated the cold war, he argues, by trying to use economic aid to force changes in Soviet policy in Eastern Europe, by failing to offer Moscow a guarantee of German disarmament in 1945, and by insisting on the Baruch plan for controlling atomic energy.

Every study of the origins of the cold war inevitably focuses on the Yalta conference of February, 1945, where the three victorious allies, in the final weeks of the war against Nazi Germany, met to work out a political scheme for the postwar world. Since that time, there have been numerous studies analyzing why the spirit of co-operation established at Yalta quickly degenerated into the armed confrontation of the cold war. However, there have been few serious accounts of the conference itself. This gap has now been filled by Diane Shaver Clemens's scrupulously researched *Yalta*. Using documents from the Soviet archives, as well as American and British records, Clemens has made a full-scale reconstruction of the Yalta conference, discussing the origins of the meeting, the issues debated and resolved there, and the significance of the proceedings.

Her method is to present the positions held by the three powers, examine the arguments made during the course of the conference, and analyze the basis for the compromises reached. From this, there emerges a narrative of the disagreements between Roosevelt and Churchill, as well as between them and Stalin, of the areas in which the Western view prevailed, and of the compromises that reflected the military and political realities during the last weeks of the war. She finds that "Soviet proposals were frequently incorporations of positions enunciated by the West", credits the Russians with a "more congenial and compromising position than postwar history has allowed", and concludes that the "decisions at Yalta involved compromises by each nation, probably more by the Soviets than by the Western nations" — a position held by many at the time, including the then Secretary of State, Edward Stettinius.

The Soviets certainly were willing to compromise on issues they deemed of peripheral importance, such as Britain's demand for the creation of a French occupation zone in Germany and the award to France of a seat on the Allied Control Commission. But where they felt vital interests were involved — such as the question of German reparations or the composition of the Polish government — they stood firm. Because these critical issues were never adequately resolved at the conference, both sides interpreted the accords as they wanted to read them, and later felt betrayed when the other side did not agree. The disillusionment with Yalta was mutual, but this was inevitable in view of the equivocal agreements on key issues — particularly reparations and the Polish question.

For Clemens the responsibility was not mutual, but the fault of the United States, which only a few months after the conference "attempted to undo those agreements at Yalta which reflected Soviet interests", while accusing the Russians of breaking the accords. Specifically, the agreements Washington sought to undo were: the dismemberment of Germany, reparations payable to the Soviet Union, and the composition of the Polish government. Why the sudden decision to renege on Yalta? Clemens offers no satisfactory explanation other than that Truman, who succeeded Roosevelt in April, just two months after the conference, was more bellicose and found himself "in a stronger position" after the successful testing of the atomic bomb.

Whether or not he dropped the bomb on Japan to scare the Russians out of Eastern Europe, as some revisionists charge, it is true that Truman cut off aid to the Soviet Union and tried to use the Soviet request for postwar credits as a pressure tactic to gain political concessions. Even before Yalta, such policies were being openly discussed. As early as 1944, Averell Harriman, then ambassador to Moscow, advised Roosevelt to cut back or even eliminate lend-lease, a measure which FDR resisted for good reason — because the US needed Russian help in defeating Germany — but which Truman implemented shortly after becoming President. Harriman's outspokenly anti-Soviet deputy, George Kennan, urged, even while the German army was still in Russia, that the time had come for a "fullfledged and realistic political showdown with the Soviet leaders."

In January, 1945, a month before the meeting at Yalta, Harriman discouraged Stalin's request for a reconstruction loan and cabled Washington that "postwar credits can serve as a useful instrument in our overall relations with the USSR." Thus, even before Yalta, powerful forces within the Administration were urging a showdown with the Soviet Union on the assumption that her economic needs were so great that she would be forced to grant political concessions in Eastern Europe.

By the time Churchill, Roosevelt, and Stalin met at Yalta in February, 1945, Russian troops were only forty-four miles from Berlin, and Soviet protégés were taking over the new government of Poland. The communist-dominated Lublin regime had already been recognized by Moscow as the sole Polish government. Churchill and Roosevelt insisted on expanding the government by including the so-called London Poles — a conservative group that would have been hostile to the USSR — and by holding free elections. Under pressure, Stalin agreed to "free elections", and to the enlargement of the Polish government — on the understanding that the Lublin group would form the nucleus. In addition, the Big Three agreed that Poland's boundaries would be shifted to the west, with Russia absorbing the territory up to the Curzon line, and with Poland being compensated by the incorporation of former German territories up to the line formed by the Oder and Neisse rivers.

According to liberal historians, Churchill and Roosevelt left Yalta apparently convinced that they had won a major concession from Stalin, and that Poland, like the rest of Eastern Europe, would be open to Western economic, political, and cultural influence. Stalin, however, had no such understanding, and the ink was barely dry at Yalta before his puppets took over Poland and shut the West out of Eastern Europe. Immediately, there were shouts of betrayal and accusations that the Russians were bent on a plan of world conquest.

Stalin, who never accepted the Western interpretation of Yalta, professed to be shocked, and could not understand why America and Britain would not grant him the free hand in Eastern Europe that he granted them in Western Europe, Latin America, and the eastern Mediterranean. Perhaps he felt that the West had not been serious at Yalta in seeking "free elections." According to Clemens, there was not even a misunderstanding. The accords on elections and the reorganization of the Polish government were only a "face-saving formula." "There had been no agreement on Anglo-American principles," she states. "Each side was aware that a different interpretation prevailed."

In view of the ambiguous nature of the accords on Poland and on free elections in liberated Europe, it is not surprising that there was soon a conflict between Russia and the West over the meaning of Yalta. Averell Harriman, in a rambling collection of speeches and reminiscences, *America and Russia in a Changing World*, maintains that "Stalin did agree at Yalta to set up an interim government in Poland, bringing in the London Poles, the free Poles from within Poland, together with the Lublin Poles, and holding 'free and unfettered' elections." He further charges that Stalin went to "extreme lengths in breaking the Yalta agreements . . . [since] it was agreed that the people in these countries were to decide on their own governments through free elections."

However, as Clemens makes clear, there was never any written agreement on the meaning or procedures of free elections, or provisions for international supervision. Furthermore, once Roosevelt and Churchill agreed to accept the Lublin group as the nucleus of the postwar Polish government (and they had little choice), it was obvious that the communists would retain control

— whatever window dressing might be devised. Churchill, who had shortly before divided up the Balkans with Stalin, well knew that military control was tantamount to political control, and Roosevelt could not have expected any less. As Stalin, according to Djilas, told Tito: "This war is not as in the past; whoever occupies a territory also imposes his own social system. Everyone imposes his own system as far as his army can reach. It cannot be otherwise."

In view of Harriman's position during this crucial period in the relations between Russia and the West, there is something disingenuous in his indignation over the imposition of a communist regime in Poland. All along, he had been arguing that the United States used its economic power to force Soviet concessions in Eastern Europe. He could hardly have imagined that the Russians, who carried the brunt of the war against Nazi Germany and who, until June, 1944, faced the bulk of Hitler's armies alone, would voluntarily give up the *cordon sanitaire* in Eastern Europe they had won at such staggering cost. As Walter Lippmann, who was an outspoken critic of the policies of confrontation being pursued by the Truman Administration, wrote:

> While the British and Americans held firmly . . . the whole position in Africa and the Mediterranean . . . and the whole of Western Germany containing 46 million Germans (compared to 18 million in the Russian zone), the greater part of the demobilized and disbanded veterans of the Wehrmacht and 70 percent of Germany's pre-war heavy industry, they undertook by negotiation and diplomatic pressure to reduce Russia's position in Eastern Europe — which the Soviet Union had won because the Red Army had defeated two thirds of the German army.

Unlike Harriman, even such an Establishment historian as Herbert Feis finds it hard to accept that Churchill and Roosevelt believed the Russians would allow the communist-controlled provisional government of Poland to be ousted in free elections. They "were not really trusting", he states in *From Trust to Terror*, but they had to face realities: "The Red Army was in occupation of Poland, and its agent, the Lublin government, with Soviet tanks in front and behind, was exercising authority throughout the country. The alternative — a major confrontation with the Soviet government while the war with Germany was still being fought — was dismaying to both the

Western military and diplomatic leaders."

Feis believes that it would have been better to risk an open break with Stalin at Yalta over the Polish question than to have maintained the alliance at such a price. That is arguable, but it is at least an honest position. It involves no mock outrage over the events whose implications were understood at the time — particularly by people like Harriman who were intimately involved in decision-making. The accords on Central Europe were a realistic basis for a postwar policy of cooperation among the victorious powers — given the will for such cooperation based on mutual spheres of influence.

It was only later, as Athan Theoharis recounts in *The Yalta Myths*, that the Democrats — stung by Republican attacks upon Yalta as a "sellout" tried to cover their flanks by protesting that they had been betrayed by the Russians. By the late 1940s, "both Democratic supporters and Republican critics had ceased to view it as a diplomatic conference that tried to achieve peace through compromise and understanding," he writes. "Instead, it had become a symbol of a mistaken or treasonous course of action."

The Truman Democrats quickly moved to establish their anti-communist credentials by instituting a vicious "loyalty" program in the civil service, and by pursuing a policy of military "containment" designed, in the words of George Kennan used at the time in enunciating the containment doctrine, to confront the Russians with counter-force "at every point where they show signs of encroaching upon the interests of a peaceful world." Under Acheson, this policy was used to justify a huge build-up of military power and its extension all over the globe. Kennan, who had been Harriman's assistant in Moscow and then the protégé of Truman's Defense Secretary, James Forrestal, later in his *Memoirs* deplored the militarization of the containment doctrine and insisted that this was a distortion of what he intended.

There is little doubt that Western policy did become harsher once Truman became President and the disillusionment over the full meaning of Yalta set in. Truman had been in office less than two weeks when he confronted Molotov on April 23 with the demand that the London Poles be integrated into the new Warsaw government and that free elections be held. The next day, Stalin wrote Truman and Churchill, expressing his puzzlement over these demands. "Poland borders on the Soviet Union which cannot be said about Great Britain or the USA. I do not know whether a genuinely representative government has been established in Greece, or whether the Belgian government is a genuinely democratic one. The Soviet Union was not consulted when those governments were being formed, nor did it claim the right to interfere in those matters, because it realizes how important Belgium and Greece are to the security of Great Britain." Stalin said he could not understand why "no attempt is made to consider the interests of the Soviet Union in terms of security as well", and found it inconceivable that the Americans should demand the return of Poland to those who ran that country before the war.

"It was difficult for other outsiders, not just Stalin, to understand the American position," Stephen E. Ambrose comments in his masterful survey, *The Rise to Globalism: American Foreign Policy Since 1938*. All during the war, the United States had never ceased talking about the need to eliminate spheres of influence and balance of power concepts and to replace them with collective security under the United Nations. But in practice America, while denouncing Soviet control over Eastern Europe — maintained hegemony in Latin America through military dictatorships, and might well have lost that hegemony if truly free elections were ever allowed.

Washington's hypocritical attitude is highlighted by an account Ambrose gives of a telephone conversation in May, 1945, between Secretary of War Henry Stimson and his assistant secretary, John J. McCloy, about how to square an American sphere of influence in the Western Hemisphere with the UN. They agreed that a Russian sphere of influence in Eastern Europe would risk war and destroy the UN's effectiveness. They further agreed that US domination of Latin America had to be maintained. "I think," said Stimson, "that it's not asking too much to have our little region over here which never has bothered anybody." McCloy added that "we ought to have our cake and eat it too . . . we ought to be free to operate under this regional arrangement in South America, at the same time intervene promptly in Europe; we oughtn't give away either asset."

Clearly we had no intention of letting the Russians have their "little region", although we were intent on retaining ours. The US demanded that the UN Charter provide for regional security groupings — to ensure our hold over Latin America — and the admission, over Stalin's vigorous protest, of Argentina to the UN in spite of its pro-Nazi wartime position. It was the Polish issue, as Ambrose points out, that provided a chance for Truman to have his cake and eat it. He was convinced by Harriman, his man in Moscow, that the Russians would have to take it, no matter how tough Truman got, because they desperately needed US economic aid for reconstruction. He put on the pressure, but as it turned out, there was a limit, and the cold war was the result.

The full story is laid out in *The Rise to Globalism*, part of the Pelican history of the United States, edited by Robert Divine, a splendid example of the impact of revisionist analysis on the reinterpretation of American wartime and postwar diplomacy. Engaged, literate, comprehensive, and always stimulating, it is among the best surveys of cold war history that have yet appeared.

Although he is free from apologetic Establishment interpretations of the cold war, Ambrose does not fully accept the radicals' assumption of Soviet good faith. On the Polish question, for example, he sees the Russians as implacably installing their own protégés. He differs sharply and convincingly with Clemens, who believes that the Russians probably would have allowed "moderately free elections in Poland as promised", but that "when Western hostility threatened everything short of war with the Soviet Union, the Russians increasingly abandoned free elections and cooperation in favor of consolidation of a defensive perimeter in Eastern Europe."

It is not necessary to go this far along the road of speculative revisionism to understand how whatever Truman's real motives may have been — the Russians could reasonably have believed that Washington was intent on reversing the spirit of cooperation established at Yalta. As Schlesinger has written:

> The Russian hope for major Western assistance in post-war reconstruction foundered on three events which the Kremlin could well have interpreted respectively as deliberate sabotage (the loan request), blackmail (lend-lease cancellation), and pro-Germanism (reparations).

In re-examining the origins of the cold war, and the perceptions and motivations of American policy makers, radical historians have helped us to understand how the United States has become an imperial, self-aggrandizing power. Their research has shown that the form the Russo-American confrontation took was not inevitable, that the United States did not simply respond defensively to Soviet aggressive moves, and that there has been nothing inadvertent in our colonial wars and our acquisition of empire.

A weakness of the radicals is their characteristically American view of America's exceptionalism. Just as conservatives see this nation as the embodiment of goodness and justice, so radicals see it as the fount of evil. Similarly, there is something sentimental about the radicals' uncritical embrace of Third World movements, and their equation of imperialism with capitalist elites. For radicals, as for everyone else, Vietnam has been a traumatizing experience. But its lesson is not, as some radicals believe, that the United States will inevitably intervene anywhere and everywhere against popular reform movements. In overdrawing the lesson of Vietnam, too many radicals, in Pfaff's words, "have unexpectedly discovered sin, but not original sin."

In using its power crudely, immorally, and imperialistically, the United States has behaved like many great powers in the past. It has done so not for the noble motives claimed by every postwar administration, but for reasons of hegemony, control, and aggrandizement. The fact that the American empire is basically non-territorial makes it no less imperialistic than its predecessors. Its major distinction is that it is considerably more hypocritical.

We now know that the professed ideals have been essentially a mask for expansionistic, and even immoral, behavior. This imperialist ambition is not fed exclusively, or even primarily, by economic need although certainly there has been a determination to use American power to impose upon the world a democratic capitalistic pattern congenial to American economic interests. The imperialistic drive also rests on a missionary impulse to mould other societies in our own image ("We're going to turn the Mekong into the Tennessee Valley," Lyndon Johnson once proclaimed), to assure ourselves of the validity of our institutions by imposing them upon others, and from a sheer will to power that comes, almost irresistibly, from the possession of overwhelming power.

Vietnam has made us aware of the American empire, and the radical historians have helped us to understand how it came into being. The ordeal society faces today is not simply how to disengage from a disastrous imperial war, but how to dismantle the empire — together with the imperial bureaucracy, the war machine, and the industrial superstructure of the warfare state — before it destroys the nation.

FOOTNOTES

1. Published October 20, 1971.
2. *Woodrow Wilson and World Politics* (Oxford, 1968).
3. *The Politics of War: The World and United States Foreign Policy 1943-1945* (Random House, 1970).
4. "The Origins of the Cold War", *Foreign Affairs*, October, 1967.
5. *Imperial America: The International Politics of Primacy* (Johns Hopkins, 1967).
6. Osgood, Tucker, et.al., *America and the World: From the Truman Doctrine to Vietnam* (John Hopkins, 1970).
7. *Nation or Empire? The Debate over American Foreign Policy* (Johns Hopkins, 1969).
8. "Laos: What Nixon Is Up To," March 11, 1971.

Works reviewed

Condemned to Freedom
by William Pfaff
Random House.

The Radical Left and American Foreign Policy
by Robert W. Tucker
Johns Hopkins.

Promises to Keep
by Chester Bowles
Harper & Row.

Architects of Illusion
by Lloyd Gardner
Quadrangle.

Yalta
by Diane Shaver Clemens
Oxford.

America and Russia in a Changing World
by W. Averell Harriman
Doubleday.

From Trust to Terror
by Herbert Feis
Norton.

The Yalta Myths
by Athan Theoharis
University of Missouri Press.

The Rise to Globalism: American Policy Since 1938
by Stephen E. Ambrose
Penguin

SECTION III: COUNTERREVOLUTION AND REVOLT IN THE THIRD WORLD

Introduction

In this section, we examine in greater detail some of the patterns and methods of counterrevolutionary intervention in the Third World. But first we must attempt to clarify what we mean by 'intervention'. As is frequently the case in this area, a precise definition is not easy to articulate. This does not matter greatly since the meaning of the term is usually evident from the context. For our purposes, interventions are positive or negative sanctions (crudely 'rewards' and 'punishments') which a state may use to achieve its foreign policy ends. In the case of the United States and the Third World, the primary thrust of US policy is the containment of revolution. To achieve this broad objective the United States has deployed a huge inventory of sanctions, ranging from the seven million tons of bombs dropped on Vietnam, to the more subtle credit embargoes deployed against Salvador Allende's Chile.

Negative sanctions (punishments) are used against regimes and political movements perceived by the US as revolutionary or pro-communist. They include: direct US military intervention (Korea, Vietnam etc.); the *threat* to use force (what used to be called 'gunboat diplomacy'); the use of surrogate troops (e.g. Cuban exiles in the C.I.A. organised Bay of Pigs invasion in 1961); and the employment by the C.I.A. of a wide variety of clandestine 'destabilising' operations against radical regimes. Finally, there is a whole range of negative economic sanctions which may be deployed. These range from the extremes of economic blockade, via trade embargoes and aid stoppage, down to relatively minor sanctions such as reducing import quotas. While negative sanctions are designed to punish and deter revolutionary regimes and groups, positive sanctions reward and sustain their enemies. Thus America's anti-communist Third World allies receive military assistance and training, generous economic aid, concessionary trade agreements and so forth.

A recent American study* examined in some depth the claim that Third World regimes which moved to the Left were punished by reductions in US trade, aid (including military assistance) and investment: regimes which shifted to the Right were rewarded. Four Third World countries (Brazil, Indonesia, Chile, Peru) which had undergone such political changes were chosen for analysis, and the relevant data were collected for an eighteen year period. As predicted, regime shifts to the Left were 'punished' and those to the Right 'rewarded'. These examples *support* the reward/punishment proposition; they do not demonstrate it as generally true. In the same study, US behaviour towards a non-Third World country (Greece) did *not* conform to the expected pattern.

The methods to which we have alluded above are not, of course, the sole preserve of the United States. The Soviet Union uses similar techniques to protect and, where possible, to extend its own global spheres of influence. However, the Soviet Union's far lower level of economic activity in the Third World means that it has less capability for using aid and trade for political manipulation than has the US. The first article in this section, by Richard Barnet, comprises a wide-ranging, and well-illustrated, discussion of US 'patterns of intervention'. Written from a liberal revisionist perspective, Barnet's paper encompasses description, explanation and a detailed critique of what the author sees as the immorality of US foreign policy vis à vis the Third World.

The United States is depicted by Barnet as having sabotaged possibilities for a peaceful post-war world order, and as having selfconsciously planned to take over Britain's 'imperial responsibilities'. Analysing the motives underlying US

*S. Rosen, 'The Open Door Imperative and U.S. Foreign Policy' in S. Rosen and J. Kurth (eds.), *Testing Theories of Economic Imperialism*, D.C. Heath, London, 1974.

expansionism, Barnet rejects the 'protection of freedom' argument as largely a rationalisation - a new version of the 'civilising mission' mythology which rationalised European imperialism of the 19th century. Is America therefore also an 'imperialist' power? On this point Barnet is ambivalent - he uses the term 'imperialism' - but differently from the usage employed by most of the theorists of imperialism discussed in the general introduction to this reader. He rejects the popular liberal thesis that interventions, such as that in Vietnam, were 'mistakes' into which a well-intentioned America blundered unawares and became inextricably bogged. But he also rejects Marxist, and other theories, which see American foreign policy as determined by economic imperatives.

Barnet believes that the US counterrevolutionary posture is neither a mistake, as claimed by liberals, nor necessary, as argued by many radicals. His own position is similar to that of the globalist theorists described in the previous section. Economic factors play a non-negligible role in foreign policy formation but they are not central. The primary determinant of US foreign policy is seen as an ideological obsession with communism, which is conditioned by a *real politik* awareness of the limits of American power. Additionally, there are the various factors to which the 'globalism' writers allude, and which 'seem to push great nations into familiar imperial patterns'. In general, Barnet's analysis provides instructive examples of the different explanatory foci which were discussed in the introductory essay on the concept of imperialism.

In the second article in this section, Andrew Mack concentrates on the *methods* of intervention rather than its causes. Like Barnet, Mack relates US foreign policy to the changed configuration of world politics in the post-war era. As we noted in the introduction to SECTION I, the mutual possession of nuclear weapons had, by the 1950s, rendered war between the superpowers suicidal and had tended to encourage proxy conflicts on the world 'periphery'. In the immediate postwar years, the focus of superpower conflict was Europe. During the 1950's, however, there was a growing de facto acceptance of the European status quo; this acceptance of mutual spheres of interest did not apply to the Third World. Whether one saw foreign policy as motivated by strategic and geopolitical factors, ideology, or economics, the gains from expanding spheres of influence, and the probable costs of their contraction, seemed obvious. But the strategic doctrine and nuclear capability, which assured the status quo in Europe, were largely irrelevant in the

Third World. This, as Mack notes in his paper, led to considerable controversy in the United States during the 1950's. But not until the early 1960's did the United States evolve a doctrine and capability designed *specifically* to crush the guerrilla uprisings against which nuclear and conventional military doctrine were useless. By the end of the 1960's that doctrine - which emphasised the use of elite American soldiers - such as the Green Berets - had been replaced by the so-called Nixon Doctrine. Vietnam demonstrated to American policy makers that the US simply could not sustain long drawn out land wars against Third World nations which posed no threat to the US itself. The Nixon Doctrine returned the responsibility for actual fighting back to America's Third World allies. The US role was relegated to supplying arms, advice and aid. In his conclusion, Mack argues that a radical new shift in US foreign policy is becoming increasingly possible. In place of the reflex hostile response to radical revolt, the United States may in the future forbear to intervene. De-emphasising counterrevolution would not derive from any belief that previous policy was immoral, but rather that it was increasingly difficult to implement successfully (Vietnam), and, at the same time, decreasingly necessary.

Patterns of Intervention

Richard Barnet

ONE

As the confrontation between the United States and revolutionary movements has come into sharper focus, the euphemistic rhetoric of American Responsibility (defending freedom, self-determination, etc.) has yielded to the starker idiom of *realpolitik*. We are readier than we were a few years ago to concede that the far-flung bureaucracies we dispatch to Asia, Africa, and Latin America are less concerned with bringing the town meeting, the ballot box, and the supermarket to their backward inhabitants than in making sure that they do not confiscate, collectivize, or chant communist slogans. The presence of a communist threat, even the *possibility* of a communist threat (as in the Dominican Republic), has supplied adequate justification for a variety of interventions. To identify the threat has been enough to preclude any further challenge to the necessity or morality of its suppression. In such cases the only questions left open for debate have been the existence of the threat: Were the fifty-three Dominican communists on the State Department list really behind the revolution? — and the propriety of the means for dealing with it: Is military repression the best way to reach the hearts and minds of the people?

The United States has become increasingly outspoken in claiming the unilateral right to make the determination whether a conflict anywhere in the world constitutes a threat to its national security or international order and what should be done about it. Only those states "with enough will and enough resources to see to it that others do not violate" the rules of international law, Secretary of State Rusk has declared, are the ones to be entrusted with enforcing the peace. When he was under secretary of state, George Ball suggested that such responsibility "may in today's world be possible . . . only for nations such as the United States which command resources on a scale adequate to the requirements of leadership in the twentieth century."[1] In other words, power is the basis of legitimacy. Conceding that the "world community" has not granted the United States the warrant to police the world in any legal sense — the United Nations Charter gives the Security Council the primary responsibility for dealing with threats to the peace — those in charge of United States national-security policy nonetheless assert that because of the deep divisions in the United Nations, which render that organization immobile, the United States must act alone. John Foster Dulles recognized that "most of the countries of the world" did not share his ideological view of international politics — "the view that communist control of any government anywhere is in itself a danger and a threat." Pointing out that it was not difficult "to marshal world opinion against aggression," he noted in the midst of the 1954 Indo-china crisis that "it is quite another matter to fight against internal changes in one country. If we take a position against a communist faction within a foreign country we have to act alone." His brother, Allen, formerly director of the Central Intelligence Agency, candidly stated the unilateral criteria by which the United States decided whether or not to intervene in a civil war:

> . . . we cannot safely limit our response to the Communist strategy of take-over solely to those cases where we are invited in by a government still in power, or even to instances where a threatened country has first exhausted its own, possibly meager, resources in the "good fight" against Communism. We ourselves must determine when and how to act, hopefully with the support of other leading Free World countries who may be in a position to help, keeping in mind the requirements of our own national security.[2]

There is nothing exceptional about powerful countries asserting the imperial prerogative of using force and coercion on the territory of another without its consent. The Athenian Empire minced no words about this. "The strong do what they can and the weak do what they must," the Athenian general reminded the Melians. Empire is its own justification, the fifteenth-century Italian humanist Lorenzo Valla advised his prince . . .

TWO

The ideology of the American Responsibility rests on a fundamental assumption concerning American self-interest. The only alternative to a Pax Americana is a Pax Sovietica or the Peace of Peking. The most powerful nation in the world has always dominated the rest. The only question is which one will emerge on top. Comforted by Talleyrand's fashionable aphorism about nonintervention — "a metaphysical term which means about the same as intervention" — the National-Security Manager concludes that the fate of the powerful is to dominate, whether they wish to do so or not. There is much to this observation. If the United States never sent a soldier or an aid dollar beyond her shores, it would still wield enormous power over other nations, particularly in the Third World, by virtue of the fact that it is the world's biggest customer. The power to cut off imports from a one-crop country is as effective an instrument of control as occupying its capital. The United States has the dominant voice in the World Bank and the International Monetary 'Fund, and private United States financial interests control much of the world money market. Countries struggling to industrialize are heavily dependent upon U.S. machinery. Most of the state-owned airlines of the world, to take one example, fly American equipment and are dependent upon U.S. corporations for servicing and replacement.

But beyond the operation of what is still termed the "private market," despite the considerable involvement of the government in these activities, is the panoply of techniques available to the national-security bureaucracy to influence the political behavior of other countries. In many countries of the world the United States is the sole supplier of the army, the primary source of training for its officers, and the educator and supplier of its police force. In addition,

through its aid program the United States is likely to have
conceived and staffed the educational system and to be the
dominant voice in its agricultural development, the
organizer of its labor movement, and the decisive influence
in setting the national priorities for economic development.
U.S. views, private and official, predominate as a consequence of
Voice of America, the armed-forces radio and
television stations, which are widely distributed, and the
increasingly wide circulation of U.S. periodicals. Many of
the individuals who provide these services do so with
generous intentions, but the effect of their efforts is to give
the United States a supreme voice in the internal affairs of
many other countries. And that, as a succession of secretaries
of state have promised Congress, is their primary purpose.
Desmond Fitzgerald, formerly a high official of the
International Cooperation Administration (predecessor of
AID), who later directed covert operations for the CIA, put it
this way:

> A lot of criticism of foreign aid is because the critic
> thought the objective was to get economic growth, and
> this wasn't the objective at all . . . . The objective may
> have been to buy a lease or to get a favorable vote in
> the UN, or to keep a nation from falling apart, or to
> keep some country from giving the Russians airbase
> rights or any one of many other reasons.[3]

In a small country like the Dominican Republic, or even a
larger one with a fairly primitive political structure and a
large contingent of American officials like Ethiopia, the U.S.
Embassy is inevitably the center of power in the country, if
only because its capacity to control communications and
intelligence is so far superior to that of the native
government. In Ethiopia, the United States dramatized this
fact by returning the emperor to his kingdom (he had been
deposed in a military coup while on a foreign visit) in a
U.S. airforce plane. John Bartlow Martin's account of his
activities in the Dominican Republic suggests that even
before the arrival of Marines, the American ambassador was
more a proconsul than an envoy.

These facts of international life are cited by the
proponents of an interventionary foreign policy as proving
the inevitability of the unilateral use of force for
"peacekeeping," i.e. police purposes. The United States is so
deeply involved anyway in the use of coercive techniques to
influence political behavior that the overt use of force,

regrettable as it is, is merely a difference in degree, not in kind. If the United States were not prepared to use violence to deal with internal political problems in other countries when it conceives that its own national interests warrant it, its chief rivals would sponsor violence to their own advantage. In short, the prevailing official view is that there is no way for a great country to relate to a small one other than as manipulator or exploiter.

History appears to support this view. All the pressures of contemporary politics seem to push great nations into familiar imperial patterns. Indeed, when the United States adopted the policy embodied in the Truman Doctrine, State Department officials quite consciously saw themselves as inheritors of Britain's imperial responsibilities, which, they assumed, they would exercise more wisely and more humanely. As a State Department publicity release would put it years later. "Strict adherence to our ideals requires us to face the challenge of reshaping the world in the image of human dignity, political freedom, and authority by consent, not decree."[4] Like their models in Whitehall, the National-Security Managers too assumed that if America could bring order to the world as a consequence of amassing an empire, that was not a bad bargain for the rest of mankind.

Thus, despite the rhetorical hopes for collective security and community responsibility which U.S. officials voice in speeches before the United Nations, back in their own offices they see no better alternative model for world order than the imperial model, to be constructed, hopefully, with as light a touch as possible. It is not surprising that they should come to this conclusion. The very nature of the nation-state, their oath of office, and their primary allegiance as well as the pressures of Congress and their superiors all require the National-Security Manager to serve the national interest, as the military, the corporations, the farmers, and the labor unions see it, rather than an abstract "world community" or so altruistic a goal as removing the grossest inequalities among the developed and undeveloped nations. He is quite free to think about a world-security system as long as he does not compromise the power of the joint chiefs of staff to decide where the forces should be deployed, what weapons should be used, and when. He is encouraged to develop an aid program, provided U.S. business benefits adequately and he can convince Congress that the United States has received sound value in influence, business concessions, or political support. Above all, he must not be so indiscreet as to sponsor a "giveaway." The pressures of various interest groups within the United States for an imperialist relationship are enormous, but one should not ignore the role of the bureaucracy itself. It is an exhilarating experience for a GS-14 to run the police force, lecture the minister of the interior, or reform the agriculture of a little country. Many Americans have found an outlet for social and political experimentation on new frontiers abroad that is denied them at home. Since the overseas bureaucracy totals some two to four million individuals, it constitutes in itself an impressive group with a vested interest in keeping the mechanics of foreign relations much as they are.[5] This means retaining control of vital decisions concerning a country's policies on defense and economic development in American hands.

THREE

Unilateralism is a more polite and perhaps less image-rich term than imperialism, which not only evokes memories of Lord Clive, Cecil Rhodes, and the French Foreign Legion but also has become saddled with Lenin's particular theories of economic causation. But they mean essentially the same thing — "the extension of control" by a single nation. Unilateralism is so much taken for granted within the national-security bureaucracy that when critics point out the discrepancy between our professed political and legal ideals as embodied in the United Nations Charter and our actual behavior as a nation, it makes very little impression. What's wrong with imperialism or unilateralism? Is there anything better?

There are two ways of trying to answer the first question. One is to look at unilateralism from the point of view of U.S. national interests. The second is to consider it from what might be called a "world-order" perspective, looking specifically toward the development of a strong legal and constitutional structure for dealing with war, hunger, disease, and other overriding global problems. I recognize that the two categories are not wholly distinct, that there are few objective criteria for determining national interests, and that a sensible government in the nuclear age would have as a primary "national interest" the development of a good system for "world order." But the categories are useful for distinguishing the most short-range and parochial considerations from longer-range perspectives.

From the standpoint of a President of the United States, thinking about re-election, concerned with solving domestic problems, and assuring himself a decent place in history, unilateralism is proving to be a disastrous policy. C. E. Black in *The Dynamics of Modernization* estimates that we must anticipate "ten to fifteen revolutions a year for the foreseeable future in the less developed societies."[6] The suppression of a single revolutionary movement in Vietnam, admittedly a long-developing and powerful one, costs the U.S. Treasury almost forty billion dollars a year, results in almost ten thousand battle deaths annually, and has stirred up political dissension unprecedented in our history. The attempt of one nation to deal simultaneously with insurgent movements in a dozen other places and to forestall still others in a variety of backward countries on three continents would tax the intellectual and political energies of the government to the breaking point.

One of the problems with imperialism is that as decision-making authority becomes centralized, the burdens on the imperialist leaders become intolerable, for along with the trappings of added power come political headaches. The Founding Fathers wisely spared the President of the United States the burden of appointing state and local officials. I suspect that they would be appalled to discover that he must now regularly pass on the qualifications of provincial governors in South Vietnam and ministers of agriculture in the Dominican Republic. There is literally no country in which the foreign-policy bureaucracy cannot discover a "U.S. interest," and since the President has at his disposal an almost infinite variety of techniques for furthering those interests, he is constantly called upon to exercise his judgment. Having no firsthand knowledge of the politics of the countries he is asked to set on one course or another, this imposes something of a strain on him. As Telford Taylor puts it, "the road to everywhere leads nowhere." The President faces a familiar problem of empire. Having asserted an interest in a faraway land, he is expected to be able to control events there. In fact, as the biographies of the commitments examined in this book reveal, the events begin to control him. Once military forces are committed, for example, it is usually impossible to limit the objectives to those which originally impelled the intervention. The commitment of national power unleashes political forces both in the country concerned and in the United States which then severely limit future choices.

The essence of unilateralism is that you recognise no limits except those of your own making. Such enlargement of the area of political discretion invites miscalculation and error. One of the functions of legal limits in a society is to provide external standards to relieve men of the responsibility to decide every issue anew. Sharing responsibility for decision with others who are also affected by it, the essence of democratic theory, is another old political device for rescuing human leaders from the dangers of distorted vision, a disability that always afflicts those who exercise power despotically. The possession of great power is not, as Secretary of State Rusk and others have suggested, a justification for using it unilaterally. It is, rather a condition, as the framers of the U.S. Constitution recognized, which cries out for legal restraints to protect the community from tyranny and the possessor from his own hubris.

The assertion of a police responsibility to prevent violent revolution and insurgency inevitably requires a militarization of a nation's foreign policy. *Webster's International Dictionary* uses the terms "militarism" and "imperialism" interchangeably, and this makes good political as well as linguistic sense, since no nation, no matter how great its economic and political resources, can hope to maintain control of events in distant lands without eventually relying chiefly on force. We have seen how, in Greece, for example, and later in Vietnam, nonmilitary strategies of "counterinsurgency" were swallowed up in the military effort. If the United States sets as a goal the prevention of regimes in the Third World which call themselves communist or which seem to lean to communism, it must be prepared to fight for that goal with its military power.

The result of such a decision, and it is one that was made a long time ago, is to make the United States Number One Enemy of a great number of people. State Department officials are privately scornful about foreign-policy criticism based on the argument that "world opinion" is turning against us. They point out, rightly, that no one knows what that means or how to measure it. The United States, however, is very much interested in those leaders of the

Third World who are convinced that only radical change can rescue their societies from political tyranny and economic stagnation. Such leaders, who are coming increasingly to see violence as the only avenue of change, are being drawn together only by their common fear and hatred of the United States. American foreign policy is providing what Marxism-Leninism has failed to offer revolutionary movements — an ideological bond to tie together nationalist revolutionary movements spread across three continents. These movements originate in the local political soil. They are primarily concerned with local issues and local enemies. But the leaders of insurgent movements are establishing international links and are attempting to help one another, despite their limited resources. They do this not because of shared ideological goals so much as because of the belief that they are partisans in the same war. What gives unity to the struggle in their analysis is "imperialism," which means chiefly the United States. To be able to characterize the enemy in an insurgent struggle as a giant White Imperialist Power helps to bring nationalists of all classes into the revolutionary coalition. Juan Bosch exaggerated only slightly when he declared that where there were fifty-three communists in the Dominican Republic before the intervention, there were now fifty-three thousand.

Nationalism and anti-imperialism are such strong forces that only those politicians, businessmen, and generals who benefit directly and personally from the American presence in their country can be counted on to oppose nationalist movements. Such movements may start, as we have seen, with the efforts of a few energetic individuals. A small minority always takes the lead. But the nationalist impulse runs through the societies of the Third World. If the United States continues to make it a policy to oppose nationalism wherever it is entwined with a radical political and economic program or with communist rhetoric, it must count on being hated and feared by political leaders, who will increasingly come to speak for a majority of the world population. It must be prepared to pay heavily to keep the loyalty of its clients. Pericles warned the people of Athens that the fate of greatness was to be hated and feared, and some of the same philosophy prevails today in the corridors of the State Department. Yet even the most powerful country in the world takes a reckless view of national security if it ignores repeated historical patterns. As Walter Lippmann has pointed out, where one nation arrogates to itself the responsibility to shape a world order, it invites others to combine against it. In a world where nuclear weapons will, in all likelihood, be widely distributed before the end of the century, this is not a reassuring road to national security for the American people.

FOUR

Now let us examine the policy of the American Responsibility — suppressing revolution — from the point of view of the world community. Assume that the two overriding minimum requirements of world order are, first, the prevention of nuclear war and such lesser violence as threatens to lead to nuclear war; and second, the creation of economic and political conditions in the southern half of the globe which can support human life there. The portion of the earth where the per-capita income is less than two hundred dollars a year is literally a giant death camp. It is possible to make reasonably accurate projections of the numbers of people within the Southern Hemisphere who are condemned to die from starvation and disease. If predictions of the growing disparity between population and resources are even substantially correct, the toll in lives that will be sacrificed by the end of the century must be reckoned in the tens of millions.

"I think what you are saying," Senator Vandenberg suggested to Secretary Acheson in an attempt to sum up the import of the Truman Doctrine, "is that whenever we find free peoples having difficulty in the maintenance of free institutions, and difficulty in defending against aggressive movements that seek to impose upon them totalitarian regimes, we do not necessarily react in the same way each time, but we propose to react." "That," Acheson replied, "I think is correct." The kind of reaction which the United States has contemplated has brought the world to the brink of nuclear war at least twice. (President Eisenhower reports that the use of nuclear weapons was seriously considered in Korea in 1953 and in Indochina in 1954). The Marines who landed in Lebanon in 1958 brought atomic howitzers with them. Had they been faced by a hostile army rather than Coca-Cola salesmen, as happily turned out to be the case, the situation would have been incredibly dangerous. In the Vietnam war, W. W. Rostow has wondered out loud how to make nuclear weapons "relevant" to the conflict.[7] There is no doubt that the chief of staff of the air force thinks he has an answer. The only successful strategy for suppressing a "war of national liberation" so far discovered has been a military strategy. (This does not mean that, as in the Philippines, nonmilitary techniques such as pacification and reform are not also used, but that the crucial element in the victory was the application of overwhelming military power.) Nor, as Vietnam suggests, does it mean that the military strategy always works. The only decisive victories over insurgents have been in Greece, Malaya, and the Philippines, and these are attributable to a combination of internal political dissension in the ranks of the insurgents combined with a military superiority of at least ten to one in the antiguerilla army . . . .

The commitment to suppress an insurgency, particularly if it is a stubborn one, leads, as we have seen in Vietnam, to a rapid rise in the level of violence. It also exerts pressure on those powers who claim to support wars of national liberation to back their rhetoric with their guns and rockets. The most plausible spark for a nuclear war (outside of Germany) is some future Haiphong (or perhaps Haiphong itself), where the giants are led by their respective clients into a direct confrontation.

There is also a world-order interest in limiting violence short of nuclear war. One consequence of a massive military intervention by a great country in a small one is that it destroys the people it is claiming to liberate. The lethal technology of the United States is so advanced and the welfare of the client population so secondary a consideration compared with winning the war that the "defense of freedom" actually requires making a desert of a primitive society. Since many of the societies facing insurgencies are living just above the subsistence level anyway, the scorched-earth strategy for dealing with the problem — destroying villages, wholesale removal of populations, destruction of crops — is particularly cruel, for it pushes poor countries further down into the depths of misery.

FIVE

There are two principal arguments advanced in support of the policy of U.S. intervention in civil wars and insurgencies which purport to rest on broad world-community interests rather than narrow nationalistic considerations. One is that the United States is defending "freedom" against "totalitarianism." If this is the policy, it is applied with something less than consistency. Many of the free governments that have received either generous U.S. military aid, friendly nods from the U.S. Embassy, or direct military intervention in their behalf constitute a group that on the whole is rather careless about civil liberties — Formosa, Korea, South Vietnam, Iran, Brazil, Paraguay, etc. Actually, a very substantial portion of U.S. aid has gone to a series of military dictatorships located at the periphery of Russia and China.[8]

Nor has the test of U.S. concern been the violent character of a government's accession to power. Military coups which seize power from constitutional regimes are consistently recognized and supported, and on occasion (Brazil in 1964, for example) encouraged. Here are a few examples of military takeovers which the United States did not oppose (and in most cases welcomed): Argentina (1955), Turkey (1960), South Korea (1961), Burma (1962), Indonesia (1966), Ghana (1966).

The defense of freedom has not even resulted in a consistent anti-communist policy. In the area under the direct control of the Soviet Union and China, United States involvement has been circumspect. After the State Department lost the diplomatic battle at the close of World War II to retain some Western influence in Eastern Europe, the United States did not take military measures to oppose the communist coup in Czechoslovakia in 1948 or to aid anti-Soviet insurgent movements, including the Berlin uprising of 1953, the Poznan riots, and the Hungarian Revolution. Low-level covert operations were conducted against the Eastern European regimes from 1946 into the 1960's, including espionage and U-2 overflights, as well as subversive propaganda over Radio Free Europe and Radio Liberation. But the rhetorical goal of "liberation" was proclaimed by Dulles only after the actual attempt to roll back Soviet power in Eastern Europe had been abandoned. With respect to China, the United States has given the Taiwan government two billion dollars with which to equip the six-hundred-thousand man army and has put U-2 aircraft at its disposal for overflights of the mainland; but for many years it has made it reasonably clear that it will not sponsor the invasion Chiang still says he will mount.

While most United States support has gone to right-wing dictatorships, in the late 1950's, and particularly in the Kennedy administration later, the United States attempted to modernize its strategy of intervention. The Truman administration and the Eisenhower administration in its first term had given wholehearted support to "legitimate" governments if they were noncommunist and friendly to the United States, no matter how oppressive or reactionary they might be. (In 1952 the United States did aid a leftist revolutionary regime in Bolivia which earned American support by lowering the price of tin and adopting a properly anti-Soviet foreign policy.) President Eisenhower symbolized U.S. willingness to support reaction in Latin America by inviting Perez Jiménez, the brutal dictator of Venezuela, to Washington and awarding him the Medal of Merit. But a few years later American intelligence agencies and private groups acting in their behalf began to support more liberal and even leftist elements in Latin America and Africa. The Central Intelligence Agency gave funds for the support of institutions like the Inter-American Centre of Economic and Social Studies and the Institute for International Labor Research in the Dominican Republic and the Institute of Political Education in Costa Rica. These institutions train, finance, and encourage political groups which often oppose their own governments for being too conservative and are also critical of official U.S. policy in Latin America but are anti-communist. It appears that resistance leaders from Mozambique and South Africa have been offered covert assistance by the CIA and in certain cases have received it. In Algeria the AFL-CIO, acting for the CIA, gave direct financial assistance to the National Liberation Front from 1957 until the successful end of the War of Independence. The American labor organization sponsored the Algerian rebels in international labor circles and arranged for membership of the FLN union in the ICFTU, the U.S.-dominated world federation of trade unions. The National Student Association, an ostensibly private organization, distributed CIA funds to Algerian resistance leaders in the form of scholarships. The operation in Algeria in support of the rebels was designed to discourage them from turning to communist countries for help. At the same time, the U.S. State Department, still officially supporting France, continued to sanction military aid for use against the FLN.[9]

The worldwide pattern of United States military involvement which emerges is thus impossible to reconcile with a global campaign to preserve freedom. For the most part, U.S. interventions have had a strong ideological thrust, either to support anticommunist regimes threatened with subversion or to subvert communist, communist-leaning, or potentially communist-leaning regimes, many of which have been at least as "free" as Stroessner's Paraguay or Ky's Vietnam. In some cases, such as Laos, the Dominican Republic, and Algeria, different U.S. agencies have intervened on both sides. The almost automatic reaction has been to commit United States military power where it appears necessary to prevent a communist takeover, except where the Soviets or the Chinese are likely to respond with a major war. The Chinese invasion of Tibet, for example, a much less ambiguous case of violent seizure of power by an external communist regime than either Greece or Vietnam, was ignored because it was so clearly beyond the power of the United States to do much about it short of a war with China. But it appears that the only areas where U.S. leaders consider it too risky to sponsor a major military intervention are the immediate rimlands of China and Eastern Europe. Elsewhere, while the dangers of escalation are growing, the experience of twenty years suggests that the communist powers will support the communist side but will not seek to deter or oppose United States intervention through a direct confrontation with American military power. Naturally, however, the United States prefers to rely on intelligence operations, aid officials, and military missions to influence the political direction of Third World governments rather than to order its counterinsurgency forces into action. U.S. National Security Managers have tried in some countries to promote reforms, but they have continually shown, as in Guatemala, Vietnam, and other places, that they are prepared to sacrifice reform to the goal of anti-communism. And by covertly supporting leftist revolutionaries in Latin America and Africa they have shown themselves to be willing to compromise ideological purity for the sake of maintaining a degree of U.S. influence and control, which often becomes the principal end in itself.

SIX

United States officials make a second claim that America

is somehow acting in the interest of the international community by undertaking a worldwide campaign against revolution. The argument is that by stamping out insurgent movements the United States is preventing World War III. With his eyes firmly fixed on the shore he has left, to quote De Tocqueville's phrase, the National-Security Manager is trying to squeeze the baffling chaos of postwar revolution into the familiar mold of Great Power politics as practiced in the 1930's. Ho Chi Minh becomes Hitler. Vietnam is the Rhineland. Negotiation is Munich. If the insurgents are not stopped in Vietnam, they will have to be stopped eventually in San Francisco.

President Kennedy's speech to the American people after his encounter with Khruschev in Vienna is a good example of this official thought process:

> He was certain that the tide was moving his way, that the revolution of rising people would eventually be a communist revolution, and that the so-called wars of national liberation supported by the Kremlin would replace the old methods of direct aggression and invasion. In the 1940's and early 50's the great danger was from communist armies marching across free borders, which we saw in Korea . . . . now we face a new and different threat. We no longer have a nuclear monopoly. Their missiles, they believe, will hold off our missiles, and their troops can match our troops should we intervene in the so-called wars of liberation. Thus, the local conflicts they support can turn in their favor through guerrillas, or insurgents, or subversion . . . [10]

The essence of the argument is that guerrillas in Vietnam, Thailand, Peru, Guatemala, and Angola are all part of the same army. If the army can be defeated in Vietnam, it will not be necessary to fight it in Thailand or the Philippines. If the insurgencies are not opposed, that will demonstrate a lack or resolve, just as Munich did, and eventually the guerillas will challenge the United States directly and then we will have to fight World War III to defend our homes and honor. The assumption that insurgencies are inspired by outside powers or that they are orchestrated by some central authority is, as I have tried to show in Part One, false. The defeat of the Vietcong will not mean that the insurgents in Thailand will surrender. Nor will a guerrilla victory in Vietnam insure a guerrilla victory in Thailand. True, revolutionary successes will encourage insurgents elsewhere.

More important, it will demonstrate to governments whose survival depends upon U.S. military aid to rule their discontented populations that since the United States cannot keep its commitments to them, their days are numbered unless they can learn to govern.

Why, however, the overthrow of corrupt feudal regimes by local insurgents should pose a danger of world war or a direct military threat to the United States is hard to see. The danger of world war arises only if the United States is committed to resisting revolution by force and is prepared to "pay any price" to do it, and then only if another major power is prepared to stand in the way. Even if we assume a wave of successful revolutions throughout Asia, Africa, and Latin America, the notion that the Castros of the future will muster an army of millions, transport them by sampan and burro, and loose them on our cities is nothing less than a psychotic fantasy, so absurd in fact that it is never explicitly stated, only hinted at in vague anxiety-producing historical analogies. (What is so sad about being ruled by such fantasies is that the diversion of money and energy to the fight which is supposed to keep Asian communists from landing on our shores helps perpetuate the conditions which have created native insurgents and guerilla warfare in American cities.)

Thus the means which the United States has chosen to deal with the phenomenon of revolution make war more likely rather than less. The idea of preventive war, that you fight a little one now to avoid a great one later, has some validity if you are facing a single adversary such as Hitler. Where there are many adversaries, each with its own local reasons for fighting, the idea can be understood only as an exercise in mysticism, not logic. In short, the arrogation by a single power of the policeman's warrant is not a solution to the problem of war . . .

The preceding discussion has assumed that the primary motivation behind America's crusade against revolution is an altruistic desire to save the people of Asia, Africa, and Latin America from the terrors of Stalinism. No doubt a few members of the national-security bureaucracy have been passionately concerned about this. But the primary allegiance of national officials in any country is to their own populations. Such considerations as the fear of $16 billion in corporate assets invested in Asia, Latin America, and the Near East as a result of expropriation by radical regimes influence policymakers at least as much as the urge to rescue undeveloped countries from one particular form of totalitarianism. Further, the National-Security Manager, who takes it as an article of faith that this is to be the American Century, is haunted by the fear that the towering event of the century, the rise of the Third World to international visibility, will not take place under United States control, that the models and the inspiration will be found somewhere else, and that, indeed, hatred of the United States and the civilization it represents may be one of the Third World's peculiar dynamics.

The best indication that the American Responsibility is designed more to ensure a sense of economic and political well-being at home than to achieve any particular lasting results abroad can be found by looking at the great Cold War successes. For years the model of a successful counterinsurgency was Greece. It was more than politeness to an old man when President Johnson called Harry Truman for his birthday and exclaimed, "We've had thirteen years to see the wisdom of your policies. There's not a right-thinking person in the free world today who would want to go back and change one of them." Greece was considered a success for many years because it ended in the surrender and disappearance of the rebels. It required no negotiation or compromise. But in the process, the political structure of the country was undermined. In the atmosphere of suppression, the extreme-right wing flourished. Twenty years after the Truman Doctrine was announced, the most reactionary military dictatorship in Europe or the Near East came to power and at present writing still rules. In the Dominican Republic, order has been purchased at the price of democratic progress. The Balaguer government suppresses and harasses political opposition and has relied on the same elements of the society Trujillo marshalled for his purposes — foreign-owned business and the military.[12] In Lebanon, where the political structure was relatively strong at the time of the U.S. intervention, progress has been made in the ten years since the Marines left. In Guatemala, Iran, Indonesia, and the Congo, on the other hand, all of which have been the scene of major U.S. interventions to change the politics of the country, it is highly debatable how much progress has been made. To say with absolute certainty whether things would have been worse or better had not the United States intervened is impossible. One thing is certain, however.

Significant progress toward the goals of stability, democracy, and substantial economic progress, for which the effort was ostensibly made, has not been achieved in any of them.

FOOTNOTES

1. George Ball, quoted in Gareth Porter, "Globalism: The Ideology of Total World Involvement," in Marcus G. Raskin and Bernard B. Fall, eds., *The Viet-Nam Reader* (New York, 1965), p. 324.
2. Allen Dulles, *The Craft of Intelligence* (New York, 1963), pp. 235-236.
3. Interview, in *United States News and World Report*, January 24, 1961, quoted in Carl Oglesby and Richard Shaull, *Containment and Change: Two Dissenting Views of American Society and Foreign Policy in the New Revolutionary Age* (New York, 1967), p. 81n.
4. U.S. Department of State, *Foreign Policy Briefs*, June 24, 1960.
5. At the end of 1965, before the major troop increases in Vietnam, the total military personnel overseas was about 800,000. The number of federal civilian employees totalled about 40,000, and the number of individuals working overseas for corporations, foundations, and other private U.S. organizations was about 100,000. See Ernest Rubin, "A Statistical Overview of Americans Abroad," in *Annals of the American Academy of Political and Social Science*, November 1966, pp. 1-10. The number of military personnel has of course grown substantially in the intervening years, as has private U.S. corporate activity, thus the number of Americans employed overseas now approaches 2,000,000. While many of the GI's do not constitute a vested interest for anything except their own desire to go home as soon as possible, the professional soldier finds great career advantages in overseas assignments, as does his counterpart in civilian agencies and corporations. But most of the members of what I call the "overseas bureaucracy" administer far-flung military, foreign-assistance, education, and private-corporate activities from the United States. Bureaucrats in the Pentagon and the State Department, executives and workers in defense industries, and managers of the mushrooming "multinational corporation" centered in the United States depend on far flung foreign activities for their livelihood and sense of purpose.
6. C. E. Black, *The Dynamics of Modernization* (New York, 1966) p. 166.
7. The Rostow paper, which circulated within the government, is only one of several "think pieces" reflecting the frustration of the world's greatest military power in its inability to bring its most lethal weapons to bear on limited wars. During the last five years, several papers have been circulated through the bureaucracy proposing the use of nuclear weapons for "demonstration effect." A leading academic analyst, Professor Thomas Schelling, was awarded a contract by the United States Arms Control and Disarmament Agency for a paper in which he discussed "the diffent use" of nuclear weapons.

8. Of a total of 24,972.3 million dollars in foreign aid, including military aid, given from the years 1946-1967, outside of Marshall Plan aid to Europe, 22,597.1 million of it has gone to Taiwan, Korea, Vietnam, Turkey, Iran, Thailand, and Pakistan. (The figure for total foreign aid does not include aid to India, Nepal, or Laos, as this information is classified.) Source: Agency for International Development, Special Report for the House Foreign Affairs Committee: *U.S. Overseas Loans and Grants, July 1, 1945-June 30, 1966* (Washington, D.C., 1967).
9. The discussion of CIA support for liberal or radical groups is based on personal interviews with U.S. union officials, African nationalist leaders, and a leading member of the Algerian resistance movement. The CIA funding of the Latin American institutes mentioned in the text was widely reported during the CIA disclosures of 1967.
10. John F. Kennedy, Report to the American People on the Vienna Meetings, June 6, 1961.
11. Lyndon B. Johnson, quoted in *The New York Times*, May 14, 1967.
12. For an account of the Balaguer regime, see S. Rodman, "The First Nine Months," in *The New Republic*, March 23, 1967.

Counterinsurgency in the Third World: Theory and Practice *

Andrew Mack

The purpose of this essay is to provide a brief overview of the theory and practice of counterinsurgency in the Third World since World War II. Given the obvious limitations of space, descriptions of particular COIN (counterinsurgency) campaigns have been avoided except to illustrate an argument. Furthermore, this essay concentrates primarily on U.S. counterinsurgency doctrines and methods. This is not to underestimate the contributions — both theoretical and practical — made by the former colonial powers in attempting to crush the impulse to national liberation in the Third World. But the European powers — with the recent exception of Portugal — had, by the beginning of the 1960s, neither the capability nor (following a number of humiliating setbacks) much enthusiasm for further military adventures in the Third World. There have, of course, been exceptions — the French in Mali, Britain in Borneo and the Anguilla affair — but these pale into insignificance when compared with the American counterinsurgency effort in the Third World, which began to gather impetus just as the major European colonial powers were

* The research for this article was in part supported by a grant from the Social Science Research Council.

abdicating their former role as Third World policemen.[1]

The attempt to cover such a wide field has also necessitated a degree of over-simplification and the exclusion of a number of key problems. For example, there is no mention made of Soviet counterinsurgency theory and practice, nor of *domestic* counter-insurgency programmes in the West which may well assume increasing importance if the current economic crisis in countries like Britain catalyses intensive class warfare. Neither is it possible within the scope of this essay to do more than suggest answers to certain crucial questions. Why, for example, should a 'counterinsurgency' programme in Vietnam which employed half a million U.S. troops and cost tens of billions of dollars fail, when 'low profile' programmes in Latin America employing only a handful of American personnel at low cost have — in the short run at least — been relatively successful? Why has the 'soft' approach to COIN so vigorously promoted by Pentagon and university social scientists failed? Why is open military intervention by the U.S. in the Third World now much less likely than previously? Is torture becoming a key weapon in the COIN practitioner's manual? These are questions to which those who formulate and carry out COIN programmes must continually address themselves. The answers to these questions are also of critical importance to those who oppose such programmes — often with their lives. It is the latter to whom this essay is respectfully dedicated.

Counterinsurgency has been succinctly defined by the Pentagon — the organization which practices counterrevolution most assiduously — as: "Those military, paramilitary, political, economic and civic actions taken by a government to defeat subversive insurgency." Since the U.S. government has itself been involved in a large number of well-documented clandestine attempts to overthrow regimes not to its liking, the Pentagon definition prudently added that: "In the current context, subversive insurgency is primarily communist inspired, supported or exploited". [2] This definition is useful since it draws attention to the essential *aims* of counterinsurgency rather than providing a catalogue of means towards these ends. The public image of counterinsurgency — small, elite units of U.S. Army Special Forces assiduously tracking guerrillas through the forests and swamps of Indochina — represents only a small and increasingly irrelevant part of the truth. Counterinsurgency also encompasses such euphemistically named "dirty tricks" as torture and assassination at one end of the spectrum, and the manipulation of aid and trade agreements at the other. Counterinsurgency is in fact the keystone of U.S. foreign policy in the Third World. The forms it takes have changed quite radically since the concept of counterinsurgency became fashionable in the early 1960s, but the aims remain essentially the same.

The aims of counterinsurgency

The consistent opposition of U.S. foreign policy to revolution in the Third World is a fact which has not been seriously questioned. The motivations which lie behind this opposition, however, have been, and continue to be, the source of considerable controversy. Some analysts have argued the objective of counter revolution is national security; others maintain the purpose is the "protection of freedom" or, alternatively, that the U.S. was protecting neither security at home nor freedom abroad, but rather that the political leadership had become blinded with an irrational obsession with the containment of communism. At the height of the Cold War the so-called Domino Theory provided the major rationalization for counter-revolutionary theory and practice. In crude terms this implied that communist influence would spread across the globe with one country serving as a springboard for subverting and then taking over the next. Like a row of dominoes which topple after the first one falls, so would Communism engulf ever increasing areas of the Third World, shifting the global balance of power and eventually posing a direct security threat to the U.S. itself.

The response to this *simpliste* evaluation of the alleged Communist Threat was a policy of containment. But this crude version of the Domino Theory had lost much of its credibility by the 1960s (which is not to say that more sophisticated versions were untenable). As the Vietnam war escalated it became increasingly clear that many of the arguments upon which containment—both in theory and practice—was based were simply rationalizations. The national security argument—"we must fight the Communists in Vietnam (or wherever) or we will be fighting them on the beaches of California"—has never been taken seriously by more than a handful of diehard militarists. The "protection of freedom" argument could only make sense if one equated anti-Communism in *any* guise with "freedom", since U.S. foreign aid and military assistance (direct and indirect) had long been used to support regimes characterized by brutal repression and a total lack of commitment to the most elementary democratic freedoms. Liberal opposition to the Vietnam war focused on the argument that the root cause of U.S.

interventionism, in Vietnam and elsewhere, grew out of a rigid and irrational ideological fixation with the dangers of communism which transcended the objective needs of national security. The Vietnam war was seen from this perspective as a "quagmire" — a mistaken venture into which the U.S. policy-makers, their vision distorted by ideology, had blundered unawares.

Finally, there is the 'revisionist' argument that it is the security of U.S. overseas *interests* rather than the territorial sovereignty of the U.S. *per se*, which forms the basic rationale for the global counterinsurgency programme. These interests are primarily economic and include not only the huge and growing U.S. investment stake in the Third World, but also the need to control access to strategic commodities. Liberal critics who have emphasized obsessive anti-communism, as the prime motivation for counterrevolutionary activity were quick to point out that this argument could not apply to Vietnam since U.S. economic interests there have always been negligible. However radical critics and U.S. policy-makers have noted that the consequences of losing in Vietnam could have serious implications (in terms of raising revolutionary expectations on the one hand, and reducing the credibility of the U.S. guarantor role for client regimes on the other) for countries where the U.S. interests *are* considerable. This constitutes a more sophisticated version of the Domino Theory.

Thus, both radicals and U.S. policy-makers, in contrast to the liberal critics, have been able to discern *rational*, rather than *irrational* and purely ideological, arguments for the Vietnam involvement and other interventions. This was forcefully emphasized in the famous memorandum on U.S. policy aims in Vietnam, by Defence Secretary MacNamara's chief assistant, John McNaughton, which was revealed with the publication of the *Pentagon Papers*. McNaughton quantifies American objectives as follows: 70 per cent to avoid a humiliating U.S. defeat (to the American reputation as guarantor); 20 per cent to keep South Vietnam (and the adjacent territory) from Chinese hands; 10 per cent to permit the people of South Vietnam to enjoy a better, freer way of life.[5] The McNaughton document was particularly important since it showed that the old-fashioned Domino Theory (the second objective noted in the memorandum) was far less important than the first (the U.S. guarantor role) and that the traditional justification for intervention — "the protection of freedom" — barely entered into U.S. calculations at all at that time.

The controversies about the 'real' motivations of U.S. foreign policy *vis-a-vis* the Third World are beyond the scope of this essay — suffice it to say that an 'obsessive' ideology of anti-communism and a more 'real-politik' concern with U.S. overseas interests are generally complementary rather than contradictory in terms of policy prescriptions. Both view-points imply a commitment to some form or other of counterinsurgency. For a Third World country to "succumb to Communism" is not merely an ideological defeat for the United States; it also implies the removal of that state from the world capitalist orbit, a shift in the global 'balance of power', the nationalization of U.S. investment interests, the denial of markets and of access to strategic raw materials.

Counterinsurgency before 1960

As will be shown later, the decade of the 1960s marked a sharp increase in interest in theories of revolution and counterinsurgency in the United States and a marked shift of military resources towards containing revolutionary activity in the Third World. However, despite the upsurge in counterinsurgency activity during the 1960s, the U.S. throughout its history has routinely employed its military forces overseas to secure American interests:

This pattern of military intervention is graphically documented in a chronology of 'The Instances of Use of U.S. Armed Forces Abroad, 1798-1945', prepared at the request of the late Senator Everett Dirksen and published in the *Congressional Record*. Of the nearly 160 occasions on which American forces were employed abroad between 1798 and 1945, an overwhelming majority involved occupation of a Third World country. Between 1900 and 1925, for instance, U.S. troops were dispatched overseas 'to protect American interests' or to 'restore order' during 'periods of revolution' no less than 46 times.[4]

...However, Third World counterrevolutionary strategy in the first decade and a half following the end of World War II was primarily the responsibility of the former colonial powers. It was a losing battle. The Dutch were forced to withdraw from Indonesia, the French from Indo-China and then Algeria, the Belgians from the Congo. The British fought a successful counterinsurgency campaign in Malaysia, but were forced to withdraw from Palestine, Aden and Cyprus. In some of the independence struggles, violent confrontation arose as a consequence of conflict over the timing rather than the principle of independence. In others — Algeria, for example — the struggle was more prolonged and savage. But by the beginning of the 1960s the former colonial powers — with the significant exception of Portugal, the oldest and weakest of them — had renounced formal political control over all but a few unimportant vestiges of their former empires. Direct and indirect U.S. involvement in counterinsurgency had by no means been absent during this period, which included not only the Korean War (usually seen as a conventional war rather than a counterinsurgency campaign) and massive economic aid to the French in their war in Indo-China, but also active support for the Philippine government in its campaign against the Huks in the 1950s; the invasion of Lebanon in 1958; operations in Quemoy-Matsu in 1958; clandestine operations in Iran in 1953; in Guatemala in 1954 and many others. However, the *scale* of the U.S. counterinsurgency effort during this era was small relative to the post 1960 period.

The passing of classical European colonialism was quite in line with U.S. interests since — like Britain in the heyday of the Free Trade era — the U.S. had always tended (with such obvious exceptions as Puerto Rico, Hawaii and the Philippines) to expand its overseas interests through aggressive trade and investment policies and *indirect* political and military control rather than through the classical colonial policy of direct territorial annexation. This approach was symbolized in the Monroe Doctrine and the Open Door Notes which applied respectively in the two major U.S. 'spheres of influence' — Latin America and Asia. The demise of classical colonialism also opened up new sources of trade and investment for the U.S. which goes some way to explaining U.S. support for independence movements in the Third World (in particular Africa) during the 1950s. This support was by no means consistent, however, as the Indo-China experience shows.

Counterinsurgency post-1960

American military doctrine during the 1950s had relied heavily on the doctrine of "massive retaliation" which was directed primarily against the Soviet Union and was essentially a war-deterring rather than a war-fighting doctrine. It laid overwhelming emphasis on nuclear weapons and was predicated on the belief that the U.S. nuclear arsenal was sufficient to deter any Soviet attack, either on the U.S. or its NATO allies, since this would result in the nuclear annihilation of the aggressor. However, critics both within and outside the military establishment were quick to point out that such a doctrine left the U.S. ill-prepared to fight 'limited wars' (like that in Korea) and almost totally unprepared to fight 'brush fire' wars in the Third World against guerrilla forces. Since the former colonial powers had to a large degree abdicated their active counterinsurgency role with the demise of direct colonial control, and since the majority of armed conflicts were now taking place in the Third World (often in areas where American interests were at stake), the critics of 'massive retaliation' had little difficulty in persuading a newly-elected President Kennedy that drastic changes were needed. The U.S. strategic doctrine for the Sixties was labelled Flexible Response. It required massive increases in counter-guerrilla and conventional war fighting capability and measures to achieve these ends were swiftly put into motion.

This shift in interest in COIN was paralleled by changes in the Military Assistance Programmes (MAP) to Third World countries which shifted abruptly in strategic focus under the new Kennedy Administration. In Latin America, for example, the rationale for Military Assistance Programmes changed "from hemispheric defense to internal security, from the protection of coastlines and from anti-submarine warfare to internal defense against Castro-Communist guerrilla warfare."[5] In 1961, Kennedy ordered a fivefold increase in Army Special Forces strength which was designed primarily for a counterinsurgency role, and the U.S. Air Force and Navy created parallel COIN groups. To increase the U.S. intervention capability — the so-called Rapid Deployment category — the Pentagon under its new Defence Secretary, Robert MacNamara, pushed through crash programmes designed to speed the deployment of men and material to obscure trouble spots in the Third World, as well as providing a rapid reinforcement capability for the NATO front. These programmes led to the procurement of the giant C-5A transport aircraft capable of transporting 700 troops; a new generation of naval military transports — the abortive Fast Deployment Logistics Ship and the Landing Helicopter Assault Ship; and the 'Instant Air Base' (ISB). The ISB was to provide for the Tactical Air Command the same degree of mobility which the C-5A offered the Army and the new 'floating garrisons' offered the Marines. With all necessary equipment self-contained in transport aircraft, the ISB was designed to turn a disused airstrip (of which the U.S. Air Force reportedly has access to some 1400 around the world) into an operational airfield for F-4 fighter-bombers within seventy-two hours.[6]

The 'soft' approach to counterinsurgency: Social Science on the warpath.

The 'fire brigade' emphasis on improving intervention capability did not in itself provide any answers to the problem of actually combating guerilla forces on the ground once an intervention had been achieved. To this end the Pentagon embarked on a huge programme of counterinsurgency research, the results of which were to be tried out in the 'laboratories' of South East Asia and Latin America. Since in the previous decades, research into the causes and means of controlling insurgency had been marked mostly by its absence, one of the first tasks of the Kennedy and Johnson Administration was to set up lavishly funded research programmes to investigate the causes of revolution in the Third World and techniques for combatting it. This led not only to a reexamination of past counterinsurgency campaigns — primarily those of Britain and France — but also to a thorough study of the works of the leading revolutionary strategists — Mao, Giap, and Guevara. By 1965 the Defence Department was spending some $10 million annually on behavioural, political and operations research programmes connnected with counterinsurgency.

The social scientists who were largely responsible for the 'software' research on counterinsurgency worked on the Defense Department research grants in both the universities and non-profit 'think tanks' like Rand, the Research Analysis corporation, the Human Resources Research office and the Centre for Research in Social Systems (CRESS). Research was co-ordinated in part through the Director of Defence Research and Engineering and in part through special horizontal advisory panels such as the Jason Division of the Pentagon's Advanced Research Projects Agency (ARPA) and various other *ad hoc* committees.

By and large the social science approach to revolution and counterinsurgency emphasized both the political and social causes of insurgency, and — initially at least — social, political and economic means of combating the insurgents. Military repression of revolutionary activity was seen as dealing with symptoms rather than causes. Such repression might be necessary in the short term in order to give the variously described 'reform', 'civic action' or 'pacification' programmes time to take effect, but it could not be a solution in the long run. Partial understanding of Mao Tse Tung's famous dictum that the 'guerrilla fish' can only survive in the hospitable 'people sea' meant that the social scientists concerned saw the key problem as separating the rebels from their social and material resource base — the people. If the masses could be persuaded to support the government rather than the guerrillas, the latter would be cut off from their sources of food, shelter and recruits, and would 'wither on the vine.'

Compared with conservative generals who advocated bombing the Vietnamese back into the Stone Age, the social scientists were liberal in their outlook, which meant in this context that they preferred non-violent techniques of counterinsurgency to military repression. They also supported whole-heartedly the U.S. government's antipathy to revolution. Additionally, they had their own professional reasons for supporting a 'soft' approach to counterinsurgency — an area in which they could lay claims to have special expertise. Not only was military repression distasteful, it was also the province of a profession over which they had no control and virtually no influence.

The high point of 'software' counterinsurgency research was Project Camelot. Originally planned as a co-ordinated research effort bringing together the talents of different academic disciplines in order to understand the causes of internal war, Camelot was ultimately concerned with "those actions which a government might take to relieve conditions which are assessed as giving rise to a *potential* for internal war" [7] (emphasis added). In other words, Camelot's contribution to counterinsurgency was to evolve a non-violent pre-emptive strike strategy — to nip insurgency in the bud with the aid of techniques of social, political and economic control before it reached the stage of manifest violence. The project, which was to have lasted three or four years and have cost some $4.5 million (the most lavishly funded social science project in history), ultimately proved abortive. Revelations in the Chilean press as to the real objectives of Camelot led to a diplomatic outcry, the cancellation of the project, a U.S. government edict that no more research was to be undertaken which could adversely effect American diplomatic relations, and considerable soul-searching within the academic community on the ethics of this type of research. Despite this, social science research on counterinsurgency has continued since Camelot, most obviously and expensively in Vietnam, but also in Thailand where the research projects of anthropologists working on Defence Department grants created a scandal within the profession, and where one

Army researcher noted: "The strategy in Vietnam was to send ten Marines for every peasant. In Thailand it's ten anthropologists."[8]

But in Vietnam where the war was continuing to escalate, there was a marked shift of emphasis on COIN research. As Samuel Huntington, one of America's leading political scientists noted of U.S. counterinsurgency theory:

Initially this doctrine, picking up the ocean and the fishes analogy from Mao, had stressed the importance of political action and "winning the hearts and minds of the people". In the mid-1960s, a 'revisionist' counterinsurgency doctrine emerged, primarily from analysts at the Rand Corporation, which like the Che-Debray revolutionary doctrine, put the primary emphasis on military organisation and military capability.[9]

Instead of studying how the peasants might be *persuaded* to support the government — a virtually impossible task in the South Vietnamese context — a 'think tank' analyst asked how they might be *prevented* from aiding the guerrillas. One of Rand's leading 'revisionists', Charles Wolf Jr., exemplified the new orientation when he wrote: "The main concern of counterinsurgency efforts should be to influence the behaviour and action of the populace rather than their loyalty and attitudes".[10] The original COIN objective of "winning hearts and minds", which had never been taken very seriously, was now completely abandoned.

Radical social scientists, inflating, like most academics, the importance of their own discipline, have sometimes made the mistake of assuming that their colleagues who sell their talents to the military have a considerable impact on the thinking of policy makers. In fact one of the primary functions of the social scientist in this field has been to provide *post hoc* rationalizations for policies which have already been chosen for quite different reasons. Social scientists most closely involved with the military have frequently complained that their advice is ignored.

The history of the Vietnam war again provides instructive evidence for the minimal effect of the 'software' approach to COIN advocated by the social scientists. From the beginning of the U.S. war effort the amount of resources ploughed into social reform programmes relative to that supplied for military programmes was minimal. Poorly funded, poorly administered and sabotaged by corrupt government officials, the inevitable failure of successive 'pacification programmes' was used by the military as an argument for pushing more resources into areas in which *their* professional expertise counted. The military, of course, started out with the initial advantage in that their resources and bureaucratic bargaining power in Washington were infinitely greater than other more 'politically' oriented government officers and the intellectual mercenaries in academia.

COIN and technology

Military strategy — as is most clearly evident in the field of nuclear warfare doctrines — tends to mould itself to the available technology. In Vietnam, as different approaches were tried and failed — from 'pacification' to 'search and destroy' — the remaining options increasingly emphasized a reliance on sophisticated technology. Thus, as Michael Klare points out:

The Kennedy brain trust originally gave equal priority to the development of non-combative programmes — such as rural development, institution building and civic action — but the failure of each successive pacification scheme has induced the military to emphasise technological means for controlling insurgency.[11]

The shift to a capital-intensive air war which marked the period from after the Tet offensive in 1968, maximised the U.S. war effort in an area in which American technological superiority was overwhelming, while minimizing U.S. manpower vulnerability. Thus, technological warfare minimized U.S. casualties which were becoming a focus for antiwar opposition in the United States. It was the cost of the war to the Americans, not the Vietnamese, which was the most powerful source of opposition to the Vietnam involvement in the U.S. Furthermore, the morale of the U.S. ground forces was deteriorating so fast that they were becoming as much a liability as an asset on the battlefield.

To continue the war required a major effort to reduce U.S. casualties. As Major-General Ellis W. Williamson put it to a Senate Sub-Committee in 1970: "We are trying to fight the enemy with our bullets instead of the bodies of our young men — 'firepower, not manpower' ".[12] Counterinsurgency warfare in Vietnam in the late 1960s and early 1970s was thus totally different in conception from that visualized by Kennedy at the beginning of the decade. The commitment to social reform — which never amounted to more than lip service — had been totally abandoned, as had the 'long haul low profile' approach which emphasized the counter-guerrilla role of the special forces. (This latter role, however, continued in Laos where the C.I.A. waged a 'secret war' with a mercenary army of Montagnard tribesmen.) Instead, the attempt to separate the guerrillas from the population was undertaken physically — by crop destruction, defoliation and carpet bombing. 'Free strike' zones were declared in which anything which moved was assumed to be hostile. In place of ground patrol surveillance, the enemy was to be located by air dropped sensor devices which could be activated by the presence of human beings or machinery and which transmitted information decoded in turn by computers to provide target data for high-flying B-52 bombers. Instead of sending in troops, vast areas could be plastered by bombs or napalm or sown with literally millions of anti-personnel mines (designed to maim rather than kill) to lie in wait for unwary intruders. For Leonard Sullivan Jr., the Pentagon's chief of Vietnam-oriented research, it was obviously an enthralling prospect. In 1968, Sullivan wrote:

These developments open up some very exciting horizons as to what we can do five or ten years from now: When one realizes that we can detect anything that perspires, moves, carries metal, makes a noise, or is hotter or colder than its surroundings, one begins to see the potential.[13]

The ultimate objective was the 'automated battlefield', articulated with great enthusiasm by General Westmoreland in an address to the Army Association in 1969:

I see battlefields on which we can destroy anything we locate through instant communications and the almost instantaneous application of highly lethal firepower.
  In summary, I see an Army built around an integrated area control system that exploits the advanced technology of communications, sensors, fire direction, and the required automatic data processing.[14]

In fact, despite the vast amount of firepower the U.S. brought to bear on peasant armies, despite the millions of refugees, and casualties and untold destruction wrought in the countryside by more than 7 million tons of bombs, the U.S. was ultimately forced to withdraw its occupation army. Thus, it followed a pattern set by the French in both Indo-China and Algeria, the Dutch in Indonesia, the British in Palestine and Cyprus and — most recently — the Portuguese in Africa. The true causes of these rather dramatic set-backs for the industrial powers concerned, have been almost completely neglected by the writers on counterinsurgency for reasons which will be discussed presently.

Most counterinsurgency studies with any pretence to sophistication stress the necessity for political and socio-economic action in addition to military repression as a means of combating guerrillas. It is, therefore, worth examining why relatively little effort has in practice been put into using socio-economic reform as a means to combating insurgency. The first point to note is that intervention is usually a response to crisis. Thus even while recognizing that the *causes* of crisis may be socio-economic, economic reform and aid (as an MIT study argued[15]) are too long-range in their impact to affect crisis management. The 'quick fix' responses are military intervention, diplomatic pressure and various types of negative economic sanction.

Secondly, there is the matter (already noted) of the relative bargaining strength of those advocating 'soft' (*i.e.* non-military) and 'hard' (*i.e.* military) strategies of counterinsurgency. Vietnam remains the most obvious case of the 'hard' approach winning, not so much the arguments, but the bureaucratic bargaining games within the polity of the intervening metropolis. The failure of poorly funded 'pacification' programmes was used as an excuse for placing increasing reliance on those techniques in which the U.S. was undoubtedly superior — advanced technology/capital intensive warfare — regardless of their actual utility in the Indo-China context.

Thirdly, there has been an almost total failure to realize that coupling 'reformist' pacification programmes with military repression means that the impact of the latter tends to negate the desired effect of the former. In the Algerian war, for example, the policies of massive repression against the FLN guerrillas achieved for the latter what they had failed to achieve for themselves through political action, namely, the politicization of the mass of the Muslim population against the French. This completely nullified the effect of the pacification programmes that the French pursued. In Northern Ireland the British government embarked on a series of genuine reforms (relative to the pre-existing situation), but the effect of these in 'winning the hearts and minds" of the Catholic population was negated by the parallel efforts (entailing disruptive house searches, internment and casual brutality) of the British Army to root out the IRA in Catholic communities. In both Ulster and Algeria the efforts of metropolitan governments to push through reforms were also bitterly obstructed by the incumbent "settler class" which correctly perceived such efforts as undermining their local hegemony.

Finally — and most fundamentally — there is the question of the nature of the reforms proposed. Invariably these are piecemeal, designed to buy off support for more radical transformations of societies which are in any case unviable. But the so-called reform programmes are *necessarily* limited. The U.S., to make the most obvious example, has been well aware that it cannot expect the client regimes in whose name it has intervened time and again in the Third World to undertake the sweeping, indeed revolutionary reforms which would be necessary to ensure the destruction of popular support for the revolutionaries. As Frances Fitzgerald has pointed out with respect to Vietnam: "... counter-revolutionaries do not adopt revolutionary strategies, not because they are too stupid to do so but because it is contrary to their interests.[16]

It is essentially for these reasons that the counterinsurgency effort of the late Sixties has increasingly neglected, not only in practice but also in theory, the 'soft' approach to combating revolution which the social science theorists have stressed to little avail. In the post-Vietnam era counterinsurgency has changed considerably, as we shall see presently. What has not changed is the essential commitment to military repression and other negative sanctions rather than socio-economic reform as a means for combating revolution.

The failures of COIN

Despite the deployment of massive force, metropolitan powers have signally failed to gain their objectives in a number of critically important conflicts in the Third World since World War II. How and why the conventionally strong can be defeated by the conventionally weak — as they have been in Indo-China, Algeria and Portuguese Africa — is something that counterinsurgency theory is, by its very nature, incapable of explaining. The reason is simple. Almost without exception COIN theorists concentrate on the insurgency itself, on its causes and a variety of means to defeat it. What these theorists do *not* examine is the impact the war has on the metropolis involved. This is a serious omission since it is clear that in none of the conflicts noted above did the insurgents have the option of defeating the metropolitan power *militarily:* they simply lacked the material capability for invading the homeland of their opponents. It is true, of course, that the Vietminh soundly defeated the French forces mustered at the battle of Dien Bien Phu in 1954. But they did not defeat *France* militarily. This would have been impossible. Since the French *material* capability to wage war was not destroyed at Dien Bien Phu (indeed only about 3 per cent of all the French forces in Indo-China at that time were involved in the battle) there was no material obstacle in the way of the French mobilizing more troops at home and shipping them out to the battle front. There were, of course, extremely powerful constraints preventing the French from doing this, but these were political, not material.

Victory for the insurgents in such struggles can only be achieved by the destruction of their opponents' *political* capability to wage war. Thus the strategic objective of the revolutionaries is *not* to decimate their opponents' troops in the field *per se* (this may or may not be useful), but rather to exacerbate those divisions in the metropolis which this type of war inevitably generates. Battles are meaningful, not in terms of the bizarre and inhumane calculus of the 'body count', but in terms of their impact on the metropolis. Thus, the Tet offensive in Vietnam in 1968 was in fact a strategic victory for the Vietnamese revolutionaries since it catalysed a growing anti-war movement in the United States and marked the turning point of the war. Political victory can even be snatched from the jaws of an unambiguous military defeat as the Battle of Algiers clearly shows. General Massu utilized the utmost brutality, including the widespread use of torture, to crush the FLN infrastructure in Algiers. But the means used to achieve this particular tactical victory created an outcry, both internationally and in metropolitan France, which was instrumental in helping shift the balance of political forces in the direction which ultimately permitted de Gaulle to withdraw from Algeria, conceding political victory to the Algerian nationalists in the process.

Counterinsurgency theorists have been aware that what they variously describe as 'war weariness' and "lack of political will" in the metropolis have been critically important in such wars, but almost without exception they have seen these as contingent factors unrelated to the conduct of the war itself. In fact the relationship has been both direct and decisive.

It is essential to understand that in the type of war under discussion there are two battle fronts, one bloody and usually indecisive in the homeland of the insurgents; the other essentially non-violent but ultimately decisive, in the homeland of the external power. The relationship between the two is intimate and the outcome of the conflict can only be understood by examining the confrontation as a whole and not by simply peering through a microscope at one end of it, as is the practice of most writers on counterinsurgency.

Guerrilla strategists have understood that politics and military strategy cannot be arbitrarily divided; that the 'theatre of war' transcends the battlefield to include the social and political institutions of their opponents; that this type of war by *its very nature* inevitably generates contradictions in the metropolis and that for this reason 'protracted warfare' must work in favour of the revolutionary side in the long run. If the enemy's political capability to wage war can be attenuated, his military strength ultimately becomes irrelevant because it is increasingly unusable. It is for this reason that the Chinese argue that in the last analysis imperialism is a 'paper tiger.'

Among writers on counterinsurgency, few have realized that the 'two front' war (the socio-political front and the military front) which COIN theory has emphasized, is also waged against the metropolis by the revolutionaries. COIN strategy has emphasized the necessity to drive a wedge between the guerrilla and their supporters. Guerrilla strategists have also attempted to drive one between the war-makers in the metropolis and *their* supporters. Nowhere has this strategy been more spectacularly successful than in the case of the U.S. and Vietnam. Among the few American writers who have shown some awareness of the revolutionary 'two front' strategy have been E. L. Katzenbach, Henry Kissinger and Robert Taber.[17]

Counterinsurgency after Vietnam

Richard Nixon's major contribution to U.S. counter-revolutionary policy was to act on the realization that the driving force of opposition to the war in Vietnam was its cost to Americans and not its cost to the Vietnamese. To the political elite which prosecuted it, the Vietnam war was (eventually) a mistake, not because it was immoral, but because its domestic costs—human, economic and political—in the U.S. were too high. The new policy which emphasizes a 'low profile' approach was already being formulated in the late 1960s when the lessons of Vietnam were beginning to sink home. As former Defence Secretary, Clark M. Clifford, told Congress in January 1969:

Clearly the overriding goal of our defence efforts in Asia must be to assist our allies in building a capability to defend themselves. Besides costing substantially less (an Asian soldier cost about 1/15th as much as his American counterpart) there are compelling political and psychological advantages on both sides of the Pacific for such a policy.[18]

What these political advantages were was not difficult to imagine. Massive troop cutbacks and a sharp reduction in direct U.S. military activity in Vietnam would placate an anti-war movement which had grown increasingly powerful as it moved from campus to Congress. In Vietnam the Thieu regime would be forced into a policy of 'Vietnamisation' of the war. The so-called Nixon Doctrine (formerly the Guam Doctrine) which in 1969 officially announced the shift in doctrine was codified in three principles, the third of which was the critical one with respect to counterinsurgency. It read:

...we shall furnish military and economic assistance when requested and as appropriate. But we shall look to the nation directly threatened to assume the primary responsibility of providing the manpower for its defence.[19]

The Nixon Doctrine was a recognition both of the political costs of direct U.S. military interventions and of the advantages of counterinsurgency by proxy, so to speak. It made a virtue out of necessity. As Defence Secretary, Melvin Laird, told Congress in 1971:

In the majority of cases, this means indigenous manpower organised into properly equipped and well-trained armed forces with the help of material, training, technology and specialised military skills furnished by the United States.[20]

In Indo-China this policy was represented by Vietnamization and massive U.S. military aid plus 'advisors', and by the use of mercenary armies — the Montagnard 'Secret Army' officially run by General Vang Pao and financed by the CIA, and the Thai and Korean troops whose operations were paid for by the U.S. government. As recent events have graphically demonstrated this policy too was doomed to fail. In other areas of the world the change was less fundamental. Vietnam had demonstrated the political risks involved in military intervention and embroilment and as a consequence this option was strongly de-emphasized. In 1965 the U.S. had intervened militarily in the Dominican Republic to prevent a mildly leftist government coming to power. By the 1970s such an action would have been unthinkable. When an avowedly Marxist government came to power in Chile, there was no suggestion that military intervention was an appropriate response: other, more sophisticated and less visible techniques of undermining the Allende government were used. As Henry Kissinger is reported to have told an executive of Deltec International in October 1970, the U.S. would give any backing *"short of a Dominican-style intervention"*[21] (emphasis added) to overthrow Allende. As we now know, the measures used included a credit blockade (operated by U.S. private banks, the Inter-American Development Bank and the World Bank), embargoes on Chile's major export of copper by the Kennecott corporation in France and other Western European countries and, most significantly, twelve million dollars worth of CIA funding to the major opponents of Allende. (Millions more had been spent previously in an attempt to prevent Allende coming to power in the first place.)

The advantages of using this type of measure need hardly be spelled out. The CIA's involvement is normally secret, with the consequence that its effects in undermining radical governments can be attributed to the inadequacies of the government, rather than the external intervention. Negative economic sanctions also have the advantage of lying below the so-called 'news threshold'. A credit blockade may have disastrous consequences for the government it is aimed at, but it is unlikely to receive more than a few paragraphs in the financial sections of the national press of the metropolis. In the post-Vietnam era any military intervention, no matter how inconsequential, would be likely to generate a storm of controversy. Economic sanctions have the further advantage of being ambiguous. Was the credit embargo brought against Chile, for example, because the Allende government was not creditworthy or because it was led by a Marxist? Since the EXimbank which denied credit to Allende's Chile was at the same time giving liberal loans to countries such as Haiti and Bangladesh (neither of which, by any stroke of the imagination, could be described as 'economically stable'), there can be no doubt that the Chile decision was politically motivated.

Thus, those radical critics who still see direct military intervention as typical of U.S. counterrevolutionary policy in the Third World are living in the past. This is not to say that future military interventions are impossible, but rather that the U.S. government would need to be assured that the political costs which such a move would inevitably generate did not outweigh the presumed strategic benefits. At the present time the most likely scenario for such an intervention would be in the Middle East, following a total cut-off of Arab oil supplies in the wake of a new Arab/Israeli war. Precisely because such a cut off would have a dramatic adverse impact not only throughout the U.S. but (to an even greater degree) among America's European allies, the possibilities of U.S.military invasion of key producer states cannot be ruled out. Indeed, a number of articles in such influential U.S. journals as *Harpers, Commentary* and *The New Leader* have appeared during late 1974 and early 1975, arguing the necessity for, and morality of, a U.S. military strike against the Gulf states.

The measures used to bring down the Allende government in Chile represent the most sophisticated of the 'low profile' techniques of contemporary U.S. counterinsurgency strategy. More typical are the classical COIN techniques utilized by Third World regimes themselves with U.S. aid, training, equipment and 'advisors'. Latin America again provides the most instructive examples, and it is there that U.S. sponsored COIN programmes have had greatest success, at least in the short term. As Samuel Huntington noted in 1971 "...revolutionary movements in Argentina, Peru, Bolivia, Columbia, Venezuela and Uruguay which flared in the 1960s were, by the 1970s, contained, weakened and in many cases decimated."[22] Richard Gott, in his wide-ranging study of guerrilla movements in Latin America, concurs with this assessment, attributing the failure in large part to the efforts of American-trained (and sometimes American-led) counterinsurgency operations. In effect, this is to argue that the Latin American guerrilla groups lacked the tenacity and strategic ability of their Vietnamese counterparts, since the latter successfully withstood a military onslaught which dwarfed in scope the relatively low profile operations which have been carried out in Latin America.

Urban guerrilla warfare and torture

A characteristic feature of guerrilla strategy in Latin America, and one which distinguishes it most sharply from Chinese and Vietnamese revolutionary strategy, has been a reliance on the so-called 'foco' theory of insurrection which (without being defined as such at the time) was used successfully by Castro to defeat the Batista regime in Cuba. The 'foco' theory, articulated by Regis Debray in his *Revolution in the Revolution*, broke with classical Maoist guerrilla strategy by insisting that military action could *by itself* create the conditions for a revolution. Che Guevara chose Bolivia to attempt to implement the 'foco' theory in practice, with disastrous results. The failure of this and other rural guerrilla operations in Latin America led Debray's critics to argue that the city rather than the countryside should be the focus of revolutionary activity, at least initially.

The strategy of urban guerrilla warfare on the 'foco' model is most clearly set out by the Brazilian revolutionary, Carlos Marighella, in his *Mini-Manual of Urban Guerrilla Warfare*. Marighella's strategy, like that of Debray and other Latin American guerrilla groups, but unlike Maoist guerrilla strategy, stresses the catalytic effect which a small dedicated band of revolutionaries can have — not in creating a revolution *per se* — but rather its preconditions. As Marighella himself put it:

It is necessary to turn a political crisis into armed conflict by performing violent actions that will force those in power to transform the political situation of the country into a military situation. This will alienate the masses who, from then on, will revolt against the army and policy and thus blame them for this state of things.[23]

One of the problems which has perplexed military strategists in general, and COIN strategists in particular, is whether or not repression will be blamed on the military who carry out the repressive acts, or the activists who catalyse it. There are no general answers to this question. In some cases, Algeria, for example, repression politicizes the mass of the population. In others, it can be divisive, as the case of French partisan actions against the German occupying army in France in World War II. Furthermore, to pose the question in this way is to create a false dichotomy, since the mass of the population may simply avoid taking sides. By doing nothing, nothing is risked. If the urban guerrillas do fail to mobilize the mass of the population behind them (as has been the case in Latin America in the 1960s), then they are peculiarly vulnerable to a counterinsurgency technique which has gained considerable notoriety on that continent during the past five years.

The *systematic* and widespread use of torture as a weapon in the counterinsurgency specialists' arsenal first came into prominence during the Algeria war. A wide range of the most barbaric tortures were successfully employed by General Massu's forces to destroy the FLN organizational infrastructure during the Battle of Algiers in 1957. Massu argued that only with the severest forms of torture could the necessary information be forced out of suspects quickly enough for it to be of use. Skilled, non-violent interrogation techniques and subtler forms of torture, such as the 'sensory deprivation' techniques employed by the British Army in Ulster against IRA suspects, were too slow. By the time the required information had been wrung from the suspect, it would be useless. But if, by using more extreme methods, information would be tortured out of suspects in a matter of *hours* rather than days, then it could be used to break the next link in the revolutionary cell-structure and so forth.

As Bernard Fall noted with respect to Algeria: "Torture is the particular bane of the terrorist, just as anti-aircraft artillery is that of the airman or machine gun fire that of the foot soldier"[24] If the urban guerrilla resistance is popularly based — as was the case in Algeria — then even these barbarous methods are unlikely to have other than a short term effect. As Trinquier, a strong advocate of the use of torture, noted of the Battle of Algiers: "Three years later, the enemy was able to re-establish his organisation and once again take control of the population. The victory of Algiers in 1957 had gone for naught."[25] But the key characteristic of the urban guerrilla groups of Latin America (and in Europe and the United States) has been precisely the lack of a popular base.

In the 1970s torture has come to play a key role in counterinsurgency programmes because, as Britain's leading COIN theorist puts it "... the problem of defeating the enemy consists of finding him",[26] and because these barbaric methods have been found to be effective, especially against urban guerrillas. New advances in the technology of torturing human beings are rapidly communicated between the military forces of regimes which employ them. The Brazilian military passed on their barbarous expertise to their Uruguayan counterparts when, under President Bordaberry, the constraints on the systematic use of torture were relaxed. When the Allende regime was toppled by the armed services, which had long boasted that they did not interfere in politics, Brazilian torture experts were reported to have flown to Chile within days of the coup's success.

The evidence for the use of systematic and 'scientific' torture by military and other right wing regimes around the world is now incontrovertible. And the growth of torture as a weapon in the COIN practitioners' armoury has been documented by Amnesty International. In its 1973 *Report on Torture* Amnesty notes: "One can state with some assurance that the practice (of torture) is both more widespread and more intense than it was fifteen years ago"[27] Furthermore, "... torture is not being used for the extraction of information alone. It is also used for the control of political dissent. Often, the two main impulses are combined in one appalling practice."[28] With respect to the spread of the use of torture, Amnesty notes: "Experts and their training, as well as torture equipment, are provided by one state for use in another state."[29] And lest anyone should think that the use of torture is in any sense arbitrary, the Amnesty report makes clear that the spread of torture reflects the evolution of "various counter-insurgency theories by military experts"[30]

That the use of torture has increased considerably during the past five years is beyond doubt. That torture is now a key technique in the counterinsurgency strategy which is the cornerstone of U.S. foreign policy in the Third World is beyond doubt. The "defence of freedom" today provides the ideological justification for the defence of torture and repression.

In the long term

Throughout the period under discussion the overriding objectives of counterinsurgency have not altered, while the means deemed appropriate to achieving those objectives have changed considerably. However, recent changes in both Soviet-American and Sino-American relations suggest that in the future counterrevolution may itself be de-emphasized as the key objective of U.S. Third World policy. If such a shift in emphasis does materialize, it would be for two reasons: first, that counterinsurgency would be unable to contain the revolutionary impulse which continues to defy the forces arraigned against it; secondly, that revolution would be seen as less of a threat to U.S. interests than has previously been the case. It is being increasingly realized by western corporate interests that the Soviet Union and Eastern Europe make excellent trading partners and offer the possibilities of extremely profitable investment outlets. In addition to offering access to investment and vital raw materials, these so-called socialist countries never renege on debts, pay their bills promptly and — above all — provide a stable investment environment, protected not only from takeover, but also from labour unrest and the ravages of inflation.

Thus in the long term it can be argued that, provided Third World countries which undergo revolutions remain within the world economic system (*i.e.* they do not opt for development programmes emphasizing autarky), then these revolutions do *not* necessarily spell disaster for U.S., European and Japanese economic interests. Such revolutions will, of course, have adverse consequences for particular corporations in the short term. But even where a revolutionary government can control production, it cannot usually control distribution and marketing. Whether socially or privately owned, commodities will still have to be transported and sold abroad. In the immediate future, one may expect strong pressures for 'tough action' from individual corporations adversely affected by revolutionary takeovers, and even stronger pressures from the powerful interests traditionally opposed to communism on 'security' and ideological grounds. In the long term, however, it would be foolish to assume that these pressures will necessarily continue to prevail.

Among the more long-sighted observers of the shifts in global power alignments since World War II, it has become increasingly obvious that a trend which was started by Yugoslavia's split from the Soviet bloc in 1948, and which became increasingly manifest with the emergence of the Sino-Soviet split, is here to stay. Communist governments can be as 'nationalist' as capitalist governments in terms of their international relations. That a country undergoes a revolution does not mean that it immediately becomes a satellite of either the U.S.S.R. or the Chinese People's Republic — a fact underlined by the determinedly independent line adopted by the new governments in Cambodia and Vietnam. Thus, neither in terms of economics (assuming that the revolutionaries do not opt for autarky), nor in terms of geo-political 'power balances' do communist revolutions necessarily spell defeat for the global capitalist system. (They may, of course, have adverse consequences for particular firms.) In fact capitalism suffers real defeats in this process only when capitalist governments persist in staking their credibility on efforts to prevent the revolutionary impulse from being realized.

For many European powers the debacle in Vietnam has only served to drive this lesson home. To date, however, there are few signs that this message is having much impact on U.S. foreign policy perspectives. But again one should caution against believing that change is unthinkable — virtue can be divined in the most unpalatable necessities, as the American about-face on its China policy graphically demonstrated. Coming to terms with revolutionary movements can be justified by the same inhuman logic of realpolitik which currently jusitifies attempts to crush and subvert such movements. If such a shift in policy does take place it would create a new set of problems for the revolutionaries, but at least it would leave behind the savage barbarisms of COIN technology and policy which have been one of the hallmarks of the post-war era.

FOOTNOTES

[1] For much of the information in this article I am indebted to Michael Klare, whose *War without End* (New York, 1972) is an admirable and paintstakingly documented study of U.S. counterinsurgency programmes.

[2] Definition taken from *Dictionary of United States Military Terms for Joint Usage*, quoted in Michael Klare, *op. cit.* p.44.

[3] Quoted in *Pentagon Papers*, New York Times Edition (New York, 1971), p. 432. McNaughton's classification of U.S. war aims in Vietnam appeared first in a policy paper dated 6 Nov. 1964 (*Pentagon Papers*, p.365). A fourth aim noted in the memorandum was "to emerge from crisis without unacceptable taint from methods".

[4] Quoted in Klare, *op. cit.* p.24.

5 Edward Lieuwen, *The Latin American Military* (Washington, 1969), quoted in Klare, *op. cit.*, p.279.
6 Klare, *ibid.* p.161.
7 Special Operations Research Office (SORO) press release quoted in Irving Louis Horowitz (ed.), *The Rise and Fall of Project Camelot* (Cambridge, Mass., 1967), p.47.
8 Quoted in Judith Coburn, 'Asian Scholars and Government: the Crysanthemum and the Sword' in Edward Friedman and Mark Selden (eds). *America's Asia: Dissenting Essays on Asian — American Relations* (New York, 1971), p.99.
9 Samuel P. Huntington, 'Civil Violence and the Process of Development' *(Adelphi Paper* No. 83, Dec. 1971), p.7.
10 Charles Wolf Jr., *Insurgency and Counter-Insurgency: New Myths and Old Realities*, quoted in Klare, *op. cit.* p.42. The argument in this paper (Rand P-3132, July 1965) is extended and amplified in the same author's *Rebellion and Authority: Myths and Realities Reconsidered* (Rand P-3422, Aug. 1966). A statistical analysis purporting to show that land distribution inequality does *not* contribute to insurgency was one of the main planks of the 'revisionist' position — see E.J. Mitchell, *Inequality and Insurgency: A Statistical Study of South Vietnam* (Rand P-3610, June 1967), Huntington's work (see above) has also clearly been influenced by the new COIN revisionism.
11 Klare, *op. cit.*, p.124.
12 *Investigation into the Electronic Battlefield Programme*, Hearings, 91st Congress, U.S. Government Printing Office, p.67.
13 Leonard Sullivan Jr., 'Research and Development for Vietnam', *Science and Technology* (Oct. 1968), pp. 35-36, quoted in Klare, *op. cit.* p.209.
14 Klare, *ibid*, p.208.
15 Lincoln Bloomfield, *et al.*, *Political Exercise II: The U.S. and the U.S.S.R. in Iran*, M.I.T., Center for International Studies (Cambridge, Mass., 1960).
16 Frances Fitzgerald, 'The Invisible Country', *New York Review of Books*, XIX, No. 6, 19 Oct. 1972, p.25.
17 Kissinger, *op. cit.*; E. L. Katzenbach Jr., 'Time, Space and Will: The Politico Military Strategy of Mao Tse Tung' in T.N. Greene (ed.), *The Guerrilla and How to Fight Him* (New York, 1962) and Robert Taber, *The War of the Flea: A Study of Guerrilla Warfare, Theory and Practice* (New York, 1965), For a more detailed exposition of the arguments presented above, see Mack, 'Why Big Nations lose Small Wars ...',*op.cit.*
18 Quoted in Klare, *op. cit.* p.322.
19 Richard M. Nixon, *U.S. Foreign Policy in the 1970s* (Washington, 1970), pp. 55-56.
20 Quoted in Klare, *op. cit.* p.324.
21 Quoted in Elizabeth Farnsworth, 'Chile: What was the U.S. Role?',. *Foreign Policy*, no. 16, 1974, p.131.
22 Klare, *op. cit.* Chs. 9 and 10.
23 Quoted in Andrew Mack, 'The Non-Strategy of Urban Guerrilla Warfare' in Johan Niezing (ed.), *Urban Guerrilla* (Rotterdam, 1974), p.42.
24 Bernard Fall, *Introduction to Trinquier, op. cit.*, p. 15.
25 Trinquier, *ibid*, p.49.
26 Frank Kitson, *Low Intensity Operations: Subversion, Insurgency and Peace-keeping* (London, 1971), p.95.
27 *Amnesty International: Report on Torture* (London, 1973), p.29.
28 *Ibid*, p.218.
29 *Ibid.*
30 *Ibid*, p.219.

SECTION IV: INTERVENTION AND THE ECONOMIC IMPERATIVES OF CAPITALISM

Introduction

In the final section of the first part of this reader, we examine, in some detail, the debate between those who argue that America's counterrevolutionary policies in the Third World stem from the economic imperatives of US corporate capitalism and those who deny this claim.

The former argument, in its strongest formulations, posits that American economic interests in the Third World are vital to the survival of the American corporate system in its present form. American capitalism requires the protection and expansion of its overseas investment outlets, markets, sources of raw materials and cheap labour. The US government which, according to this theory, rules in the interest of the corporate capitalist class, will intervene overseas whenever necessary to protect the interests of this class.

Theories which seek to explain America's counterrevolutionary policies in economic terms are often, but not always, and certainly not necessarily, Marxist. The best known proponent of the economic approach, Harry Magdoff, is certainly a Marxist; his work is referred to in all three articles in this section and is the principal object of criticism in the third. But Theodore Moran's argument in the second paper in this section is based on a decidedly non-Marxist model of corporate growth behaviour, while Heather Dean, in a paper on US raw material dependency, written six years before the 1973 oil crisis, seems to distance herself from what she calls 'the Marxist left'.

Dean argues that US corporate necessity for secure access to strategic, Third World raw materials is the 'dynamic of American imperialism', but the logic of her argument applies equally to socialist economies. The US economy is not dependent on overseas raw materials because it is capitalist, but because it is a *high growth*, mass consumption economy. Thus it has been argued that a high growth, mass consumption *socialist* America would face exactly the same problem, and would also act 'imperialistically' if threatened with denial of access to its sources of vital foreign raw materials.

The debate has other important political implications. Both Moran, and Miller, Bennett and Alapatt, draw our attention to the difference between those theorists who argue that overseas economic expansion is, to use Moran's words, an 'institutional necessity' for US corporate capitalism, and those who argue that such expansion, although profitable, is in *no sense* necessary. The difference is not merely semantic, since, in the former case, it implies that no fundamental reform of US foreign policy is possible. The US, according to the 'institutional necessity' argument, has no choice but intervention in areas where US economic interests are threatened, since those interests are crucial to the survival of the capitalist system. Only when capitalism is overthrown in the United States will the interventionary imperative disappear. For Miller, Bennett and Alapatt, who are also critical of US interventionism, reform *is* possible because the alleged economic imperatives simply do not exist. They quote from official statistics which, they claim, show that US economic interests in the Third World *cannot* be crucial to the survival of American capitalism because they are simply too small. The sums involved may appear huge in absolute terms, but *relatively* they are insignificant. Since, according to their analysis, there are no economic imperatives for intervention, and since the irrational anti-communism of the Cold War is ebbing, Miller *et.al* view the prospects for reform as excellent.

Although the papers which follow cover most of the arguments in the debate between economic vs. non-economic explanations, a few additional points are worth noting. Miller, Bennett and Alapatt make much of the fact that the U.S. global economy is so huge that it can in no sense be said to depend on its (relatively) tiny Third World component. They argue that

American capitalism will *not* collapse if denied access to its Third World investments/markets/raw materials - Harry Magdoff, the major target of their attack, would agree. But we can see that, although intervention may not be *necessary* for the survival of capitalism in America, it may still be both *convenient* and *profitable* for American capitalists. In other words, counterrevolutionary policies *may* be economically motivated without being essential for the survival of capitalism.

However, recent surveys* of the attitudes of corporate executives in the United States would seem to support Miller, Bennett and Alapatt's conclusions. The businessmen surveyed were generally 'dovish', and few favoured the use of American military forces *anywhere* in the Third World. Among those who *did* support intervention, there was an overwhelming consensus that it should only be used if important U.S. *political* or *strategic* - not economic - interests were threatened. Corporate executives with business interests in the Third World were naturally concerned about the security of these interests and they wanted them protected. But what they wanted was U.S. government guarantees of compensation for any foreign expropriations, and *not* U.S. military action against the expropriators.

If these surveys are accurate and representative, and we have no reason to believe that they are not, then it seems clear that the cruder versions of the 'capitalist imperatives' thesis are false. But this still does not mean that the link between capitalism and foreign policy can be dismissed. Miller, Bennett and Alapatt quote English Marxist, Michael Barratt Brown, as follows:

> While there may be good *original* economic grounds for policies pursued, the whole structure of institutions, ideas and purposes built up from these grounds *takes on a life of its own* and becomes its own justification. (our italics)

According to Barratt Brown there is an important relationship between imperialism (exemplified by intervention) and capitalism, but it is not necessarily the obvious and direct one usually proclaimed by vulgar Marxists. Here we have an example of the 'level of analysis' problem referred to in the introduction. Many similar problems are raised when dealing with these complex issues and the fact that much of the debate is

---

*B: Russett and E.C. Hanson, *Interest and Ideology: The Foreign Policy Beliefs of American Businessmen*, Freeman, San Fransisco, 1975

intensely politicised only compounds the readers' difficulties. As the (Marxist) editor of a recent anthology of articles on imperialism has noted, this makes the task of evaluation even more problematic. Arguments often become highly polemical, theories are parodied to the point of absurdity, and the complexity of opponents' positions is often deliberately ignored.

Scarce Resources: The Dynamic of American Imperialism

Heather Dean

"That empire in Southeast Asia is the last major resource area outside the control of any one of the major powers on the globe.. I believe that the condition of the Vietnamese people, and the direction in which their future may be going, are at this stage secondary, not primary."

Senator McGee (Wyoming), U.S. Senate, February 17, 1965.

FOUR THEORIES OF IMPERIALISM

Lenin's

Lenin wrote at a time when domestic markets in Europe were saturated, leading him to predict that the industrialized countries would war among themselves for overseas outlets for investment capital and for overseas markets. The Social Democrats argued that alternate solutions would be found — the crisis of "over-production" would be ended by increasing domestic demand by wage increases, welfare payments, etc. Lenin dismissed with two words (under capitalism!) this notion that the greedy capitalists would give the workers money.

However, the development of capitalist economies has shown an almost limitless capacity for internal expansion. Legalized unions, welfare, public works, defense spending, planned obsolescence, space programs, consumer credit, ad-created markets and fad spending — techniques beyond the wildest dreams of the Social Democrats — lead one to suspect that the last cataclysmic convulsion of capitalism just isn't coming.

Not only have capitalist economies succeeded in expanding internally, but they have observably *not* exploited market and investment opportunities in the underdeveloped countries. The feudal economic and political structures of the Third World provide neither purchasing power nor opportunities for investment in industry and, liberal disclaimers to the contrary notwithstanding, American policies are directed at maintaining such structures. (For example, the Alliance for Progress specifically forbids use of its funds for any sort of land reform program.) There has been no effort to duplicate the European expansion sparked by investment in the industrialization of North America.

Yearly American investment overseas is approximately five per cent of domestic investment, and the major part of that is in Europe and Canada. Only two fifths of American overseas investments is in underdeveloped countries; only a negligible amount on the Asian mainland.

American investors do make a tidy sum each year on their overseas investments, and it would be naive to suppose that the corporations involved would be too altruistic to fight to maintain them. But the degree of expansion has been so limited, the profits so peripheral to the American economy, that it takes a peculiar sort of demonology to believe that they are in themselves adequate justification of the three wars and countless lesser military actions by which the United States has gained and maintained control of the Third World.

Neo-Marxist

Some modern Marxists argue that America's overseas investments are indeed negligible to the survival of the American economy, but that the domestic economic effects of imperial wars are crucial. The figures lend more weight to this argument. American investments in her domestic war industries each year are more than sixty times her investments in underdeveloped countries.

However, there is nothing magical about the kind of economic waste implied in needless war spending. Other forms of waste such as space programs are equally effective sources of investment, and many other forms would be easier to sell politically than wars against fictitious invaders.

Liberal

In response to this sort of argument, the majority of the American liberal-left denies that the Marxist theories of imperialism explain American foreign policy today, although they credit it (when they know it at all) with some degree of accuracy in interpreting the earlier part of the century. Their most common explanation of America's military domination of Asia, Africa and Latin America suggests there is *no* rational motive for it. Imperialism belongs to America's economic past; however, the ideology and bureaucracy that supported these outdated interests have a blind momentum of their own that has made them endure beyond their moment in history.

This understanding leads to a politics of petition — the Quaker "Speak Truth to Power" approach. Its analysis of American power is filled with words like "irrational fear," "blunder," "paranoia," or "fixation." So the solution is seen in effecting a change in the personal qualities of the men at the helm, running peace candidates or helping those in power see the illogic of "the system in which they are trapped."

Scarce Resources

The research for this paper was based on the premise that American policy is rational and successful. It may not be directed at *our* goals, but it is goal-directed, and the goals are not anachronisms of the American system but are essential to the maintenance of existing power relations. I have looked for this motive in the aspect of imperialism that is usually footnoted in considerations of the American economic influence in the Third World — the massive extraction of raw materials.

While not denying the existence of other economic motivations which are stressed by the Marxist left, I would argue that they are secondary to the total dependency of American production on foreign resources, that this dependency is sufficient in itself to explain U.S. policy, and that it leads to a fundamental conflict between the survival of the American economy in its present form and the drive for development in the Third World.

U.S. MATERIALS POLICY STUDIES, 1950-1960

"Has the United States of America the material means to sustain its civilization?"

In 1952, the U.S. President's Materials Policy Commission opened its report with this question. Its answer shattered forever the myth of cornucopian natural resources on the North American continent, and introduced a new alarm into the consciousness of policy makers: the U.S. depended on foreign sources for every significant industrial resource except molybdenum and magnesium.

The Commission, headed by William S. Paley, Chairman of CBS and life trustee of Columbia University, hired a phalanx of experts to predict U.S. demand for natural resources for the next 15 years, and to advise the President on legislation necessary to ensure that these resources would be available.

Its report is far from a dry compilation of statistics; its principal author seems to see himself as something of a philosopher-poet. In the introduction he reflects on the wry workings of fate which makes materials a key factor in the struggle between the Spirit of Man and the Forces of Materialism. The Report concluded that the materials would not be lacking. However, it found domestic reserves adequate to meet only a small and shrinking fraction of American needs.

The Third World is expected to supply the bulk of the raw materials used by U.S. industry. In another burst of lyricism the Report details the mutual benefits to arise from this Free World division of labor. Each nation has its appointed role: that of the underdeveloped countries is to produce, that of the U.S. is to consume. (It's highly reminiscent of the speeches on peaceful coexistence that the Russians keep delivering to the Chinese.) By selling to U.S. markets, Third World nations will accumulate the capital necessary to finance their own industrialization. But this eventuality appears only in the rhetoric of the report. Their statistical projections do not allow for a significant increase in consumption of industrial raw materials in the underdeveloped countries.

In response to the Paley Report, defense stockpiling was undertaken on a massive scale to safeguard against such supply shortages as had occurred during the Korean War. Government subsidies (since largely discontinued) encouraged exploitation of inferior domestic ores in hopes of making technological breakthroughs. Government commissions were set up to give early warning of financial or political threats to foreign sources of defense materials.

Most important, and probably most successful, an organization was established with Ford Foundation money to refine and expand the work of the Paley Commission. "Resources for the Future" (RFF) was incorporated to do research, publish, and make policy recommendations. Paley was joined in its administration by such pillars of the American Establishment as George P. Brown (United Shoe Machinery, Boston Herald-Traveller Corp., First National Bank of Boston, New England Tel & Tel, Old Colony Trust Co.), Frank Pace (Time, Inc., Colgate-Palmolive, Continental Oil, Banker's Trust, Eurofund, etc.), and Laurance Rockefeller (Rockefeller Brothers Fund, Rockefeller Brothers, Inc., etc.).

The major publication of RFF is "Resources in America's Future." It is a massive collection of statistics and extrapolations that attempts to predict patterns of American consumption to the year 2000, allowing for substitutions, probable technological innovations, etc. In tone its publications seem to be one half of a debate with Rachel Carson. One feels the presence of an unseen Conservationist Lobby proposing crimps in the style of the barons of the extractive industries, many of them on the board of RFF. This report, too, concludes that the raw materials America needs will be available. But for those of us to whom "America's interests" are not the whole spectrum of concern, the means by which this conclusion was reached are ominous. The introduction warns:

> It should be pointed out clearly, however, that our conclusion that there is no general resource shortage problem for the balance of the century applies specifically to the United States; it cannot be extended automatically to other countries. In many less developed countries, especially in Asia, Africa and Latin America, population presses hard on available natural resources; for them a sustained increase in living levels can by no means be guaranteed with the assurance it can be for the United States and other more advanced industrial countries.

In plainer words, the surpluses of industrial raw materials which America expects to import from Asia, Africa and Latin America are illusory. They would vanish from world markets if the intolerable stagnation of Third World economies were ended. To ensure their continued availability will require complete political and economic control of Third World countries — a control exercised against the most elemental interests of their populations.

THE EXTENT OF SCARCITY

In 1963, the Minerals Year Book supplied a table of figures for U.S. imports for consumption.

This gives some idea of the magnitude of U.S. reliance on other than domestic sources, but the figures are distorted in two directions. In some cases they minimize the shortage because current needs are being met by uneconomic government-subsidized exploitation of small deposits of inferior ore. In other cases, notably iron, the U.S. imports are of sufficiently high quality to compensate for shipping costs, but apart from the price differential, the U.S. has quite adequate supplies of ore.

Mineral	% of consumption imported	% of world production
Iron	22%	—
Manganese	94%	—
Chromite	100%	14%
Cobalt	98%	—
Nickel	86%	35%
Tungsten	43%	—
Copper	25%	23%
Lead	35%	—
Zinc	44%	—
Uranium	38%	—
Tin	78%	—
Aluminium	—	45%
Bauxite	85%	31%

Taken to the end of the century, the relative significance of the shortage shifts, but the overall picture is sufficiently alarming that it is certain that scarce resources are a significant determinant of government policy. The U.S. has between one per cent and ten per cent of the reserves necessary to meet demand from now to the year 2000, and will require between 50 per cent to 100 per cent or more of known reserves in the "non-Communist world" (the RFF amendent of Paley's "Free World").

All terms and statistics are drawn from the RFF report, 'Resources in America's Future':

USCD—US Cumulative Demand (total demand from 1960 to 2000), often in three projections, low, medium, high;
NCW — non-Communist world;
reserves — minerals contained in ore that can be mined with present technology (this includes ores which are not commercially feasible at current prices but which are technically easy to mine and about 50% less rich than ores currently marketable);
resources — minerals that could be mined if cost were no object, or given a technological breakthrough (such as oil in tar sands.)

Electricity and steel will continue to be the irreducible basis of any advanced civilization for at least a century. The imponderables of shifts in consumption patterns, technological innovations and substitutions are held to a minimum in considering the following minerals: the ferro-alloys, and copper and aluminium, the two conductors of electricity.

Manganese is absolutely essential to the manufacture of steel; it strips it of the major impurity, sulphur. There is no possible substitute. Most of the world's reserves of manganese are in the USSR and China. There will probably be discoveries in Africa, however, which could double the figure of 185 million tons in NCW reserves.

USCD—48 million tons (low) — 73 million tons (medium) — 107 million tons (high)
US reserves — 0.9 million tons
Total NCW demand — 300 million tons (Medium projection)
Total NCW reserves — 185 million tons

Tungsten has the highest melting point of any metal. It is used for high speed steels, and steels that must withstand constant friction like bits and drills. It imparts the necessary hardness to cutting tools, and is a major electrical and electronic component.

USCD — 250,000 tons — 460,000 tons — 800,000 tons
US reserves — 71,000 tons (low-grade ore)
NCW demand — 1,000,000 tons
NCW reserves — 320,000 tons

Molybdenum is a possible substitute for tungsten in steel.

Nickel is the single most important alloy mineral, currently used in over 3000 alloys. It gives steel strength, hardness and resistance to corrosion or deformation at high temperatures. It is found in quantity only in Indonesia, New Caledonia, Canada and Cuba. Le Nickel of Europe (French Rothschilds) controls the New Caledonia mines, so the North American market is supplied almost entirely from Canada.

USCD — 7 million tons — 11.7 million tons — 19.3 million tons
US reserves — 0.5 million tons
NCW demand — 37 million tons
NCW reserves — Canada, 6 million tons; New Caledonia, 4.6 million tons; Indonesia 5-8 million tons total proved — 11.3 million tons (+ inferred)

Chrome steels are extremely hard for their weight, and of course are resistant to corrosion.

USCD—40 million tons
US reserves — 4 million tons (very inferior ore)
NCW demand — 200 million tons
NCW reserves — 450 million tons (estimates of reserves are tentative while exploration continues in Africa; reserves in South Africa may run from 80 to 800 million tons, in Southern Rhodesia from 175 to 200 million tons).

Cobalt is used in steels that must resist corrosion at extremely high temperatures. It is used in jets, missiles, gas turbines, and generators. Actual use has been less than the projects so far due to the political instability of the Congo.

USCD-450,000 tons (medium) — 700,000 tons (high)
US reserves — 45,000 tons
NCW reserves — 900,000 tons plus inferred reserves in Africa.

The only mineral that conducts electricity as well as copper is silver. However, a more plausible substitute is aluminium, with 60% of the conductivity of copper. Copper shortages are worldwide. Neither the USSR nor China has a potential surplus.

USCD—60 million tons — 112 million tons — 181 million tons
US reserves — 30 million tons;US resources, 20 million tons, Canada, 9 million tons
NCW demand — 500 million tons
NCW reserves — 200 million tons proved; 200 million tons inferred.

Although it is rare in North America, aluminium is a fairly common mineral throughout the world. One major strike was made when a farmer sent a sample of poor soil for analysis. As it is produced by electrolysis, the ore has moved to power; this is why Canada has been a leading aluminium producer. Control of major hydro-electric power projects in the third world is more critical to securing aluminium supplies than is control of the source of the ore.

USCD—140 million tons—255 millions tons—480 million tons
US reserves — 13 million tons (plus 98 million tons resources)
NCW demand -- 900 million tons (medium)
NCW reserves — 800 million tons

IS THERE ENOUGH TO GO AROUND?

With approximately eight per cent of the NCW population, the United States is presently planning to reserve for her own industries and her own consumption between 50 per cent and 100 per cent of the world's mineral resources. Her assurance that these resources will be available to her use is hard to explain. Even using the figures given for NCW demand, there would appear to be a bitter competition for resources imminent. And those figures are predicated upon continuing desperate poverty for one-half of the world.

NCW demand was calculated by assuming a growth rate of consumption of industrial raw materials of between three per cent and six per cent, most of it to come from Europe. To see these figures in proper perspective, consider the past history of developing nations.

United States

Between 1867 and 1905, steel production increased an average of 25 per cent per annum. This average reflects even higher rates of increase in boom times, followed by severe depressions. After a period of stagnation, World War I sparked another surge in production of 15-20 per cent per annum.

Japan

In arming for World War II, Japan increased her steel production from 2.5 million tons in 1932 to 8 million tons in 1943. Due to deliberate occupation policy, her steel-making capacity was reduced to 3 million tons until 1949. In 1964 she produced 40 million tons — an average rate of growth over 15 years of more than ten per cent.

China

Production in Metric Tons

Commodity	1952	1957	1958	1959
Coal	66,000	128,000	270,000	335,000
Oil	440	1,444	2,260	3,500
Copper	10	50	70	80
Iron	4,290	15,000	30,000	45,000
Manganese	191	700	850	1,000
Aluminium	0	20	27	60
Lead	7	45	60	75
Steel	1,350	5,350	8,000	12,000

Based on the U.S. Bureau of Mines Special Supplement 25, March, 1960.

What surpluses of raw materials would be available to the U.S. if the U.N. undertook a development program designed to bring the Third World to the consumption level of a poor European country by the Year 2000? (By which time the U.S. GNP will have quadrupled.) The obvious pattern consumption would follow, from the examples above, would be far from a stately three per cent of nothing increase per annum. For the first few years, reflecting the smallness of the base, production and consumption would increase by 50 per cent to 300 per cent per annum, and then settle to a steady ten per cent growth rate.

What will the year 2000 find in fact? Surely not the world predicted in the U.S. studies, where half the world is swept with plagues and famines as they trudge out to the mines to dig up raw materials for an American affluence of science fiction proportions! The rate of development I have hypothesized is possible. The Third World knows it. They know that the much-vaunted roads, railways and telegraphs that American money has gifted them with lead from the mines to the ports. If they refuse to accept the division of labour on American terms, there will be far too little to go around.

The U.S. represents approximately eight per cent of the "non-Communist world" population. Europe and Canada are approximately twice that. But they need the greater part of all known reserves to maintain their current level of consumption; in some cases they need more than all known reserves, as with copper and tungsten. Is the enemy the U.S. confronts really Communism — or is it in fact industrialization?

IMPLICATIONS FOR U.S. POLICY

It must be a conscious and primary aim of American foreign policy to ensure that the flow of raw materials from the Third World is never interrupted.

Imagine a situation in which pro-Peking Community Parties controlled all overseas sources of raw materials for America's steel industry. They could cripple the U.S. as an economic and military power.

But America runs the risk of political opposition from many strains of political opinion besides the Maoist. And the important conclusion to be drawn from the first part of this paper is that there are economic reasons for any honest and independent government — communist, socialist, liberal democratic or even revolutionary-right — to stop selling raw materials to the United States. An examination of all the possible contingencies that could motivate a government to cut off American supplies makes it quite clear that American dependency on foreign suppliers makes it necessary for her to maintain regimes in power that are under her total control.

First, and most vital, a country may wish to conserve its resource base for its own industrial development. It will not be impressed by arguments that the necessity of containing communism requires economic sacrifices from the underdeveloped countries.

Second, there will be competition for what surpluses they may wish to sell, and they will have no reason to hand America a monopoly of their exports. America will have to compete with capitalist and socialist Europe, and with other Third World countries. Since her competitive position will not be strong, she will probably lose open competitions. Primary producers will sell raw materials in those markets from which they can purchase back finished goods at the lowest prices. This is much more likely to be Japan, for instance, than it is the United States.

Third, there will inevitably be anti-American sentiments associated with any independence Movement, and that may provide a political motive for giving preference to non-American buyers, as a symbol of independence or an expression of a legacy of bitterness.

Fourth, there might be sanctions in protest against American foreign policy in other Third World nations. For example, an independent Asian government such as Sihanouk's in Cambodia would be unlikely to sell war material to the United States while it was engaged in a counter-insurgency war such as in Vietnam.

A military consideration makes it equally imperative, from the American viewpoint, to maintain American puppets in Asia. Any number of Asian countries are located along the shipping routes by which the U.S. obtains strategic materials. If any one of them were to collaborate with a country (guess who) with whom America was engaged in a protracted land war, it could seriously interfere with American war industry.

HOW U.S. SECURITY IS GUARANTEED

There are three dangers against which American policy-makers will guard which arise from reliance on foreign sources of raw materials: political control of strategic locations by potentially hostile regimes, trade sanctions for political reasons, and loss of supplies for economic reasons.

Tactics to forestall these eventualities are varied. The ultimate weapon of government, and perhaps the best understood one, is the military coup, instigated by the CIA and backed by the Marines or the Seventh Fleet.

Short of this, American aid to the armed forces of tottering regimes gives the U.S. *de facto* political control. When Americans train and select the armed forces' officers, and service and repair military equipment, the effective control of such an army lies outside its own territory. This amounts to occupation by proxy.

American aid also means that the capital equipment of a country — its transportation system and industries — rely on American parts; and thus the country is extremely vulnerable in the short run to sanctions.

Stock-piling of scarce resources is used to maintain political and economic orthodoxy in the poor nations, as they are too close to the verge of complete economic collapse to withstand the dislocation of suddenly losing American markets. Since their margin of survival is so slight, they have no bargaining power, even when facing what appears to be a seller's market.

A final barrier to independent development is the lack of any source of development capital that is ear-marked for the priorities of mankind, and not controlled by the handful of great, inter-locking financial empires that are most rewarded by the status quo.

HOT SPOTS, OR, GOD SAVE AFRICA

If you make a list of troubled areas around the world — South Korea, Indonesia, Brazil, Congo, Rhodesia, Chile, Ghana, British Guiana (Guyana), Philippines — you have also made a list of sources of critical raw materials.

At the moment we seem to be trading Africa for Asia, which is cruel for the Africans, but may move us one step from the brink. Africa is particularly valuable, not only for the vast reserves of copper, chromium, manganese, and cobalt, but also for power. The Volta project, whose future has just been taken from Kwame Nkrumah's hands, will generate enough power to take aluminium production out of the hands of the northern hemisphere.

We may expect to see Africa and Asia firmly in the hands of "responsible" leadership, who will stress traditional agriculture and fiscal stability over industrialization. Or else.

THE CORNUCOPIANS

Some economists, known to the Conservationists as "the

Cornucopians" see in each exploited raw material not the use of an irreplaceable resource, but the forging of a key to even greater resources. They point to past history and current trends to show that technological innovations have made possible substitutions or mining of inferior ores at lower costs than earlier exploitation of high-grade ores.

In considering the impact of scarce resources on American foreign policy two questions arise. How far can technology deliver us from the Law of Diminishing Returns, and how many of U.S. policy makers are Cornucopians abroad as well as at home?

Theoretically, the whole earth is exploitable as a source of industrial minerals; the barriers are cost in dollars, and cost in time, training and machines. If the U.S. were presented with a *fait accompli*, if all her colonies were denied her and she were thrown back on her own and Canada's reserves, she could probably find ways of surviving as an advanced civilization. She has the knowledge, the training centers, the tax base, the power, the tools.

But short of that, will she do it, or will she continue to loot the poor countries of the earth?

At least three times in man's history, great civilizations have grown stagnant and been destroyed because they lacked the social forms that would realize the potential of their sciences. Steam powered the doors of temples while slaves rowed ships.

The capacity of American technology to solve the resource problem is not in question. It is in the selection of priorities, not the capacity for research, that our civilization is failing.

The space race is everybody's prime example of misallocation of our human and technical resources. Throughout the fifties reformers cried, "In some countries in the Far East and Africa 50 per cent of the population is blind! Forget the moon, and find a cure for trachoma". Immunization against the trachoma virus was finally developed through a breakthrough in virological research comparable to the development of the Salk vaccine — by the Chinese.

The system as it is presently structured will not lead to creative alternatives to imperialism as solutions to the resource problem. So long as ownership and control lie in the hands of the great international cartels, and so long as research priorities are determined by market mechanisms, looting will remain the logical solution to a problem with such initial components.

Although the human race as a whole is going to have to find means of using the less accessible and less-easily reduced ores, at any given point, a strong competitive advantage will accrue to whomever has the cheapest raw materials. It is technically feasible for the United States to find ways of mining manganese from the ocean bottom, but as long as Indian coolies are scratching 50 per cent ore out of the ground with wooden spades, it is economically ridiculous to produce it at twenty times the cost. The Russians and the Chinese both possess substantial deposits of most of the minerals America and Europe lack. As long as their low-cost ores are on the market, Americans will purchase on world markets, and keep secondary sources in Asia, Africa, and Latin America "on ice". But since the *status quo* in these countries is a standard of living below subsistence and declining, the *status quo* can only be maintained by force.

VESTED INTERESTS

(no, I am not now, nor have I ever been ...)

What this phrase means is simply demonstrated. The East India Company made enormous profits out of the maintenance of India as a British colony. It did not make as much in profits, however, as it cost to hold India by means of a vast administrative system, an overseas army and a Pacific fleet. So for Britain as a whole, it was not profitable to hold India, at least by force. *But*, the people who made the profits were not the same people who paid the price. And the people who made the profits, and had a vested interest in maintaining the *status quo* controlled the foreign policy of Britain against the interests of its people.

The situation may now exist where enclaves of power depend on a productive system that has become obsolete for the nation as a whole. More concretely, it will be possible to substitute agricultural fuels (alcohol) for mineral fuels. So it is no longer in the interests of the American people to support a war for oil, but it may well be in the interests of the Rockefellers.

A parallel and more perplexing problem is the phenomenon of vested psychological interests. If we know enough to make competition for the earth's resources a closed chapter in the evolution of human culture, will the legislators of the great powers undergo the shift in consciousness that will make fear of shortages obsolete in fact as a determinant of policy?

If some of these flying saucers would stop to offer some otherwordly benevolent guidance, they would probably suggest a world-wide program of search, research and development. The needs are obvious; how to get there from here is not.

We need an exhaustive geophysical survey, under U.N. auspices of Canada, Africa, Latin America, and all areas where reserves are suspected but not proved. With an expanded and scattered reserve base the risks of losing political control over any one country would be minimal.

"Do I understand, Senator, that you are prepared to take those risks with the security of the United States and the Free World?"

The U.N. should also provide development capital, so that owner countries will not run into a credit squeeze in the international capital market, and be forced to sell to the controllers of international credit, who just happen to include the same people who currently own most of the earth's resources (Morgan, Rockefeller, Rothschild).

International aid should be reallocated from currency stabilization to industrial development.

With Russia and China both self-sufficient and probably able to produce for export, there is probably enough to go around, at least potentially. But we are considering the motivations and probable decisions of groups of men committed to the security, and the competitive advantage, of a particular political and economic system that they wish to preserve unchanged. However great an abundance of raw materials is discovered in this century, the political considerations remain critical as long as one government has political control over the resources necessary to another government. It means that the resource-poor country must control the producing country, or be in some degree dependent on its good will.

A supranational body in control of prices and allocation of scarce resources might lessen the political tensions involved, but there would still be risk, still insecurity, for the developed countries. And a fair allocation would involve surrender of economic advantages that the United States is currently securing by military and paramilitary means.

"Do I understand, Senator, that you are suggesting placing the security of the United States and the Free World in the hands of the one-worlders, Black Africans, communists, and assorted riff-raff who inhabit the United Nations?"

Unfortunately, the economic motives for enforced poverty and economic stagnation in the Third World are easily elided into the "Great Black Blot" theory of communist expansion which U.S. congressmen seem to find so compelling. They overthrow governments to defend freedom, not our inflated levels of consumption. Political unrest in an area of strategic importance is easily rationalized into a military tactic by which the international communist conspiracy is attempting to cut our supply lines. (There's a marshall's baton in every attache case.) "Our interests" and "our commitments" are logically identical, but psychologically polar opposites.

It is past time that we made the leap in moral imagination that would let us understand that we are rich because they are poor. Guerilla movements are swelling throughout the Third World, and the lines are becoming clearly drawn. We must commit ourselves to the creation of a system of international distribution that will permit the industrialization of the Third World, or visit more Vietnams on the poor of the earth.

Foreign Expansion as an 'Institutional Necessity' for U.S. Corporate Capitalism
The Search for a Radical Model

T.H. Moran

Is foreign economic expansion in some sense an "institutional necessity" for corporate capitalism in the United States? Is there something inherent in the internal dynamics of American capitalism that creates such strong pressures for foreign private investment that the U.S. Government must consider the creation and preservation of an international system that facilitates such expansion to be among our most vital national interests? What yardstick can measure the opportunities, the needs, the necessity of investing abroad, or the cost and risk if the option of foreign private investment is threatened?

Traditional theories of imperialism have traced the impetus for foreign economic expansion to the need of an outlet for surplus capital generated in advanced capitalist states.[1] Underconsumption, or the presumed inability of mature capitalist economies to generate enough profitable opportunities to absorb the investment fund created by private corporations, leads to crises. Conspicuous consumption, military expenditures, and foreign investment are ways in which advanced capitalist nations try to deal with the problem of surplus capital.[2]

The models of foreign investment emphasizing surplus

capital or declining profit opportunities in mature industrial economies have received scant empirical support.

Historically, developed countries have traded and invested first and most heavily with each other. Foreign investment has not flowed from regions of capital abundance to regions of capital scarcity as vigorously as it has flowed from one region of relative capital abundance to other regions of relative capital abundance. And when foreign investment does take place in countries of capital scarcity, the bulk of the financing is frequently raised locally.

Relative profitability of foreign operations as between developed and underdeveloped economies is almost impossible to evaluate adequately on the basis of available data and conventional concepts — for reasons discussed within this paper — but there are strong indications that the most developed economies offer more and higher profit opportunities for investment to their own and foreign investors than do less developed countries.

The more developed the country, the more attractive it appears to be for investors. Developed economies have both the capital and the markets. Surplus capital is not pushed out of advanced economies because they have difficulty absorbing it.

Dependence on scarce natural resources from the underdeveloped world would seem to be the strongest argument why the most important corporations and their governments might "need" to maintain the option of direct foreign economic penetration. Yet, for the United States, domestic substitutes, synthetics, new techniques of low-grade extraction, and new methods of recovery and recycling suggest that the economy has a variety of alternatives other than the traditional pattern of foreign direct investment for supplying internal needs at acceptably higher prices. And, even in the unlikely event that all American natural resource companies in the Third World were nationalized and all exporting countries could maintain producers' cartels, these countries would still have to sell the bulk of their primary products to the United States and other developed capitalist countries at (perhaps)[3] higher prices. Thus, it can be argued that direct economic penetration to secure natural resources is not a compelling need for the functioning of corporate capitalism in the United States.

Considerations about the relative independence and self-sufficiency of the large capitalist economies (especially the United States) have led some analysts — Deutsch, Heilbroner, Waltz, Tucker, Miller, and others — to conclude that direct foreign expansion (above all, the expansion of non-natural resource companies into the underdeveloped world) cannot or should not be considered to be a vital national interest.[4] If feelings of economic necessity ever did dictate the Open Door policy in Asia or the Big Stick policy in Latin America, those feelings were "mistaken"; foreign investment has always been and will continue to be a "convenience" more more than a "necessity", and foreign economic expansion is not an "institutional need" of U.S. corporate capitalism.

Magdoff and others bypass the question of convenience or necessity by simply pointing to the sheer size of direct foreign investment — which, for the United States, represents production equivalent to the third- or fourth-largest economy in the world.[5] This accumulated stake is huge and extremely important — from both a balance-sheet and a cash-flow perspective — to those large international corporations who are likely to have the most influence on governmental policy. Foreign investments are large. They are profitable. They will be defended and expanded because they are there.

In this paper I will argue that an emphasis on the stake that multi-national corporations have in direct foreign expansion is more plausible than the models of surplus capital. But revelations about the accumulated stake in foreign investments do not explain the dynamics of how such a stake gets built up, or why it will continue to be built up in underdeveloped as well as developed countries. Indeed, any interpretation of an *accumulated* stake far understates the interest that the most dynamic domestic corporations have in keeping the possibility of foreign expansion open to them in *their future*. Recent studies of the growth of American manufacturing firms confirm that the largest, the most diversified, the fastest growing, and the most technologically advanced corporations have considered the option to invest in foreign countries to be a need vital to their corporate strategies in the past, that they continue to do so today, and will fight to preserve the option in the future.

Concentrating only on U.S. manufacturing companies, I will show why the pressures to invest abroad are much stronger and the costs of giving up the foreign option are much higher in corporate decision-making than conventionally understood by either neoclassical or neo-Marxist analysts.

The study of the growth of the firm in the United States suggests that corporate managers have felt, and will continue to feel, that pressures for foreign economic expansion are much more a compelling need or even an institutional necessity than merely a profitable convenience. And in the future such needs or necessities may dictate corporate strategies for stronger penetration into the Third World than that which has already taken place in the developed countries.

I

The classical theory of the firm and the classical theory of foreign trade and investment assumed free availability of information, stable production functions, and no significant returns to scale. Foreign investment, like domestic investment, is made on the basis of marginal return on capital.

Recent models of the growth of U.S. firms in manufacturing industries, however, have assumed that technology and information are tightly controlled, that production processes are characterized by large economies of scale, and that products undergo predictable changes in production and marketing over time.[6] Foreign investment is viewed as the strategy of corporations to expand or defend barriers to entry which are repeatedly challenged and eroded.

According to these later models of the growth of the firm, corporations begin with control over some combination of skills (technology, management, differential access to capital or other factors of production) that gives them a competitive edge in (stimulating and) responding to demand. From this control comes their power to exact an economic rent from customers. The development of new products or a new line of products is usually characterized by tightly held technology, short production runs, and sales to a close-by, ill-defined market. As aggregate demand in that market expands, or as the geographical servicing of demand spreads, the technology becomes more standardized and the production runs become longer and more stable. This lowers average cost. The uncertainties of marketing are lessened as price- and income-elasticities of demand are more thoroughly explored. The standardized technology is more easily imitable. Almost inevitably, the result is increasing competition in the initial market as more firms enter into production. The originator of a new product or a new production process loses a portion of his ability to exact economic rents to rivals. If barriers to entry are sufficiently high, the erosion of oligopoly control proceeds relatively slowly. But even in those cases where stable oligopoly shares of the market can be maintained for some period of time (perhaps decades), the growth of profitability for the individual firm becomes a function of growth of aggregate demand in the market and slows considerably from the initial expansion of the product. Studies of the product cycle show that firms thus face repeated "closing[s] of the continental frontier" as significant as William A. Williams supposes the 1890's were for the expansion of the economy of the United States.[7]

During the period of product development and technological standardization in response to the market opportunities nearby, some foreign orders come from countries with similar demand structures. These orders create the first opportunity for firms to extend the exploitation of barriers to entry in the face of increasing competition and their inability to maintain dynamic growth at home. Exports become an increasingly important part of the firms' production and marketing strategies.

After a short time, however, the same process occurs in the foreign market as occurred in the original domestic market. The standardization of technology, the wider possibilities of technological diffusion and technological imitation, the clearer knowledge of demand and cost characteristics all serve to lower barriers to entry into the market. Local competitors begin to challenge the position of the foreign exporters. They do not have the transportation costs of the foreign exporters; they may be able to combine local factors of production as efficiently or more efficiently than foreign exporters; and they can seek governmental protection.

This again challenges the ability of the original producers to maintain the potential to exploit their oligopolistic edge. At that point, they must make the decision of whether to give up the overseas market and settle back down to a shrinking share of the market in the home country, or take the big step of investing within the foreign country to defend their positions as exactors of oligopoly rents.

Foreign investment defends a market already built up through exports. It allows the firm to average overhead and R & D costs over a larger production run, and to extend the payoff the parent company receives on initial costs sunk into technology without having to make any additional investment of this type in the foreign country.[8] It also allows the firm to maximize returns on an increasingly experienced (but costly) multinational management staff: There are increasing returns to scale for management organization which can only be realized by multinational expansion.[9]

Recent studies of U.S. corporate expansion, aimed at testing the model of the product cycle and the growth of the firm, have found overwhelming evidence in support of the model.[10] American manufacturing enterprises typically began by producing for domestic consumption, and then expanded abroad through exports to countries that had similar demand characteristics. As production processes became more standardized in the United States, the most frequent sequence for foreign expansion from the late nineteenth into the twentieth century consisted of a response to sales opportunities in Canada, then Great Britain, Germany and France.

Subsequently, foreign competition imitated or duplicated the technology of products first introduced in the United States. National companies threatened to combine local factors of production in efficient ways while avoiding transportation costs. More importantly, they threatened, through governmental protection, to exclude exports. U.S. exporters were thereby forced to make an investment in foreign production in order to maintain their market position. Wilkins and Vernon find that frequently, corporations discovered that local production costs were lower than those at home. However, they did not move into local production in the foreign countries until their exports were threatened by tariffs.[11] The flow of American direct private investment in manufacturing again typically proceeded in the Canada-Great Britain-Germany-France pattern — with capital flowing toward areas of relative capital abundance in response to a challenge to the possibility of exploiting the original barriers to entry.

Mira Wilkins cites the example of International Harvester which, like companies in the automobile industry, began exporting early in the twentieth century.[12] By 1911, in response to "tariffs and the possibility of competition developing behind the tariff walls," Harvester had followd up its exports by building five foreign plants — in Canada, Sweden, France, Germany, and Russia. Foreign business by that time constituted 40 per cent of the company's total revenues and a greater share of net earnings.

Similar histories have been traced for General Electric, Kodak, Ford, IBM, Singer, Westinghouse, and other major companies in reapers, typewriters, cash registers, pumps, telephone apparatus, film, drugs, electrical equipment, elevators, explosives, and so on.[13]

The same cycle has been evident in the pattern of economic relations with countries that are less familiar to the United States than Canada and Western Europe. Products created in response to demand in the U.S. market were exported to Latin America

GROWTH OF U.S. FOREIGN INVESTMENT IN MANUFACTURING

Number of Foreign Manufacturing Subsidiaries of 187 U.S. Controlled Multinational Enterprises

	1929	1939	1950	1959	1967
Total	467	715	988	1891	3646
Europe (incl. U.K.)	226	335	363	677	1438
Canada	137	169	225	330	443
All other areas	104	211	400	884	1765
Ratio: All other areas to Total	22.3	29.5	40.5	46.7	48.4

Number of Product Lines Introduced by Foreign Manufacturing Subsidiaries of 187 U.S.-Controlled Multinational Enterprises

	1920-29	1930-39	1940-50	1951-59	1960-67
Total	365	438	473	1345	2921
Canada, Europe, U.K.	276	271	209	666	1581
All other areas	89	167	264	679	1340
Ratio: All other Areas to Total	24.4	38.1	55.8	50.5	45.9

Book Value of Direct Foreign Investment of U.S. Enterprises In Manufacturing Subsidiaries (In Millions of Dollars)

	1929	1940	1950	1957	1969
	$	$	$	$	$
Total	1,813	1,926	3,831	8,009	29,450
Europe (incl. U.K.)	629	639	932	2,195	12,225
Canada	819	943	1,897	3,924	9,389
All other areas	364	343	1,003	1,890	7,836
Ratio: All other Areas to Total	20.1	17.8	26.2	23.6	26.6

Sources: Vaupel and Curhan (fn.10), chap. 3; Vernon (fn.6), tables 3-3 and 3-4; U.S. Department of Commerce, *U.S. Business Investments in Foreign Countries* (Washington, D.C. 1960), and *Survey of Current Business*, various issues.

RATIO: U.S. FOREIGN INVESTMENT IN MANUFACTURING OUTSIDE CANADA, EUROPE, AND U.K. TO TOTAL U.S. FOREIGN INVESTMENT IN MANUFACTURING

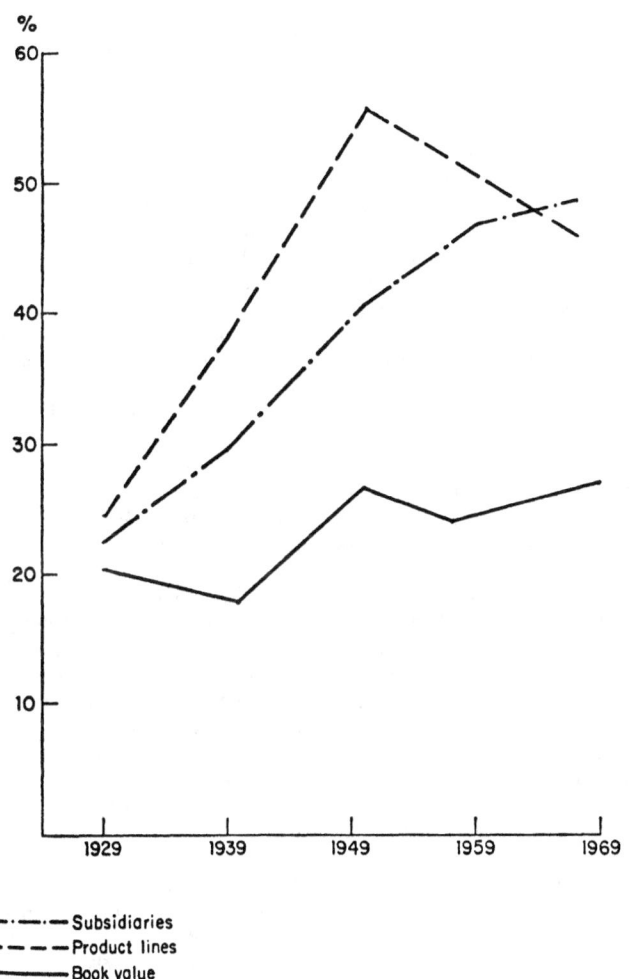

—·—·— Subsidiaries
— — — Product lines
———— Book value

and the Far East (but largely excluded from Africa and India by European colonial pressure). The struggle over the Open Door policy in China was waged precisely to prevent that market from becoming the exclusive sphere of influence of the European powers in the pattern of India and Africa.[14] With the achievement of the Open Door policy, China's demand was served by import, like Latin America's, rather than through direct investment — despite potentially lower labor costs if production had been carried out locally.

Only in Japan, where the supersession of unequal treaties in 1899 gave that country the chance to introduce tariff protection, did American businessmen face the clear choice of either investing in local manufacturing or losing their export market. Professor Wilkins points out that it was in Japan, rather than in China, that companies such as Westinghouse, American Tobacco, and General Electric had their "key investments".[15]

Direct private investment by the United States in manufacturing subsidiaries located outside Canada, Europe, and the United Kingdom did not begin to grow with any dynamism until the Depression threatened to cut off exports. According to the Harvard Business School study of 187 U.S. multinational corporations, the number of foreign manufacturing subsidiaries and the number of product lines introduced in new areas outside Canada, Britain, and continental Europe doubled between 1929 and 1939, in contrast to the much slower growth of manufacturing activity in the old familiar countries.

During the process of import-substituting industrialization after the second World War, this process of direct foreign investment by American firms accelerated in new areas. U.S. manufacturing assets located outside Canada, Europe, and Britain reached a high of 26 per cent of all U.S. foreign manufacturing assets in 1950, and managed to maintain that level even during the celebrated American "penetration" of Europe in the 1960's. During the same period the ratio of U.S. manufacturing subsidiaries located in new areas to the total number of foreign manufacturing subsidiaries rose from 30 per cent to 48 per cent.

Again, American companies followed exports with investments in the drive to maintain their oligopoly positions and preserve the ability to exact economic rents from barriers to entry that were repeatedly being challenged. Clearly, not all industries invested abroad. Some were content to sit at home and collect the proceeds from a declining share of a slowly growing market. But the largest, most rapidly growing, most technologically advanced industries — the ones with the greatest competitive edge to exploit and the greatest ability to absorb the informational and managerial costs of multinational expansion — did feel compelled to defend themselves and grow in the only way they could: through direct foreign investment.[16]

II

The study of corporate growth in the United States shows that economic expansion abroad results from the struggle to expand and defend the capacity to exact oligopoly rents.

This model has received support not only from historical analyses of extraterritorial investment, but also from contemporary studies of product cycles and international trade.

In a pioneering study of the petrochemical industry, Robert Stobaugh has found that prices for bulk organic chemicals go through a clearly defined cycle that begins at a high point when new products are first introduced and then declines as production becomes more standardized and domestic competition increases.[17] Innovators find that after a certain time lag — a time lag that has become shorter with each decade of this century — they are faced with a declining share of the domestic market, slower aggregate growth, and limited manoeuverability within the oligopoly. The servicing of foreign demand begins with exports. After a time lag narrowing from twenty-seven to seven years, competition will spring up in the foreign markets — competition that includes firms who have purchased (or licensed) the standardized technology from the original country in which the product was developed. The result has been massive foreign investment on the part of the petrochemical industry to defend its position in foreign markets and pursue its increasingly threatened opportunity to exact an economic rent from the product. Of 105 direct foreign investment decisions in Stobaugh's study, not one direct foreign investment was made *before* a foreign competitor had commenced production. But by the mid 1960's the petrochemical industry was second in total value of United States foreign investments and first among U.S. manufacturing groups in net capital outflows to affiliates abroad.

In the electronics industry - from radios through computers to lasers — Seev Hirsch has found the same product and investment cycle.[18] U.S. exports have been highest over time in whatever are the newer, higher growth sectors of the industry.

But as the product groups assume more mature characteristics — as production processes become more stable, as specifications become more standardized, as the importance of skill content declines — foreign manufacturers duplicate or license the technology, adapt it to their environment, and challenge the position of the original producer. The only option for the marginal producer is to expand abroad with his more mature, standardized line to meet the competition.

G.C. Hufbauer, in examining the production of synthetic materials, argues in a similar vein: leading countries have an initial competitive advantage which they lose, after a time lag, to national producers who have bridged the technological gap.[19] For the erstwhile leader who thinks he still has an advantage to exploit against local producers who enjoy tariff protection or lower costs, the answer must be direct foreign investment within the others' national market.

In a study of companies from nine industries that account for over 90 per cent of U.S. direct foreign investment in manufacturing — food products (Standard Industrial Classification 20), paper and allied products (SIC 28), chemicals and allied products (SIC 28), petroleum (SIC 29), rubber products (SIC 30), primary and fabricated metals (SIC 33 and 34), non-electrical machinery (SIC 35), electical machinery (SIC 36), and transportation equipment (SIC 37) — a team of investigators at the Harvard Business School has shown that exports preceded direct foreign investment, and that direct foreign investment took place as a defensive reaction when production could no longer be expanded (for domestic or foreign markets) at home.[20]

This is the dynamic that accounts for most foreign investment in manufacturing by American firms — the pursuit of opportunities to exploit some barrier to entry in the face of repeated challenges to those opportunities. The result has been the spread of U.S. corporate investment abroad, in both developed and underdeveloped countries, without direct regard for regions of relative capital scarcity or significant concern about where capital is actually raised to finance the foreign expansion.

III

Studies of the product cycle and the growth of the firm do not deny that corporations invest abroad as part of their search for profits.[21] But there are important empirical and conceptual complications in trying to evaluate how profitable foreign operations are.

In the first place, corporations seldom publish disaggregated data that permit identification of returns from specific product lines in specific countries which could be compared to the same product lines in the home country. Such disclosure would allegedly reveal too much information to competititors. Occasionally, the U.S. Department of Commerce publishes statistics by regions and activity.

RETURN ON U.S. FOREIGN INVESTMENT IN MANUFACTURING IN 1965[22]
(Millions of Dollars)

	Earnings	Assets (book value)	Return (%)
Far East (incl. Japan)	$101	$893	$11.3
Europe (incl. U.K.)	855	7,570	11.2
Latin America	269	2,741	9.9
Canada	606	6,855	8.8
Africa (excl. South Africa)	4	55	7.2

However, even when available, such numbers are of limited use in evaluating the return generated by various foreign investments. A second difficulty springs from the fact that international corporations inevitably exercise some discretion in deciding where they will show their profits. This discretion extends from comparatively simple decisions about how to allocate common R & D costs, to more perplexing decisions created by a substantial degree of vertical integration across national boundaries. The company that sells to or buys from its own subsidiaries must establish some transfer price for the internal transaction when making out its tax form for the host government. If there is no open arms-length market to indicate what the price should be, then the point where profits are shown to occur is a matter of pure discretion depending on the corporation's internal strategy. Two major goals of corporate strategy are to minimize its global tax burden and to protect itself from competition. Therefore, companies will tend to show low profits where tax rates are high, or at stages in the vertical chain where there are insignificant barriers to entry. Whether these considerations will mean that low profits are generally being declared in underdeveloped countries as opposed to developed countries, or in foreign countries as opposed to the home country, cannot be predicted *a priori*.[23]

The third problem in evaluating how attractive or enticing a foreign investment will appear to an individual firm can be illustrated by looking at the real alternatives open to that firm. Most analysts of corporate behavior reject the assumption of classical economics that information and accumulated experience are free commodities. A firm begins, as I have argued in this paper, with control over some technique, managerial ability, and/or corporate knowledge which it seeks to exploit in domestic markets, through exports, and in foreign production. This control over information, experience, or technology creates what Richard Caves calls "sector-specific capital" or "low inter-industry mobility of capital" — indicating that the firm can use its resources only with diminishing returns as it moves away from the type of behavior with which it is familiar.[24] Thus, although an economist might find that there is some "average" marginal profitability of 15 per cent (after taxes) on operations within the United States, many individual American firms may face the choice of investing abroad in their familiar line of operations with a marginal return of 12 per cent, or investing at home with a marginal return of 4 per cent or less. In fact, if an expansion of output in the firm's home market will bring retaliation from competitors, the marginal return from increasing capacity at home may be negative. Thus, one can predict that foreign investment will exercise a great pull on the funds of many firms, even though the typical marginal profitability of such an investment might be substantially lower than some average marginal profitability of "an investment" in the home country.

Finally, the evaluation of the profitability or the importance of making a foreign investment must take into consideration how corporations react to the actual or potential actions of their fellow oligopoly members. Those industries that have some barrier to entry to exploit at home are precisely the ones who are most likely to move abroad in close follow-the-leader patterns. If one company invests abroad to protect its export market, other members in the home market must worry not only about being shut off from exports by a tariff wall, but also about the first investor getting a significant jump on them in the foreign market — in terms of national good will, product identification, familiarity with local officials, and so forth. Thus, to a calculation of profit rate on incremental investment overseas, they must add — once the first firm has made its move — an even higher probability of losing their export market.

The calculation of potential loss which must be added to the calculation of potential profit to indicate the appeal or the need of a foreign investment will become much more important, as we shall see, when we examine the trend toward re-exporting back into the home market. The firm that does not follow its competitors into other countries may face not only the loss of an export market but a share of its domestic market as well.

In conclusion, it is difficult to get data giving the return on foreign investment, and such data are of only marginal use when obtained. The only adequate way to estimate the profitability, the appeal, or the "need" of foreign investment is to ask what would happen to the firm if the investment were not made.

Potential loss of export markets, low opportunity cost for capital in the home market, the threat of losing a large part of the global ability to exact oligopoly rent — all indicate high values to be put on foreign investment, and strong reactions against the risk of losing the option of foreign investment in the future. For large American firms operating in a setting of unstable imperfect competition, foreign expansion has appeared to corporate decision-makers — accurately — more as a compelling institutional need than a profitable convenience.

With the trend running toward foreign investment to produce goods (or components) for export back into the home market, this compelling need to go abroad has become an "institutional necessity."

IV

The model of the product cycle and the evidence of United States expansion in manufacturing industries was begun by considering foreign production only as a means of supplying a foreign domestic market. But U.S. direct foreign investment has increasingly aimed not merely at supplying the local market, but at exporting to third countries, most notably back into the United States. Hirsch has documented this for electrical and electronic products; [25] Wells for textiles and standard computer components; [26] Vernon for transportation equipment, office machines, telecommunications equipment, and food products.[27] In Latin America, for example, U.S.-controlled companies accounted for 12 per cent of the exports of manufacturers in 1957, but 41 per cent in 1966. In absolute terms, the exports of manufacturers from Latin America grew by $904 million in the same period, of which $585 million were exports of subsidiaries of U.S. firms.[28]

In 1968, U.S. foreign manufacturing subsidiaries produced almost $120 billion worth of goods, of which 22 per cent were then exported out of the country of production; U.S. foreign subsidiaries have become an exporter as large as Germany and twice the size of Japan.[29] Eight per cent of the production of U.S. foreign manufacturing subsidiaries was imported back into the United States, accounting for about one-fourth of all U.S. imports, and making the subsidiaries a trading partner almost equal in size to all importers from Europe and twice the size of all importers from Japan. Even if the huge imports from subsidiaries of the United States automakers in Canada are ignored, imports into the United States still amount to 5 per cent of all U.S. foreign production, or almost one billion dollars more than the value of all imports from Japan.

Again, the kinds of firms that are beginning to scan the globe for possibilities of rationalizing production and trade are generally the kinds of firms that move in close follow-the-leader patterns in response to each other's behavior. The common fear is that some one oligopoly member will come to dominate a low-cost source of production and leave them all at a serious disadvantage. When one invests abroad, all feel compelled to follow.

If costs in the new area prove too high for export back to the home market, or if the new local market does not grow as rapidly as expected, the market shares of all the oligopoly members will be maintained with the loss of a relatively small investment. This small investment is an *option* on a potentially very great source of profit and an *insurance policy* against a potentially very great risk of loss. The producer who is left behind and finds not only his export market but even his home market swamped with low-cost imports produced overseas by his domestic rivals sees the specter of his own death. Leading or following his competitors abroad becomes an "institutional necessity."

V

The study of the product cycle and the growth of the firm explains why the the largest, the fastest growing, and the most technologically advanced American manufacturing companies have been under intense pressures to expand into other countries, both developed and under-developed. This intensity is far greater than is revealed by conventional figures on relative profitability; it is an intensity that has indeed been intrinsic to the dynamics of unstable imperfect competition in the United States.

This does not mean that foreign economic expansion has been the most compelling national interest at every point in time, or that economic considerations have always dominated military or political or religious strategies. But it does suggest the working hypothesis that, during the last hundred years, powerful corporate decision-makers, responding with good judgment to opportunity and to risk, have brought what pressures they could to keep the option of foreign economic expansion open to them in their companies' futures. The dynamics of foreign penetration by American business did not follow a lackadaisical course of convenience or adventure in the pursuit of profits. Ours was not an accidental empire.

It is of course possible to imagine a future far different from a steady unimpeded corporate multinationalization of the globe. Regional trading and investing areas could develop. Protectionist groups seeking security could prevail over competitive groups wanting to use their talents in technology and organization for expansion—for a time.[30] Large sections of the underdeveloped world could successfully shut themselves off from foreign exports or foreign investments—for a time. In fact, broad protectionist moves in the United States or broad exclusionary moves in the underdeveloped world that would serve to render unstable imperfect competition more stable could probably be quite easily tolerated by U.S. multinational corporations in the short run, provided domestic competition could be restrained simultaneously.

But there *is* something fundamental to American corporate capitalism—the capitalism of tightly held technology, uncertain information, large economies of scale, and unstable imperfect competition, rather than the capitalism of perfect competition and portfolio investment—that creates strong pressures for foreign investment. As long as American corporations exercise their virtues of inventiveness and aggressiveness, their government will feel intense, even frantic pressures to create and preserve an international system that facilitates foreign economic expansion.

FOOTNOTES

[1] J.A. Hobson *Imperialism* (Ann Arbor 1965); V.I. Lenin, *Imperialism, The Highest Stage of Capitalism* (New York 1930); Paul M. Sweezy, *The Theory of Capitalist Development* (London 1942); Paul A. Baran, *The Political Economy of Growth* (New York 1957); Paul A. Baran and Paul M. Sweezy, *Monopoly Capital* (New York 1966).

[2] In their last work, *Monopoly Capital*, Baran and Sweezy suggested that none of these methods could absorb surplus capital very effectively. On foreign investment, see *ibid.*, 104-11.

[3] It is by no means certain that the prices of all primary products would rise with the nationalization of operations at the production stage. Cf. Moran, "New Deal or Raw Deal in Raw Materials", *Foreign Policy*, No. 5 (Winter 1971/72)

[4] Karl W. Deutsch and Alexander Eckstein, "National Industrialization and the Declining Share of the International Economic Sector, 1890-1959," *World Politics*, XIII (January 1961); Robert I. Heilbroner, "Counter-revolutionary America," in Irving Howe, ed., *A Dissenter's Guide to Foreign Policy* (Garden City, N.Y. 1968); Kenneth N. Waltz, "The Myth of National Interdependence, " in Charles P. Kindleberger, ed., *The International Corporation* (Cambridge, Mass. 1970); Robert Tucker, *The Radical Left and American Foreign Policy* (Baltimore 1970); S.M. Miller, Roy Bennett, and Cyril Alapatt, "Does the U.S. Economy Require Imperialism?" *Social Policy*, (September-October 1970).

[5] Harry Magdoff, *The Age of Imperialism* (New York 1969), and "The Logic of Imperialism" *Social Policy*, I (September-October, 1970); Frank Akerman, "Magdoff on Imperialism" *Public Policy*, XIX (Summer 1971).

Since the end of the 1960's, total production of foreign firms controlled by U.S. corporations has been close to the total production of the Japanese economy, making them third or fourth behind the U.S. and the U.S.S.R.

[6] The most important body of this literature deals with the theory of the product cycle: Raymond Vernon, "International Investment and International Trade in the Product Cycle," *Quarterly Journal of Economics*, LXXX (May 1966), and *Sovereignty at Bay* (New York 1971); Louis T. Wells, Jr., "Test of a Product Cycle Model of International Trade," *Quarterly Journal of Economics*, LXXXIII (February, 1969) and *International Trade: The Product Cycle Approach* (Basic Books, forthcoming).

Related to this approach to the growth of the firm are Edith T. Penrose, *The Theory of the Growth of the Firm* (Oxford 1966); Raymond Vernon, "Organization as a Scale Factor in the Growth of Firms," in J.W. Markham and G.F. Papanek, eds., *Industrial Organization & Economic Development* (New York 1970)

On oligopoly behavior and the theory of foreign investment, see Stephen H. Hymer, "The International Operations of National Firms: A Study of Direct Foreign Investment," unpub. Ph.D. thesis (MIT 1960); Stephen Hymer and Robert Rowthorn, "Multinational Corporations and International Oligopoly: The Non-American Challenge," in Kindleberger (fn. 4); Richard Caves, "International Corporations: The Industrial Economics of Foreign Investment," *Economica*, New Series, XXXVIII, No. 149.

This paper does not attempt to deal with the dynamics of foreign investment and oligopoly behavior in natural resource industries. For some approaches to this subject, see Moran, *El Cobre es Chileno — The Multinational Corporation and the Politics of Development: The Case of Copper in Chile* (Harvard Center for International Affairs 1972); Vernon, *Sovereignty at Bay* (see above); John E. Tilton, "The Choice of Trading Partners: An Analysis of International Trade in Aluminium, Bauxite, Copper, Lead, Manganese, Tin, and Zinc," *Yale Economic Essays*, VI (Fall 1966).

There is also no attempt to look at the behavior of multinational manufacturing enterprises that are not based in the United States. Preliminary investigations suggest that there may have been systematic differences in their behavior related to the amount of instability and competition in the home market — although their strategies may be converging with those of U.S. enterprises.

[7] William A. Williams, *The Tragedy of American Diplomacy* (New York 1962).

[8] Cf. Harry Johnson, "The Efficiency and Welfare Implications of the International Corporation," in Kindleberger (fn. 4); Raymond Vernon, "U.S. Controls on Foreign Direct Investments — A Reevaluation," Financial Executives Research Foundation (April 1969).

[9] Penrose (fn. 6); Vernon, "Organization as a Scale Factor in the Growth of Firms" (fn. 6).

[10] Mira Wilkins, *The Emergence of Multinational Enterprise* (Cambridge, Mass. 1970); Vernon, *Sovereignty at Bay* (fn.6); James W. Vaupel and Joan P. Curhan *The Making of Multinational Enterprise* (Boston, 1969).

[11] Cf. Wilkins (fn.10), esp. chaps, IV, V, and X; Vernon (fn.6) chap.3 and tables 3-5

[12] Wilkins (fn. 10), 102-103.

[13] *Ibid.*, 65, 68, 212-13.

[14] In addition to William A. Williams's well-known thesis (fn. 7), see supporting data in Wilkins (fn. 10), chap. IV.

[15] *Ibid*, 75, 205.

[16] The most comprehensive discussion of the key characteristics of foreign investors in the Harvard Business School sample of 187, in the *Fortune* 500, and in the U.S. Commerce Department statistics can be found in Vernon (fn. 6), chap I, and in Vaupel and Curhan (fn. 10), chap. I.

Studies by Stobaugh and Hirsch (see fns. 17 and 18) of the petrochemical and electronics industries go further in relating foreign investment to rate of growth.

The argument is also made that U.S. foreign investors are the most sophisticated in managerial organization. Cf. John M. Stopford, "Growth and Organization Change in the Multinational Firm," unpub. D.B.A. thesis (Harvard Business School 1968); Lawrence E. Fouraker and John M. Stopford, "Organizational Structure and Multinational Strategy," *Administrative Science Quarterly*, XIII (June 1968).

[17] Robert B. Stobaugh, Jr., "The Product Life Cycle, U.S. Exports and International Investment," unpub. D.B.A. thesis (Harvard Business School 1968).

[18] Seev Hirsch, *Location of Industry and International Competitiveness* (Oxford 1967), and "The United States Electronics Industry in International Trade," in Wells (fn. 6)

[19] G.C. Hufbauer, *Synthetic Materials and the Theory of International Trade* (London 1965)

[20] Robert Stobaugh, Jose de la Torre, Robert Hayes, James Tucker, Richard Moxon, Rita Rodriguez, and others, *U.S. Multinational Enterprises and the U S. Economy*, Harvard Business School report prepared for the U.S. Department of Commerce (January 1972).

[21] The argument of this paper can be translated directly into profit-maximizing terms if one admits discontinuous opportunity costs to the firm and if, to the calculation of marginal return on investment, one adds a measure of the risk of loss to the enterprise if the foreign investment is not made.

[22] U.S. Department of Commerce, *Survey of Current Business*, Foreign Investments 1965-66 (September 1966).

[23] All other things being equal, there should be a presumption that when they get the chance, U.S. firms will declare more of their profits to be on foreign operations than at home, especially in the case of foreign investment in underdeveloped countries. The deferral feature of the U.S. foreign tax credit in effect provides

foreign subsidiaries of American businesses with an interest-free loan amounting to the U.S. tax liability of unremitted profits. Also, in less developed countries, the absence of a "grossing-up" requirement means that taxes paid to a host government relieve a company of much more of its global tax liability than taxes paid to the U.S. Government.

[24] Caves (fn. 6). Caves's finding that direct foreign investment does *not* tend to equalize rates of return in any country *between* industry sectors is consistent with and supportive of the model of corporate growth advanced here.

How firms have evaluated the choice between diversifying at home and expanding abroad is not clearly understood. It appears that considerations of accounting rather than of economics have been responsible for many of the conglomerate mergers in the United States. And, in any case, domestic diversification has been seen as an aid to foreign expansion rather than as an alternative in the strategy of some of the largest conglomerates, such as ITT or Litton.

[25] Hirsch (fn. 18).

[26] Wells, *Q.J.E.* (fn. 6).

[27] *Sovereignty at Bay* (fn. 6), chap. 3.

[28] Council for Latin America, *The Effects of United States and Other Foreign Investment in Latin America* (New York 1969).

[29] The figures on exports of U.S. foreign manufacturing subsidiaries for 1968 are cited in Stobaugh (fn. 20), 28. Comparisons with export and import figures for the countries in the text are taken from *International Financial Statistics* of the International Monetary Fund and the *Statistical Abstract of the United States*.

[30] For those who favor a behavioral model of the firm, it can be argued that managers of the fastest growing divisions within a large diversified corporation can ally themselves with managers of research and development divisions and with those production managers who want access to cheap foreign inputs against the managers of "mature" divisions who might press for protection.

Does the U.S. Require Imperialism?

S.M. Miller, Roy Bennett and Cyril Alapatt

The United States, it is charged, is imperialist, neo-imperialist, neo-colonialist.

The well-being of the economy, it is contended, requires the economic exploitation of and the draining of superprofits from weaker countries. Vietnam was no "accident". It was a logical continuation of inevitable economic drives that will be followed by "many more Vietnams".

If these contentions are valid, if the internal inconsistencies or the inherent contradictions of the American economy inexorably drive it to solve its problems through the exploitation of weaker countries, it follows that it would be extraordinarily difficult, if not impossible, to change U.S. foreign policy without first changing its economic and social system.

But if factors other than a basic economic thrust for foreign trade, sources of raw materials, and super-profits are involved, if political or military considerations are also levers — possibly prime levers — then a change in overseas policies might be possible without the prior shattering or destruction of the system itself.

The charge that economic imperialism is a necessity seems to have surface validity. How else can one explain the ubiquitous economic and military presence of the United States?

Starting with the premise that simple economic imperialism does not adequately explain U.S. foreign policy and the military interventions consequent to that policy, we have undertaken to question whether this theory's fundamental assumption is, in fact, valid.

Since the conclusion that imperialism is economically imperative for the United States is reached from a variety of viewpoints, it is therefore important that we specify what phenomena we are investigating.

1. The domestic significance. We are here concerned *only* with the domestic significance of U.S. overseas activity. We do not attempt to analyze its impact on the countries affected, however distorted their economies may be by the pattern of U.S. economic policies. We seek only to discover how important overseas activities are to this country without considering the extent to which the American economy dominates that of other nations. An asymmetry might prevail: while U.S. overseas economic activities may not be of overriding importance to this country, they may still be deeply significant and distorting to the nations at the other end.

2. The Third World boundary. Our concern is with the importance of U.S. economic activity with low-income, or Third World, countries. We are not appraising the importance of its role in Western Europe, Japan, and other high-income or high-industrial countries.

Why this distinction? Because direct military intervention by the United States for economic reasons in the high-income countries has become highly unlikely. (Indeed, with the economic "miracles" of the Common Market countries and Japan, the 1970s will face the United States with serious competition abroad in the field of foreign-investment flows originating from Germany and Japan, among others.) The danger of military intervention or U.S.-directed coups is to the low-income countries. While we recognize that for other purposes it would be important to consider all U.S. overseas economic activity, with our objective of assessing the likelihood of direct military activity, the primary question is: Do U.S. economic interests in low-income countries compel military-interventionist action?

3. Separating military and economic activities. We do not presume that every economic activity necessarily requires, or can draw upon, military support, or that military action necessarily leads to expanding the economic importance of a territory for the United States. We wish here to examine economic reasons for intervention separately from military reasons. Obviously the two often coincide and it is worth examining when and why they do, but we do not attempt that important job in this paper.

Doubtless, some will assert that if these three perspectives shape our analysis, there is little sense in reading further. But bear with us. It is important to review data from many perspectives if we wish to have action programs that can change policy rather than merely sloganize against it.

Magdoff's approach. The most detailed analysis of the imperatives of economic imperialism for the United States is that presented by Harry Magdoff in his study *The Age of Imperialism*. Magdoff aggregates his data on overseas economic activity to show the importance of all foreign economic activity to the U.S. economy; thus, he lumps together trade and investment with high-income nations and with Third World countries. We do the opposite; that is, we disaggregate the data on overseas economic activities in order to see how important economic activity with low-income countries is to the United States.

High-income and low-income countries. In examining data on overseas economic activities, we have divided nations into high-income and low-income categories. We have included in high-income countries Canada, Western Europe, South Africa, Australia and New Zealand, and Japan. Low-income nations include all of Latin America (although countries like Venezuela, Mexico and Argentina are on the borderline of the United Nations definition of developed countries) and all of Asia and Africa, except Japan and South Africa. Eastern Europe and the Soviet Union, which are not significantly involved economically with the United States are considered outside these two categories.

Exports. The most common argument used to prove that export trade is not of central consequence to the American economy is its small relative size. While not a conclusive argument, it is not unimportant.

In 1968 U.S. exports were $34.7 billion, while GNP was $860.6 billion. Exports, then, constituted about 4 percent of total product. So it has been for generations: foreign demand takes a small relative percentage of the total output of U.S. goods and services.

But, more important, two-thirds of these exports were to high-income rather than low-income nations;[1] that is, most of our trade is with rich competitors, not weak dependencies.

Moreover, exports to low-income areas dropped, between 1955 and 1968, from 37.1 percent of all exports to 31.4 percent, and preliminary figures for 1969 and 1970 indicate that this tendency continues.

Some point out that overall percentages may disguise the importance of foreign exports for particular U.S. industries. No doubt they do. But it is our view that the rise or decline of a particular industry, firm or groups of firms does not necessarily have special significance unless it can be shown that this industry or group controls, or strongly influences, U.S. foreign policy.

In 1958 only two industries exported more than 20 percent of their output: chemicals and fertilizers (20.5 percent), and construction, mining and oil-field machinery (26.9 percent). These are not, in dollar volume, large industries; nor are they politically potent groups.

In most industries exports furnished less than 10 percent of demand. When one takes into account that these figures are for all countries, *the actual market sales to low-income countries do not exceed 3 to 3.5 percent of the output of American industry.*

A more detailed breakdown demonstrates, surprisingly, that agricultural products constitute a very significant component of total exports. In 1970 farm exports are expected to total $6.5 billion, almost 20 percent of all overseas shipments.[2] This is a continuation of a peculiar structural change in the U.S. export pattern, away from sophisticated goods and toward agricultural and primary products, an export pattern characteristic of the less, rather than the more, developed nations.

Of the six major commodity groups, the one showing the highest percentage of exports to low-income countries is the agricultural group: 46.7 percent in 1968. High-income nations receive at least half the exports of all other types; and in the case of sophisticated products — motor vehicles, auto parts, civilian aircraft, and pulp-paper manufactures — the high-income nations receive 73.4 percent of these exports.[3]

It should also be noted that the existence of high or low levels of trade does not, in itself, demonstrate anything about imperialism. All nations of all social systems trade. The United States, although in absolute numbers a large trader, is, in relation to its economy, one of the smaller trading nations. It is outranked by Japan, England, Germany, Italy, France and a number of other countries. The important issue is the use to which a nation puts its trade. Therefore, it is not enough to show that a nation trades; one must show that trade exploits weaker nations. Thus, while it can be shown that the terms of trade favour *all* developed nations, the question to be answered is whether these benefits are so vital to the continued existence of the high-income imperialist nations that they cannot, for economic reasons, change this relationship.

Investments. Many find the strongest argument for the existence of economic imperialism to be the size of overseas direct investments. *In 1968 the total amount of overseas investment was $64.8 billion, a small percentage of the trillion dollars of all investments.*[4]

In 1964 low-income nations were the home of only 31.4 percent of all U.S. overseas investment — while the high-income nations absorbed almost 70 percent.[5] Furthermore, this percentage has declined since 1960, when low-income countries had 36.44 percent of overseas investment. This much-noticed changing trend indicates that the richer nations are finding it more profitable to do business with one another than with poorer nations.

In a comparison of the values of direct investments abroad in 1968 by selected countries and industries, one striking fact stands out.[6] In that year more than $2 out of every $5 (42.2 per cent) of U.S. investments in low-income nations were in petroleum. *If this were excluded, investment in all the poorer nations would be only 16.7 percent of U.S. total investments abroad. Yet, with this very high concentration of oil investments in low-income countries, absolute dollar investments are still greater in high-income than in low-income nations.*

Although the Latin American republics do contain considerable non-petroleum investments (particularly Brazil, Mexico and Argentina), these investments appear less massive when broken down by countries than when viewed in the aggregate for the region as a whole.

But are they at a level that requires the United States, for sheer economic reasons, to intervene to protect its investors from the threat of loss? Recent experiences with investments in Peru and Bolivia, and in Zambia and Libya in Africa, suggest that the State Department and the White House are less than eager, at this point to intervene militarily to prevent nationalization of U.S. privately owned properties. No Latin American country — with the exception of Venezuela (oil) — had in 1968 a very high percentage of U.S. investments in any particular field. Even the Venezuelan investment is less than 10 percent of all U.S. overseas holdings in petroleum — a figure that surprised us.

For the Third World the general conclusion is that, with the exception of some Latin American countries, non-petroleum investments are not high enough in any one country to warrant great economic concern by the United States. (The development of joint ventures, in which the poor country retains title to the enterprise, shares in its output, and at an agreed time assumes complete control, is a new factor and promises to affect the future investment picture importantly).

The effect on individual corporations. At this point it might be useful to point out again that we do not contend investments are not high for an individual U.S. company. When Chile nationalized Anaconda's copper mines in 1968 (and promised $500 million indemnification, which few expect will ultimately be paid), it cost Anaconda a large proportion of its earnings; its stock dropped over 60 percent in value. But that did not make it a national problem. It will help solve a national problem for Chile — which is good — but it is not of big enough proportion to affect negatively an economy the size of the United States. When Cuba, in 1960-61 unceremoniously liberated a billion dollars in U.S. fixed assets, not a ripple appeared in the U.S. economy.

A counterargument could be a version of the domino theory: investment in one nation may be low, but if it is lost in one, then other nations within the region may do likewise; therefore, an instructive lesson in deterrence is necessary. This is as much a political issue as a narrow economic one. We shall consider political issues in our concluding section, but we should point out here that the United States is already the victim of the domino effect. In financial circles there is considerable talk about the nationalization of the International Petroleum Corporation in Peru, Anaconda Copper in Chile, Occidental Petroleum in Libya, Roan Selection in Zambia; but there is no panic, except among speculators in those particular securities.

Income from investments. Magdoff points out that two other types of analysis strengthen the case for the importance of overseas activity to the domestic economy. One is the level of income from overseas investment; the other is the importance of imports.

The total of overseas investment income in 1968 was *just under $5 billion*,[7] compared with *approximately $90 billion* from domestic operations of companies. But this figure is for all countries. Income from low-income nations totalled $2.9 billion, *about 3 or 4 percent of the total income of companies in* *the United States.* In relation to 1968's GNP of $850 billion, "imperialist earnings" in the same years from the underdeveloped countries amounted to *a little more than .033 percent.*[8] In addition, this represents a steady decline in the importance of investment income from low-income countries. In 1950 they furnished 65.1 percent of the income from all overseas investment;[9] in 1964, 60.4 percent;[10] in 1968, 59.5 percent.[11] But the most striking fact is that *71 percent of the investment income from low-income nations derives from petroleum!*[12] *If we exclude petroleum, only a little over 14 percent of overseas investments income, or less than $500 million total, comes from low-income areas.*

These recomputations weaken the impact of Magdoff's startling statement: "By 1964, foreign sources of earnings accounted for about 22 percent of domestic nonfinancial corporate profits." We have not succeeded in breaking down this figure on earnings, but our previous analysis strongly suggests that rich countries make the substantial contribution to this outcome and that petroleum is the overwhelming source of profit from low-income countries.

Imports. A very strong argument can be made for the importance of overseas raw materials in American industrial production. Indeed, in "Scarce Resources: The Dynamics of American Imperialism," a Radical Education Project pamphlet, Heather Dean dismisses the arguments we have been analyzing and stresses the raw materials question exclusively:

> While not denying the existence of other economic motivations which are stressed by the Marxist left, I would argue that they are secondary to the total dependency of American production on foreign resources, that this dependency is sufficient in itself to explain U.S. policy, and that it leads to a fundamental conflict between the survival of the American economy in its present form and the drive for development in the Third World.

Magdoff, too, emphasizes the role of raw materials in U.S. overseas activities, but he does not consider it the dominant factor.

In both accounts, one is struck by the extent to which U.S. industries require basic materials, especially metals, from abroad and by the fact that projections of potential need increase U.S. dependence upon materials produced or extracted in other nations. Of course this argument cuts both ways. The low-income countries are vulnerable because they are low-income. But the high-income countries are also vulnerable because they are big consumers of raw materials. This suggests that low-income countries have some leverage against the imperialists. In recent years this has become evident in the Zambian copper nationalization, in much higher percentages for the low-income countries in petroleum deals, and in the nationalization of U.S. oil and copper properties in Bolivia, Chile and Peru.

We have not gone into this question in depth, but we believe we first have to learn which U.S. industries depend upon raw materials from which other nations. Of course, "depend" is an unspecific term; an item which is but 1 percent of the elements of a production process may be more significant than one which provides 20 percent of the process if it is difficult or very expensive to substitute another element for it.

This issue is basic to the question of "dependency", for it may be possible to shift the process of production to accommodate changes in the availability of costs of particular materials. Thus, the issue is not only the current significance of materials, but the difficulty or ease of substituting other materials for them. (Some obvious examples of substitutions are: synthetic rubber for natural, ceramics for high-temperature steel, aluminium for tin, and plastics for almost anything, including copper, especially in corrosive petroleum chemistry.) Nor should it be assumed that a particular product is used because it is the only one available. Cost factors are important in making choices. The unavailability of a particular commodity may not be a great problem; another may do as well, although at a higher price. And since raw materials are usually a small part of total costs, the resulting price rise may not be great. Even if it were, it need not be the main issue. U.S. publicly owned domestic shale oil reserves in the Rocky Mountain states are huge, amounting to 1.8 trillion barrels, 40 times other domestic reserves; and in the unlikely hypothesis that Latin American oil were not available, investment would be made in research and development to bring down the price.

Finally, on the question of oil dependency, Middle East petroleum, which is by far the largest income earner, is the one product on which the United States is *not* dependent. Middle East oil goes to Europe. The American source is domestic and Latin American. In the future it probably will be Alaskan and Rocky Mountain shale.

The question of substitution is also affected by possible shifts in the end-products of American industry which, in turn, determine what materials are needed. The main change, of course, could be a reduction in military production. Magdoff cites a 1958 U.S. Department of Defense list of strategic materials indicating the high importance of imports for military production. If public pressure is effective in reducing military expenditures and in changing military technology, many of these materials would become less significant. The need for nickel, tungsten, titanium, tantalum and other exotic metals for super-high-temperature military products would diminish markedly. Thus the demand for these and other materials is not unchanging.

It is, of course, wrong to approach the question of substitution as if one were suggesting the United States could or would adopt a policy of self-sufficiency. The substitution question is more serious for the low-income countries than it is crucial for the raw materials needs of the imperialist countries, as the matter is often placed. The issue is to find a way for the developing nations to exploit their own resources, deriving much greater revenue thereby, while recognizing that the market for this large raw materials output, for some time to come, will be in the developed — i.e., imperialist — nations. One does not expect Anaconda or the petroleum companies to cooperate in any such endeavor. But that does not mean it cannot be done without them. However, this is a political, not an economic, question and requires a separate study.

Implications. Let us recapitulate. Out of a total of direct investments abroad of $64.7 billion in 1968, 70 percent was invested in high-income countries — the Common Market, England, Canada, Australia and to a small extent, Japan. Only 30 percent, 18.6 billion, was invested in *all* the low-income countries. Out of the $18.6 billion invested, repatriated income was $2.9 billion.

What we question is that an economy approaching a trillion-dollar gross national product can, from any point of view, regard this $2.9 billion annually as critical to its existence. (Of the $2.9 billion in returned profit and interest, $2.1 billion is from petroleum investments, mainly in the Middle East).

If one were to believe that this less than $3 billion income is vital to the existence of imperialism, one would have to accept that it is a mighty extraordinary tail to be able to wag a trillion dollar dog.

We have been making a case against the imperialism argument, but a special kind of case. Our interest is focused on one question: How important is U.S. economic activity in low-income nations for the general level of economic production and growth in this country? We emphasize "general" for, obviously, particular firms or industries depend heavily on their activities in low-income countries, but the economy as a whole may not benefit to a marked extent from these activities. *Our conclusion — subject to closer study of the import question — is that the economy as a whole does not have a heavy dependence upon activities in low-income nations.*

This conclusion is similar to that of John Strachey in *The End of Empire*, and of Michael Barratt-Brown in *After Imperialism*, on British imperialism in the 19th century. Barratt-Brown argues that imperialism *retarded* the economic growth of Britain over the long run and that trade and investment in Europe and America and the developed parts of the Commonwealth (Australia, Canada, New Zealand, South Africa) were more significant than were trade and investment with the colonialized part of the Empire. Strachey stresses that the costs of maintaining the empire far overshadowed the economic gains from it. These arguments seem to have considerable validity in application to the United States. Foreign aid has been a cost to secure foreign trade. And the huge military costs so far outweigh the economic benefits of exploitation of weaker nations that one is compelled to consider whether political miscalculations rather than economic greed are not at the root of policy.

Much earlier this same perspective was debated at the Stuttgart Congress (1907) of the Second International. Both at the Congress and later, Rosa Luxemburg's contention that imperialism was a "historical necessity" of capitalism was attacked by Karl Kautsky. Kautsky argued, in the words of one of Luxemburg's recent interpreters, "that imperialism was not a necessary outgrowth of capitalism, but an abscess which the capitalist class as a whole would more and more wish to get rid of."[13] Kautsky's theory was that imperialism was a method of expansion supported by certain powerful capitalist groups (the banks and the armament kinds), contrary to the needs of the capitalist class as a whole; that expenditure on armaments reduced available capital for investment in the domestic economy. He argued further that the majority of the capitalist class would progressively increase its opposition to armed imperialist expansion. (We suggest the current attitude of Wall Street and big business to the Vietnam war is worthy of note, especially when Charles B. McCoy, president of DuPont, attacks the war for taking "a terrible toll in human life" and raises questions about the preservation of democratic values.[14] Or when Thomas B. Watson, Jr., of IBM tells a Congressional committee that the war presents "a major obstacle" to economic health and threatens "irreparable damage to society".[15] Or when Henry Ford II uses the forum of stockholders' meeting to attack the Administration war policy as harmful to American business.)

The Kautsky position, as thus described, comes close to ours, in contrast to the neo-imperialist position, which continues to stress Lenin's 1917 analysis of imperialism. It is our belief that it is *economically* possible to curtail military production and U.S. interventionism. To do so presents a political problem, but it is not economically foreclosed.

Put another way, it has been the inability of critics, up to this point, to develop sufficient political support — rather than the heavy weight of economic necessity — which has kept U.S. policy moving in one direction rather than another.

Barratt-Brown has stated the problem forcefully:

> While there may be good original economic grounds for policies pursued, the whole structure of institutions, ideas and purposes built up from these grounds takes on a life of its own and becomes its own justification. Those who claim to be Marxists need to be at least as Marxist as Marx in this matter and should not cite Marx's authority for the crudest type of economic determinism.[16]

For example, despite the importance of the oil companies and their overseas investments, they have not had unequivocal influence on U.S. policy in the Middle East since the formation of Israel. A strong case can be made that sheer economic interests and the political might of the oil companies should have led to Washington's support of the Arab nations rather than limited but unmistakable American support of Israel. Domestic political — not economic — considerations and the cold war led to the Pro-Israel outlook of U.S. foreign policy.

We do not argue that economic interests are unimportant, or that they do not at times influence or determine U.S. policies. Obviously they do. Our argument is different: we are unconvinced that the U.S. economy so depends on overseas activities that it must protect them, even by military actions.

How then explain U.S. interventionism — in Cuba, in

Vietnam? We think that today's interventionism springs much more from political-military than from economic roots. The cold war climate led to the imposition of "vital" military-political centers around the world, as in Southeast Asia, and to the defense or strengthening of those centers. A mindless anticommunism has considered any step toward radical change or revolution a pro-Russian, pro-Chinese, anti-American threat — a challenge to the American system — that must be confronted.

With the waning of the cold war, the prospective lowering of the "American profile" abroad, this counterrevolutionary reflex may also wane. Vietnam need not be followed by "other Vietnams". *If it is, the failure is political, not the result of inexorable economic necessity.*

The one clear-cut case where "economic necessity" appears vital is the oil industry. This is one mighty industry dependent on overseas profits, especially from low-income nations. Greater sensitivity to the behavior of this industry, particularly abroad; is urgent. As the recent Peruvian, Bolivian and Libyan examples show, there is already unwillingness, even in a Nixon Administration, to intervene militarily on behalf of oil companies. Close watch on the oil industry is essential, so that its imperatives do not become "economic necessity" and then political-military necessity for the nation. The oil industry should be totally nationalized, or turned into a public utility and regulated in the public interest. If progressive groups properly raised this issue, they would expose the very small political constituency of the oil barons.

The oil industry is politically vulnerable; they know it, and Congress knows it.

By the same logic, the armaments industry should also be nationalized. The public pays for it. Why shouldn't they own it?

Underlying our perspective is the contention that the U.S. economy could adapt to lower military budgets and a nonexpansionist policy abroad. Whether it does so or not largely depends, first, on the political strength to adopt policies that would expand the economy in other ways. If military outlays were cut, we do not doubt that policies could (not necessarily would) be followed which would produce growth rates of a relatively high level. We are less optimistic about policies to reduce inequality or improve the quality of life at home. For we do not see the problem of the U.S. economy as one of imminent crisis or collapse, but more in terms of whether or not it meets qualitative goals we think should be its target.

In general, we believe the economy has more flexibility than many left critics suggest. This does not mean that we are unmindful of the profound structural bias that operates against social change. However, this is not the place, nor is it our intention, to deal with the political strategy and tactics of turning the social system around.

We are aware that to assert that a billion dollars here or a billion dollars there is not significant sounds like playing with stage money. Any such sum is significant to those involved. Therefore, we are not arguing that economic activity between the United States and low-income nations is insignificant. Rather, our point is that this activity alone is not so dominating within our economy that political groups could not develop and offset the demands made by narrow, economically motivated interest groups. We do not think that the economy would collapse if particular economic interest groups were unable to control overseas U.S. political-military activities in certain areas.

A further note about high-income and low-income nations is in order. Our stress upon the relatively low significance of economic relations between low-income nations and the United States is not intended to downgrade foreign activities in the U.S. economy. The spectacular growth in U.S. foreign relationships is, however, with high-income nations. The most significant international economic institution — the multinational corporation — chiefly involves these countries. This development is likely to affect the American economy in many important ways. And one of its unfortunate effects may be, not further economic involvement with poor countries — which has helped as well as harmed them — but greater neglect of them. Rather than growing in importance for the rich nations, the poor countries are likely not only to fall further behind the rich but to become of even less concern to them. The rich will need one another more than they need the poor. Interventionism may be supplanted by unbenign neglect.

Fundamental changes. Finally, we believe a 19th-century approach to imperialism, or even the 20th-century variant of neo-imperialism, misses the truly fundamental changes that are going on in the contemporary capitalist states. Galbraith tried to deal with the new phenomena in domestic terms in his *The New Industrial State*, but the task remains for analysts to deal with the virgin territory of foreign economic relations and their meaning.

Surely there is something new in the fact that 25 years have passed since World War II and no major economic crisis has occurred in the United States. Something is new when some Western capitalist nations are growing faster than the socialist growth states of China and the Soviet Union; something is new when contradictions and struggles among the rich nations for markets and sources of raw materials have diminished rather than sharpened.

All this is not to suggest that the developed capitalist Western nations have resolved their contradictions. It is to contend that papering over Lenin's *Imperialism* with neo-imperialism does not begin to get at the new trends and developments taking place in the substructure of the world's economy.

A discontinuity, an abrupt change, has occurred in the functioning of the big industrial states since World War II. A simple linear projection of the past is not enough to explain the new phenomena. The degree of revolutionization of technology — its social, political and economic implications — requires a comparable revolution in thinking.

Along with Barratt-Brown we do not hold that imperialism has never been a paying proposition. As in Great Britain, there were periods when it paid, and very well indeed. But periods change. What we are suggesting is that classical 19th-century economic imperialism has become a costly luxury that is far more politically than economically oriented, and that this is especially true for the United States.

The qualitative character of the change is dramatically illustrated in the following: In the 19th century a brigade of British soldiers easily and inexpensively held an entire Indian province; and a handful of gun-boats dominated the whole of Mainland China. Today over a half million U.S. troops and $100 billion cannot hold a half sliver of a tiny nation in Southeast Asia, an area where the United States has no foreign investment at all.

A deeper study may suggest that U.S. imperialism since the 1890s was a product of a misperceived economic analysis, a belief that the domestic market problem could be solved only by expansion abroad.

The tempestuous growth of Japan and Germany in the postwar period, without foreign investments or colonies, suggests that solutions — other than the colonial, semicolonial and neo-colonial answer — are available for markets and raw materials. No one suggests that either West Germany or Japan has become less capitalist. But they may have become less imperialist, when imperialism is defined in the old terms.

It is worth examining whether some "unsolvable" internal market problems have not become susceptible to mitigation by different varieties of capitalist planning, as practiced in Western Europe or Japan. Japan's growth in living standards and GNP is rivaled only by the growth of her government-business-financial cohesion, to a degree unknown in the West. Indeed, there is some question whether there is as much directed, central planning in Peking or Belgrade as there is in Tokyo.

This question raises issues far beyond the scope of this small paper. But we hope the narrow slice we have chosen to point up will encourage others to delve more deeply than we have into what is manifestly a new and developing phenomenon.

FOOTNOTES

[1] Calculated from *Statistical Abstract of the United States*, 1969, p.808.
[2] Address of Assistant Secretary of Agriculture C.D. Palmby to the Sugar Club of New York, *The New York Times*, June 5, 1970.
[3] Calculated from data in *Statistical Abstract of the United States*, 1969, p. 805.
[4] *Survey of Current Business*, October 1969, p. 28.
[5] $13.6 million out of $44.3 billion total. This is $13 billion less than 2 percent of all U.S. invested capital at home and abroad. U.S. Department of Commerce, *Statistical Abstract*, 1967.
[6] *Survey of Current Business, op.cit.*
[7] *Ibid*
[8] We know that official figurs might be underestimates. But there is no way of adjusting for this. The point, however, is that even if one were to increase the return by doubling the figures, the relative importance of income or earnings remain small. The corporation profit figure (profit from all sources) does not include approximately $20 billion in interest income, $20 billion in rental income, and approximately $60 billion income of nonincorporated business.
[9] U.S. Department of Commerce, *Balance of Payments Statistical Supplement, 1950-1960*, rev. ed., 1963, pp. 186-187.
[10] *Ibid*
[11] *Survey of Current Business, op. cit.*
[12] *Ibid*
[13] Tony Cliff, *Rosa Luxemburg*, London, 1969, p. 34.
[14] *The New York Times*, June 4, 1970.
[15] *Ibid*
[16] Michael Barratt-Brown, *After Imperialism*, London, 1963, p. 204.

PART II

IMPERIALISM AND DEVELOPMENT

Introduction

Part II concentrates on a range of issues which today tend to be lumped together under the omnibus label, 'North/South conflict'. This complex conflict syndrome centres on the growing economic gap between the rich industrialised nations ('North') and the poor 'developing', 'under-developed', or 'less-developed nations', ('South').

Development

Various 'indicators' are used by contemporary theorists to describe the level of 'development' attained by a particular society. One of the most common, though in many ways least satisfactory, is that of g.n.p. (gross national product) per capita. (g.n.p. per capita simply measures the ratio of total societal wealth to that of the total population - it tells us absolutely nothing about the equality of distribution of that wealth. It is quite possible for a country to sustain high rates of growth of g.n.p. per capita while the income of large sections of the peasantry actually declines. This has been the case, to give just one example, during much of Mexico's economic 'boom' during the past decade.) Other indices of development measure the people's access, and equality of access, to such 'goods' as health care, housing, education, adequate nutrition, or employment. But whatever combination of indices is used, the situation of

Third World countries appears equally depressing. On almost every count the nations of Asia, Africa and Latin America which make up the Third World, are worse off than the industrialised world (we include here the Soviet Union and Eastern Europe). Compared with most Europeans, Americans or Australians the inhabitants of Third World countries endure far higher rates of infant mortality, susceptibility to disease, malnutrition, unemployment and illiteracy, while their income levels, life expectancy, and access to welfare services are all far lower.

The Third World

Some writers argue that the differences *between* Third World countries are so great as to render the term 'Third World' devoid of descriptive utility. The differences certainly exist and are important, there remain however, common characteristics which *do* serve to separate Third World countries quite sharply from those of the industrialised North. Certainly the governments of the Third World see *themselves* as having common problems and common goals vis-a-vis the industrialised nations and they use the term Third World for self-description. Among these governments there exists a fairly widespread consensus that moves towards 'closing the gap' are necessary; that the present international economic order is unjust and works to the disadvantage of an already disadvantaged Third World; and that the growing inequalities derive primarily from the selfish policies of the rich nations. On issues of common interest, Third World countries often vote as a bloc in the United Nations and at various international economic fora. The following characteristics taken together would make up the 'typical' Third World country. In noting these, it should be remembered that there are very many exceptions to the patterns described.

Economically Third World societies are predominantly rural, and dependent on farming techniques with low levels of productivity. There is little industrialisation and much of what exists is devoted to 'import substitute' industries whose main purpose is often to save foreign exchange rather than build up any developmental infrastructure. As a consequence some Third World countries build cigarette, beer and Coca Cola factories before fertiliser plants. To pay for those imports which are not easy to produce locally, and which tend to be consumed by service sectors and the members of the burgeoning state bureaucracies, Third World countries have to develop their own export sectors. Typically these rely on one or more commodities, such as coffee, cocoa, sisal, palm oil, or minerals (copper, bauxite, tin, diamonds). In contrast to the prices of the manufactured goods which they import, the prices of such primary goods and minerals tend to fluctuate widely with (according to the United Nations) a long term tendency to decline. This has the consequence of making long term planning difficult while causing much short term disruption.

Demographically Third World countries, with a few exceptions, have achieved a degree of death control without a commensurate progress in the area of birth control. The obvious consequence is the so-called population explosion, with Third World populations doubling every 25-35 years. Rates of population increase tend to cancel gains in economic growth. As a consequence of these trends, Third World countries in contrast to rich countries) have demographic profiles skewed towards youth, with around 50% of the population in many countries under the age of 20. Most countries (again with important exceptions) lack widespread basic literacy, while unemployment (and *under*employment) amongst the young is increasing.

In the *political* sphere we find high degrees of instability, frequent extra-legal changes of governments and a steady increase in military rule throughout the 1960s and 1970s. Civilian governments are now the exception rather than the rule in Africa and Latin America. Levels of inequality are consistently higher than in the industrialised countries and corruption is endemic - the latter often actively fostered by multinational corporations as illustrated by the recent Lockheed scandals.

Exacerbating the absolute deprivation of Third World poverty is the growing Third World awareness of increased *relative deprivation* vis-a-vis the industrialised countries. In 1972, the developing countries with 74% of the world's population, disposed of only 26% of its wealth. This inequality is increasing, indeed the 'growing gap' is the primary focus of the North/South conflict. In 1970, the average g.n.p. per capita in Africa and Asia was just over US$100; that of the developed capitalist states just over US$2,000. By the year 2000 if the present trends continue the poor country figure will stand at around US$500 while the rich country average will have arisen to nearly US$8,000. In the short and medium term, even those countries with *higher rates of growth* than rich countries are little better off. Even making the heroic assumption that the growth rate differential which favours the poor country can be maintained it would, in many cases, take hundreds, even thousands, of years to bridge the gap.

Aware of the implications of such projections, radical and some liberal development theorists have argued the need for a New International Economic Order (NIEO). In their most radical formulations, the NIEO proposals entail a massive redistribution of wealth from rich to poor nations. But in North/South negotiations in 1976 and 1977 the rich nations have shown the greatest reluctance to agree to even the mildest measures of redistribution. Many Marxist theorists would argue that it would be naive to expect anything else and that the way forward lies not in modifying the exploitative exchange relationships between the developed and underdeveloped nations but breaking them completely.

Overview of Part II.

The central questions pursued in each of the sections of Part II are those of *causation*. Why does the gap between rich and poor countries continue to grow? What *are* the underlying causes of Third World poverty? Answers to such questions range from crude racism - 'Africans/Asians are inferior/stupid/lazy' etc., to econometric models of Byzantine complexity and dubious relevance. The papers chosen in the second part of the reader contribute to the ongoing development debate from a number of different perspectives. The first two sections (i.e. Section V and VI) introduce two contending views of the causes of underdevelopment.

During the late 1960s and early 1970s many of the underlying assumptions of the previous decade's development theories were subjected to increasingly trenchant criticism. Oversimplifying considerably one can argue that the liberal development theorists (economists, sociologists, psychologists and political scientists) of the 1950s and early 1960s had tended to locate the causes of underdevelopment *within* the institutions of Third World countries, or the cultures of their peoples. The radical critique of this position argued a very different case. 'Underdevelopment' was not a state of being but a *dynamic process* the radicals argued. Third World countries were actively *underdeveloped* by rich country exploitation.

Liberal development theorists argued that the causes of underdevelopment were *endogenous* - that is *internal* to the countries concerned. The roots of the problem lay in the inadequacies of Third World social, political and economic institutions, plus a lack of capital. The solution was *external* - the diffusion of the missing ingredients - ideas, experts, technology and capital - from the rich nations to the poor.

For the radicals (sometimes Marxists but not always) the primary cause of underdevelopment was *external* exploitation. The prescribed solution however, was *internal* - a socialist revolution, the breaking of exploitative ties with the capitalist West, and (often) the emulation of China's autonomous development approach.

The papers in Section V examine the traditional view - that the primary barriers to development are located within the Third World itself. Those of Section VI introduce some of the arguments which locate the causes of underdevelopment in imperialist exploitation.

Section VII presents a collection of articles which centre on the most crucial problem facing a majority of Third World countries over the next two decades - the global food and population crisis. Once again we move into an area where virtually no scholarly consensus exists - even with respect to the severity of the problem. The critical questions include the following — Does 'overpopulation' cause underdevelopment or is it a *consequence* of underdevelopment? Is the problem lack of access to birth control technology or unwillingness to utilise this technology even when it is available? Can the problem of low agricultural productivity in the Third World be overcome by the Green Revolution - new inputs of high yield seeds plus improvements in irrigation and fertiliser application. Liberals have tended to believe that western provided technology, whether for birth control or the 'Green Revolution', *does* provide solutions to these problems; radicals disagree completely. The real issues, argue the latter, are not technological and political and the food crisis simply *cannot* be solved by Western capitalism's favoured technological solution - the Green Revolution. Poor peasants simply can't themselves afford the expensive 'inputs' which the Green Revolution requires, neither can they afford to buy the produce of the rich farmers. Secondly, it is claimed that the very notion of a 'food crisis' is mistaken. The *real* problem is the distribution of food within and between nations. With equitable distribution the 'food crisis' would disappear. But the problem of the *re*distribution of food - or wealth or land - is a problem of power, a problem of politics, and *not* simply a technical problem. Thus, argue the radicals, there can be no solutions to the basic problems of development without revolutionary political and social changes within Third World countries themselves.

In Section VIII we examine the Chinese approach to development and its relevance for the Third World.

SECTION V: INSIDE THE THIRD WORLD

Introduction

We now turn to examine some of the dimensions of the so-called North/South conflict. As noted in the introduction to this part of the reader, a very rough division can be made between liberal democratic theories, which locate obstacles to development *within* national boundaries, and radical theories which claim that development is blocked by external exploitation. The papers in this section concentrate on the former theories.

'Development', like 'imperialism', is a concept to which many different meanings have been assigned. Some theorists - and statesmen - equate the term largely with economic growth, others have stressed national independence and intra-national equality. However, there would be a general consensus that, whatever else it may mean, development must entail increases in the material wellbeing of the mass of the people. This in turn requires large increases in the production of goods and services.

It is occasionally argued that the redistribution of wealth and income can substitute for increased production. This is not the case. While the need for far greater equality - on a whole range of grounds - is unquestionable it is, in itself, not enough. In many Third World countries much of the wealth is tied up in artefacts which simply *cannot* be redistributed equitably - Mercedes Benz, motorways and prestige office blocks for example. Nonetheless, the often maligned indicator of g.n.p. per capita does serve one useful purpose - it tells us exactly what each person's income would be in any country if there were perfect equality of incomes. And a real income per head of less than $US200 - into which category fit 54% of the world's population - is inadequate under any conception of 'development'. Thus - with the exception of a few middle class ecologists in the West - there is almost universal agreement that more efficient and more productive economic systems are necessary. Furthermore, population increase and social change also mean that material progress cannot be achieved via the methods of 'traditional society'.

Among the liberal democratic theorists there has never really been any question of 'alternative paths' to development - capitalism and development were seen as synonymous - socialism was rarely mentioned. Achieving successful capitalist development required importing the ideas, institutions, technology and capital which the Third World countries lacked, and the absence of which formed the principal obstacles to economic betterment. According to liberal democratic theory, *under*development and the capitalist mode of production are *inversely* related. The greater the penetration of capitalist relations of production, the less the underdevelopment (radical theories make the opposite claim). The failure of Third World countries to achieve their development targets arises because 'traditional' social formations are continuing to resist the modernising imperatives of western-induced capitalism. To the problem thus defined the liberal theorists prescribe further diffusions of aid, technology, and so forth. Underdevelopment, according to this view, does not arise from too much foreign investment, but not enough. In this context it is sometimes argued that if the US aid programmes to the Third World were as generous as its aid to Europe after World War II, many of the problems of underdevelopment would disappear. The Marshall plan allocated 2.5% of America's g.n.p. to rebuild western Europe. Today a much richer United States gives only 0.25% of its g.n.p. to a Third World which is much poorer than was Europe immediately after the War.

However, the first two papers in this section are concerned primarily with the obstacles to development rather than solutions.

Peter Marris' paper focuses mainly on Africa although he claims that his central points have a wider validity. Marris argues that the constraints on development derive in part from the persistence of traditional values and the difficulties of adaptation to the modern world. But he also notes that the heritage of a now defunct colonial system has bequeathed political boundaries, institutional frameworks and values which may be inimical to progressive national capitalist development programmes. Marris seems to imply that *past* contacts with the West have left a legacy which often *constrains* capitalist development, while *present* contacts *facilitate* it. However, Marris is less concerned with the legacies of colonialism, than with the problems of transition from the traditional to the modern world. He argues that, 'The new institutions existed side by side with the old, eroding them but not replacing them, creating growing confusion and insecurity.' It is in the area of adaptation from old to new, of building new institutions and creating new values, that the major obstacles to development lie.

While Marris' paper examines what he believes to be universal problems of developing countries, economist J.K. Galbraith makes a different argument. There is no such thing as a typical underdeveloped country, Galbraith claims, and since the problems differ, so too must the solutions. However, there are common obstacles to development in different *regions* and Galbraith sets out three 'models of underdevelopment' which exhibit these. Model I is typical of the countries of sub-Saharan Africa. Here the *central* difficulty is diagnosed as a lack of education. Lacking sufficient graduates and technicians, the so-called modernising élite lacks the skills necessary to push through successful economic development programmes. Confronted by a small and ineffectual élite and inadequate infrastructures, the forces of 'traditional society' (on which Marris concentrates) successfully impede the modernising impulse.

Model II is typical of Latin America, and a number of countries in the Middle East and elsewhere. Here the problem is neither lack of education or training, nor lack of investment capital, but rather the parasitic nature of the ruling élites. The political powerbase of these élites derives from a range of economic activities (e.g. absentee landlordism, corruption, or investments overseas) which are 'non-functional' - i.e. antithetical to economic growth. Whereas Model I countries have élites which are too small, Model II countries have élites with the wrong values.

In the case of Model III, which is typical of South Asian

countries, there is an *over*production of the teachers, administrators, scientists and engineers which Model I countries lack, but there is also an overproduction of people generally. Overpopulation and the related land pressures, together with some of the 'non-functional' economic activities of Model II, form the core obstacles to development here.

While Marris and Galbraith are concerned essentially with problems and causes, President Julius Nyerere of Tanzania, focuses on solutions. Nyerere argues that while 'development' must increase consumption, the fruits of this increase must be equitably distributed, and the developmental process must be independent. Since capitalism produces the opposite - namely, domestic inequality and external dependency - the capitalist road to development must be rejected. In place of mass production there must be production for the masses; development must conform to the basic human needs of the people rather than the people being forced to conform to the needs of 'development'. An emphasis on basic human needs, rather than increasing economic growth, is now commonplace among development specialists whether in universities, United Nations agencies, or the World Bank. But few would accept Nyerere's flat affirmation that capitalism exacerbates development problems and that 'the rational choice' for development must be socialism.

Social Perspectives

Peter Marris

Long ago, a Kikuyu soothsayer predicted the coming of an iron snake spitting fire. The snake would bring a strange race, whose skin was the colour of a pale frog, and their dress like butterflies' wings. These fierce strangers, with the lethal magic sticks, would rule the Kikuyu until a certain giant fig tree died. The tree has duly withered and fallen, and the white rulers have gone. But the snake — the East African railway — remains, linking the highlands of Kenya to Lake Victoria and the Indian Ocean, carrying tea, cement, bags of maize, bacon and cotton cloth — goods unknown in the soothsayer's time — to countries he could scarcely have imagined. In less than one man's lifetime, the civilization of western Europe — in its greed and idealism, curiosity and aggressive nationalism — thrust itself upon the small-scale, self-sufficient societies of eastern Africa, destroyed for ever the traditional boundaries of their lives, and surrendered its responsibility. It brought a wealth of knowledge and technical skills: and their counterparts, awareness of ignorance and poverty. The colonial experience was both liberating and humiliating, denying what it seemed to promise, and profoundly disruptive — not only of ideas and relationships, but of the ecological balance of populations.

Nowhere else, perhaps, has the transition been as abrupt or

recent as in tropical Africa. Elsewhere an earlier history of trade or colonial settlement had established states or empires, sometimes created a more sophisticated aristocracy of landowners, a unifying religion, or washed a community of international traders on to the shores of an agricultural hinterland. And even within Africa, the scale of effective social organization varied — from the city states of the Yoruba to the Ibo villages, from the kingdom of Buganda to the intimate hills and valleys of Kikuyu country. But for all the diversity of their history and traditions, the possibilities of nationhood in a technologically sophisticated world seem to impose on all societies the need, for their own survival, to achieve a much larger scale of social organization than ever before. And those countries most conscious of their backwardness, where the need is most urgent, are also those where the obstacles are greatest.

Even to maintain the present standard of living of their people, many of the poor nations of Asia and Africa must exploit their resources more intensively, since their populations are growing by 2 or 3 per cent a year. At the height of her industrial expansion, Britain never faced so hectic a growth: nor did the children born in the slums of Manchester or London expect the rights which every nation now tries to promise to its children — education, medical care, protection from the exploitation of their labour. In the new nations schools and hospitals, humane industrial laws, have preceded the industrial growth that might sustain them. To educate and feed and care for this abounding population, to fulfil, even within a generation, some of the promises of nationhood, these poor countries have no choice but to expand their resources at a far higher rate than has ever been achieved before. And they cannot do this, unless they also reintegrate their societies upon a much wider scale.

Economic growth cannot, for the most part, be realized by extending the traditional manner of cultivation: there is now little idle land to bring into use. It depends upon specialization in marketable crops, the aggregation of land-holding, mobility of labour, diversification of occupation, the establishment of industry. And none of this will be possible without creating a pattern of social relationships far more wide-ranging, differentiated and complex, than those which served a society of peasant farmers, craftsmen and cattle-keepers. This specialization and diversification has to take place within a system of economic exchange international rather than national in scope. It means flying out-of-season strawberries to Fortnum and Mason, turning grazing land into tourist hotels for viewing wild game, mass-producing craft goods for shops in New York, London and Frankfurt. It means that those who can no longer subsist on family farms travel to sell their labour and their skills hundreds of miles from home, learning new trades, starting new businesses. There must be, too, a political and administrative structure wide enough in scope to gather and redistribute the product of this enterprise, allocating schools, hospitals, roads, development capital: and powerful enough to defend its trading interests in a competitive international community.

But the new nations face far more daunting obstacles than the industrial empires which set their aspirations, and established the system of international exchange through which they must realize them. Many of them are made up of heterogeneous populations of different language, race, culture and very unequal resources, contained within arbitrary boundaries. A tribe may be split by frontiers, while each part is expected to identify with fellow nationals who are wholly alien to their traditions. In Europe nationhood grew out of awareness of a common language and culture; linguists and collectors of folktales were the first heroes of the nationalism which broke up the Austro-Hungarian empire and remade the map of Europe. In Africa and Asia it was imposed from without, by the accidents of conquest.

The political boundaries of new nations do not, then, usually correspond with any tradition of social organization on so large a scale. Even where, in the past, an indigenous people have built an empire — as the Inca in South America or the Fulani in West Africa — they have seldom bequeathed much more than a romantic memory, or more insidiously, an essentially feudal structure incompatible with the development these nations are now seeking. Political leaders, especially in Africa, have sometimes appealed to the traditions of their society, seeing in customs of cooperation an example of the socialist principles they hope to establish: but the appeal is to an analogy, rather than a model. To translate the quality of village relationships to a nation, altogether new institutions will have to be created to embody them: the traditions of a tribe can be of little direct guidance.

The institutions of the colonial period are often unsuitable too, since they were not designed to promote a progressive economy under indigenous control. Until the last few years, most people in colonial Africa were discouraged or forbidden to take part in political life, education was preoccupied with training junior administrators, clerks, and technicians; economic policy was pre-occupied with a few primary products of value to the imperial power; and the administration was an alien bureaucracy, owing its first loyalty to the colonizing nation. Few new nations can find, either in their recent or more distant past, relevant models for their present needs — especially since older nations, too, as the inventiveness of technology carries us towards strange opportunities and strange problems, are less than ever confident of their own principles of organization.

The profound social changes which the poor countries of the world are now undergoing arise from the progress of a transition from small scale peasant societies to nations with a specialized but diversified commercial agriculture, feeding a complex of industrial production; where the pressure for quick results and the obstacles to be overcome are equally formidable; and where there is little experience to guide them. At the same time, these pressures generate their own reaction, as people seek to escape the demands of new and complex relationships they cannot handle. Tribalism, linguistic nationalism, nepotism, racialism all seek to limit involvement, to reduce the scale of life once more to manageable proportions, however crippling the economic cost.

In the pages which follow, I have tried to explore some aspects of this tension between the compelling need to expand and diversify the range of social relationships, and the desire to retreat, to simplify and guard oneself against its disturbing implications. The circumstances of poor countries of course vary greatly. Most of tropical Africa is free of any inherited caste or class system to constrain mobility, but unlike Asia has few traditions of highly developed crafts. The Caribbean has complexly intermingled race and class antagonisms, a legacy of slavery, but a longer experience of modern institutions. The states of Latin America are older than many in Europe. No general discussion can take account of all these differences. My examples are mostly taken from Africa. But the theme, I believe, is universal, and the struggles of emerging nations centre on it.

The Range of Economic Relationships

The changes in the conception of social relationships that must accompany this transition run very deep. In an African society of the past, for instance, where the economy was based on subsistence agriculture, economic, political and social organization were characteristically determined largely by lineage. A man's place amongst his kin, in one way or another, decided his entitlement to land, the authority to which he was subject, the women he might marry, his rights and duties. Even where no ties of blood or marriage were traced, terms of kinship often served to define relationship: by virtue of his age grade, or his clan, a man would salute as mother or brother members of his community outside his family. Elaborate — and very varied — systems of relationship structured the whole society, so that while some might be enemies, none were strangers; and every relationship embodied familiar rules of behaviour. Some of these rules seem to us bizarre — like the ritual hostility of 'joking' relationships, the acting out of kidnap when a bride (after months of negotiation between the families of the couple) is carried by force from her father's house, the avoidance of personal names in address. But they symbolize an understanding of the nature of society — of the balance of conflict and cooperation, the ordering of power and responsibility, the cross-cutting of allegiance — within which everyone could know his place. At the same time, the rules expressed through conventional behaviour were reinforced by myth and ritual, representing more abstractly the order of the universe and the legitimacy of the social order which reflected it. The system of thought and behaviour formed a whole. This tribal life is now disintegrating, sometimes only gradually, sometimes wholesale.

If the people who subsisted on this land are now to exploit it more intensively for national and international markets, they will have to master a far more complex social organization, extending to include more different kinds of people towards whom a person must behave with competence. They begin to form part of different systems of relationship which may have little in common, and may even be based on incompatible principles. In different situations, they may need to act from quite different conceptions of the nature of social organization.

Farming itself comes to involve cooperative societies — with registered members, committees, accounts, audits — marketing boards, produce inspectors, cesses, compulsory spraying, byelaws, land titles, planned investment and calculated returns. To manage his affairs, the farmer has to understand, and react appropriately to, strangers as well as neighbours, and an elaborate hierarchy of specialized institutions, each with its own system of permits, forms, regulations and personnel. As a member of a cooperative society, he has to vote in accordance with a constitution, guard his interests against fraud and appeal to courts of law or a government ministry if he is dissatisfied. It matters to him what happens in international crop auctions, what his government can negotiate at trade conferences. The relationships that govern his life are not only far more wide-ranging, but more limited to particular purposes, and more impersonal. And the same process of differentiation takes place within his family. Brothers and sons leave home in search of education and jobs, and become part of different occupational structures with different styles of life. Kinship is no longer the basis of society, but one strand amongst the many which draw people together or twist them apart. Behaviour is determined as much by the employment structure, the commercial network, the hierarchy of educational qualifications, the systems of justice, administration and political authority — each with its own pattern of relationships, values and institutions. This increasing scale and complexity of society means, too, that people have to react regularly to people whom they have never seen before, and may never see again; whose familiarity rests only on the position they hold — and who may be of other tribes, races, languages and cultures.

To master this new social environment, people have to be able to distinguish the behaviour appropriate to one system from another, even when the actors are the same — as when a nephew applying to his uncle for a public post must be treated simply as a candidate. And they have to agree on the nature of the relationship; and the expectations which should govern it. At the same time, since the transformation of society is continuous, they need to be quick to identify new kinds of relationship, establish their form, and to abandon those which no longer serve.

Consider, for instance, the progress of a village carpenter, as by shrewdness and determination his business grows. He may never have been to school, but learned his craft by casual apprenticeship from a friend of his father. He begins by selling to his neighbours, and buying his timber from local pit-sawyers. At first, his business is bounded by the village community, his commercial relationships contained within a familiar world. But if it is to expand, he outgrows the resources of this narrow circle. He needs capital which only a bank or government agency can provide, skilled employees, wider markets, machinery imported from abroad. These new assets are no longer provided informally within a system of intimate personal relationships, but by contract between strangers. He has to establish these commercial relationships on a basis of mutual trust, though his wholesaler, his employees, his bank manager may be of different tribes or races. At the same time, for his own protection, he has to segregate these commercial relationships from the claims of kinship. If now he agrees to oblige a friend or relative by employing his son, he risks a loss through bad work which may ruin him. Wasted wood and broken machinery cut his profit, raise his overheads, and land him in debt or without money to buy timber to fulfil his contracts. As a businessman, he has to treat kinsfolk as he would strangers, just as, in his commercial transactions, he has to treat strangers with the same sense of obligation as he bears towards his family. If the business grows still larger, the structure of relationships may change again, as personal ownership gives way to a limited company, with a formal directorate, audited accounts, shareholders' meetings, and the search for new markets.

The change implied by economic growth is not then, simply a change from one set of values to another — from love of cattle to love of money, from respect for seniority to respect for education, from faith in customs to faith in science — but a more profound change in the nature of social skills. Instead of absorbing, throughout childhood, a conception of the social world as static, bounded, and governed by principles which intermingle in every aspect of life, men and women grow up into a social world continually evolving, whose limits vary from situation to situation, whose principles are ordered differently for each kind of relationship, and change as functions are differently rationalized. To survive, they will need to be endlessly adaptable, to abstract underlying principles of organization from any particular time or place or purpose.

Reactions to Uncertainty

The older order was, by its nature, adapted rather than adaptable. Its conception of life was expressed through specific acts, rituals, myths, externalizing and particularizing its understanding. It could have little immediate resilience in the face of new circumstances. The intrusion of alien institutions — schools, hospitals, money — at once shook its foundations. Education began to offer to a few young men authority and wealth which affronted the political rights of elders, and challenged the accepted meaning of seniority. Money changed the nature of control, substituting a fluid resource for a fixed asset. Where, for instance, bride-wealth was traditionally paid in cattle, it served as a bond between two families, guaranteeing their concern for their children's marriage. For if the young bride behaved badly, her parents would lose the cattle they had received for her, and if the fault lay with the husband, his family stood to lose both daughter-in-law and the bride-wealth they had paid for her. But once money was substituted for cattle — or cattle became readily saleable — the bride-wealth became hard to reclaim: it disappeared into someone's pocket. And the same with means of livelihood: if a wife was entitled to land, for cultivation, from her husband and his family, she was secure in her possession, As this became instead a right to support from her husband's income, she was much more at his mercy. She could turn for redress only to the alien system of courts and maintenance orders, which lay outside her experience, and were as likely as not unenforceable.

But though schools, money, taxes, trade goods were at once disruptive, they did not put any viable alternative in the place of the relationships they were undermining. They formed part of the social system of the colonizing nation, but they intruded upon the colonized piecemeal, as fragments of an alien society, whose consequences were scarcely considered. Children went to school to discover the powerful secrets locked in written words: no one foresaw, or even wanted, perhaps, the overthrow of the whole basis of tribal authority. The new institutions existed side by side with the old, eroding them but not replacing them, creating a growing confusion and insecurity.

This uncertainty about the nature of relationships is very hard to tolerate. In order to survive, a man must be able to predict how others will react to his behaviour, and how they expect him to react to theirs. Unless he can do this, more or less successfully, his behaviour disintegrates: he becomes increasingly withdrawn, or frantic, ultimately becomes apathetic and even dies. In the Nazi concentration camps, for instance, the administrators deliberately created a capricious and unpredictable social environment, to destroy the personality of their prisoners: very few could withstand for more than a year or two this relentless social bafflement. Life becomes a nightmare, once the obligations and expectations of relationships cannot be foreseen with any confidence. An African farmer, on trial for murder before a colonial court, cried out 'For God's sake kill me and have done with it, I can't stand any more of this': the artificial procedures of British justice were to him incomprehensible, and therefore cruel, even while they attempted to protect his legal rights. The new and unfamiliar therefore generates profound anxiety, which must quickly be contained, either by avoidance or by assimilating these relationships to something intelligible from the stock of experience. However great the potential advantage, however stagnant or crumbling the old order, change is a threat to the integrity of personality: nor are those who have most to gain necessarily the same as those whose confidence in their mastery of the social situation will be most painfully disrupted. The reaction against change is obstinate and continuous, arresting and distorting the process of evolution.

At the outset, a society may refuse altogether to respond to the demands of economic development, protecting its traditional ways — as, for instance, amongst the Masai of East Africa. The cost is isolation, increasing relative poverty and political impotence. Any member of the society who rejects this conservatism can no longer find a place within it, so that a way of life becomes a policy of resistance, unable to meet the forces it opposes on any common ground.

But more common, and more insidious, is a kind of conservatism which tends towards rigidity. It does not reject new institutions, but in the anxiety to re-establish stable relationships, emphasizes their formal structure at the expense of their purpose, and clings obstinately to them. Schoolteachers resist changes in teaching methods and curriculum; administrators perpetuate the conventions of colonial bureaucracy; professionals and technicians trained abroad follow the practices they have learned without re-examining them in their home environment. This displacement of concern from the ultimate aims of an organization, to the preservation of the organization for itself, is the universal disease of bureaucracy. But the newer and more insecure these organizations are, the greater the risk that routine will become an end in itself — a brace to hold up the fragile confidence of the insecure official, and free him from the burden of personal decision. Policy, interpreted in organization, quickly becomes ritual. An Indian agricultural training centre, say, intended to give practical guidance, dwindles into a course of irrelevant formal lectures bounded by the classroom, and no amount of encouragement will get the teachers out into the fields, demonstrating their techniques. Institutions which may be neither appropriate nor efficient obstinately survive.

Most damaging of all, people may give up the attempt to integrate their behaviour on a scale large enough to sustain development, restricting their concern to some smaller and more homogeneous group. The group may be an elite, seeking to pre-empt educational opportunities and the best jobs; a race or privileged class; a tribe or a family. Even nationalism itself, where it retreats from the need for international cooperation, frustrates the chances of economic growth. This tendency towards secession has been the most obvious threat to new nations — in the Congo, Nigeria, the break-up of the Caribbean Federation, linguistic nationalism in India — and it represents, best of all, perhaps, the social dilemma of people in new nations.

For tribalism, in this broad sense, is both a rejection of the wider society, and a means of defining one's place within it.

Tribalism as Adaptation and Rejection

In an account of his father's life, a Nigerian Ibo writer has described the career of a village pioneer of change.[1] His story shows very clearly how tribal loyalties can adapt under the stress of change to fulfil new functions, and how tribal membership begins to acquire a new meaning within the framework of a nation. But the recent history of Nigeria also shows how disastrous the consequences can be.

This village pioneer was the first child of his community to seek an education from the missionaries. He met strong disapproval. His parents refused to support him, and he was driven to cultivate tabooed bush to feed himself while he studied. With courage and determination, he withstood the hostility of his family and the ostracism of his age-mates, and learned enough to become in time a post office manager. So, as a young man, he fought the prejudices of his community, willing to become an outcast rather than abandon the promise of new ideas. But later he began to see how these ideas, and the administrative changes of the colonial regime, were threatening to demoralize his people. Respect for traditional authority was giving way as chiefs became corrupt, and colonial government distorted the former basis of their legitimacy. Disputes which had once been settled by discussion now went into litigation. And as people left the village to settle in cities like Lagos and Port Harcourt, they neglected home affairs. So he, and local leaders like him, set out to re-establish the unity of their community — to restore its ability to handle conflict, overthrow corrupt authority, and bind together those who stayed at home and those who had gone in search of new opportunities in the towns. In the 1940s they formed an association, to which every villager was to belong, whose aims were both integrative and progressive. It forbade anyone to take disputes to court, without first submitting them to the association for settlement, and instituted a 'general return home' every third year — when everyone, whether he was working in Lagos, Enugu, Port Harcourt or the north was to return with his family, or face a substantial fine. The association also promoted a market and postal agency in the village, raised money for scholarships, and contributed several thousand pounds towards a cottage hospital. Its branches sprang up in every major city, meeting regularly, attending to the welfare of its members, and collecting contributions for development at home.

Tribal unions of this kind grew up all over Eastern Nigeria, and became an important basis of organization, not so much to conserve a cultural tradition as to meet a variety of new needs. They served to integrate city and village, to mediate between colonial institutions and traditional ways, and to recruit resources to exploit new opportunities for education and health. But their very success tended to forestall the possibility of integration on a larger scale — not because these unions were intrinsically hostile to national unity, but because the effectiveness of their organization seemed to threaten that they might dominate the whole of Nigeria. The adaptability of their sense of community, which had been so powerful an advantage, also stamped that advantage with a tribal mark, and made them tragically vulnerable.

Tribalism, as a sense of identity with people of the same language and culture, or local patriotism, can in itself be integrative and constructive — though it seems that only some peoples, whose traditions of social organization were always relatively individualistic and flexible, are able to exploit it as effectively as the Ibo. But it has also a more negative aspect: the rejection of outsiders. In this sense, tribal membership no longer defines the structure of relationships within which a person acts out his life; rather, it defines an aspect of his relationship to others in a social environment which includes many different tribes. When a newcomer arrives in a city, in search of work and shelter, it provides an immediate frame of reference by which to find his place. Where is he to stay? Who can he approach for help? Where should he inquire about a job? The obvious answer is his countrymen. At the same time, he can make at least a crude adjustment to the strangers about him, in terms of tribal stereotypes.

Stereotyping seems a universal device for structuring an unfamiliar environment. It enables one to make assumptions about a stranger's behaviour from the most casual acquaintance. Accent, dress, race, language are taken to imply a whole range of characteristics, arranging others in degrees of acceptability. But these stereotypes are always more or less hostile, since their purpose is to rationalize avoidance: other tribes eat disgusting food, follow dirty practices, are lazy or lying or thieving. The stereotypes can therefore be very tenacious. People cling to them to excuse their inability to establish relationships of mutual understanding with people who speak different languages and follow different customs. The unsophisticated may never make enough acquaintance outside their own people to challenge their prejudices. But even amongst the most educated, every frustration — quarrels at work, disappointment in promotion, being cheated of a bargain — is likely to revive them. This pervasive latent hostility to strangers, once it becomes associated with tribal or racial classification, is profoundly dangerous. In the face of insecurity and disappointment, people project the threat outwards, so that the danger is no longer within themselves — an inability to meet the demands of their environment — but from outside. Tribal stereotypes provide ready-made enemies against which to turn. Contempt becomes anger, and people begin to see other tribes — often quite irrationally — as the source of their difficulties. The appalling atrocities committed on the Ibo in Northern Nigeria were possible partly because the northerners saw the Ibo as scarcely human: their stereotype had been distorted into something that no longer deserved ordinary human decency.

Even so, the tragedy might never have happened if the Ibo had not also been conspicuously associated with a position of advantage. They held many of the clerical and administrative positions in the north, pre-empting jobs which the northerners felt should be for them. In the same way, the Asians of East Africa were vulnerable because of their control over commerce. Where an economic grievance can fasten, with more or less justification, on a tribal or racial group, the combination can easily lead to a violent outburst so disruptive that it destroys the very economic opportunities at issue.

The Ibo experience illustrates both the value and risks of tribal identity as a principle of adaptation. Confidence in and respect for the culture in which he grew up helps a man to master new situations without feeling that his essential personality is going to pieces. And there are aspects of life to which this identity remains appropriate within a wider society — the economic progress and welfare of his home district, local politics, the introduction of newcomers to city life. But if it extends to become an all-embracing principle of organization, it turns into separatism. Whenever an inherited structure of relationships successfully adapts to new functions, there is a risk that some kinds of activity will become restricted to the racial or cultural group from which this structure arose, and sharpen group antagonisms. Tribalism has to be contained by cross-cutting loyalties based on other principles. The evolution of a society able to carry the demands of economic development depends, then, on the ability to discriminate the system of relationships appropriate to each activity, and find your identity within it — as a member of a tribe, as a professional responding to the principles of a vocation, as an entrepreneur responding to the demands of a commercial system. The danger is that people will be unable to handle the strain of these multiple identities, and try to merge them. The danger is all the greater, because their past has handed down to them so little in common.

The Disjointedness of Change

So far we have discussed the transition to a larger scale of social organization in terms of the insecurity it generates. But the defences against perplexity and disintegration — withdrawal, rigidity, separatism — are compounded by the disjointedness of change. Innovators are always adapting to a society not yet created, at the risk of making their situation untenable in society as it is. The farmer who plants crops for sale may stand to earn more. But he may also thereby opt out of a traditional system of exchange by which people supported each other in times of want. In times of distress, he finds himself without friends. Even his prosperity may generate so much jealousy that his plans are defeated. The risks of innovation can, then, look very different to the agricultural planners in a government ministry, and the farmers who are expected to implement them. As chapter nine describes, traditions of cultivation are a subtle and expert adaptation to the circumstances which govern a subsistence farmer's life, and he will not abandon them lightly for the advice of an agronomist who does not know his community or understand the constraints under which he takes his decisions. The planners are thinking of yield per acre in the long term: the farmer has to consider what will happen if his crop fails next year, or if envious rivals burn down his grain store.

Nor are the risks of innovation always borne by those who choose them. A sophisticated couple who marry across caste lines may live happily enough in a Bombay suburb, while their families at home are ostracized. Between city and village, between economic systems and systems of social insurance, the unevenness of change leaves incompatible principles of organization unreconciled.

Just as vainglorious governments sometimes build pretentious monuments to their modernity, which stand incongruously amongst the shacks and rutted lanes, waiting for the nation to catch up with them, so the institutions of the state may be sharply at variance with the prevailing standard of life. In most African nations, the salary and privileges of the civil service remain those of the colonial regime, and within that salary structure, conform to a continuous gradation of reward. In the context of African society, they represent not two or three times the average wage, but ten or twenty times. The disparity between the style of life of the urban elite, who govern and educate the future governors, and those they govern is profound; and in future generations there will no longer even be the bond of a common childhood experience. For those in power, like everyone else, herded their father's goats, and walked barefoot to the village school between their mothers' plots of maize and beans. But there are children growing up in Africa now, to whom it is natural to go to school in a Mercedes-Benz, and to come home to cake and Coca-Cola on the drawing-room carpet, watching television. These privileges have not grown up from a selfish exploitation of power, however self-interest may help to sustain them. They arise because different parts of society are framed in quite different orders of value. A university graduate who enters the civil service, works with foreign advisers, prepares reports for representatives of the World Bank, attends international conferences, does not see himself as privileged, but only as living the life of government servants anywhere in the world. To deny him this is an affront, implying that he is not as worthy as his international colleagues — and a humiliation for his country too, that it cannot sustain a sophisticated modern bureaucracy. The values against which he judges his self-respect, and what is due to it, have only the most tenuous links with the world of a peasant farmer. Each conceives life in different terms, and though they work for each other, their behaviour may be mutually unintelligible.

The Range of Language
Most of these problems of change are not peculiar to new nations. Bureaucratic rigidity, racial antagonisms, separatism, conflicts over redundancy and growing disparity of incomes are familiar enough in the most industrialized countries, and seem to arise from a similar reaction against the growing scale and complexity of the economic system on which society is based. The difference lies partly in the abruptness of the transition. The son of a village elder represents his country at the United Nations: in one generation, the scope of relevant relationships breaks out from a circle of hills, a plain, to cover the whole world. There is a crippling shortage of people with knowledge or experience to master the problems of transition. Some countries faced independence with scarcely a single university graduate trained to take over the responsibilities of administration. But

there is one crucial handicap, characteristic of these new nations, which makes the problems of integrating a national society very much more difficult. Unlike the industrial countries, they lack an established common language which everyone can read and write.

Unless most people are literate in a national language, it becomes much harder to communicate ideas at every level, and much more expensive. If a farmer cannot read the instructions on a tin of insecticide, an agricultural officer must call and explain them — and this might be an assistant who cannot read them himself and who, in the process of memorizing them translated into his own language, has got them wrong. The quality of what is communicated becomes distorted by translation, cruder and more fragmented, and more readily misunderstood. Once the scale of society outgrows the range of personal relationships, written words become the vital link between individuals and the institutions of their society. And these words must embody, not only practical instructions but the conception of the social order which the nation is struggling to evolve. It would be virtually impossible to convey these through the language of any small-scale society, let alone communicate them in several languages at once. For the language of the nation must express, not only new ideas, but a different logic from the languages of the past.

In tribal society, the principles of life are conveyed through ritual and conventions of behaviour, not abstracted from them. In a relatively static society, with familiar boundaries of experience, proverbs, myths, the natural environment provides elements of argument from which a skilled orator can elaborate a subtly structured speech. But the logic of this structure can scarcely be grasped by an outsider, even when the literal sense is translated. The juxtaposition of the elements of the argument are meaningful only within a particular world of experience. The language lacks the kind of abstract concepts which can be universally applied, irrespective of a familiar situation. But it is impossible to interpret the principles of life in a large-scale, complex, changing society except in these more abstract terms. Even the ideas of political independence and freedom themselves could often be conveyed in the languages of the people who fought for them only in a sense which profoundly distorted their meaning. And conversely, if different tribes are ever to understand each other, their different cultures will have to be interpreted in terms which make sense to them all. Thus the language in which people communicate becomes one of the most powerful forces binding or dividing groups, making intelligible their structure and variety, and defining their limits.

But to achieve a society literate in a common language, there must be competent teachers with a relevant and adaptable curriculum, and therefore good colleges to teach them, and able administrators in the ministry of education. The more urgently schooling is extended, the worse its quality is bound to be, while talent is so scarce. If untrained teachers, unable to master their role, reduce their classes to a ritual incantation, if success in formal examinations of artificial knowledge become the accepted ladder to positions of power, then the conservative rigidity we discussed earlier can cripple the progress of society as well as ignorance itself. Educational policy is caught between the need for an intelligent elite, able to guide society through its evolution, and the risk that such an elite may be unable to communicate or even sympathize with the mass of the people they are leading. All the frustrations and promises of change converge upon education, so that who should get schooling, for how long and in what language are passionately debated.

The Search for National Integration

Throughout this discussion, we have tried to trace the social implications of an economic logic which impels poor countries towards a larger, more complex, more differentiated and adaptive structure of relationships, where in the recent past there existed neither common institutions, nor even the words to conceive their present situation. This structure cannot help but be at first very fragile and disjointed. Its uncertainties and unfamiliar demands generate powerful reactions, which can stultify progress, and break the nation into pieces, as people seek refuge in a more manageable world of experience. In the face of these threats, there are essentially two conceptions of how an integrated national society can evolve. One concentrates on unity, the other exploits the conflicts of diversity, and each largely excludes the other. Each derives from a different aspect of the problems we have discussed. There is a need for a common language, a common set of principles by which to articulate the relationships of society as a whole: there is also a need to differentiate the conventions and interests proper to each activity, to separate the loyalties which should govern one kind of relationship from those of another. In styles of government, in argument and development strategy, one or the other aspect seems to preoccupy attention. So, for instance, Tanzania and Kenya, though their problems have much in common, approach them with a consistently different emphasis. Tanzania stresses a common language and an articulate national ideology, impatient of tribalism, sectional interest, independent trade union pressure or the claims of an administrative elite. All activities are ideally subordinate to an over-riding party which embodies the national purpose. Kenya pursues the politics of coalitions of interest, encourages private enterprise, tolerates the independence of trade unions, and is moving towards vernacular teaching in its primary schools. Not that either nation, by its history and the complex of its political circumstances, could freely have chosen to follow the example of the other. But in each of them, the sense of how the nation should evolve seems to be dominated by a different principle, with strengths and weaknesses the other lacks.

The preoccupation with national unity leads towards the goal of a radical transformation of every section of society, based on common principles. Such a policy assumes a national ideology persuasive enough, and backed by sufficient sanctions, to bring about a fundamental reconstruction of social relationships. Its boldness is attractive, especially in former colonies where so much of the accretion of recent history can be seen as a humiliating alien imposition. And since it is seldom possible to make fundamental changes in one aspect of life without parallel changes in many others, its universality promises escape from the interlocking constraints of accepted ways of life. But it has also serious drawbacks.

If the nation is to be integrated by pervasive ideology, nothing that formerly defined relationships can any longer be taken for granted. A new, comprehensive code of behaviour extends to every aspect of life, and people must redefine their part according to it. New rules are needed for husbands and wives, parents and children, for the arts and sports, as much as for economic and political relationships. If people are to understand each other these rules must be propagated explicitly and unambiguously, and everyone must accept them, just as they must accept the rules of language. Any radical social reconstruction, undertaken consciously as a coherent whole, is necessarily dogmatic and intolerant. Otherwise it claims to invalidate all past experience, without replacing it by any sufficiently predictable code of behaviour to govern relationships.

But there are all kinds of issues which cannot be solved by any dogmatic prescription — centralization or decentralization of organization; priority for agricultural or industrial development; mass participation or the training of an elite.

Society has to alter course as it runs into difficulties. The dogmatic style of a unifying ideology makes these adjustments difficult. The need to replace the certainty of the familiar with a corresponding certainty of doctrine makes for a rigidity which adapts awkwardly and abruptly to its mistakes. A definition of social relationships, explicit enough and enduring enough to give their citizens a secure sense of their own identity within the system, also imposes a constraint which handicaps adjustment to circumstances and experience.

The pursuit of national integration through a common language, a common framework of ideas leads on towards an authoritative ideology. It centres the structure of relationships on a core of master principles which, if they are not viable, bring everything down with them. The alternative is to integrate society through the cross-cutting loyalties to which everyone is subject, and ally him now with one grouping, now another. As a member of an occupation, a man is loyal to his trade union; as a churchgoer, loyal to his denomination; as a tribesman, loyal to his compatriots. So long as each brings him into association with a different group, the potential disruptiveness of the conflicts into which any one such loyalty may draw him is checked by his need to maintain his ties also with others. The conflicts themselves then become integrative rather than disruptive, because the over-riding need to reconcile them creates means of arbitration. And acts of arbitration are amongst the most sensitive means of evolving pragmatically the principles of a social order.

As a conception of how a national society can evolve, this alternative calls for a great variety of formal associations — professional bodies, tribal welfare societies, trade unions, student groups, chambers of commerce, cooperative unions — each concerned with a specific aspect of life; and secondly facilitating agencies, such as advisory services, to help people understand the demands of unfamiliar relationships. It is little help to a man to be formally a member of a trade union, a shareholder in a company, a cooperative farmer, if he does not understand how it can serve his interests, and how to exercise his rights. And he must understand too what interests it cannot serve — that it concerns him only as an employee, a shareholder, a farmer, relating him to society in that aspect of his life alone. The gravest danger to this whole conception of integration arises when these various interests converge. So long as the tribe, for instance, is only one amongst many groups which lay claim to loyalty, it is no more disruptive than religion, class, politics or profession.

But if tribe and religion, or tribe and occupation, come to coincide, if political loyalties are based on ethnic ties, or members of a tribe are identified with a privileged class, then too many conflicts, rational and irrational, are drawn together in a single confrontation.

There is a risk, too, that a society integrated through the cross-cutting loyalties of functional groupings will correspondingly lack means to sustain faith in its underlying unity. Because its manner of integration is structural rather than ideological, and emphasizes the arbitration of conflict, its symbols of national unity and purpose may be poorly articulated and unimpressive. Impatience with the frustrations of conflict and compromise may provoke a reaction towards more authoritarian rule. Indeed, the evolution of society seems likely to proceed at first by violent swings between the stress on over-riding unity, and the encouragement of autonomous institutions representing the diversity of interests and functions. But in the long run, as the mediation of conflict creates over-arching principles of law and constitution, or a revolutionary movement settles into an established division of functions, the two approaches to integration must converge. Otherwise, either remains precarious.

If this is so, we can begin to see the kind of social criteria which should be most relevant, in assessing a country's chances of sustaining economic development. Is there a common language, and how many people can read and write it? Are there means of communication — newspapers, radio, advisory services, political discussion — which reach the villages, and can they also carry the villagers' response? Within an income group, an occupation, how well are the different tribes, races or religions of the society represented? Do associations representing different activities and interests exist, and if so, are they genuinely differentiated and autonomous, or merely instruments of an extraneous, more powerful interest — political, perhaps, or tribal? Are there means to resolve conflicts by principles and procedures independent of personal political authority? Is education open to children irrespective of their class or region? Is recruitment to occupations governed by criteria relevant to their performance, or by some other standard of acceptability? And finally, we can ask just the same kind of questions about the institutions of international relationships, on which the chances of development equally depend.

The Causes of Poverty: A Classification

J.K. Galbraith

I

As concern with the problem of economic development increased in the years following the Second World War, and especially as it became a subject for research, for what is called research and of instruction in the universities, there appeared also a tendency to divide the world according to the state of well-being. The rich countries were the developed countries. The poor were the underdeveloped or — where tact was thought more important than accuracy — the developing countries. (Many of them were not, in fact, developing very much and none of the developing countries was developing as rapidly as the developed countries.) It became the habit, both in looser political discussion and prescription as well as in ostensibly more precise pedagogy, to speak of the needs and problems of *the* underdeveloped country. They were assumed to have enough in common so that as 'the descriptive literature on such countries suggests ... we may confidently describe "a representative underdeveloped country".'[1]

This tendency to speak of a typical underdeveloped country, and to prescribe for it, has, with some modifications, continued.

The corollary is the supposition that there is roughly common therapy applicable to such countries as a class. Men will devise policies that are meant to be applicable generally to underdeveloped countries; they will continue to say, as they often do now, 'This is what an underdeveloped country should do.'

Or this will be the tendency. But, in fact, there has long been a considerable differentiation in the prescription for the poor countries. India, in *per capita* income, is almost as poor as any country in Africa. Yet we recognize that her capacity to use capital is much greater than most of them enjoy. In the years since the Second World War she has absorbed, in the main usefully, somewhere between a third and a half of the capital assistance available through public channels to the poor countries. And with mention of India, the problem of population comes almost immediately to mind.

The African countries, for their part, have been strongly interested in education. And gradually a design for development is emerging which places primary emphasis on this. And this is in contrast, in turn, with the seeming requirements of many of the Latin American countries where social reform occupies a place of particular urgency. Though in analysis we still speak of the underdeveloped country, for purposes of prescription we make important distinctions. There is need, evidently, for bringing the analysis abreast of the differentiation that practical judgement requires.

II

Some years ago at Harvard, we began experimenting with a classification of underdeveloped countries that is based on the obstacle or combination of obstacles which, in the given case, is the decisive barrier to economic advance.[2] The classification is a fourfold one. Three classes are important for present purposes; the fourth embraces the countries where there is no strongly operative obstacle to development and where, accordingly, it proceeds more or less reliably. It is useful for fixing thought to give each of the classes or models not only a number but an identification with the part of the world to which it is most applicable. Its application is not, however, confined to the geographical or other area in the designation. The three models of underdevelopment are:
    Model I. The Sub-Sahara African Model
    Model II. The Latin American Model
    Model III. The South Asian Model

There are also, as might be expected, intermediate or mixed cases. And the geographical designations do not include all of the countries of the area. Ceylon is not typical of the South Asian Model; Ghana, Nigeria and Kenya are not fully characteristic of the Sub-Sahara African Model; Mexico, Costa Rica and Cuba do not conform to the Latin American Model; and Brazil, a notably difficult case, conforms more closely to that model in the northern than in the southern states.

III

In the Model 1 or Sub-Sahara countries, the principal barrier to development is the absence of what I shall call a minimum cultural base. It is important, both for reasons of tact and precision, that this should not be misinterpreted; the problem is not absence of aptitude but absence of opportunity. Most of the countries that are described by this model have recently emerged from colonialism, sometimes of the more regressive sort. More fortunate countries have had decades and centuries of preparation for the tasks of economic development. These have had only a few years.

To an extent unmatched in most of the underdeveloped world, positions of skill and responsibility [in Africa] were until recently in the hands of non-Africans ... As late as 1958 there were only about 8,000 Africans graduated from all the academic secondary schools below the Sahara, and only about 10,000 others were studying in universities — more than half of these in Ghana and Nigeria ... in 1962 there were still few African countries where more than two hundred Africans received full secondary diplomas.[3]

When the Republic of the Congo gained independence, there were fewer than 25,000 Congolese with any secondary education and only about thirty Congolese university graduates. The first university, Lovanium, had opened only in 1954 and only thirteen Africans had graduated by 1960.[4]

The consequences of an inadequate cultural base are comprehensive — on government, the economy, internal security, communications, even foreign policy. But the most visible manifestation is on the apparatus of government. People with the requisite education, training and honesty for performing public tasks are unavailable. As a consequence, taxes are collected in haphazard or arbitrary fashion and public funds are spent inefficiently or for no particular purpose except the reward of the recipients. Where this is the case, government will ordinarily be unstable; those who do not have access to public income will have a strong incentive to seek to oust those who do. As a further consequence, law enforcement is unreliable; and so, at a minimum, are essential public services. In this context, in turn, there can be no economic development that involves any sophistication in technique or organization.[5] Primitive and local trade will flourish under almost any handicaps. But larger-scale commerce and industry — the modern, large, technically advanced corporate enterprise — are more demanding in their environment; their persons and property must be reasonably secure; their property cannot be hidden and if taxed merely because it is visible, it soon becomes inoperative; their business cannot be transacted in the absence of posts, telephones and common carrier transportation. In the colonial era, firms were allowed to provide for their own security and establish the services essential to their existence. With independence, such extraterritorial administration ceased, in most cases, to be admissable.

The inadequacy of government reflects the absence of schools, colleges and cultural environment for producing or preparing people for public tasks. All discussion of economic development involves difficult problems of sequence and circularity. This is an example: how does a country get an educational system without an adequate government? How does it get a government without the qualified people that an educational system provides? There is no obvious answer. But it helps to have narrowed the problem to this point. For we then recognize that little is accomplished by action that does not break into this particular circle. Assistance in the form of capital funds will not be useful if there is no one with the technical competence to employ it, and if the environment is hostile to the resulting enterprises. Technical assistance will not be useful if there is no one to advise or assist. In the next model, progress waits on reforms which reduce the power of a vested ruling elite. Here there is no such elite.

There is a measure of overstatement in any attempt to establish categories. No country is without some small group of honest and competent people in some area of economic activity or government. But in those countries where colonialism was exploitive and regressive — where there was no liberalizing urge that sought to prepare people for some role other than that of primitive agriculture — this group is very small. As a result, this model — as in the classic case of Haiti — can readily become one not of advance but of disintegration with eventual reversion to tribalism or anarchy. All that is needed is for the perilously small group of competent and honest people to be overwhelmed by those who see government in predatory and personal terms. Once the latter are in possession of the available instruments of power — the army, government payroll, police — it is not clear when (or even whether) the process of disintegration can be reversed by internal influences. This disintegration, not Communism for which these countries are as little prepared as for capitalism, is the form of failure in this model.

IV

I come now to Model II — What I have called the Latin American case. The great mass of the people in these countries is also very poor. But there is a sizable minority that is well-to-do. And associated with this well-to-do minority is a rather larger number of people with a diverse assortment of qualifications and skills — lawyers, physicians, accountants, engineers, scientists, economists and managers. As compared with the Model I countries, the cultural base is quite wide. And supporting it is a limited, undemocratic and otherwise imperfect, but still substantial, educational system. Peru, Ecuador and Guatemala are, by any calculation of *per capita* income, very poor countries. Argentina, Brazil, and Chile are well below North American and European levels. But all have trained and educated people and facilities for their replacement that are more adequate than in the new African states. As a further aspect, they have a strong intellectual tradition. As is also true of the United States, they could use more people of the highest calibre and training. Public servants of high competence are rarely in surplus. But in these countries — as also in the Arab states where the pattern is similar — the absence of trained and educated people is not the obvious barrier to development.

The far more evident barrier is the social structure and the way it tends to subvert economic incentive and production. The élite, though sizable, depends for its economic and social position on land ownership, or on a *comprador* role in the port or capital cities, or on government employment or sinecure, or on position in the armed forces. Beneath this élite is a large rural mass and, in some cases, an unskilled and often semi-employed urban proletariat. The rural worker, in the characteristic Latin American situation, either earns the right to cultivate a small plot of land by giving service to the estate on which he resides or he is part of the *minifundia* — cultivator of a small plot on which he has some form of permanent tenure. In either case he has no effective economic incentive. He thoughtfully renders the landlord the minimum service that will earn him the right to cultivate his own plot. The latter plot was anciently arranged to be of the minimum size consistent with more or less temporary survival. The same tends to be true of any holding to which he has title. So any possibility that he might improve his position by increasing output is excluded by what amounts to a systematic denial of incentives. In a number of countries — Peru, Guatemala and Ecuador, for example — the fact that most of the rural mass is Indian adds a sense of racial exclusion to this denial.

But the elimination of economic incentives is not confined to the rural masses. Beginning with them, it tends to become comprehensive. The landlord, since he has a labour force that is devoid of incentive, cannot do much himself to increase production. Often he lives in the capital city and does not try. Instead of the revenues of a small area farmed efficiently, he enjoys those of a large area that is farmed with extreme incompetence. (It is strongly characteristic of this model that agriculture, some plantation operations apart, is technologically stagnant.)

Income derived from government position or the armed forces is also unrelated to economic service. It depends, rather, on distribution of political or military power, and this leads to the further likelihood of struggle over the division of power. Feudal agriculture is so constituted as to survive unstable or avaricious government. Modern industry — again unless under external protection — is much more vulnerable. So instability in government and its use as a source of personal income has a further adverse effect on industrial incentives. In this model, substantial rewards accrue to traders. But this is more dependent on a strong monopoly position — the franchise for the sale of a North American or European branded product (cigarettes, radios, motor vehicles, pharmaceuticals) or a similar control over the financing, procurement and export of some local product — than on efficient economic service.

It is the normal assumption of economists in advanced communities that income rewards economic effort. Since it induces that effort, it is functional. There has been ample dispute over whether particular functions are over- or under-rewarded, and this is the foundation of the eternal quarrel between Marxians and non-Marxians. But the adequacy of reward for service is not the central issue in this model; the problem is that numerous claimants — landlords, members of the armed services, government functionaries, pensioners — render no economic service at all.[6] And the best-rewarded businessman is not the one who performs the best service but the one whose political position or franchise accords him the most secure monopoly. It is useful to have a term for the income which is so divorced from economic function, and one is readily at hand. It may be called non-functional income.

Not only is the non-functional income large but strong forces act to limit the amount of functional income. The rural worker gets the maximum established by custom; greater endeavour brings him no more. The landlord, as noted, is confined by a labour force that is without incentive. He cannot be more functional. The efficient urban enterpreneur risks being regarded as a better milch cow by those who live on the state. He can protect himself only by developing the requisite political power; this means that his income comes to depend not alone on economic performance but also on political power. His return, or that part of it which derives from political influence, thus also becomes economically non-functional.

The power of the controlling élite is commonly thought to result from the ownership of land — from the control of wealth and access to livelihood that this provides. Traditionally this has been the case. But it is a mistake to identify land in this model as the exclusive or even the primary source of power. Membership in the armed forces, control of hierarchical wealth from sources other than land, possession of trading monopoly, even bureaucratic position can all be sources of power over the state. And government in the interest of those who have such power, since they are non-functional, will be unrelated and unconducive to economic development.[7]

In a number of countries of this model, most notably Argentina, Brazil and Chile, the non-functional groups are in competition with each other and with more recently franchised economic groups for the available income. (In each of these countries an incomplete revolution accorded political power to urban white-collar and working classes without disestablishing the old non-functional groups.) The total of these claims bears no necessary relationship to the income that is available. Since productivity is low, the tendency is for claims to exceed what is available, and invariably they do. The easiest way of reconciling competing claims is to meet that of each group in money terms and allow them to bid against each other for real product in the market. As a result, in these countries inflation is endemic. In countries such as Ecuador and the Central American countries, where the urban white-collar and working classes are weak, inflationary pressures are much less strong. This, however, reflects the weakness of these classes, not their better position under non-inflationary conditions.

V

With variations as to the composition of the non-functional élite, and its source of power, Model II has general application in Central and South America and in Iraq, Syria, ~d elsewhere in the Middle East. In few if any of these countries — two or three Central American and Caribbean countries are possible exceptions — is the cultural base the decisive factor; economic advance is not barred by the absence of trained and educated people. A shortage of capital is assumed almost intuitively by economists to be the normal barrier to advance. Iraq and other Arab states have rich sources of income from oil and Peru from oil and minerals. This has not rescued them from backwardness and some of the oil-rich countries are among the poorest in the world.[8]

In Latin America three countries break decisively with this pattern — Mexico, Costa Rica and Cuba. Mexico, by revolution, destroyed its old power structure based on land ownership. Costa Rica was always, in the main, a country of modest land holdings. Costa Rica has no army; the Mexican army is insignificant in size and cost. Neither country has any other strongly vested non-functional group which uses its power to exercise a major claim on income. In consequence, income in both countries is — by all outward evidences — far more closely related to economic performance than in the remainder of Latin America. They are the two countries which enjoy the most favourable rate of economic development. The case of Cuba is so far less clear. Its land system before the revolution, somewhat exceptionally, was socially regressive but technically proficient. Since the revolution it has lost markets and suffered the costs of much social experiment, not all of it successful. In the longer run, it is impossible to suppose that the Cuban revolution will be regarded as less to the advantage of economic development than the Mexican revolution.

VI

For purposes of identification, I have associated Model III with South Asia. The clearest prototypes are, indeed, India and Pakistan, although it has application to the United Arab

Republic, in limited measure to Indonesia, and, since its characteristics transcend political organization, to China.

In this model, the cultural base is very wide. India and Pakistan have systems of primary and secondary education that are far superior to those of Latin America. There are at least as many full-time professors in the University of Delhi alone as in all Latin America. Both countries tend to a surplus rather than a shortage of teachers,[9] administrators, scientists and entrepreneurs. In recent years, these countries have been substantial, if inadvertent, exporters of medical and scientific talent to the United States and the United Kingdom. Without the doctors provided by this informal educational exchange, the hospitals of both countries would be even more inimical to health.

In both India and Pakistan, there is a substantial volume of non-functional income. But it is not, as in Latin America, associated with political power. In India, the political power and non-functional claims on land revenues of the princes, *jagirdars, zamindars* and large landlords were terminated or greatly curtailed at the time of independence or in the ensuing land reforms. The armed forces, though costly, do not have decisive political power.[10] In consequence, in agriculture there is a rough and imperfect but still real relation between effort and return. Economic incentive is thus reasonably operative. The endemic inflation which characterizes many of the Model II countries is absent. The social structure in these countries is not at the highest level of compatibility with economic advance. But it is clearly not the operative barrier.

The barrier in this model is drastically bad proportioning of the factors of production. Demographic history, still imperfectly explained, has given these countries a large and dense population. The supply of arable land in India, Pakistan and Egypt has been subject to repeated and very great increases through irrigation. But this increase has been followed, as harvest follows planting, by a relentless increase in population. As a result, *per capita* agricultural production and incomes have remained small and, as a further consequence, savings are limited and so consequently is the supply of capital. Capital shortage, in turn, has retarded and continues to retard industrial development. The small land and capital base provides effective employment for only part of the available labour force. People who live close to the margin of subsistence, as I have noted, cannot afford any risk that they might fall below subsistence levels. This is a further inducement to backwardness.

The Model III countries are, in some respects, the most comprehensible in their lack of development. They conform most closely to the standard explanations of the economists; because of their education and cultural sophistication, their people tend to speak for all of the underdeveloped lands. (At any conference on economic development the most persuasive speaker is usually an Indian.) Their case, in consequence, is frequently and erroneously generalized to all instances of underdevelopment.

VII

It is now evident, I think, how dangerous it is to treat the poor countries as a class. The poverty that produces so many common tendencies in behaviour — and which also gives such stark uniformity to the village hut or urban slum — proceeds from very different causes. For purposes of prescribing economic policy, it is at least as unwise to associate sub-Sahara African countries with India as to prescribe a common policy for India and the United States. There is at least equal error in associating for purposes of policy countries with a regressive social structure such as Ecuador, Iran or Peru with the African countries where social structure is not a primary obstacle to advance.

In recent years, economists have prided themselves on the progress that they have made in refining the concept of economic growth and in developing the theory that explains it and the policies that promote it. We are inclined to believe that we are becoming much more scientific about the whole business, although in an established tradition of the discipline there is some tendency to identify scientific precision with mechanical elegance rather than reality. But the claim to progress in these matters is not above reproach so long as underdeveloped countries are treated as a class and one theory is assumed to cover all. Science must be a trifle suspect if it involves unscientific generalization.

FOOTNOTES

[1] Henry J. Bruton, 'Growth Models and Underdeveloped Economies', *Journal of Political Economy*, August, 1955. Reprinted in A.N. Agarwala and S.P. Singh, *The Economics of Underdevelopment*, Oxford University Press, Bombay, 1958, pp. 219-220.

[2] I have drawn heavily, and gratefully, on seminar and class discussion of this classification. I first presented it at the Third Rehovot Conference in Israel in August 1965.

[3] Elliot J. Berg, 'Socialism and Economic Development in Tropical Africa', *Quarterly Journal of Economics*, November 1964, p. 561 (Mr. Berg argues with much effect that this shortage of qualified talent has not prevented — and has possibly encouraged — a number of these countries to commit scarce administrative resources to demanding experiments in socialism and planning at heavy cost to themselves.)

[4] Ernest Lefever, *Crisis in the Congo*, Brookings Institution: George Allen & Unwin, 1965, p.9.

[5] Cf. George H. Kimble, *Tropical Africa*, vol. II, 'Society and Policy', Doubleday, New York, 1962, pp. 469 ff.

[6] In certain philosophical or political contexts, this may be held to be true of the armed forces of any country. They are said to serve the wrong foreign policy, be part of the wrong defence strategy, serve only the arms race, or what not. But the armed forces are committed to the service of the disapproved philosphical or political goals. In Latin America no serious observer supposes that the armed services are seriously important for national defence, territorial integrity or any other military or foreign policy objective. Their role is exclusively related to domestic politics and income.

[7] This is a matter of much practical importance, especially as regards the armed forces. Generally in the United States there has been recognition of the bearing of a regressive or feudal land system on economic development. That *caudillo* government, either by itself or in association with other non-functional groups, can be equally inimical has not been so readily seen. As a consequence, conservative, often simplistically traditionalist, officials regularly turn up defending army dictatorships in Latin America. And, in the past, military aid funds have regularly gone to support armies, which were a source of political power, at the same time that economic assistance was being given to development or even (hopefully) to land reform. It would be difficult to find a policy with a greater element of self-contradiction and this is not lessened by the tendency of those who espouse support to the Latin American military to assume that pragmatism, professionalism and even an element of righteousness are on their side.

[8] Venezuela also has rich income from oil but may gradually be breaking the hold of a regressive social structure which for a long time led to the dissipation and waste of this revenue.

[9] Although not in all categories of teachers or those with a sufficient willingness to serve in rural villages.

[10] The army has political power in Pakistan. However, it is not a recognized avenue to political power and economic advantage as in Latin America. The armed *coup* which brought President Ayub Khan to power in 1959 (like his subsequent administration) bore little or no resemblance to the Latin American phenomenon.

The Rational Choice

Julius Nyerere

My job today is to give a starting point for discussion and thought. And my subject is an examination of the alternative economic and social systems which are open to Third World countries.

In order to keep this discussion within reasonable bounds I must make certain assumptions. It is important that these should be clear before I begin; for if the assumptions are not shared, then much of what I say will be irrelevant.

Fortunately, my assumptions are not very controversial — at least within Africa.

The Assumptions

My first assumption is that any discussion about the appropriate economic and social organization must, for the time being at least, be conducted within each nation state, and the decision must be made exclusively by the people of that nation. Thus, it is the people of Tanzania as a whole, or the Sudan as a whole, who will decide the path for their country. Tanzania cannot decide for the Sudan, nor vice versa — and I hope that nothing I say today will be understood to imply otherwise! The fact that, for example, Zanzibar within the United Republic of Tanzania, and the Southern Provinces within Sudan, have autonomy in certain matters means that in these respects the smaller units will be the unit of choice rather than the nation as a whole.

Secondly, I take it to be axiomatic that all the peoples of the Third World desire to govern themselves, and want their country to be completely independent from external control. This does not rule out the possibility of political or economic links between two or more countries; nor does it exclude a possible voluntary merger of sovereignties, provided that these things are agreed upon after discussions based on the equality of all participants.

Thirdly, I shall assume that, to everyone in the Third World, the present degree of poverty, and the general lack of economic development, is completely unacceptable. We have to increase our production of wealth so that we may increase the level of our collective and individual consumption.

My fourth and final assumption is that our struggles for independence were national struggles, involving the rights of all the inhabitants. We were not aiming to replace our alien rulers by local privileged *elites*, but to create societies which ensure human dignity and self-respect for all. The concomitant of that is that every individual has the right to the maximum economic and political fredom which is compatible with equal freedom for all others; and that neither well fed slavery nor the necessity to beg for subsistence are acceptable human conditions.

I have said that these assumptions are not very controversial within Africa. It is equally true that they do not represent the present situation. They represent aspirations rather than facts. That is obvious from an examination of world affairs, or from the briefest visit to any of our rural areas — or even to those urban areas where our unskilled labourers live.

Yet because these stated assumptions are also a list of our fundamental aspirations, they must be the basis for our choice of policies. If a policy militates against the achievement of these conditions, then its acceptability must be questioned. Even more, if a social and economic system is incompatible with these goals, then it must be rejected.

In the modern world there are two basic systems of economic and social organization — capitalism and socialism. There are variations within these broad classifications, like welfare capitalism or humanistic socialism; but the broad distinction between the two systems remains, and our first choice has to be between them.

Remnants of feudalism and of primitive communalism do, of

course, still exist in the world; but neither of these are viable systems when challenged by the organized technology of the twentieth century. Sometimes, as in Japan, these old systems influence the organization of capitalism for a while; but the influences are subordinate to the logic of the later organization, and will eventually be completely eradicated. For, in the last resort, anything which detracts from the profit of an individual capitalist enterprise will be abandoned by that enterprise; and anything which militates against the efficiency of the capitalist system will be uprooted.

Primitive communalism is equally doomed. The moment the first enamel pot, or factory woven cloth, is imported into a self-sufficient communal society, the economic and social structure of that society receives its death blow. Afterwards it is merely a question of time, and of whether the members of that community will be participants or victims in the new economic order.

Thus the choice for new nations lies effectively between socialism and capitalism. It is not a completely free choice, for all of us inherited certain patterns of trade, and have been to a greater or lesser extent indoctrinated by the value systems of our colonial master. Further, the great powers continue to regard us as being within the sphere of influence of one or other of them — which usually demonstrates its displeasure if we refuse to conform to the expected pattern of behaviour. But ultimately, if we so determine, and if we are prepared to overcome our recent past and the difficulties which others may place in our way, we can move towards the growth of one system or the other within our society.

Yet having said that I now propose to argue that there is no real choice. In practice Third World nations cannot become developed capitalist societies without surrendering the reality of their freedom and without accepting a degree of inequality between their citizens which would deny the moral validity of our independence struggle. I will argue that our present poverty and national weakness make socialism the only rational choice for us.

Capitalism and Independence

Under a capitalist system the purpose of production and distribution is the making of profit for those who own the means of production and exchange. The need for goods is subsidiary to the profit involved in making them. Therefore the owner of the machines and equipment used in production — that is, he who provides the money for these things — is the one who determines whether there shall be any p.oduction, and of what kind, and in what quantity. Neither the men who provide the labour for the production, nor the men who need the goods which could be produced, have any say in these decisions. Under capitalism, money is King. He who owns wealth owns also power. He has power over all the workers who he can employ or not, and power over the governments which he can paralyse by withholding vital production, or sabotage by the manipulation of men and machines.

That has always been the essence of capitalism. But there is a further relevant fact in these decades of the twentieth century. That is that this power is now concentrated in very few hands. For whereas one hundred years ago a quite small amount of money sufficed to establish an industrial or commercial enterprise, modern technology now precludes this in all important areas of production. Thus, for example, Henry Ford could begin his manufacture of cars in a bicycle repair shop, and build up his capacity bit by bit. But now, in the 1970s, anyone who decides to begin making vehicles must be prepared to make a multi-million dollar investment before the first one rolls off the assembly line. Mass production techniques make small units uneconomic — they go bankrupt in an attempt to compete with the giants, or else sell out to a larger business. Therefore, instead of having a very large number of small capitalists, we have a very small number of large capitalists. 'Small men' exist; but they initiate an insignificant proportion of the total wealth produced, and usually confine their attention to the luxury trades.

This development is part of the dynamic of capitalism — for capitalism is very dynamic. It is a fighting system. Each capitalist enterprise survives by successfully fighting other capitalist enterprises. And the capitalist system as a whole survives by expansion, that is, by extending its area of operations and in the process eradicating all restraints upon it, and all weaker systems of society.

Consider now what this means for the new nations of the Third World.

According to capitalist theory, if we choose capitalism our citizens would be free to establish capitalist enterprises, and these Tanzanian or Sudanese capitalists would compete — that is, would fight — all other capitalist enterprises, including the foreign ones. In practice, however, two questions immediately arise. First, where in our lands are those citizens who have sufficient capital to establish modern industries; and second, how would our infant industries fight other capitalist enterprises?

I believe the answer to these questions is clear in all Third World countries. For Tanzania is no exception in not having within its borders the kind of wealth which is necessary to establish modern industrial units. As a general rule no individual, or group of individuals, from within any of our nations has the capacity to establish even a large modern textile mill, much less to operate a diamond mine, put up a steel mill, or run a large-scale commercial enterprise. That amount of money, and that kind of expertise, just do not exist. Certainly, the most which could be done by Tanzanians is the establishment of little workshops, which either assemble imported components, or which undertake simple processing of locally produced crops. Our citizens can establish small retail shops; wholesaling on any economic scale is likely to demand more resources than they have.

When Britain experienced its industrial revolution at the end of the eighteenth century, that was enough. It is not enough now! How could these little Tanzanian capitalists compete with I.C.I., Ford, Nippon Enterprises, and the other big multi-national corporations — or even with Walls Food Products? The answer is simple: they could not! The best they could do would be to become agents of these international capitalist concerns. And this would not bring progress in the attack on our underdevelopment; for the result would not be modern factories producing necessities, but local agents importing and processing those things — and only those things — which were profitable to both the local agents and the overseas enterprise.

In fact, Third World capitalism would have no choice except to co-operate with external capitalism, as a very junior partner. Otherwise it would be strangled at birth. You cannot develop capitalism in our countries without foreign capitalists, their money and their management expertise. And these foreign capitalists will invest in Third World countries only if, when, and to the extent that, they are convinced that to do so would be more profitable to them than any other investment. Development through capitalism therefore means that we Third World nations have to meet conditions laid down by others — by capitalists of other countries. And if we agreed to their conditions we should have to continue to be guided by them or face the threat of the new enterprises being run down, of money and skills being withdrawn, and of other economic sanctions being applied against us

In fact, a reliance upon capitalist development means that we give to others the power to make vital decisions about our economy. The kind of economic production we shall undertake; the location of factories, offices and stores; the amount of employment available in any area; and even the kind of taxation system we adopt; all these matters will be determined by outsiders.

It is claimed that this would be a temporary phenomenon, as foreign capitalist investment in a Third World country would be a catalyst for local capitalist enterprise. To some extent this is true; small local businesses may grow up in the shadow of a major, foreign-owned, factory. But all such businesses would have the purpose of providing service to the workers of the big industry, or of making small components for it. They would therefore be absolutely dependent upon it, flourishing when it expanded and collapsing if it closed down. Local business would thus be the puppets, not the enemies of the foreign enterprise — the subsidiaries, not the competitors. They would be forced to identify themselves with all demands made by the foreign capitalists. The loss of real national self-determination would therefore be increased — not decreased; for the foreign owners would have secured a local political base to back up their economic power.

This is very easy to understand. If the Government for example, proposes to lay down new minimum wages, or to raise revenue from a tariff on goods of interest to the factory, the big employer may say — politely or otherwise — that in such a case they will close their factory. They can point out that this will not only result in a loss of livelihood for all those directly employed; it will also force into bankruptcy a number of ancillary units. Of course, the independent government can still go ahead with its proposals; but it will then have to deal with the consequences — and they are not likely to be pleasant either for that government or the people it wishes to serve.

Nor is this all. Foreign policy questions will also be affected by reliance upon foreign capitalists for economic development. It is true that American, British, or Japanese capitalists have no patriotic loyalty to their country of origin. But they do have loyalty to their largest investments — and these are unlikely to be inside any one underdeveloped country! Therefore, a poor nation's quarrel with one of the imperialist countries about, for example, its support for Zionist expansionism, or for South Africa, Rhodesia, or Portuguese colonialism, can easily lead to the withdrawal of capitalist expansion plans, or even to the contraction and eventual closing of established enterprises.

What I am saying is that, given the present inequalities between nations, capitalist development is incompatible with full national independence for Third World countries. For such development will be foreign owned, and foreign controlled; local capitalists will be subsidiary, and will remain subsidiary.

There can be no question about this — the foreign domination is permanent, not temporary. It is the big enterprise which will make the large profits and have large monies available for the next investment. The small ones will remain small — or be bought out! For confirmation of this fact, and its meaning, it is only necessary to look at what has happened within the major capitalist countries. One sees that medium size enterprises gobble up small ones, and are themselves gobbled up by large ones. Finally, the giants fight among themselves for ultimate supremacy. In the end the rich governments of the big capitalist countries find their own freedom of action is restricted by the economic power of the capitalist giants. Even if they are elected to fight capitalism, they find it necessary to ensure the raw materials, and the profitability, of the big corporations, or face mass unemployment and major economic crises.

The fact that a number of competing big capitalist institutions may invest in a particular developing country — perhaps from different foreign bases — does not invalidate this simplified analysis. As a general rule the meaning is that the poor country has given several hostages to fortune instead of one. In theory it can endeavour to play one enterprise off against another; but in practice it is much more likely to discover that its economic destiny has been determined by enterprise conflicts which originate outside its own borders, and about which it knows nothing! A 'take-over bid', or a rationalization scheme, or a new cartel arrangement, can undo years of local negotiation, and the independent government may well hear about the prospect only if one giant or the other hopes to use it in order to get better terms for its own shareholders!

Capitalism and the nature of society

This inevitable loss of real national freedom is, however, only one of those results of capitalism which I believe to be incompatible with the national purposes of all Third World governments. For capitalism does not only imply a fight between capitalists, with the developing nations' capitalists inevitably being worsted. It also involves a permanent fight between capitalists on one side and workers on the other.

This is a very important matter for us, coming as most of the African Third World countries do, out of primitive communalism into the modern world. For it means a new factor of national division at a time when all of us are still fighting to overcome the divisive forces of tribalism, religion, and race. It also means that the fruits of independence will be denied to the mass of the people who worked for it, or in whose name it was demanded.

There is no escaping this effect of capitalism. For the purpose of capitalist enterprise is the making of profit. To do this, the capitalist must keep his costs of production as low as possible, and get the maximum return from the sale of the products. In other words he must pay the lowest wages for which he can get workers, and charge the maximum price at which he can sell the goods produced. A permanent conflict of interest between the worker and the employer inevitably follows. The former want to get high wages, so as to live decently — and perhaps buy some of the goods they work to produce. The latter needs to pay low wages so as to maximize his profit, that is, the return on the money he has invested.

Thus capitalism automatically brings with it the development of two classes of people: a small group whose ownership of the means of production brings them wealth, power and privilege; and a very much larger group whose work provides that wealth and privilege. The one benefits by exploiting the other, and a failure in the attempt to exploit leads to a breakdown of the whole system with a consequent end to all production! The exploitation of the masses is, in fact, the basis on which capitalism has won the accolade for having solved the problem of production. There is no other basis on which it can operate. For if the workers ever succeeded in obtaining the full benefits of their industry, then the capitalist would receive no profit and would close down the enterprise!

What this means for the masses of people in the Third World countries should be obvious. Their conditions of employment, and their return from employment, will be just sufficient to maintain the labour supply. Further, if the nation is dependent upon capitalist investment for all its desired economic expansion, the workers will have to be prevented from organizing themselves to fight for their rights. For an effective trade union struggle might lead the employer to argue once again that his factory has become uneconomic. The resultant threat of a close down may well prompt the government to intervene on the side of the employers in order to safeguard the economic growth rate and its own miserably small, but vital, tax revenue.

Development through capitalism is thus basically incompatible with the fourth aspiration I listed — that of human dignity and self-respect for all, with equal freedom for all inhabitants of the society. For capitalism means that the masses will work, and a few people — who may not labour at all — will benefit from that work. The few will sit down to a banquet, and the masses will eat whatever is left over.

This has a further implication. With a capitalist system the production of goods, measured statistically, may well go up considerably; if it happens to possess certain mineral resources, the Third World country may even find itself high on the list of 'successful states' as regards the growth rate of its gross national production. But the mass of the people, who produce the goods which are measured, will be without sufficient money to buy the things they need for a decent life. Their demand will exist, but it will not be effective. Consequently, the production of basic necessities — decent houses, food, and nice clothes — will be limited; such production would be less profitable to the capitalist investor than the provision of 'luxury goods'. It was no accident, for example, that one of the early post-independence investments in Tanzania was a drive-in cinema. Much more profit could be made from using cement that way than in producing worker's houses!

For on top of everything else, the choice of capitalism as the road to development means a particular kind of production, and a particular kind of social organization. Rural water supplies will have a low priority, regardless of the fact that they are needed for the health of the people. The importation, and perhaps even the production, of air conditioners, of private cars, and of other 'consumer durables' will have a high priority. The former brings no profit; the latter does.

To see the real meaning of this we can once again look at the developed capitalist societies. Then we can see the malnutrition among the people of the Appalachian mountains and of Harlem contrasted with the gadgetry of suburban America; or in Britain we can see the problem of homelessness while colour television sets are produced endlessly; and in the same societies we can observe the small resources devoted to things like education and health for the people as compared with those spent to satisfy the inessential desires of the minority.

The Alternative of Socialism

To argue, as I have been doing, that capitalism is incompatible with the aspirations of the Third World does not mean that the alternative of socialism is an easy one, nor that success under it is automatic. But socialism can be compatible with our aspirations; by adopting socialist policies it is possible for us to maintain our independence and develop towards human dignity for all our people.

The vital point is that the basis of socialist organization is the meeting of people's needs, not the making of profit. The decision to devote the nation's resources to the production of one thing rather than another is made in the light of what is needed, not what is most profitable. Furthermore, such decisions are made by the people through their responsible institutions — their own government, their own industrial corporations, their own commercial institutions. They are not made by a small group of capitalists, either local or foreign — and the question of foreign domination through economic ownership is thus excluded. Further the workers of the nation can receive — directly or indirectly — the full fruits of their industry; there is no group of private owners which constantly appropriates a large proportion of the wealth produced.

None of this means that great inequalities within the society, or the exploitation of groups, or even the seizure of power and privilege by a small minority, is automatically ruled out in a society which opts for socialism. Looking around the world we can see so-called socialist countries where all these things happen. But my point is that such things mark a failure to implement socialism, they are not inherent in it in the way that they are inherent in capitalism.

The major argument used against socialism for the developing world is, in fact, that it will not work, and that all socialist states are poor states because of their socialism. Without speaking for as long again as I have already spoken — which I do not propose to do — it is not possible to refute this argument in any detail. There are, however, three very fundamental points which I would ask you to consider in this respect.

The first is that to measure a country's wealth by its gross national product is to measure things, not satisfactions. An increase in the sale of heroin, in a country where this is legal, would be recorded as an increase in its national wealth; if human well-being was the unit of measurement, such an increase of sales would be a negative factor. Similarly, the spread of good health through the eradication of endemic diseases may, or may not, be recorded as an increase in statistical national wealth; it is certainly better for the people if it has happened!

My second point is that a successful harlot, or favoured slave, may be better off materially than a woman who refuses to sell her body, or a man to sell his freedom. We do not regard the condition of the harlot or slave as being consequently enviable — unless, of course, we are starving, and even then we recognize the possible amelioration in our circumstances as being uncertain and insecure.

Thirdly, I do not accept that the so-called unworkability of socialism has been proved. Capitalism has been developing for about two centuries. The first national commitment to socialism was made in 1917, by a backward and feudal nation devastated by war, which has subsequently suffered greatly from further civil and international conflict. Even so, few people would deny the material transformation which has been effected in the USSR during the past fifty-five years. And in fact, despite the major criticisms which can be made of all the socialist countries, it is difficult to argue that their peoples are worse off than the late capitalist starters — countries like Greece, or Spain, or Turkey, for example. On the contrary, they are clearly better off in the vital matters of health, education, and the security of their food and shelter. Whether or not they have the same number of television sets seems to me to be much less important!

Conclusion

It cannot be denied that many difficulties face a Third World country which chooses the socialist alternative of development. Not least among these are its own past, the dynamism of capitalist initiative techniques, and the gambler instinct which every human being seems to possess, so that we all hope we shall be among the privileged not the exploited! But I believe that we can choose the socialist path, and that by so doing we can develop ourselves in freedom, and towards those conditions which allow dignity and self-respect for every one of our citizens.

I believe that this prospect must be pursued, with vigour and determination. We shall not create socialist societies overnight; because we have to start from where we are, we shall have to make compromises with capitalist money and skill, and we shall have to take risks in our development. But I am convinced that Third World countries have the power to transform themselves, over time, into socialist societies in which their peoples can live in harmony and co-operation as they work together for their common benefit.

SECTION VI: THIRD WORLD POVERTY AND THE WEST

Introduction

In the articles by Marris and Galbraith in the previous section, the roots of underdevelopment were located within the political, social and economic institutions of the Third World countries themselves. According to this perspective the perpetuation of 'traditional' values creates barriers which the externally-induced forces of 'modernisation' have to struggle to overcome. The problems are internal; the prescribed remedy comes from without—and consists of the importation of the 'missing ingredients' necessary to achieve the development ideal—the 'take-off' to 'self-sustained' growth: Technical assistance, training and investment capital (public and private) and even the development theory itself must be imported from the developed capitalist nations. If progress towards development goals is inadequate it is either because the obstacles of 'traditionalism' are too stubborn to be overcome, and/or insufficient aid and other forms of assistance have flowed in from abroad to overcome them.

Radical theories of development, as the papers in this section explain, reject the above views almost totally. The radicals turn the liberal theories upside down. What for the liberals is the solution—the relationship with the developed capitalist economies—for the radicals constitutes the essence of the problem. Lack of progress derives not from poor country inadequacies but from the various forms of Western capitalist domination and exploitation described in the three papers in this section.

The first article by Rosen and Jones provides a brief, but graphically illustrated, introduction to some of the main arguments of radical theorists. Mack and Leaver in the second paper, extend the discussion somewhat, while also providing a detailed empirical critique of some prevalent radical assumptions. The final paper by Illich takes a 'Third Worldist' perspective, and constitutes a sustained polemic against what has become known as 'growth without development'—the situation in which the already affluent benefit disproportionately from the fruits of economic growth, while the standard of living of the poor stagnates or actually worsens. Illich is an advocate of a radical form of the 'redistribution with growth' approach which is described in the paper by Mack and Leaver.

In this section and the previous one the key *differences* between radical and liberal theories have been highlighted, yet it is clear that the two perspectives are not *necessarily* incompatible. Economic progress *may* be checked by the factors the radicals claim are crucial, *and* by those which the liberal theorists emphasise.

The Radical Theory of Development

S. Rosen and W. Jones

The radical theory of development fundamentally disagrees with this conventional view regarding both the cause and cure of underdevelopment. To the conventional theorist, the *cause* is internal inefficiency and the *cure* is outside help from the developed states. To the radical, the cause is international *exploitation* by exactly these developed "friends", and the cure is a fundamental change of international relations between the poor and the rich. Indeed, the very medicine proposed by the conventional theorist — foreign investment, trade, and aid — is considered the root of the disease by the radical, for whom investment, trade and aid are extractive mechanisms that systematically siphon away the wealth of the LDC's.

The two schools disagree on basic assumptions regarding the global inequality of life. To the conventional theorist, the rich are ahead of the poor because of uneven endowments of intellectual capacity, dedicated effort, and managerial skills. To the radical, the Western peoples achieved their advantage, "not by the laws of the market, but by a particular sequence of world conquest and land occupation." [1] It follows from the conventional view that when the poor make up the gap in productive skills (with the help of foreign aid, and so on) the economic gap will close. It follows from the radical view that only cutting the international relationship will end the unjust division of the world's wealth.

The conventional view posits an essential similarity between the development problems of the LDC's today and the problems successfully mastered by the now rich states in earlier periods. It says in effect, "Just as the United States and Europe developed yesterday and Japan and Mexico are developing today, so will you, the late starters, develop tomorrow." Development is portrayed as a linear process in which every economy passes through certain known stages of economic growth.[2]

Radical analysis rejects this portrayal of the LDC's. The economies of the big capitalist states started as largely autonomous markets under domestic control, though international trade and investment were conducted within careful limits. The economies of the Third World, however, enter the modern development epoch as mere subsystems of global capitalism, having long ago been penetrated by foreign interests and been made economic satellites of the dominant states of the North. The global system consists of a "center" — Europe, America and Japan — and a "periphery" — the dependent economies of Latin America, Africa and Asia. The basic economic institutions of the dependencies were formed in response to the insistent demands of the industrial world, rather than in relation to local needs and interests. The typical dependency economy is geared to the export of commodities needed by the industrial center and the import of products from the center. This is known as the pattern of "foreign-oriented development," in which external rather than domestic influences shape the society, economy, and political structure.

What produced this lopsided and unnatural development, so heavily dependent on foreign interests? In the earliest period, it was caused by massive raw material hunger on the part of the industrial nations. The underdeveloped regions, subdued and controlled by the superior military force of the center, were reduced to cheap suppliers of raw materials, useful mainly for their wells or mines or tea or rubber. Cuba became a sugar plantation, Bolivia a tin mine, the Arab world an oil field, Southeast Asia a rubber plantation, Gabon (in Barbara Ward's phrase) "a faint appendage to a mineral deposit." In many cases, local impulses to produce industrial goods for home consumption were quelled by the dominant foreigners, as the dependency was needed as a secure market for exactly these products from the center. Thus, foreign domination served to channel LDC economic activity into a high degree of forced specialization.

In general, *one* main export item accounts for a much higher portion of foreign sales by poor nations than by rich nations — 46 percent compared to 17 percent. Thus, it is fair to say that the typical LDC is a one- or two-product exporter, while the typical developed nation has a diversified economy.[3] Venezuela exports 90 percent oil; Colombia depends on coffee; Cuba has not escaped sugar dependence; two-thirds of Chilean exports are copper. Should the mineral be exhausted (as is happening to Bolivia) or a cheaper source be found for the national product (such as the seabed?), or should changing consumer preferences reduce demand, dependent LDC economies could be destroyed. What if people stop drinking coffee? In other words, highly specialized economies are dangerously subject to the vicissitudes of the world market.

The "Terms-of-Trade" Problem

The export commodities in which the LDC's specialize tend strongly to be "primary products"— minerals, fuels, and crops taken more or less directly from the earth with minimal processing. Approximately 80 per cent of the exports of poor countries in 1973 were primary products, compared to about 20 percent for rich countries Conversely, 80 percent of the exports of the rich countries were manufactures, compared to only 20 percent for the poor countries. The poor sell to the rich raw materials and buy from them finished goods.

This commodity composition of trade adversely affects the developing countries. One reason is the tendency of primary-product export prices to fluctuate substantially and sometimes extremely in world markets, as illustrated in Table 5-3, while the prices of industrial product imports tend to rise relatively consistently over time. One hundred pounds of Burmese rice, for example, fetched $7 in 1968 but only $3 in 1971. This means that to pay for a $5,000 imported International Harvester tractor, Burma had to sell thirty-six tons of rice in 1968. In 1971, the same tractor cost at least the equivalent of eighty-three tons of rice and probably more because of inflation in the price of the industrial product. Of course, in a boom year the price fluctuation may be quite favorable, In 1974, at $17 a hundredweight, Burma had to export only fifteen tons to earn $5,000. But when a large portion of the labor force and economic activity of a small country is tied to the export of a single product, the wild "boom and bust" cycles illustrated in Table 5-3 are socially hazardous and detrimental to orderly economic development.

Table 5-3   Price Fluctuations of Selected Primary Commodities

Nigeria cacao (100 pounds)		Brazil coffee (100 pounds)	
1968	$31	1968	$32
1970	43	1970	44
1972	30	1971	34
1974	59	1973	53

Chile copper (100 pounds)		Malaysia rubber (100 pounds)	
1968	$47	1968	$17
1969	61	1969	22
1972	44	1972	15
1973	71	1973	35

Philippines copra (100 pounds)		Burma rice (100 pounds)	
1970	$ 8	1968	$ 7
1972	5	1971	3
1973	10	1974	17

Source: International Monetary Fund, *International Financial Statistics*, August, 1975.

Moreover, the price fluctuations of primary commodities do not necessarily average out over time to a general rate of increase comparable to the incessant inflation of industrial goods. Indeed, Third World economists such as Raul Prebisch and leading Marxists such as Arghiri Emmanuel have argued that there is an inherent inequality in international trade, and as a result the prices of primary products tend to "decay" over time relative to industrial goods.[4] That is, the prices of primary commodities have not risen as rapidly as finished industrial goods, and in some cases they have declined absolutely. Figure 5-6 compares the "terms of trade" for developed and less developed countries by using indices based on export prices divided by import prices. The figure shows that, particularly during the 1950's and early 1960's, market prices strongly favored the advanced industrial exporters to the disadvantage of the less developed primary exporters, and that even by 1973 substantial losses in LDC terms of trade had not been recovered. (See also Figure 5-7.) The United Nations Conference on Trade and Development estimated the magnitude of terms-of-trade losses to the LDC's at $13 billion for a six-year period from 1961 through 1966. This drain, significantly, results *not* from explicit imperialism and exploitation, but rather from the quiet operation of market laws seemingly beyond anyone's control, so-called objective world market prices. Billions of dollars are implicitly taken from the poor and given to the rich through the impersonal mechanism of freely negotiated international trade pricing. Even the Soviets were accused by Che Guevara of using these unfair world market pricing advantages.

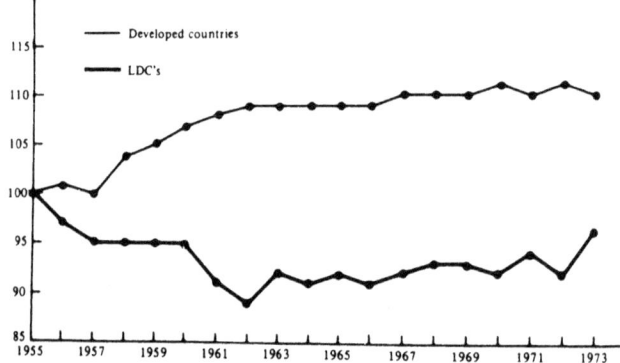

FIGURE 5-6 The Terms of Trade: Unit value index of exports divided by unit value index of imports

Productivity increases. The terms-of-trade factor puts the LDC.'s in a position that cannot be compared to that of the rich states in an earlier period. The now advanced states achieved rapid increases in productivity during their "takeoff" stage, and these are regarded as the key to their success. But today, the primary price decay erodes productivity gains. Malaysia, for example, increased its rubber exports almost 25 percent from 1960 to 1968 — from 850 to 1100 thousand tons — while reducing its plantation labor force significantly. This is a notable gain in productivity. But its *income* from rubber sales *declined* by about 33 percent during these years as prices fell. In effect, productivity increases were passed along to foreign consumers in the form of lowered prices, rather than to Malaysian workers in the form of higher wages and living standards. The terms-of-trade problem can be a treadmill on which it is necessary to run faster and faster just to stand still.

Inelastic demand. Explanations of this phenomenon are based on disadvantages of primary products against finished goods. One is the relative "inelasticity of demand" for primary goods — only so many bananas will be consumed no matter how many are produced, tending to reduce prices after the market is saturated.

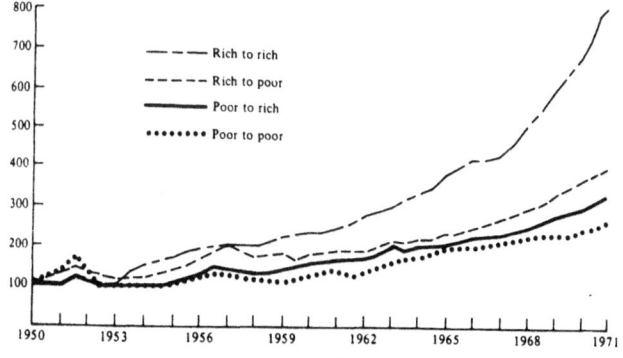

FIGURE 5-7 Export Value Indices for Developed and Developing Countries, 1950–1971

Source: World Bank Group, *Trends in Developing Countries 1973*, Table 5-5

Unorganized labor. Another factor is the position of labor in the LDC's compared to the industrial countries. Workers in the advanced states are relatively well organized into trade unions, and can command a share of the gains from productivity increases. The comparative weakness of labor organizations in the LDC's, however, allows productivity gains to be taken by management in the form of profits or to be passed on to consumers in the form of lower prices. Productivity gains in the center are taken at home, but productivity gains in the periphery tend to flow away — to the center — in the form of lower prices or in profits remitted to foreign owners. The deck is stacked in favor of the already developed world, and mere productivity advances of the type advocated by the conventional theorists will not change the unfavorable rules.

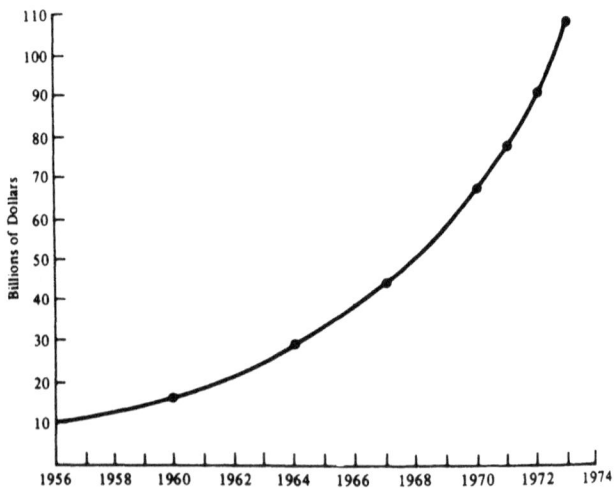

FIGURE 5–8 External Debt of Developing Countries

The Radical View of Foreign Investment

While the conventional theorist views the multinational corporation as an agency for the transfer of capital and technology for the betterment of the developing countries, the radical theorist sees it as an instrument of foreign control extracting exorbitant profits. U.S. investment, for example, puts about $1 billion in new capital into the LDC's annually, but takes out each year $2.5 billion in profits — in effect substantially *de*capitalizing the host countries. Moreover, each incoming dollar buys four times that amount of control over the local economy, since foreign firms borrow from local banks about $2 for every $1 of new money that they bring in plus the reinvestment of a fourth dollar of local earnings from past investment. The result is a geometric rate of expansion of foreign economic penetration. It is estimated that American foreign holdings in all countries grow in value by $8 billion yearly from reinvestment alone, with no real contribution of funds from the United States. In Latin America, U.S. investors have taken out more than three times as much as they put in since 1945, and yet the book value of American holdings continues to grow. Profit rates in some sectors are still increasing despite the imposition of restrictions by many countries. United States returns on direct investment in Latin America mining and smelting went from 9 percent in 1951-55 to 11 percent in 1956-60, 15 percent in 1961-65 and 23 percent in 1966-68.

Multinational firms use several devices to evade legal restrictions on excess profits. For example, one foreign subsidiary of a multinational conglomerate typically buys some of its intermediate components from other branches of the same parent located in other countries. The internal "prices" of such sales may be manipulated by the parent for optimal bookkeeping results, taking losses in one subsidiary where profits are restricted and showing them in another where they are not. Other devices include the manipulation of royalties, management fees, and other internally negotiated "costs". The multinational enterprise has a variety of options to remit profits without defying legal limits.

Another objection to foreign capital is its effect on the social and class structure of the host society. The foreign firm is at first typically an isolated enclave of modern economics in a sea of underdevelopment, but eventually a network of subcontractors extends the patterns of dependency outside the company gates. Often the multinational guest dwarfs all local enterprises — the sales revenue of the United Fruit Company, for example, exceeds the entire national budgets of Panama, Nicaragua, Honduras, Guatemala, and El Salvador. The pure economic power of such an entity opens the doors of the middle and even the top strata of the official bureaucracy and creates at the same time a dependent class of local merchants and bankers. In addition, the foreign firm develops a special relationshp with certain privileged sections of the labor force, sometimes by paying wages slightly above the depressed local rates. United States firms in northern Mexico, for example, are able to pay 75 cents an hour, which is more than three times the local average but at the same time only a third of the rate in nearby southern Texas. Local workers are co-opted by the competition for these prized jobs. In effect, foreign capital creates satellite classes whose interests are tied to the *dependencia* syndrome.

Even if the economic and social effects of foreign investment were entirely positive, patriots of developing countries could be expected to resist the control of national industries by foreign interests. In Malaysia in 1968, for example, the share of foreign-controlled subsidiaries and branches was 75 percent of rubber plantations, 54 percent of other agriculture, 69 percent of mining, 49 percent of manufacturing, 30 percent of construction, 60 percent of wholesale and retail trade, 28 percent of other industry and 57 percent of all industries as a whole. Such unrestricted penetration by outsiders gives foreign investment the image of neocolonialism, whatever the economist may conclude from the arithmetic of cost-benefit calculations.

Objections to Foreign Aid

It may seem surprising that even foreign aid is regarded with suspicion in the radical theory. If we concede that dependence on foreign capital and primary product exports is disadvantageous, wouldn't it seem to follow that aid as a form of capital transfer would give the recipient some relief?

There are several objections to this simple view. First, most foreign aid consists not of simple grants but of interest-bearing loans that must be repaid. The typical less developed country runs a chronic payments deficit because of the unfavorable balance of trade and the drain of excess profits to foreign firms. Borrowing foreign "aid" to make up the gap in current bills leads to mounting indebtedness and simply defers the day of reckoning, accumulating losses to be repaid in some future golden age. Borrowing from Peter to pay Paul (or "rolling over" the debt) does not break the pattern of dependency, but reinforces and perpetuates it. Foreign debt service cost the developing countries 11 percent of their export earnings in 1971 and will go to 20 percent by 1980. Some countries are especially hard hit — foreign debt service preempted over one-sixth of Egypt's total public revenue in 1972.

The emergence of LDC dependence on aid makes these nations vulnerable to political influence in new ways. For if aid is terminated, not only is development slowed, but even bare necessities that are imported will be halted, the nation will face a balance of payments crisis, and the economy will be capsized. Chile was faced with such an "invisible blockade" when the government of Salvadore Allende moved in directions perceived as hostile by the U.S. On the other side, obedient dependencies are permitted to have periodic debt crises during which the rich states generally allow payments moratoria for short periods to allow the LDC's to "catch their breath." Thus, the accumulation of foreign debts creates new forms of dependence. This problem grows in significance as indebtedness mounts. Figure 5-8 shows that the foreign public debt of the Third World quadrupled in twelve years, while that of the developed world stood still.

A second objection is that radicals object to the political conditions under which aid is given. More than half of American aid, for example, went to a handful of client states of dubious political character in the radical view: Vietnam, Laos, Taiwan, Thailand, Philippines, Spain, Portugal, Greece, and Turkey. These states also get the most favorable terms, including a high proportion of straight grants. Aid is given by the United States in the name of promoting international "stability" — that is, reinforcing the very relationships that keep the LDC's enslaved. Aid is part of the web of imperialism.

Third, the principal economic benefits from aid go not to the developing countries but to agricultural and industrial interests within the advanced countries themselves. Most aid is "tied" to purchases from the donor country, resulting in substantial sales for industries such as capital goods, fertilizers, defense, and railroad equipment. More than 90 percent of American foreign aid is spent within the borders of the United States. Purchases financed by aid account for more than $1 billion per year in United States industrial exports and an equal amount in agricultural exports. Indeed, PL 480, renamed the Food for Peace programe by President Kennedy, was originally called the Agricultural Surplus Support Program. Significantly, United States agricultural and industrial lobbyists generally give their firm support to maximum congressional appropriations of foreign assistance. On the Department of Commerce assumption of 60,000 jobs for every $1 billion in industrial exports, we may estimate that well over 100,000 American workers owe their employment to foreign aid.

Subsidised sales to LDC's under the aid program also have the effect of creating permanent trade links and a market infrastructure. Replacement parts will later be needed. Aid is the foot in the door for other forms of economic penetration.

Even the celebrated Green Revolution does not escape suspicion in the radical theory. We noted earlier that scientific agriculture may actually increase class conflict by concentrating land ownership. It also tends to increase reliance on machinery, chemical fertilizers and insecticides, and large investment of capital, much of which must be imported. Thus, even domestic agriculture begins to depend on foreign factors. Over a third of nitrogen, phosphate, and potash fertilizers must be imported as consumption increases. American exports of tractors and agricultural supplies are in fact booming as a result of this new development. Radical analysts are divided as to whether the food production advantages of the new methods are sufficient compensation for this new form of trade dependence.

FOOTNOTES

[1] See Ward et al., *The Widening Gap*, pp. 152-64, where the two views are eloquently contrasted.

[2] See Walt W. Rostow, *The Stages of Economic Growth* (London: Cambridge University Press, 1960)

[3] Thomas Weisskopf, "Capitalism, Underdevelopment, and the Poor Countries," in Jagdish Bhagwati, ed., *Economics and World Order* (New York: Macmillan, 1972), p.73.

[4] Two recent classics developing this view from different perspectives are United Nations Conference on Trade and Development, *Towards a New Trade Policy for Development* (UN: 1964), universally known as the Prebisch Report, and Arghiri Emmanuel, *Unequal Exchange: The Imperialism of International Trade* (New York: Monthly Review Press, 1972).

Radical Theories of Underdevelopment: An Assessment

Andrew Mack and Richard Leaver*

> It is international monopoly capital, most of which originates in the U.S.A., which creates and maintains the present world structure of underdevelopment ... Development and underdevelopment are two sides of the same coin ...[1]

> ... this existing international order is hierarchical and exploitative, it produces affluence for the rich, central developed countries and it provides dependent underdevelopment for the Third World countries.[2]

> The problem of the poor countries ... is not that they lack resources, technological know-how modern institutions, or cultural traits conducive to development, but that they are being exploited by a world-wide capitalist system and its particular imperialist agents, both foreign and domestic.[3]

There are many different radical theories which seek to explain Third World underdevelopment, but almost all assume that 'underdevelopment'[4] is a consequence of, or at least is perpetuated by, relationships with the capitalist West. Poor

---

* Thanks for helpful comments on an early draft of this article to, Richard DeAngelis, John Anglim, Bill Brugger, Ursula Doyle, David Plant and Steve Reglar.

countries are poor, it is argued, not because their economic, social and cultural institutions are somehow inadequate, but because they are exploited; the ultimate causes of underdevelopment do not lie within Third World societies themselves, but in the exploitative 'dependency' relationships which bind them to the Western capitalist metropoles. Radical theorists stress the *integrated* nature of the world capitalist system and argue that underdevelopment can only be understood in the context of this system.

The non-radical, mainstream development theorists of the 1950s and 1960s had generally assumed that the key causes of underdevelopment were located *within* Third World social, cultural, economic and political structures. To generate development the capital, technology and expertise which were both necessary and absent could be 'diffused' via public aid programmes and private investment from rich to poor countries.

This transfer of resources would stimulate economic 'take-off' into 'self-sustained' growth. According to this view, the 'malady' of underdevelopment is internally caused; the prescribed cure comes from without.

Radical theorists, however, not only claim that the causes of underdevelopment are external in origin, but also that the 'solution' advocated by the non-radical diffusion theorists is in fact an integral part of the problem. The net flow of resources is not, they argue, from rich nations to poor, but from poor to rich. Third World countries give economic aid to the West not vice versa. Indeed many argue that genuine economic development can only take place when the exploitative linkages are broken and policies of self-reliance are adopted. The major differences between the two approaches can be shown diagrammatically.[5]

UNDERDEVELOPMENT

		Cause	Remedy
TYPE OF THEORY	Diffusionist	internal (societal 'inadequacies')	external (diffusion of capital etc.)
	Radical	external (western exploitation)	internal (self-reliance)

Traditional Marxist Theory and Radical Development Theory

Both Marx and Lenin held views considerably closer to modern diffusion theorists than to today's radical theorists. Thus as French Marxist, Argihiri Emmanuel, has noted:

> The notion of the diffusion of development by the movement of capital is one of the oldest theses of Marxism.[6]

Marx believed that, although it involved cruelty, destruction and was motivated by greed, the penetration of capitalist modes of production into the Third World was a historically *progressive* process. While grossly exploitative, capitalism generated new productive forces; it represented a clear social and economic advance over the feudal and other pre-capitalist modes of production which it swept aside. The evolution of capitalism also provided the necessary, but not sufficient conditions for socialism. Today's radical theorists are almost unanimous in rejecting the traditional Marxist view. In sharp contrast to their mentor they have stressed:

> the impossibility of vigorous national development for the Third World within a capitalist framework—or alternatively have argued that the development of capitalism in the Third World is impossible except as a distorted and feeble caricature of western capitalism.[7]

A most significant dissent from what might be called the new radical conventional wisdom is found in the work of the late Bill Warren, a distinguished English Marxist theorist. Warren argues against the widely held pessimism of most development theorists and has been attacked for so doing.[8] Third World economic growth has, Warren claims, been quite remarkable during the post-war period. With relatively few exceptions *per capita* growth rates have also grown—i.e. economic growth has kept ahead of population increases (contrary to the claim made by Ivan Illich in the article which follows).[9] Furthermore Warren argues that this economic progress is not simply 'growth without development', as Illich maintains; in general the fruits of economic growth *do* trickle down to the poorest strata of Third World countries.

Similarly, and again in contrast to the prevailing consensus, Warren argues that the 'basic needs' of Third World peoples—health, education, nutrition and housing—are also increasingly being satisfied. Warren is not of course claiming that contemporary Third World conditions, with malnutrition, famine and disease still rife, are satisfactory, merely that they are, with some exceptions, improving rather than deteriorating. Other researchers have reached very different conclusions. Adelman and Morris, in a study published in 1973, claimed that '... development is accompanied by an *absolute* as well as a relative *decline* in the average income of the very poor.'[10] (The term 'very poor' usually refers to the bottom 40% of the population.)

We do not seek to evaluate the debate between Warren and his critics in this paper, simply to point out that the belief that capitalism may be an historically progressive force is not the sole preserve of apologists for the overseas activities of multinational corporations. But even if Warren's data (which he draws largely from U.N. sources) are correct, it may still be true that Western capitalist exploitation is preventing a *more rapid* improvement in the conditions of the Third World's poor. In this case many of the radical theories about the negative impact of western capitalism on the Third World may still be valid. It is with these theories that we are concerned in this paper.

Dependency Theories

Dependencia theory is Latin American in origin and has made a cosiderable impact in U.N. agencies such as UNCTAD (United Nations Commission for Trade and Development) and ECLA (Economic Commission for Latin America).[11] The theory, which originated as a critique of the non-radical diffusion theories, argues that the problems of underdevelopment arise from the *dependence* of poor nations on the rich. What is meant by 'dependency' in this context? The usual measures relate to the importance and nature of trade and foreign investment levels in LDCs. If a large percentage of a particular Third World country's national income (gross national product—gnp) arises from exports; if the exports are concentrated in one or two commodities (say cocoa or copper), and if the 'commanding heights' of the economy are dominated by foreign multinationals, we would then say that that country is highly dependent. Thus economic decisions taken beyond the nation's boundaries, and thus outside its control, may determine its economic fate. There is no doubt that many Third World countries are highly dependent using these criteria, and it is also clear that dependency may impose limitations on political sovereignty. What has not been demonstrated, is that economic dependency *per se* has negative consequences for capitalist development. Some Western capitalist countries are clearly highly dependent; they are also rich. Canada, economically dominated by, and dependent on, the United States is an obvious example. In the Third World some of the *least* dependent countries, including Bhutan, Nepal, Chad, Burundi and Afghanistan, are among the poorest and have the lowest rates of per capita economic growth. By contrast, some of the most dependent countries (using the above criteria), including Taiwan, South Korea, and Singapore are highly successful (using any of the usual measures of development.) These measures relate primarily to material well-being and do not include any reference to degrees of political liberty, civil rights, or religious freedoms. The absence of any clear causal relationship between economic dependency and either developmental success or failure, casts some considerable doubt on the validity of the theory. In fact the whole *dependencia* approach is itself currently undergoing a sustained critique.[12]

How Rich Nations May 'Underdevelop' the Third World

To see how the capitalist West might exploit poor nations and/or block or 'distort' the process of capitalist development within them, we need to look more closely at the economic and political relationships which link the LDCs (Less Developed Countries) to DCs (Developed Countries).

Very crudely we can outline three means by which DC/LDC relationships may obstruct capitalist development in the latter. These are (i) 'exploitation' or unequal exchange, (ii) trade barriers, (iii) 'blockage'.

Exploitation and Unequal Exchange

> Exploitation has to do with the direct exchange relationship between two countries. Broadly speaking there is exploitation if one country gets more out of the exchange than the other.[13]

> Exploitation [is] ... an exchange process in which one party unfairly acquired most of the value.[14]

The problem with these definitions, as their authors are doubtless aware, is that the notion of 'unfair' is left undefined. Take the case of trade—can an exchange be 'unfair' if both parties are happy with it? Or, to put it another way, is there a criterion for 'fairness' independent of the attitudes of those who are doing the trading? Some theorists believe there is:

> Marxist theory ... provided a criterion—that is, the labour theory of value. To state it simply, the answer to the question "How much is commodity X worth?" is "It is worth the amount of labour put into it."[15]

Suppose LDC workers labour for eight hours to produce a particular commodity, while DC workers only work one hour to produce another good; suppose also that the international trading price for each good is the same. If the two nations trade with each other in just these two comodities, then it follows that the LDC workers are going to have to work eight times as long as the DC workers in the exchange process. This is not a fanciful example since, as Argihiri Emmanuel has argued, the LDCs:

> ... whatever they undertake and whatever they produce [LDCs] always exchange a large amount of their national labour for a smaller amount of foreign labour.[16]

This idea forms the basis of Emmanuel's theory of 'unequal exchange'.[17] In this theory Emmanuel does not seek to explain why poor countries were poor in the first place, simply how they may be relatively disadvantaged in their trading relationships with rich countries. Conventional economics rejects the Marxist labour theory of value and with it any notion of necessarily 'unequal' exchange. In conventional economic theory a 'fair exchange' is that determined by 'free market' forces—the laws of supply and demand under conditions of perfect competition. However there are severe restrictions on real competition between DCs and LDCs. As we shall see later, highly disadvantageous limitations are imposed on some Third World goods crossing DC frontiers. There are also extremely strict barriers to the free movement of people across international frontiers. Immigration regulations keep very low paid Third World nationals out of high wage DC labour markets thus blocking a migration process which might otherwise greatly reduce international wage inequalities. Immigration policies in rich countries admit small numbers of workers from low wage countries to perform the most unpleasant tasks that DC workers no longer wish to perform. Opposition to looser immigration controls has, not surprisingly, often been led by DC trade unionists whose wage levels would be most directly affected by any large migrant influx.

Unequal Exchange and Deteriorating Terms of Trade

The idea that there is a fundamental inequality in trade relationships between rich and poor nations has few non-radical adherents, but the belief that the LDCs' trading position is deteriorating from some previously acceptable baseline has wide currency. The idea of a deterioration in the 'terms of trade' (also described in the Rosen and Jones paper in this reader) is best illustrated with an imaginary example. Suppose a Third World country exports one commodity only—say cocoa—and imports only one manufactured good—say tractors. Suppose that the price of cocoa falls by a half over a certain period (as has in fact happened on occasions) and that the price of the tractor doubles over the same period (which is also plausible). At the end of the period the Third World country will have to produce four times as much cocoa to buy one tractor as it did at the beginning of the period. Our somewhat exaggerated example shows what is meant when it is claimed that Third World countries' 'terms of trade' deteriorate. Compared with the previous datum point the exchange is now relatively more disadvantageous to the poor country.

It is certainly possible to find a number of examples for specific countries over particular time periods where there have been dramatic deteriorations in the terms of trade. But for this argument to provide a *general* explanation of Third World poverty one must show—at the very least—that there has been a *long term* deterioration in the terms of trade against poor countries—yet this is extraordinarily difficult. The argument is extremely complex, but the very fact that experts can disagree so bitterly about the long term trends suggests perhaps that there has been neither a large deterioration of Third World terms of trade as some radicals imply, nor the continued improvement which classical economic trade theory predicted.[18]

However there is no doubt that in the relatively short run—say ten years—terms of trade *can* decline for LDCs, and that this means a loss of purchasing power. As the relative value of LDC exports falls, their ability to buy needed imports is reduced. How important are such losses? Radical theorist, Pierre Jalée in his, *The Third World in World Economy*, quotes Paul Bairoch as estimating an LDC deterioration in the terms of trade of some 12% between 1954 and 1965 leading to a total 1954-65 loss of resources of the order of $4.3 billion.[19] Over an eleven year period this gives an average annual loss of *$0.39 billion*. This is a not inconsiderable sum, but whether or not it has any real significance for the development process depends on the proportion of Third World gnp which it represents. Jalée, whose detailed figures for various international economic exchanges we will be using throughout this paper, gives the total 1965 Third World gnp as $230 billion.[20] Thus the 1965 $0.39 billion terms of trade loss equals approximately *0.2 of one percent of total 1965 Third World gnp*. (We discuss the significance of such percentages later.)

This does not seem to be a very large amount but we need to add to it various other losses which LDCs may incur in their dealings with DCs during 1965. (We will be using 1965 as a test year to evaluate some of the radical claims.) The addition of other losses will give us an idea of total Third World economic losses. There can then be set against the total flow of economic resources *to* the Third World *from* the DCs. The two totals combined will give us the net flow of resources. If this net flow of resources is from poor to rich nations, and if the amount is sufficient (in proportion to total Third World gnp) to affect Third World development programmes negatively, then one of the major radical claims will be vindicated. Following this assessment, we will move on to examine the 'trade barriers' and 'blockage' arguments.

Exploitation and the 'Sucking Out of Wealth' Argument

Third World losses through deteriorating terms of trade show up as a loss of LDC purchasing power—there is no *direct and visible* transfer of cash from poor nations to rich, although the effect is as if this were the case. Direct and visible transfers of wealth from DCs to LDCs, primarily via multinational corporation(MNC) profit remittances, are the most obvious and most criticised form of LDC capital drain. Profit remittances have been a central feature of radical claims that DC-based multinationals exploit the Third World.

The argument runs roughly as follows: the purpose of the initial flow of foreign capital to the 'satellite' LDC is simply to create the infrastructure for the subsequent pumping of profits back to the Western metropolis. Thus foreign investment does not *create* wealth as the 'diffusionists' claim; it creates the machinery to *remove* wealth from the LDC—it acts, in Paul Sweezy's words, as 'a giant pump for sucking surplus out of the underdeveloped countries'.[21] The reversal of private capital flows takes some time as Peter Evans has pointed out:

> Initially a less developed country may receive more investment than it must pay out in remitted (MNC) income, but over the years the balance is likely to shift to its disadvantage. A comparison of Latin America, where United States investment has a long history, with Africa, where it is relatively recent, will serve as an illustration. From 1965 to 1969 Africa received about as much new capital from the United States as it remitted in income. Remitted income from Latin America, on the other hand, was over three and one-half times the amount of new capital received.[22]

The wealth thus removed from the LDC is a form of economic

aid to the rich countries. As Gunder Frank has argued:

> ... the metropolis expropriates economic surplus from its satellites and appropriates it for its own economic development. The satellites remain underdeveloped for lack of access to their own surplus.[23]

We should point out here that there is no controversy on the question of private capital flows—it is widely accepted that the net flow of private capital has been from poor nations to rich. It might seem therefore that the radical case is proven, but net private capital flow figures on their own cannot do this. The reason is simple. Comparing the difference between what goes in (MNC investment), and what comes out (MNC repatriated profits), ignores what happens in between—i.e. we need to look at possible beneficial effects of the initial investment *within* the LDC economy. Corporate growth arising from a portion of profits being reinvested locally may provide increased jobs, increased government revenues through royalties, etc. It is *possible* that these benefits would (a) not have been forthcoming without the initial foreign investment, and, (b) that they would exceed by a considerable margin any losses through repatriated profits. Warren produces figures to show that, in 1957, of the total income from sales of US-controlled DMNCs in Latin America, only *2.7%* was repatriated as profit, while *81.7%* was spent locally on wages, taxes, raw materials and services. Warren describes as 'ridiculous' the notion that, 'because the outflow of profits and dividends exceeds the original investment the host country has lost.'[24]

Nevertheless for the purposes of our argument we propose to ignore the alleged benefits noted above and to concentrate simply on the net capital flows. Note that in so doing we are deliberately ignoring an argument which could well undermine the radical 'sucking out of surplus' critique of private foreign investment.

What sort of sums are involved in this 'pumping out' of wealth? Jalée's calculations suggest that in 1964, total DC corporation profits repatriated from the LDCs amounted to US$4.9 billion. This was three times the total private capital *inflow* to the LDCs from the DCs in the same year. (Confusingly Jalée sometimes gives data for 1964 and sometimes for 1965, however the small differences between various figures for the different years will not affect the conclusions we will draw from these data.) To the total of US$4.9 billion in 1964, Jalée adds his This amounts to US$1.1 billion; a further US$1.35 billion is

added for the receipts from the maritime shipping of Third World goods by the vessels of the developed countries'.[25]
goods by the vessels of the developed countries'.[25]

It is questionable how legitimate the inclusion of these last two entries in Jalée's LDC capital outflow balance sheet is. For example, interest payments on debt should take into account the effects of inflation—which benefit the LDC debtor not the DC lender, e.g. if a loan has to be repaid at 10% interest during a period with 10% inflation the loan is effectively interest free. Jalée does not take the effects of inflation into account. But once again we will accept his figures for the purpose of our argument.

There is one more source of wealth drain from LDCs which is, by its very nature, impossible to measure—the clandestine movement of capital. This takes two forms—first the so-called 'Swiss Bank factor' which involves the *illegal* transfer of funds from poor to rich countries—often undertaken by corrupt politicians; and secondly the phenomenon of 'transfer pricing'. Losses via transfer pricing take place without any actual cash moving across frontiers—as is also the case with LDC terms of trade losses. Transfer pricing works as follows. When the corporate headquarters of a Western multinational company trades with one of its subsidiaries in a Third World country, the prices which the parent charges the subsidiary are frequently determined by management in the parent company's head office and not by market forces. The parent company can thus charge its subsidiary either more or less than the cost price of any item which is traded.

Being able artifically to manipulate *costs* between two countries also means being able to manipulate *profit* figures. This means that the MNC can 'transfer prices' so that it declares high profits in countries with low rates of corporation tax, and low profits in areas of high corporation tax. When this happens the result is that the corporation's *total* tax bill is lower than it would have been otherwise.

The high tax country has *lost* taxes it would otherwise have gained; but the low tax country has *gained* more MNC taxation than would have been the case with no 'transfer pricing'. Thus 'transfer pricing' constitutes net gain for corporations and for low tax states, and a net loss for high tax states. If DC corporate taxes are higher than those of LDCs, then 'transfer pricing' will lead to a 'hidden' transfer of wealth from rich to poor. LDC governments frequently offer tax 'holidays' to entice foreign companies to invest in their economies—i.e. they lower corporate taxation levels. Given low taxation levels LDCs may actually *benefit* from the transfer pricing that takes place. However Barnet and Muller in their major study of the activities of multinational corporations in the Third World argue that transfer pricing *does* disadvantage LDCs,[26] and again, for the purpose of argument, we will accept this assumption. But even if we accept that transfer pricing is disadvantageous for LDCs, the problem of determining the *amount* of the loss is enormous.

Emmanuel quotes unnamed experts as evaluating these losses as high as US$2.0 billion per annum for Latin America alone.[27] Since Latin America has approximately one third of total Third World gnp, we can multiply the estimated loss for Latin America by three in order to get an estimate for *global* LDC transfer pricing losses of some US$6.0 billion. We emphasise that this figure is, of necessity, *highly* speculative but the error is likely to favour the radical argument.

The Net Flow of Wealth

We are now in a position to add together *all* the claimed LDC capital losses for our nominal test year, 1965. They are as follows:

LDC Outflow

Terms of trade loss	US$0.39 billion
MNC profit remittances	US$4.90 billion
Various interest payments	US$1.10 billion
Shipping costs	US$1.35 billion
Transfer pricing etc. losses	US$6.00 billion
	US$13.74 billion

We should note in passing that we believe that Jalée makes a simple error in his calculations (which incidentally do not include any transfer pricing loss estimate). Under the terms of trade lose heading he appears to list the eleven year *total* loss of purchasing power for the one year period in 1965, instead of the average *annual* loss figure.

$13.74 billion is 6% of the total Third World gnp of $230 billion. But of course this is simply the LDC wealth *outflow* figure and must be set against the *inflow* of private capital and foreign aid to get the *net* flow figure. Jalee's figures for the *inflow* of capital into the LDCs are as follows.

LDC Inflow

Foreign (Public) Aid—bilateral, multilateral,
  gifts and loans .... US$6.27 billion
Private Flows—investment, loans, private
  export credits .... US$3.88 billion
Other Flows .... US$0.81 billion

                                              US$10.96 billion

Thus for 1965 we have an estimated total
  outflow of .... US$13.74 billion
An estimated total inflow of .... US$10.96 billion

The *net* flow is thus: .... US$2.78 billion
from LDCs to DCs.

Thus the radical claim appears to be validated, but *only* because we have included a *highly* speculative figure for transfer pricing losses that no other radical theorists have attempted to quantify. Without this inclusion the balance sheet appears very different and the net flow is then from rich nations to poor to the tune of approximately US$3.0 billion.

Before assessing the significance of this US$2.84 billion estimated capital 'drain', we will review briefly the points at which we have given this particular radical theory the benefit of the doubt.

(a) *The case to be answered:* If it could be demonstrated that LDCs *were* undergoing quite rapid rates of economic growth, and that the fruits of that growth *were* not restricted to the elite, then the case against capitalism and against imperialist economic penetration of the Third World could not be that it brings about what Gunder Frank calls the 'development of underdevelopment'. It may be that socialist development programmes would do better, but that is a different question. We have already noted English Marxist Bill Warren's highly optimistic views about Third World economic progress. Michael Lipton, a liberal theorist, in an important recent study which echoes some of Warren's optimism, wrote:

> First, the poor countries have enjoyed a long period of unprecedented economic growth: the true value of output and income available per person in poor countries has almost doubled in the last quarter-century, after many preceding centuries without any long term upward tendency. Second, this is not 'growth without development' ... Third ... the condition of the really poor has undergone little improvement except in important areas of social provision, especially health and education.[28]

Lipton, Adelman and Morris and World Bank president, Robert McNamara, (see fn. 10) all seem to concur that the real problem lies with the poorest of the poor—the mostly rural, bottom 40% of the Third World's population, who tend to be over-represented in the so-called 'Fourth World' countries (the poorest of the LDCs). It is within this stratum that we find stagnation and even economic regression rather than growth. We will return to the problem of the poorest of the poor later.

(b) *Terms of trade:* Here we pointed out that, contrary to many radical claims, it is by no means clear that the *long term trend* is for LDC terms of trade to decline. Indeed, according to Warren, the argument that LDC primary commodity exports tend to decline in value relative to DC manufactured goods has been refuted, '... time and time again, but has behind it a mighty edifice of vested interest, including in a sense the entire personnel of UNCTAD'.[29]

(c) *Private capital flows:* Here we deliberately ignored the well-made criticism that simply measuring *net* capital flows ignores possible income-generating activities of MNC activity *within* Third World countries.

(d) *Transfer pricing:* There were, we argued, good *a priori* grounds for suspecting that transfer pricing by MNCs might actually benefit LDCs (assuming, not unrealistically, that LDC taxation levels are lower than those of the parent company's home nation). We have, however, assumed the opposite to be the case.

In other words, in arriving at our final highly speculative estimate of the amount of wealth siphoned out of the LDCs for 1965, i.e. US$2.8 billion, we have systematically ignored potentially highly damaging counterarguments to the thesis that LDC poverty persists because of exploitation. The mechanisms for transferring wealth discussed here—i.e. direct and visible (e.g. profit remittance), or indirect and invisible (terms of trade and transfer pricing) are the *only possible* means by which LDCs can be exploited by DCs.

How important *is* this estimated loss of US$2.8 billion for the LDCs in 1965. The sum is equal to 1.2% of total LDC gnp for 1965. But the significance of this $2.8 billion dollars lies not in its relationship to total gnp but to LDC *investment*. Without investment economic growth is impossible. According to economist Robert Heilbroner, most LDCs, 'have investment rates that are closer to 5 than to 10 percent [of gnp]'.[30] Let us assume that the figure is in fact 7%. If the estimated LDC wealth 'drain' (1.2%) were checked, and if the wealth thus saved were invested, then the rate of investment would increase by 1.2%— from 7 to just over 8 percent. What difference in LDC growth would such an increase in the investment rate create? To determine this, conventional economists use what they call the 'marginal capital-output ratio'. In simple terms, this ratio tells us how much extra economic growth we can expect from each extra increment of investment. If, as Heilbroner claims, the marginal capital-output ratio is one third,[31] then every extra 10 dollars of investment will give rise to three dollars of additional output. Thus an increase of just over one percent in investment (our $2.8 billion dollars) will mean an increase of just over *one third of one percent* in Third World rate of economic growth.

We have now arrived at the end of our attempt to test the thesis that LDC developmental progress is prevented by western capitalist exploitation. We have found that *even when we do not* attack obvious weaknesses in the various hypotheses about terms of trade, transfer pricing, the measurement of capital flows and so forth, we finish up with data which suggest that at most the 'guesstimated' loss of LDC wealth is just over one percent of LDC gnp. This represents a *potential* increment of investment which would yield one third of one percent increase in the average LDC growth rate. We conclude by arguing that the 'exploitation' hypothesis thus described is weak, highly susceptible to attack and, even in its strongest formulation, not particularly convincing.

Trade Restrictions and Galtung's Theory of Imperialism

One of the most characteristic features of the economic relationships between the rich nations and the poor is the so-called 'international division of labour'. Broadly speaking this means that the Third World functions as a supplier of raw materials to the rich countries and buys manufactured goods from them. 75% of the LDC's income from trade comes from 'primary commodity' exports, i.e. food, beverages, minerals, fuels, etc.; only 25% is derived from the export of manufactured goods.[32]

Thus Third World raw materials are exported to the DCs where they undergo processing; this is where LDCs lose out since, the greater the amount of processing a commodity undergoes the higher the price of the final product. (Think of the difference in value between a kilo of iron and some carbon, and a kilo of stainless steel razor blades). As World Bank economist, Mahbub ul Haq pointed out in 1975:

> The developing countries, unlike the developed, receive only a small fraction of the final price that consumers in the international market are paying for their [LDC] produce ... A rough estimate indicates that final consumers pay over $200 billion (excluding taxes) for the major primary products (excluding oil) of the developing countries (in a more processed, packaged, and advertised form), but these countries receive only $30 billion ... [If] the poor nations were able to exercise the same degree of control over the processing and distribution of their exports as the rich nations presently do, and if they were to get back a similar proportion of the final consumer price, their export earnings from their primary commodities would be closer to $150 billion.[33]

The difference between current earnings of $30 billion and those potential earnings of $150 billion is $120 billion. These figures are from the early 1970s and we note that in 1973 Third World gnp amounted to some $680 billion. The increase in income ul Haq is discussing is thus equivalent to nearly *20% of LDC gnp.* This figure makes the 1.2% estimated *possible* loss from 'exploitation' appear insignificant. The major reason that LDCs do not get access to this extra income is that they are prevented from so doing by DC trade barriers. Here the argument is not, as previously, that LDC development is being held back by DC *exploitation*—by wealth being removed—directly or indirectly from the LDCs; rather it is claimed that, LDC processed goods are, deliberately and selfishly, being *denied access to* DC markets.

Johan Galtung, as the following summary of his theory of imperialism suggests, has taken the argument a stage further. He argues that more is at stake in processing than simply the extra *money* generated:

> The processing stages also generate positive "spinoffs". They *necessitate*—and thus stimulate—high levels of technology, skill and education and sophisticated systems of transportation and communication. Processing on a large scale has a multiplier effect, generating subsidiary industries ... It also encourages a basic psychology of self-reliance and loosens up the social

structure as the demands of industry breakdown traditional socioeconomic patterns, thus increasing social and geographical mobility.[34]

To exemplify the argument, consider the following hypothetical case. A Swedish multinational corporation extracts ore from Liberian iron mines. The MNC employs Liberian workers at high wages, it pays the Liberian government large sums in royalties, but it also repatriates a percentage of its profits. The iron ore is sent to Sweden where it is processed into steel; the steel is made into tractors. In order to improve its agriculture, Liberia needs the tractors which its own iron ore has produced. But, in buying the tractors, Liberia has to pay the Swedish company part of the costs of extracting the ore from Liberia and shipping it to Sweden. The price of the tractor also includes the costs of the extremely high wages and social security benefits of Swedish workers; the profits of the Swedish steelmakers, and tractor and tractor component manufacturers; and the costs of shipping the iron ore (now transformed into the form of a tractor) back to Liberia. But the processing which took place in Sweden does not simply generate more income for Swedes. Processing also requires, and further stimulates, technological progress in Sweden. Sweden gains what Galtung calls the 'spin-off' effects of processing. Liberia gains none of the advantages of this 'virtuous circle' (to use Galtung's phrase), meanwhile its source of tractor-buying funds—the iron ore—is rapidly being used up, leaving nothing but an increasingly large hole in the ground.

If, as Galtung claims, processing has so many developmental advantages why don't Third World countries themselves get into the act? The answer is that trade barriers are deliberately erected around the rich nations which systematically discriminate against LDC processed goods, severely limiting their entry. DCs want to retain the value which is added by processing. DC manufacturers and workers in industries with which LDC processed goods would compete insist that their government erects tariff or quota barriers to protect domestic industries and jobs. Raw materials (unless produced locally, as is the case with sugar in the European Community) are usually admitted free of duty, but tariffs rise as the level of processing increases.

Consider the following 1966, European Community Common External Tariff structure for some typical LDC exports.

Tariff Percentages on LDC Imports

	Degree of Processing		
	None (raw)	Low	Higher
Peanuts	0	10% (raw oil)	15% (refined oil)
Cotton	0	6% (spun)	14% (woven)
Jute	0	8% (spun)	19% (woven)

[35]

Galtung argues that:

> Under this type of structure the colonial system worked for years ... the 'customs tariffs' are an institutionalisation, expressed in cool percentages, of the robbery and brutality of former times.[36]

And as Robert McNamara, certainly no radical, has pointed out this process of discrimination is by no means restricted to Europe or just to tariffs:

> In the United States, hides and skins enter duty-free, but tariffs of 4 to 5 percent apply on leather and 8 to 10 percent on shoes ... Finally, and perhaps worst of all, non-tariff barriers to trade have proliferated throughout the rich countries in recent years. Restrictions on market access exist in a variety of administrative and fiscal measures, including quotas, subsidies, valuation techniques, and preferential buying arrangements under government procurement.[37]

Furthermore, DCs put up higher tariffs against the entry of LDC manufactured goods than they do against the entry of other DC exports of manufactured goods. In 1972 the average tariff protection on *all* manufactured goods into the rich countries was 11.1%; for manufactured goods from all poor countries it was 22.6%—twice as high.[38] Multinational corporations operating in the Third World also act to protect their metropolitan domestic markets. Barnet and Muller note in their highly critical study, *Global Reach: The Power of the Multinational Corporations*, that:

> A study of 409 "transfer of technology" contracts between global corporations and their subsidiaries in Ecuador, Bolivia, Peru, Chile and Colombia shows that *almost 80 percent of them totally prohibited the use of the transferred technology for producting exports.*[39]

Galtung suggests two more ways in which the DCs ensure that their economic advantages are not wrested from them—these are "penetration' and 'fragmentation'.[40]

Fragmentation

Galtung argues that the international system has a 'feudal' structure. By this he means that whereas DCs communicate and interact with each other with great facility, LDCs do so with great difficulty. In the case of the LDCs, this phenomenon is most clearly visible in Africa where it is in large part a function of the colonial era. For example, many West African nation states are simply too small to be economically viable, consequently it would be economically rational for them to institute policies of inter-state economic co-operation—common markets and so forth. This does not happen, partly because there is no regional transportation of communication intrastructure. Roads, railways and rivers continue to fulfil their former colonial function of transporting raw materials to the coast—to the shipping points to Europe. Trade *between* black African states accounts for less than 10 percent of total African trade, and in 1969 telephone calls from the Central African Republic to Kenya were still being routed via the former colonial capitals of Paris and London! 'Fragmentation', a policy consciously pursued by DC elites, helps to prevent united Third World 'trade union' action such as that attempted with stunning success by the Organisation of Petroleum Exporting Countries—OPEC. Between 1971 and 1975, and stimulated by the 1973 Arab/Israeli 'October War', the OPEC states *quadrupled* the posted price of oil thus boosting their export earnings enormously. OPEC's victory was due to successful collusion among producers (i.e. the breakdown of Galtung's fragmentation phenomenon) and stimulated LDC hopes that other producer cartels, such as the Intergovernmental Committee of Copper Exporting countries, the International Tin Council and the Union of Banana Exporting Countries, could emulate OPEC's success. Currently no other commodity is as indispensable and unsubstitutable to the West as oil and OPEC's success has not been repeated. There are a number of reasons for this failure,[41] but the 'fragmented' nature of LDC interests and deliberate DC 'divide and rule' tactics have certainly played their part.

'Penetration'

Galtung sees 'penetration' as a form of cultural imperialism. Under colonialism European control was based on direct political rule backed by military coercion where necessary. Under *neo-colonialism* western dominance is much more subtle. During the period of colonial rule, native elites were built up by the colonial administrations. These elites were usually western-educated, aspired to western lifestyles and, when their countries achieved independence, became the new rulers. The period of colonial rule was also used by the colonial powers to:

> ... reshape the social and economic institutions of many of the dependent countries to the needs of the metropolitan centres.[42]

In 'traditional' LDC economies, agricultural production had been oriented towards domestic consumption; under colonialism the emphasis switched to production of agricultural raw materials for export to the DCs. This pattern has persisted since independence. These exports provide the foreign exchange which the new elites must have in order to buy the western consumption goods, from Mercedes to Coca Cola, which they have been socialised to demand. Thus Galtung is arguing that the 'penetration' of western values into LDC elite culture helps to attenuate LDC/DC conflict. There is, he argues, a certain identity of interest between the LDC elite and that in the DC. LDC elites, with their Western motor cars, Western lifestyles and materialistic aspirations, have more in common with their former colonial masters than with the majority of their own exploited and often miserably poor subjects. While Galtung does not rule out the possibility of elite conflict between DCs and LDCs (to do so would be to defy history), he does suggest such inter-elite conflict is less frequent and much less salient than the conflict of interests between what he calls the 'centre' (elite) and the 'periphery' (mass) *within* the LDCs.

Galtung's and ul Haq's positions may be briefly summarised as follows:
(a) the global international division of labour is such that the LDCs are denied easy access to DC markets for their processed goods, and this denies them a huge potential increase in their export earnings—equivalent to approximately 20% of their gnp according to ul Haq.
(b) The international division of labour also involves what Galtung calls the 'asymmetric distribution of spinoffs'. Processing generates growth-enhancing spinoffs, but it is concentrated in the DCs and (largely) denied to the LDCs.[43] Galtung believes these spinoff benefits to be so great for the DCs that it would pay them to more than compensate the LDCs for any losses they might incur via the terms of trade.
(c) This system, which denies LDC's opportunities for economic growth, is maintained in large part via the mechanisms of 'fragmentation' and 'penetration'.

Blockage

In the first section of this paper we examined arguments which claimed that LDCs were underdeveloped because DCs appropriated their wealth. In the second section the growth-inhibiting factor was the DC denial of market access to LDC manufactured goods. Finally we deal with what, for want of a better word, we have called 'blockage'. This is the third way in which relationships between DCs and LDCs may obstruct the development process in the latter. The basic idea behind the concept of blockage is that various forms of western aid to LDCs shore up regimes which, (a) are not pursuing economic programmes likely to promote development for the mass of the population and (b) without such aid might collapse as a consequence of internal opposition.

Consider the following example. A Third World country is well endowed with natural resources and has an educated and energetic population capable of utilising those resources to stimulate growth. One of the major barriers to economic advancement in this country is the concentration of land ownership, but those who oppose land reform—the latifundistas (landowners)—also control the government, while the reformists are left-leaning radicals. To the U.S. State Department, the latter look as though they might become communists (Fidel Castro looked like a social democrat in 1958), while the former are staunchly anti-communist. Although the U.S. would prefer a liberal anti-communist regime, the Administration decides that the reactionary incumbents must be supported (via aid, military training and perhaps even military intervention) in order to prevent the possibility of a latent communist threat (represented by the left reformists) becoming manifest. Thus in helping to maintain the conservative regime in power, the U.S. assists in the 'blocking' of the development process within the LDC even though this may mean no 'exploitation' at all in the sense of a net flow of resources from poor country to the rich

The idea that foreign aid may actually obstruct the development programmes, which it is (ostensibly) intended to promote is by no means novel. The critics of diffusion theory, as already noted, claim that foreign aid serves simply to 'prime the pump'; to set up institutional mechanisms which will later be used to siphon LDC wealth back to the Western metropoles. But there is no need to make *any* assumptions about exploitation in the above sense for 'blockage' to take place—and we will not make this assumption here. If a particular regime (in good or bad faith) is pursuing policies which are inimical to development (though no exploitation need take place) the foreign aid will block progress and may actually worsen the situation. Foreign aid does not go directly to the people who most need it, but to LDC governments which may or may not use it in the best interests of the mass of the population. If not, then the flow of foreign aid will increase the total resources of the LDC state (whether in terms of military hardware for repressive control, or economic resources for patronage purposes) and this will increase the *power* of the state *vis a vis* any potential opposition.

This criticism of the political functions of aid within the LDC comes from conservative development theorists as well as from radicals. Thus Professor Peter Bauer of London University has written

> ... official wealth transfers go to Third World governments, not to the population at large. Inevitably, this increases the power of the ruling groups over their people.[44]

The essence of Bauer's objection is that foreign aid increases the power of the state sector in the economy and thus weakens (relatively) the power of the free market, the unfettered operation of which Bauer sees an essential for economic development. While not sharing his enthusiasm for the free market, many radicals would agree with Bauer's assertion that foreign aid often helps swell the size of vast and unproductive LDC bureaucracies. The main political function of such bureaucracies is to provide a source of patronage jobs for governments to dole out to their supporters.

A more general criticism of foreign aid is not simply that it has channelled resources to LDC governments, but that aid programmes have also been heavily biased towards the *urban* areas and not to the rural sector where the needs are greatest. The idea that 'urban bias' is the major cause of the continued poverty and economic stagnation of the poorest two fifths of the Third World's population has been elaborated at some length in an important recent study by Michael Lipton.[45] The bottom 40%, writes Lipton, are:

> .. overwhelmingly rural: landless labourers, or farmers with no more than an acre or two, who must supplement their income by wage labour. Most of these countryfolk rely, as hitherto, on agriculture lacking irrigation or fertilisers or even iron tools. Hence they are so badly fed that they cannot work efficiently, and in many cases are unable to feed their infants well enough to

prevent physical stunting and perhaps even brain damage ... One in four dies before the age of ten, the rest live in the same overworked, underfed, ignorant and disease-ridden lives as thirty, or three hundred or three thousand years ago.[46]

Why is it that the countryside remains in a state of abject and often worsening poverty while the cities (relatively speaking) thrive?[47] The answer is to be found in the 'urban bias' of development planning. Urban bias is the orientation of development resources—cash, expertise, personnel, and research away from the countryside and towards the city.

> *... the 60 to 80 percent of people dependent on agriculture are still allocated barely 20 percent of public resources;* even these small shares are seldom achieved; and they have, if anything, tended to diminish. So long as the elites interests, background and sympathies remain predominantly urban, the countryside may get the 'priority' but the city will get the resources.[48]

Lipton points out that 'urban bias' can exist, albeit in somewhat different forms in non-capitalist planned economies. Thus, in the USSR under Stalin:

> Russia's peasantry was sacrificed to industrialisation on a much more massive scale than today's ... [LDC governments] however urban-biased, would contemplate.[49]

Furthermore, there seems to be no general law equating capitalism *per se* with 'urban bias'. As noted above, it may occur in non-market economies, but, as Lipton points out, a few capitalist LDCs have successfully countered urban bias by using state intervention to steer resources to the rural sector where they are most needed.

This transfer of resources increases both equity and productivity.[50] Recognition of the problems inherent in 'urban bias' has led to an increasing rejection of so-called 'trickledown theory', and a growing emphasis on what is currently labelled 'redistribution with growth'.[51]

'Trickledown' theorists saw 'urban bias' as a positive virtue. As Peter Berger has written:

> It is argued that the co-existence, in sharp contrast, of wealth and poverty is a necessary stage in the process of development. This is the stage during which capital must be rapidly accumulated in preparation for the 'take-off'. Once a certain level of accumulation is reached, the benefits will supposedly be distributed in a more equitable fashion, again because of the intrinsic economic dynamic of the development process.[52]

Berger notes that, 'this tenet has been called the "trickledown effect", more optimistically the "spread effect" '.[53] Trickledown theory, which had long been criticised by radical theorists such as Gunder Frank, has recently come under sustained attack from liberal development theorists who argue the 'redistribution with growth' case.[54] These theorists argue that there is no evidence that wealth will 'naturally' percolate down to the poorest strata in the countryside as a consequence of the 'free play of market forces'. Indeed, if anything, there is a tendency for wealth to 'trickle-up' from the periphery to the LDC metropolitan centre as Frank has argued.

Among LDCs, Brazil represents an extreme case of 'urban bias' and a good test case for the 'trickledown' thesis since Brazil's rates of economic growth throughout the 1960s were extremely high. Taiwan on the other hand, has adopted development policies closest to those advocated by the 'redistribution with growth' theorists—i.e. the state has actively intervened to redistribute resources to the rural poor. A comparison of the developmental progress of the two countries during the decade of the 1960s is thus most instructive.

Development Indicators	Taiwan	Brazil
per capita income	1960: $174	268
	1969: $334	348
gnp growth rate in 1960s	10%	6%
unemployment and gross underemployment	10% in 1963	
	4% in 1968	10-12%(1970)
annual increase in industrial jobs	10%(1963-1969)	2.8%(1966-9)
Income improvement of poorest 20% over past 20 years	200%	Negligible
Effective land reform?	Yes	No
Yields per acre in food grains	3,570	1,280
% of farmers belonging to co-operatives (late 1960s)	100%	28%
literacy	85%	67%
life expectancy	68	64
birth rate (births per thousand)	41 (1947)	41 (1950)
	26 (1970)	38 (1970)

[55]

It is quite clear from the table that the Brazilian reliance on "trickledown" via 'free market forces' has not benefited the Brazilian poor at all. But in Taiwan a deliberate government policy of channelling much-needed resources—i.e. rural credit, agricultural extension services, rural electrification programmes etc.—to poor farmers has been highly successful in reducing inequality and raising the standard of living of the bottom 20% of the population. Taiwan's policy is a good example of 'redistribution with growth'.

Concluding this section we can say that 'urban bias' appears to be a powerful explanation for the perpetuation of rural LDC poverty. According to this theory, the rural poor are poor, not because they are inadequate or 'traditional', but because they are denied resources by the urban dwellers. Thus Lipton argues:

> ... the basic conflict in the Third World is not between capital and labour, but between capital and the countryside, farmer and townsmen ... [and] while the urban centres of power and government remain able and willing to steer development overwhelmingly towards urban interests, development will remain inequalising.[56]

Why don't the underprivileged and exploited rural populations fight back? Central to the problem is the fact that the rural poor:

> ... constitute an almost voiceless, largely illiterate, dispersed unorganised rural mass. It seldom combines, articulates its needs, or backs them with effective political or trade union power.[57]

Thus, the 'fragmentation' of the rural sector enhances its weakness, while the 'penetration' of western 'trickledown' theories of development has convinced urban elites that selfishness is a virtue. Furthermore, the political capability of the elites which propagate anti-rural development programmes is strengthened by the resources which flow to LDC metropoles in economic and military aid programmes. It is in this sense that we may talk of DC/LDC relationships acting to 'block' development.

Conclusion

In this paper we have examined three ways in which DC/LDC relationships can obstruct the progress of capitalist development in the Third World. We argued first, that evidence for the exploitation thesis—that the development process is hampered by the removal of wealth from the Third World—was not convincing.

Second, we examined the Galtung/ul Haq theories concerning the international division of labour. These theories claim that the denial of DC market access to LDC processed goods tends artificially to perpetuate an international division of labour which (a) denies LDCs a huge potential increase in export earnings (ul Haq), and (b) denies them the positive growth-generating 'spinoffs' associated with processing (Galtung). Here wealth is not being *removed* from the LDCs by DCs, but *denied* to them by the trade barriers which the DCs erect to protect their domestic markets. There is no doubt that these theories point to a major barrier to greater LDC economic progress.

If the barriers to which Galtung and ul Haq draw attention were removed, LDC manufacturing industries would be given a huge boost but the resultant industrial growth would most probably be located in the *urban* areas. And unless we accept the largely discredited 'trickledown' theory, there is no reason to assume that this growth would benefit the poverty-stricken countryside—indeed it might well increase urban/rural inequality still further. This brings us to the third theoretical approach discussed, that of 'urban bias'. Lipton's 'urban bias' theory is by no means immune to criticism (see fn. 37), but the central thesis, that rural poverty (*the* development problem) is a result of a highly-skewed allocation of resources in favour of particular classes in the urban areas, is more convincing than the theories discussed previously.

In concluding this discussion there is one more theoretical issue to which the reader's attention should be drawn. it concerns the so-called 'level of analysis' problem and is extremely important. Most of the radical arguments examined in this paper have analysed relationships between *nations*. We have discussed theories which claim that poor nations may be disadvantaged in their relationships with rich nations, via falling LDC terms of trade, transfer pricing, profit remittances and denial of access to DC markets, etc. In each case the *unit of analysis* was the nation state—rich *nations* exploit poor *nations* and so forth. A general problem with this level of analysis is that it may obscure as much as it reveals. Instead of, or at the very least in addition to, using the nation state as a unit of analysis we should use the concept of *class*. Galtung's theory of imperialism represents one attempt to move away from the practice of treating nation states as homogenous entities and examining only the relationships which exist between them. Galtung argues that there is an identity of interest between the elite of the DC and the elite of the LDC, and that this identity of interest is more important than the apparent *conflict* of interest between the LDC nation-as-a-whole and the DC nation-as-a-whole. Both the DC and the LDC elites may profit from various unequal economic exchanges, even though the LDC *as a whole* is economically disadvantaged. If this is the case then the real victims are the LDC poor. A recent trend in radical analysis has been to argue that the primary focus of the analysis of underdevelopment should be the relationships between *classes* at both the inter and intra-national levels and *not* the relationships between nations.

Finally we return to the question of the increasingly inequitable global division of wealth. In the short term the bargaining power of the Third World is not very great—OPEC's success remains exceptional. But in the long run, the balance of power may begin to shift in the direction of the LDCs. Mahbub ul Haq points out that the population of the rich countries is continually shrinking relative to the population of the poor. By the turn of the century the DCs will compose only 20 percent of the world's population, while increasing numbers of the LDCs will have acquired nuclear weapons. With the mutual possession of nuclear weapons neutralising the nuclear threat, sheer numbers of people may again become politically salient:

> Throughout history, the only way a small minority has continued to exercise control over human affairs is through its monopoly over some form of human destruction: once this advantage is neutralised, the minority begins to realise how dependent it is on the goodwill of the majority for its continued existence.[58]

FOOTNOTES

1. R. Jenkins, *Exploitation* (Paladin, London, 1971) pp. 160-1.
2. D. Bhattacharya, quoted in *Political Economy of Development* (ABC publications, 1977) p. 34.
3. P. L. Berger, *Pyramids of Sacrifice* (Penguin, London, 1977) p. 29.
4. Gunder Frank and some other radical theorists distinguish 'underdeveloped' from 'undeveloped' nations. The latter are (or were) 'traditional' Third World societies untouched by western influences. '*Under*developed' societies are those which have been penetrated and transformed by western capitalist intervention which in many cases has existed for centuries.

5. For a good summary of the various arguments of the liberal development theories of the 1950s and early 1960s plus a hard-hitting critique see G. A. Frank, 'Sociology of Development and Underdevelopment of Sociology' in J. D. Cockcroft, A. G. Frank and D. L. Johnson, *Dependence and Underdevelopment* (Anchor Books, New York, 1972). Note that we use the terms 'liberal', 'non-radical' and 'diffusionist' interchangeably in the text.
6. A. Emmanuel, 'Myths of Development', *New Left Review* (May/June, 1974) p. 74.
7. B. Warren, 'The Postwar Economic Experience of the Third World', *Journal of Australian Political Economy*, No. 3 (September, 1978) p. 38.
8. See B. Warren, 'Imperialism and Underdevelopment', *New Left Review*, No. 81, and 'The Post War Economic Experience of the Third World', *op.cit.* For a useful discussion of the Marxist views on the possibility of capitalist development in the Third World which Warren criticises see, B. Sutcliffe, 'Imperialism and Industrialisation in the Third World' in R. Owen and B. Sutcliffe, *Studies in the Theory of Imperialism* (Longman, London, 1972). For radical critiques of Warren's views see A. Emmanuel, 'Myths of Development' and P. McMichael, J. Petras and R. Rhodes, 'Imperialism and the Contradictions of Development', *New Left Review*, No. 85 (May/June 1974).
9. Warren's figures indicate that, between 1960 and 1973, out of 98 Third World nations with a population of more than one million (between 1960-73) less than 12% suffered negative per capita growth rates. See 'Post War Economic Experiences ...', *op.cit.*, pp. 12-13.
10. I. Adelman and C. Morris, *Economic Growth and Social Equity in Developing Countries* (Stanford, 1973) p. 189. (our emphasis). Robert McNamara, the World Bank's president, has also 'focussed attention on the stagnant or *worsening* lives of the bottom 40% of people in poor countries', M. Lipton, *Why Poor People Stay Poor* (Temple Smith, London, 1977) p. 15. Lipton's own contribution to this debate is worth reading, see pp. 27-30.
11. See, S. Bodenheimer, 'Dependency and Imperialism: The Roots of Latin American Underdevelopment', and T. dos Santos, 'The Structure of Dependence' both in K. T. Fann and D. C. Hodges, *Readings in U.S. Imperialism* (Porter Sargent, Boston, 1971); O. Sunkel, 'Big Business and "Dependencia": A Latin American View', *Foreign Affairs* (April, 1972); B. J. Cohen, 'Dependence and Exploitation', Chapter VI in his, *The Question of Imperialism* (Macmillan, London, 1974); G. A. Frank, 'Economic Dependence Class Structure, and Underdevelopment Policy' and 'The Development of Underdevelopment' both in J. D. Cockcroft, *et.al.*, *Dependence and Underdevelopment* (Anchor Books, New York, 1972); R. H. Chilcote, 'Dependency: A Critical Synthesis of the Literature' in *Latin American Perspectives*, Vol. 1, 1974.
12. See C. Leys, 'Underdevelopment and Dependency: Critical Notes', *Journal of Contemporary Asia*, Vol. 7, No. 1 (1977); B. Warren, 'Postwar Economic Experience ...', *op.cit.*, pp. 29-32; Cohen, *op.cit.*
13. J. Galtung, *The European Community: A Superpower in the Making* (Allen and Unwin, London, 1973) p. 38.
14. J. Caparaso, 'Methodological Issues in the Measurement of Inequality, Dependence and Exploitation' in S. Rosen and J. Kurth (eds.), *Testing Theories of Economic Imperialism*, (DC: Heath, Boston, 1974) p. 107. For another attempt to define exploitation see Cohen, *op.cit.*
15. Caparaso, *op.cit.*, pp. 91-2.
16. Quoted in A. Mack, 'Theories of Imperialism: The European Perspective', *Journal of Conflict Resolution*, Vol. XVII, No. 3 (September, 1974) p. 529.
17. A. Emmanuel, *Unequal Exchange: A Study of the Imperialism of Trade* (New Left Books, London, 1972).

18. Part of the problem here is that the choice of starting point for measuring changes in the terms of trade can affect the outcome. For example, because of the Korean War, 1950 was a boom year for Third World commodities and a relative fall in commodity prices subsequently was to be expected. Thus 1950 was hardly a legitimate starting point for the measurement of any *long term* trend. Yet 1950 to 1961 *was* the period which UNCTAD, unfairly according to Professor Bauer of London University, used to measure long term trends. Not surprisingly this period showed a decline for the LDCs. Bauer argues that had the period 1938 to 1950 been chosen, an *improvement* of some 40% in LDC terms of trade would have been noted. See P. Bauer, *Dissent on Development* (Weidenfeld and Nicholson, London, 1971) p. 256. Emmanuel on the other hand quotes U.N. figures to demonstrate a deterioration in LDC trade terms of 40% between 1900 and 1939. See his discussion in *Unequal Exchange, op.cit.*, p. xxiii to xxv.
19. P. Jalée, *The Third World in World Economy*, (Monthly Review Press, New York, 1969) p. 75.
20. *Ibid.*, p. 12.
21. Quoted in R. Owen and B. Sutcliffe, *Studies in the Theory of Imperialism* (Longman, London, 1972) p. 323.
22. P. B. Evans, 'National Autonomy and Economic Development', *International Organisation*, No. 25 (1971).
23. G. A. Frank, *Capitalism and Underdevelopment in Latin America* (Penguin, London, 1971) p. 33. Note the use of the terms metropolis and satellite—implying dominance/dependency relationships, rather than DC/LDC.
24. B. Warren, 'Postwar Economic Experience ...', *op.cit.*, p. 31. See also A. Emmanuel, 'The Multinational Corporation and Inequality of Development', *International Social Science Journal*, 28:4 (1976).
25. Jalée, *op.cit.*, p. 117.
26. R. Barnet and R. E. Muller, *Global Reach: The Power of the Multinational Corporations* (Simon and Schuster, New York, 1974) pp. 157-162.
27. A. Emmanuel, 'Myths of Development', *op.cit.*, p. 77. Emmanuel, writing in 1974, gives no dates for this estimate. One suspects that they are probably for the early seventies. We should also point out that other Third World statistics used here are also often highly suspect.
28. Lipton, *op.cit.*, p. 28.
29. Warren, *op.cit.*, fn. 134.
30. R. Heilbroner, *The Making of Economic Society* (Prentice Hall, Englewood Cliffe, 1975) p. 253. For a simple exposition of the relationship between savings investment and growth see P. Donaldson, *Worlds Apart* (Penguin, London, 1973) pp. 87-94.
31. Heilbroner notes that this, 'seems to be *roughly* what the marginal capital-output ratio of new investment in the underdeveloped areas may be.' *Ibid.*, p. 253.
32. See R. D. Hansen (ed.), *The U.S. and World Development: Agenda for Action, 1976* (Praeger, New York, 1976), p. 179, for detailed breakdown of trade composition.
33. M. ul Haq, *The Third World and the International Economic Order*, Overseas Development Council Development Paper, No. 22 (Washington, Sept. 1976) p. 4-5.
34. A. Mack, *op.cit.*, p. 522-3.
Galtung's concept of 'spinoff' seems to encompass the following concepts of conventional economic theory: 'the multiplier'; 'backward linkages'; 'forward linkages'; 'horizontal linkage' and 'externalities'. See P. Streeten and F. Stewart 'The Little-Mirrless Method and Project Appraisal' in P. Streeten, *The*

Frontiers of Development Studies. (Macmillan, London, 1972) pp. 349-355, for discussion of these concepts.
35. Source, J. Galtung, *op.cit.*, p. 74.
36. *Ibid.*, p. 74.
37. R. McNamara, *One Hundred Countries, Two Billion People* (Pall Mall, London, 1974) p. 84-5.
38. H. Singer and J. Ansari *Rich Countries and Poor Countries* (Allen and Unwin, London, 1977) p. 81.
39. R. Barnet and R. Muller, *Global Reach: The Power of the Multinationals* (Simon and Schuster, New York, 1974) p. 163. Our emphasis.
40. See J. Galtung, *The European Community*, *op.cit.*, and 'A Structural Theory of Imperialism' *Journal of Peace Research* XIII No. 2 (1971).
41. For a rundown of reasons for this see S. D. Krasner, 'Oil is the Exception', *Foreign Policy* (Spring, 1974).
42. H. Magdoff, 'Imperialism Without Colonies' in R. Owen and B. Sutcliffe, *op.cit.*, p. 164.
43. It should be pointed out that this situation appears to be changing. In 1960, according to Galtung's own figures, 14% of the exports were composed of processed goods (there is some difficulty in defining 'processed'); by 1969 this proportion had increased to 24%—a highly significant increase of about 70% in nine years.
44. P. Bauer, *Spectator* (25 June 1977) p. 13. For a more detailed exposition of Bauer's views see his *Dissent on Development* (Weidenfeld and Nicholson, London, 1971). Chpt. 2.B.
45. M. Lipton, *Why Poor People Stay Poor: Urban Bias in World Development* (Temple Smith, London, 1977).
46. *Ibid.*, p. 15.
47. Of course not *all* urban dwellers thrive, but Lipton somewhat controversially treats the so-called 'informal sector'—the recently arrived immigrants from the countryside—as a temporary phenomenon. Either these people will return to the countryside or be fully absorbed in the urban sector. For a critique of this argument and other aspects of Lipton's book see R. Leaver, 'Agriculture and Economic Development in the Second Development Decade: Is Reformist Development Possible?', paper presented to the 20th Annual Conference of the Australasian Political Science Association. Adelaide, August 1978.
48. Lipton, *op.cit.*, p. 17-18. Our emphasis.
49. *Ibid.*, p. 122.
50. *Ibid.*, p. 77.
51. Recent development literature arguing the 'redistribution with growth' thesis includes Lipton's own book, *ibid.*, Adelman and Morris, *op.cit.*, H. Chenery et.al., *Redistribution with Growth* (Oxford University Press, London, 1974); R. Jolly et.al. *Third World Employment: Problems and Strategy* (Penguin, London, 1973); E. Owens and R. Shaw, *Development Reconsidered* (D. C. Heath, Boston, 1972); A. Birou et.al., *Towards a Re-definition of Development* (Pergamon Press, Oxford, 1977) and J. W. Mellor, *The New Economics of Growth* (Cornell University Press, 1976).
52. P. Berger, *Pyramids of Sacrifice* (Penguin, London, 1977) p. 65.
53. *Ibid.*, p. 65.
54. For a good example of this criticism see J. P. Grant 'Development the End of Trickledown', *Foreign Policy* No. 12 (1973-4).
55. Statistics from S. George, *How the Other Half Dies* (Penguin, London, 1976) p. 64-5.
56. Lipton, *op.cit.*, p. 67.
57. *Ibid.*, p. 37.
58. ul Haq, *op.cit.*, p. 14.

Outwitting the 'Developed' Countries

Ivan Illich

It is now common to demand that the rich nations convert their war machine into a program for the development of the Third World. The poorer four-fifths of humanity multiply unchecked while their per capita consumption actually declines. This population expansion and decrease of consumption threatens the industrialized nations, who may still, as a result, convert their defense budgets to the economic pacification of poor nations. And this in turn could produce irreversible despair, because the plows of the rich can do as much harm as their swords. US trucks can do more lasting damage than US tanks. It is easier to create mass demand for the former than for the latter. Only a minority needs heavy weapons, while a majority can become dependent on unrealistic levels of supply for such productive machines as modern trucks. Once the Third World has become a mass market for the goods, products and processes which are designed by the rich for themselves, the discrepancy between demand for these Western artifacts and the supply will increase indefinitely. The family car cannot drive the poor into the jet age, nor can a school system provide the poor with education, nor can the family icebox ensure healthy food for them.

It is evident that only one man in a thousand in Latin America can afford a Cadillac, a heart operation or a Ph.D. This restriction on the goals of development does not make us despair of the fate of the Third World, and the reason is simple. We have not yet come to conceive of a Cadillac as necessary for good transportation, or of a heart operation as normal-health care, or of a Ph.D. as the prerequisite of an acceptable education. In fact, we recognize at once that the importation of Cadillacs should be heavily taxed in Peru, that an organ transplant clinic is a scandalous plaything to justify the concentration of more doctors in Bogota, and that a Betatron is beyond the teaching facilities of the University of Sao Paulo.

Unfortunately, it is not held to be universally evident that the majority of Latin Americans — not only of our generation, but also of the next and the next again — cannot afford any kind of automobile, or any kind of hospitalization, or for that matter an elementary school education. We suppress our consciousness of this obvious reality because we hate to recognize the corner into which our imagination has been pushed. So persuasive is the power of the institutions we have created that they shape not only our preferences, but actually our sense of possibilities. We have forgotten how to speak about modern transportation that does not rely on automobiles and airplanes. Our conceptions of modern health care emphasize our ability to prolong the lives of the desperately ill. We have become unable to think of better education except in terms of more complex schools and of teachers trained for ever longer periods. Huge institutions producing costly services dominate the horizons of our inventiveness.

We have embodied our world view into our institutions and are now their prisoners. Factories, news media, hospitals, governments and schools produce goods and services packaged to contain our view of the world. We — the rich — conceive of progress as the expansion of these establishments. We conceive of heightened mobility as luxury and safety packaged by General Motors or Boeing. We conceive of improving the general well-being as increasing the supply of doctors and hospitals, which package health along with protracted suffering. We have come to identify our need for further learning with the demand for ever longer confinement to classrooms. In other words, we have packaged education with custodial care, certification for jobs, and the right to vote, and wrapped them all together with indoctrination in the Christian, liberal or communist virtues.

In less than a hundred years industrial society has molded patent solutions to basic human needs and converted us to the belief that man's needs were shaped by the Creator as demands for the products we have invented. This is as true for Russia and Japan as for the North Atlantic community. The consumer is trained for obsolescence, which means continuing loyalty toward the same producers who will give him the same basic packages in different quality or new wrappings.

Industrialized societies can provide such packages for personal consumption for most of their citizens, but this is no proof that these societies are sane, or economical, or that they promote life. The contrary is true. The more the citizen is trained in the consumption of packaged goods and services the less effective he seems to become in shaping his environment. His energies and finances are consumed in procuring ever new models of his staples, and the environment becomes a by-product of his own consumption habits.

The design of the 'package deals' of which I speak is the main cause of the high cost of satisfying basic needs. So long as every man 'needs' his car, our cities must endure longer traffic jams and absurdly expensive remedies to relieve them. So long as health means maximum length of survival, our sick will get ever more extraordinary surgical interventions and the drugs required to deaden their consequent pain. So long as we want to use school to get children out of the parents' hair or to keep them off the street and out of the labor force, our young will be retained in endless schooling and will need ever-increasing incentives to endure the ordeal.

Rich nations now benevolently impose a straitjacket of traffic jams, hospital confinements and classrooms on the poor nations, and by international agreement call this 'development'. The rich and schooled and old of the world try to share their dubious blessings by foisting their pre-packaged solutions on to the Third World. Traffic jams develop in Sao Paulo, while almost a million northeastern Brazilians flee the drought by walking 500 miles. Latin American doctors get training at the New York Hospital for Special Surgery, which they apply to only a few, while amoebic dysentery remains endemic in slums where 90 percent of the population live. A tiny minority gets advanced education in basic science in North America — not infrequently paid for by their own governments. If they return at all to Bolivia, they become second-rate teachers of pretentious subjects at La Paz or Cochibamba. The rich export outdated versions of their standard models.

The Alliance for Progress is a good example of benevolent production for underdevelopment. Contrary to its slogans, it did succeed — as an alliance for the progress of the consuming classes, and for the domestication of the Latin American masses. The Alliance has been a major step in modernizing the consumption patterns of the middle class in South America by integrating them with the dominant culture of the North American metropolis. At the same time, the Alliance has modernized the aspirations of the majority of citizens and fixed their demands on unavailable products.

Each car which Brazil puts on the road denies fifty people good transportation by bus. Each merchandised refrigerator reduces the chance of building a community freezer. 'Every dollar spent in Latin America on doctors and hospitals costs a hundred lives,' to adopt a phrase of Jorge de Ahumada, the brilliant Chilean economist. Had each dollar been spent on providing safe drinking water, a hundred lives could have been saved. Each dollar spent on schooling means more privileges for the few at the cost of the many; at best it increases the number of those who, before dropping out, have been taught that those who stay longer have earned the right to more power, wealth and prestige. What such schooling does is to teach the schooled the superiority of the better schooled.

All Latin American countries are frantically intent on expanding their school systems. No country now spends less than the equivalent of 18 percent of tax-derived public income on education — which means schooling — and many countries spend almost double that. But even with these huge investments, no country yet succeeds in giving five full years of education to more than one-third of its population; supply and demand for schooling grow geometrically apart. And what is true about schooling is equally true about the products of most institutions in the process of modernization in the Third World.

Continued technological refinements of products which are already established on the market frequently benefit the producer far more than the consumer. The more complex production processes tend to enable only the largest producer to continually replace outmoded models, and to focus the demand of the consumer on the marginal improvements of what he buys, no matter what the concomitant side effects: higher prices, diminished life span, less general usefulness, higher cost of repairs. Think of the multiple uses for a simple can opener, whereas an electric one, if it works at all, opens only some kinds of cans, and costs one hundred times as much.

This is equally true for a piece of agricultural machinery and for an academic degree. The midwestern farmer can become convinced of his need for a four-axle vehicle which can go 70 m.p.h. on the highways, has an electric windshield wiper and upholstered seats, and can be turned in for a new one within a year or two. Most of the world's farmers don't need such speed, nor have they ever met with such comfort, nor are they interested in obsolescence. They need low-priced transport, in a world where time is not money, where manual wipers suffice, and where a piece of heavy equipment should outlast a generation. Such a mechanical donkey requires entirely different engineering and design than one produced for the U.S. market. This vehicle is not in production.

Most of South America needs para-medical workers who can function for indefinite periods without the supervision of an MD. Instead of establishing a process to train midwives and visiting healers who know how to use a very limited arsenal of medicines while working independently, Latin American universities establish every year a new school of specialized nursing or nursing administration to prepare professionals who can function only in a hospital, and pharmacists who know how to sell increasingly more dangerous drugs.

The world is reaching an impasse where two processes converge: ever more men have fewer basic choices. The increase in population is widely publicized and creates panic. The decrease in fundamental choice causes anguish and is consistently overlooked. The population explosion overwhelms the imagination, but the progressive atrophy of social imagination is rationalized as an increase of choice between brands. The two processes converge in a dead end: the population explosion provides more consumers for everything from food to contraceptives, while our shrinking imagination can conceive of no other ways of satisfying their demands except through the packages now on sale in the admired societies.

I will focus successively on these two factors, since, in my opinion, they form the two co-ordinates which together permit us to define underdevelopment.

In most Third World countries, the population grows, and so does the middle class. Income, consumption and the well-being of the middle class are all growing while the gap between this class and the mass of people widens. Even where per capita consumption is rising, the majority of men have less food now than in 1945, less actual care in sickness, less meaningful work, less protection. This is partly a consequence of polarized consumption and partly caused by the breakdown of traditional family and culture. More people suffered from hunger, pain and exposure in 1969 than they did at the end of the Second World War, not only numerically, but also as a percentage of the world population.

These concrete consequences of underdevelopment are rampant; but underdevelopment is also a state of mind, and understanding it as a state of mind, or as a form of consciousness, is the critical problem. Underdevelopment as a state of mind occurs when mass needs are converted to the demand for new brands of packaged solutions which are forever beyond the reach of the majority. Underdevelopment in this sense is rising rapidly even in countries where the supply of classrooms, calories, cars and clinics is also rising. The ruling groups in these countries build up services which have been designed for an affluent culture; once they have monopolized demand in this way, they can never satisfy majority needs.

Underdevelopment as a form of consciousness is an extreme result of what we can call in the language of both Marx and Freud *'Verdinglichung'* or reification. By reification I mean the hardening of the perception of real needs into the demand for mass manufactured products. I mean the translation of thirst into the need for a Coke. This kind of reification occurs in the manipulation of primary human needs by vast bureaucratic organizations which have succeeded in dominating the imagination of potential consumers.

Let me return to my example taken from the field of education. The intense promotion of schooling leads to so close an identification of school attendance and education that in everyday language the two terms are interchangeable. Once the imagination of an entire population has been 'schooled', or indoctrinated to believe that school has a monopoly on formal education, then the illiterate can be taxed to provide free high school and university education for the children of the rich.

Underdevelopment is the result of rising levels of aspiration achieved through the intensive marketing of 'patent' products. In this sense, the dynamic underdevelopment that is now taking place is the exact opposite of what I believe education to be: namely, the awakening awareness of new levels of human potential and the use of one's creative powers to foster human life. Underdevelopment, however, implies the surrender of social consciousness to pre-packaged solutions.

The process by which the marketing of 'foreign' products increases underdevelopment is frequently understood in the most superficial ways. The same man who feels indignation at the sight of a Coca-Cola plant in a Latin American slum often feels pride at the sight of a new normal school growing up alongside. He resents the evidence of a foreign 'license' attached to a soft drink which he would like to see replaced by 'Cola-Mex'. But the same man is willing to impose schooling — at all costs — on his fellow citizens, and is unaware of the invisible license by which this institution is deeply enmeshed in the world market.

Some years ago I watched workmen putting up a sixty-foot Coca-Cola sign on a desert plain in the Mexquital. A serious drought and famine had just swept over the Mexican highland. My host, a poor Indian in Ixmiquilpan, had just offered his visitors a tiny tequila glass of costly black sugar-water. When I recall this scene I still feel anger; but I feel much more incensed when I remember UNESCO meetings at which well-meaning and well-paid bureaucrats seriously discussed Latin American curricula, and when I think of the speeches of enthusiastic liberals advocating the need for more schools.

The fraud perpetrated by the salesmen of schools is less obvious but much more fundamental than the self-satisfied salesmanship of the Coca-Cola or Ford representative, because the schoolman hooks his people on a much more demanding drug. Elementary school attendance is not a harmless luxury, but more like the coca chewing of the Andean Indian, which harnesses the worker to the boss.

The higher the dose of schooling an individual has received, the more depressing his experience of withdrawal. The seventh-grade dropout feels his inferiority much more acutely than the dropout from the third grade. The schools of the Third World administer their opium with much more effect than the churches of other epochs. As tne mind ot society is progressively schooled, step by step its individuals lose their sense that it might be possible to live without being inferior to others. As the majority shifts from the land into the city, the hereditary inferiority of the peon is replaced by the inferiority of the school dropout who is held personally responsible for his failure. Schools rationalize the divine origin of social stratification with much more rigor than churches have ever done.

Until this day no Latin American country has declared youthful under-consumers of Coca-Cola or cars as lawbreakers, while all Latin American countries have passed laws which define the early dropout as a citizen who has not fulfilled his legal obligations. The Brazilian government recently almost doubled the number of years during which schooling is legally compulsory and free. From now on any Brazilian dropout under the age of sixteen will be faced during his lifetime with the reproach that he did not take advantage of a legally obligatory privilege. This law was passed in a country where not even the most optimistic could foresee the day when such levels of schooling would be provided for only 25 per cent of the young. The adoption of international standards of schooling forever condemns most Latin Americans to marginality or exclusion from social life — in a word, underdevelopment.

The translation of social goals into levels of consumption is not limited to only a few countries. Across all frontiers of culture, ideology and geography today, nations are moving toward the establishment of their own car factories, their own medical and normal schools — and most of these are, at best, poor imitations of foreign and largely North American models.

The Third World is in need of a profound revolution of its institutions. The revolutions of the last generation were overwhelmingly political. A new group of men with a new set of ideological justifications assumed power to administer fundamentally the same scholastic, medical and market institutions in the interest of a new group of clients. Since the institutions have not radically changed, the new group of clients remains approximately the same size as that previously served. This appears clearly in the case of education. Per pupil costs of schooling are today comparable everywhere since the standards used to evaluate the quality of schooling tend to be internationally shared. Access to publicly financed education, considered as access to school, everywhere depends on per capita income. (Places like China and North Vietnam might be meaningful exceptions.)

Everywhere in the Third World modern institutions are grossly unproductive, with respect to the egalitarian purposes for which they are being reproduced. But so long as the social imagination of the majority has not been destroyed by its fixation on these institutions, there is more hope of planning an institutional revolution in the Third World than among the rich. Hence the urgency of the task of developing workable alternatives to 'modern' solutions.

Underdevelopment is at the point of becoming chronic in

many countries. The revolution of which I speak must begin to take place before this happens. Education again offers a good example: chronic educational underdevelopment occurs when the demand for schooling becomes so widespread that the total concentration of educational resources on the school system becomes a unanimous political demand. At this point the separation of education from schooling becomes impossible.

The only feasible answer to ever-increasing underdevelopment is a response to basic needs that is planned as a long-range goal for areas which will always have a different capital structure. It is easier to speak about alternatives to existing institutions, services and products than to define them with precision. It is not my purpose either to paint a Utopia or to engage in scripting scenarios for an alternative future. We must be satisfied with examples indicating simple directions that research should take.

Some such examples have already been given. Buses are alternatives to a multitude of private cars. Vehicles designed for slow transportation on rough terrain are alternatives to standard trucks. Safe water is an alternative to high-priced surgery. Medical workers are an alternative to doctors and nurses. Community food storage is an alternative to expensive kitchen equipment. Other alternatives could be discussed by the dozen. Why not, for example, consider walking as a long-range alternative for locomotion by machine, and explore the demands which this would impose on the city planner? And why can't the building of shelters be standardized, elements be pre-cast, and each citizen be obliged to learn in a year of public service how to construct his own sanitary housing?

It is harder to speak about alternatives in education, partly because schools have recently so completely pre-empted the available educational resources of good will, imagination and money. But even here we can indicate the direction in which research must be conducted.

At present, schooling is conceived as graded, curricular, class attendance by children, for about 1000 hours yearly during an uninterrupted succession of years. On the average, Latin American countries can provide each citizen with between eight and thirty months of this service. Why not, instead, make one or two months a year obligatory for all citizens below the age of thirty?

Money is now spent largely on children, but an adult can be taught to read in one-tenth the time and for one-tenth the cost it takes to teach a child. In the case of the adult there is an immediate return on the investment, whether the main importance of his learning is seen in his new insight, political awareness and willingness to assume responsibility for his family's size and future, or whether the emphasis is placed on increased productivity. There is a double return in the case of the adult, because not only can he contribute to the education of his children, but to that of other adults as well. In spite of these advantages, basic literacy programs have little or no support in Latin America, where schools have a first call on all public resources. Worse, these programs are actually ruthlessly suppressed in Brazil and elsewhere, where military support of the feudal or industrial oligarchy has thrown off its former benevolent disguise.

Another possibility is harder to define, because there is as yet no example to point to. We must therefore imagine the use of public resources for education distributed in such a way as to give every citizen a minimum chance. Education will become a political concern of the majority of voters only when each individual has a precise sense of the educational resources that are owing to him — and some idea of how to sue for them. Something like a universal GI Bill of Rights could be imagined, dividing the public resources assigned to education by the number of children who are legally of school age, and making sure that a child who did not take advantage of his credit at the age of seven, eight or nine would have the accumulated benefits at his disposal at age ten.

What could the pitiful education credit which a Latin American Republic could offer to its children provide? Almost all of the basic supply of books, pictures, blocks, games and toys that are totally absent from the homes of the really poor, but enable a middle-class child to learn the alphabet, the colors, shapes and other classes of objects and experiences which ensure his educational progress. The choice between these things and schools is obvious. Unfortunately, the poor, for whom alone the choice is real, never get to exercise this choice.

Defining alternatives to the products and institutions which now pre-empt the field is difficult, not only, as I have been trying to show, because these products and institutions shape our conception of reality itself, but also because the construction of new possibilities requires a concentration of will and intelligence in a higher degree than ordinarily occurs by chance. This concentration of will and intelligence on the solution of particular problems regardless of their nature we have become accustomed over the last century to call research.

I must make clear, however, what kind of research I am talking about. I am not talking about basic research either in physics, engineering, genetics, medicine or learning. The work of such men as Crick, Piaget and Gell-Mann must continue to enlarge our horizons in other fields of science. The labs and libraries and specially trained collaborators these men need cause them to congregate in the few research capitals of the world. Their research can provide the basis for new work on practically any product.

I am not speaking here of the billions of dollars annually spent on applied research, for this money is largely spent by existing institutions on the perfection and marketing of their own products. Applied research is money spent on making planes faster and airports safer; on making medicines more specific and powerful and doctors capable of handling their deadly side-effects; on packaging more learning into classrooms; on methods to administer large bureaucracies. This is the kind of research for which some kind of counterfoil must somehow be developed if we are to have any chance to come up with basic alternatives to the automobile, the hospital and the school, and any of the many other so-called 'evidently necessary implements for modern life'.

I have in mind a different, and peculiarly difficult, kind of research, which has been largely neglected up to now, for obvious reasons. I am calling for research on alternatives to the products which now dominate the market; to hospitals and the profession dedicated to keeping the sick alive; to schools and the packaging process which refuses education to those who are not of the right age, who have not gone through the right curriculum, who have not sat in a classroom a sufficient number of successive hours, who will not pay for their learning with submission to custodial care, screening and certification or with indoctrination in the values of the dominant elite.

This counter-research on fundamental alternatives to current pre-packaged solutions is the element most critically needed if the poor nations are to have a liveable future. Such counter-research is distinct from most of the work done in the name of the 'year 2000', because most of that work seeks radical changes in social patterns through adjustments in the organization of an already advanced technology The counter-research of which I speak must take as one of its assumptions the continued lack of capital in the Third World.

The difficulties of such research are obvious. The researcher must first of all doubt what is obvious to every eye. Second, he must persuade those who have the power of decision to act against their own short-run interests or bring pressure on them to do so. And, finally, he must survive as an individual in a world he is attempting to change fundamentally so that his fellows among the privileged minority see him as a destroyer of the very ground on which all of us stand. He knows that if he should succeed in the interest of the poor, technologically advanced societies still might envy the 'poor' who adopt this vision.

There is a normal course for those who make development policies, whether they live in North or South America, in Russia or Israel. It is to define development and to set its goals in ways with which they are familiar, which they are accustomed to use in order to satisfy their own needs, and which permit them to work through the institutions over which they have power or control. This formula has failed, and must fail. There is not enough money in the world for development to succeed along these lines, not even in the combined arms and space budgets of the super-powers.

An analogous course is followed by those who are trying to make political revolutions, especially in the Third World. Usually they promise to make the familiar privileges of the present elite, such as schooling, hospital care, etc., accessible to all citizens; and they base this vain promise on the belief that a change in political regime will permit them to sufficiently enlarge the institutions which produce these privileges. The promise and appeal of the revolutionary are therefore just as threatened by the counter-research I propose as is the market of the now dominant producers.

In Vietnam a people on bicycles and armed with sharpened bamboo sticks have brought to a standstill the most advanced machinery for research and production ever devised. We must seek survival in a Third World in which human ingenuity can peacefully outwit machined might. The only way to reverse the disastrous trend to increasing underdevelopment, hard as it is, is to learn to laugh at accepted solutions in order to change the demands which make them necessary. Only free men can change their minds and be surprised; and while no men are completely free, some are freer than others.

SECTION VII: THE WORLD POPULATION/FOOD CRISIS

Introduction

Of all the issues which make up the North/South conflict none has generated more controversy than the population/food crisis. In this section, we examine some of the fierce debates over the relationships between poverty and population growth. It was noted in Section V, that the liberal democratic development theorists tended to prescribe Western *technological* solutions for problems which the radical theorists saw as essentially political. This tendency is nowhere more evident than in the liberal enthusiasm for the Green Revolution and western birth control technology as means for helping solve the food and population crises.

The dramatic increase in Third World population during the past half century is due primarily to western-induced public health programmes and the medical control of major tropical diseases like malaria. The death rate has been reduced without commensurate reductions in the birth rate, and it is this combination of death control without birth control which creates the 'population explosion'. With the majority of the population of many Third World countries living at the subsistence level, the $\frac{food}{population}$ equation is obviously far more critical than in affluent industrialised societies. In the last two decades, a combination of rising populations and a succession of crises in Third World food production led many observers to predict widespread global famines in the 1970s and 80s. To forestall such disasters the liberals prescribed measures which were essentially technological. The population crisis would be alleviated by the export of birth control technology, and the food problem would be resolved by transfers of the new seed strains, plus fertiliser and irrigation inputs which had become known as the Green Revolution.

Conservative development specialists, like Garrett Hardin and the Paddock brothers, argued that the liberal prescriptions were naive and would not work. Many areas - India with an unsuccessful national birth control programme going back more than two decades was an obvious example - were simply beyond hope. The only solution for such countries, argued the conservatives, was the Malthusian one of raising the death rate. Developed countries had achieved population equilibrium by lowering their birth rates to match low death rates. Underdeveloped countries which could not lower the former rates would have to raise the latter.

The radicals in this debate argue that many of the problems articulated by liberals and conservatives simply do not exist, while others are wrongly formulated. Thus, with respect to the 'food crisis', it is pointed out that there is no crisis of food *supply*, only crises of *distribution* and *waste*. If food reserves were more equitably distributed between, and within, nations, the alleged problem would disappear. Even in India, in the famine year of 1965, there was more than enough food to feed the entire population, yet thousands died of starvation. Furthermore, global malnutrition could be largely abolished if the grain protein currently fed to livestock in the United States were made available to the malnourished in poor countries. The Green Revolution, argue the radicals, *cannot* solve the hunger problem, even if it solved the alleged production problem. This is because the cost of the irrigation and fertiliser 'inputs' and the new seed strains, has put Green Revolution technology beyond the reach of the poorest peasants. The new technology may well produce more food, but the people whose need is greatest will still lack the money to buy it. On the question of underdevelopment and population growth, the radicals claim that high birth rates are not a *cause* of Third World poverty but one of its *effects*. Having many children is rational for individual poor families in Third World countries. it is a form of insurance. Increases in the standard of living, the spread of basic literacy, reducing infant mortality and improving the status of women and, above all, increasing equality, bring the birthrate down - birth control programmes, on their own, will not. The best 'Pill' is development, say the radicals, and once again China is seen as a model for other developing countries to follow in this respect.

In the first article in this section, Barry Commoner, critically reviews some of the liberal and conservative arguments while making a strong argument for the radical case. The surveys by *The Economist*, and *Survey of International Development*, review some of the latest findings in demographic and food production research. The final article, by Else Skjønsberg, also discusses the role of food production but with particular reference to the crucial, but much neglected, role of women in the rural development process.

How Poverty Breeds Overpopulation
(and not the other way around)

Barry Commoner

The world population problem is a bewildering mixture of the simple and the complex, the clear and the confused.

What is relatively simple and clear is that the population of the world is getting larger, and that this process cannot go on indefinitely because there are, after all, limits to the resources, such as food, that are needed to sustain human life. Like all living things, people have an inherent tendency to multiply geometrically — that is, the more people there are, the more people they tend to produce. In contrast, the supply of food rises more slowly, for unlike people it does not increase in proportion to the existing rate of food production. This is, of course, the familiar Malthusian relationship, and leads to the conclusion that the population is certain eventually to outgrow the food supply (and other needed resources), leading to famine and mass death unless some other countervailing force intervenes to limit population growth. One can argue about the details, but taken as a general summary of the population problem, the foregoing statement is one which no environmentalist can successfully dispute.

When we turn from merely stating the problem to analyzing and attempting to solve it, the issue becomes much more complex. The simple statement that there is a limit to the growth of the human population, imposed on it by the inherent limits of the earth's resources, is a useful but abstract idea. In order to reduce it to the level of reality in which the problem must be solved, what is required is that we find the *cause* of the discrepancy between population growth and the available resources. Current views on this question are neither simple nor unanimous.

One view is that the cause of the population problem is uncontrolled fertility, the countervailing force — the death rate — having been weakened by medical advances. According to this view, given the freedom to do so, people will inevitably produce children faster than the goods needed to support them. It follows, then, that the birthrate must be deliberately reduced to the point of "zero population growth".

The methods that have been proposed to achieve this kind of direct reduction in birthrate vary considerably. Among the ones advanced in the past are: (a) providing people with effective contraception and access to abortion facilities and with education about the value of using them (i.e. family planning); (b) enforcing legal means to prevent couples from producing more than some standard number of children ("coercion"); (c) withholding of food from the people of starving developing countries which, having failed to limit their birthrate sufficiently, are deemed to be too far gone or too unworthy to be saved (the so-called "lifeboat ethic").

It is appropriate here to illustrate these diverse approaches with examples. The family planning approach is so well known as to need no further exemplification. As to the second of these approaches, one might cite the following description of it by Kingsley Davis, a prominent demographer, which is quoted approvingly in a recent statement by "The Environmental Fund" that is directed against the family planning position: "If people want to control population, it can be done with knowledge already available . . . For instance, a nation seeking to stabilize its population could shut off immigration and permit each couple a maximum of two children, with possible license for a third. Accidental pregnancies beyond the limit would be interrupted by abortion. If a third child were born without a license, or a fourth, the mother would be sterilized." (Quoted from the Environmental Fund's Statement "Declaration on Population and Food"; original in *Daedalus,* Fall, 1973).

The author of the "lifeboat ethic" is Garrett Hardin, who stated in a recent paper (presented in San Francisco at the 1974 annual meeting of the American Association for the

Advancement of Science) that: "So long as nations multiply at different rates, survival requires that we adopt the ethic of the lifeboat. A lifeboat can hold only so many people. There are more than two billion wretched people in the world — ten times as many as in the United States. It is literally beyond our ability to save something for our grandchildren."

Actually, this recent statement only cloaks, in the rubric of an "ethic," a more frankly political position taken earlier by Hardin: "Every day we (i.e., Americans) are a smaller minority. We are increasing at only one percent a year; the rest of the world increases twice as fast. By the year 2000, one person in 24 will be an American; in one hundred years only one in 46 . . . If the world is one great commons, in which all food is shared equally, then we are lost. Those who breed faster will replace the rest . . . In the absence of breeding control a policy of 'one mouth one meal' ultimately produces one totally miserable world. In a less than perfect world, the allocation of rights based on territory must be defended if a ruinous breeding race is to be avoided. It is unlikely that civilization and dignity can survive everywhere; but better in a few places than in none. Fortunate minorities must act as the trustees of a civilization that is threatened by uninformed good intentions." *(Science,* Vol. 172, p. 1297; 1971).

The Quality of Life

But there is another view of population which is much more complex. It is based on the evidence, amassed by demographers, that the birthrate is not only affected by biological factors, such as fertility and contraception, but by equally powerful *social* factors.

Demographers have delineated a complex network of interactions among these social factors. This shows that population growth is not the consequence of a simple arithmetic relationship between birthrate and death rate. Instead, there are circular relationships in which, as in an ecological cycle, every step is connected to several others.

Thus, while a reduced death rate does, of course, increase the rate of population growth, it can also have the opposite effect — since families usually respond to a reduced rate of infant mortality by opting for fewer children. This negative feedback modulates the effect of a decreased death rate on population size. Similarly, although a rising population increases the demand on resources and thereby worsens the population problem, it also stimulates economic activity. This, in turn, improves educational levels. As a result the average age at marriage tends to increase, culminating in a reduced birthrate — which mitigates the pressure on resources.

In these processes, there is a powerful social force which, paradoxically, both reduces the death rate (and thereby stimulates population growth) and also leads people voluntarily to restrict the production of children (and thereby reduces population growth). That force, simply stated, is the quality of life — a high standard of living, a sense of well-being and of security in the future. When and how the two opposite effects of this force are felt differs with the stages in a country's economic development. In a pre-modern society, such as England before the industrial revolution or India before the advent of the English, both death rates and birthrates were high. But they were in balance and population size was stable. Then, as agricultural and industrial production began to increase and living conditions improved, the death rate began to fall. With the birthrate remaining high the population rapidly increased in size. However, later, as living standards continued to improve, the decline in death rate persisted but the birthrate began to decline as well, reducing the rate of population growth.

For example, at around 1800, Sweden had a high birthrate (about 33/1000), but since the death rate was equally high, the population was in balance. Then as agriculture and, later, industrial production advanced, the death rate dropped until, by the mid-nineteenth century, it stood at about 20/1000. Since the birthrate remained constant during that period of time, there was a large excess of births over deaths and the population increased rapidly. Then, however, the birthrate began to drop, gradually narrowing the gap until in the mid-twentieth century it reached about 14/1000, when the death rate was about 10/1000.* Thus, under the influence of a constantly rising standard of living the population moved, with time, from a position of balance *at a high death rate* to a new position of near-balance *at a low death rate*. But in between the population increased considerably.

This process, *the demographic transition*, is clearly characteristic of all western countries. In most of them, the birthrate does not begin to fall appreciably until the death rate is reduced below about 20/1000. However, then the drop in birthrate is rapid. A similar transition also appears to be under way in countries like India. Thus in the mid-nineteenth century, India had equally high birth and death rates (about 50/1000) and

* This and subsequent demographic information is from: Agency for International Development. *Population Program Assistance*, December, 1971)

the population was in approximate balance. Then, as living standards improved, the death rate dropped to its present level of about 15/1000 and the birthrate dropped, at first slowly and recently more rapidly, to its present level of 42/1000. India is at a critical point; now that death rate has reached the turning point of about 20/1000, we can expect the birthrate to fall rapidly — provided that the death rate is further reduced by improved living conditions.

One indicator of the quality of life — infant mortality — is especially decisive in this process. And again there is a critical point — a rate of infant mortality below which birthrate begins to drop sharply and, approaching the death rate, creates the conditions for a balanced population. The reason is that couples are interested in the number of *surviving* children and respond to a low rate of infant mortality by realizing that they no longer need to have more children to replace the ones that die. Birth control is, of course, a necessary adjunct to this process; but it can succeed — barring compulsion — only in the presence of a rising standard of living, which of itself generates the necessary motivation.

This process appears to be just as characteristic of developing countries as of developed ones. This can be seen by plotting the present birthrates against the present rates of infant mortality for all available national data. The highest rates of infant mortality are in African countries; they are in the range of 53-175/1000 live births and birthrates are about 27-52/1000. In those countries where infant mortality has improved somewhat (for example, in a number of Latin American and Asian countries) the drop in birthrate is slight (to about 45/1000) until the infant mortality reaches about 80/1000. Then, as infant mortality drops from 80/1000 to about 25/1000 (the figure characteristic of most developed countries), the birthrate drops sharply from 45 to about 15-18/1000. Thus a rate of infant mortality of 80/1000 is a critical turning point which can lead to a very rapid decline in birthrate in response to a further reduction in infant mortality. The latter, in turn, is always very responsive to improved living conditions, especially with respect to nutrition. Consequently, there is a kind of critical standard of living which, if achieved, can lead to a rapid reduction in birthrate and an approach to a balanced population.

Thus, in human societies, there is a built-in control on population size: If the standard of living, which initiates the rise in population, *continues* to increase, the population eventually begins to level off. This self-regulating process begins with a population in balance, but at a high death rate and low standard of living. It then progresses toward a population which is larger, but once more in balance, at a low death rate and a high standard of living.

Demographic Parasites

The chief reason for the rapid rise in population in developing countries is that this basic condition has not been met. The explanation is a fact about developing countries which is often forgotten — that they were recently, and in the economic sense often still remain, colonies of more developed countries. In the colonial period, western nations introduced improved living conditions (roads, communications, engineering, agricultural and medical services) as part of their campaign to increase the labor force needed to exploit the colony's natural resources. This increase in living standards initiated the first phase of the demographic transition.

But most of the resultant wealth did not remain in the colony. As a result, the second (or population-balancing) phase of the demographic transition could not take place. Instead the wealth produced in the colony was largely diverted to the advanced nation — where it helped *that* country achieve for itself the second phase of the demographic transition. Thus colonialism involves a kind of demographic parasitism: The second, population-balancing phase of the demographic transition in the advanced country is fed by the suppression of that same phase in the colony.

It has long been known that the accelerating curve of wealth and power of Western Europe, and later of the United States and Japan, has been heavily based on exploitation of resources taken from the less powerful nations: colonies, whether governed legally, or — as in the case of the U.S. control of certain Latin American countries — by extra-legal and economic means. The result has been a grossly inequitable rate of development among the nations of the world. As the wealth of the exploited nations was diverted to the more powerful ones, their power, and with it their capacity to exploit, increased. The gap between the wealth of nations grew, as the rich were fed by the poor.

What is evident from the above considerations is that this process of international exploitation has had another very powerful but unanticipated effect: rapid growth of the population in the former colonies. An analysis by the demographer, Nathan Keyfitz, leads him to conclude that the growth of industrial capitalism in the western nations in the period 1800-1950 resulted in the development of a one-billion excess in the world population, largely in the tropics. Thus the present world population crisis — the rapid growth of population in developing countries (the former colonies) — is the result not so much of policies promulgated by these countries but of a policy, colonial exploitation, forced on them by developed countries.

A Village in India

Given this background, what can be said about the various alternative methods of achieving a balanced world population? In India, there has been an interesting, if partially inadvertent, comparative test of two of the possible approaches: family planning programs and efforts (also on a family basis), to elevate the living standard. The results of this test show that while the family planning effort itself failed to reduce the birthrate, improved living standards succeeded.

In 1954, a Harvard team undertook the first major field study of birth control in India. The population of a number of test villages was provided with contraceptives and suitable educational programs; birthrates, death rates and health status in this population were compared with the comparable values in an equivalent population in control villages. The study covered the six-year period 1954-1960.

A follow-up in 1969 showed that the study was a failure. Although in the test population the crude birthrate dropped from 40 per 1,000 in 1957 to 35 per 1,000 in 1968, a similar reduction also occurred in the control population. The birth control effort had no measurable effect on birthrate.

We now know *why* the study failed, thanks to a remarkable book by Mahmood Mamdani *(The Myth of Population Control,* Monthly Review Press, New York, 1972). He investigated in detail the impact of the study on one of the test villages, Manupur. What Mamdani discovered is a total confirmation of the view that population control in a country like India depends on the economically-motivated desire to limit fertility. Talking with the Manupur villagers he discovered why, despite the study's statistics regarding ready "acceptance" of the offered contraceptives, the birthrate was not affected:

"One such 'acceptance' case was Asa Singh, a sometime land laborer who is now a watchman at the village high school. I questioned him as to whether he used the tablets or not:

'Certainly I did. You can read it in their books — From 1957 to 1960, I never failed.' Asa Singh, however, had a son who had been born sometime in "late 1958 or 1959.' At our third meeting I pointed this out to him . . . Finally he looked at me and responded. 'Babuji, someday you'll understand. It is sometimes better to lie. It stops you from hurting people, does no harm, and might even help them.' The next day Asa Singh took me to a friend's house . . . and I saw small rectangular boxes and bottles, one piled on top of the other, all arranged as a tiny sculpture in a corner of the room. This man had made a sculpture of birth control devices. Asa Singh said: 'Most of us threw the tablets away. But my brother here, he makes use of everything.' "

Such stories have been reported before and are often taken to indicate how much "ignorance" has to be overcome before birth control can be effective in countries like India. But Mamdani takes us much further into the problem, by finding out why the villagers preferred not to use the contraceptives. In one interview after another he discovered a simple, decisive fact: that in order to advance their economic condition, to take advantage of the opportunities newly created by the development of independent India, *children were essential.* Mamdani makes this very explicit:

"To begin with, most families have either little or no savings, and they can earn too little to be able to finance the education of *any* children, even through high school. Another source of income must be found, and the only solution is, as one tailor told me, 'to have enough children so that there are at least three or four sons in the family.' Then each son can finish high school by spending part of the afternoon working . . . After high school, one son is sent on to college while the others work to save and pay the necessary fees . . . Once his education is completed, he will use his increased earnings to put his brother through college. He will not marry until the second brother has finished his college education and can carry the burden of educating the third brother . . . What is of interest is that, as the Khanna Study pointed out, it was the rise in the age of marriage — from 17.5 years in 1956 to 20 in 1969 — and not the birth control program that was responsible for the decrease in the birthrate in the village from 40 per 1,000 in 1957 to 35 per 1,000 in 1968. While the birth control program was a failure, the net result of the technological and social change in Manupur was to bring down the birth rate."

Here, then, in the simple realities of the village of Manupur are the principles of the demographic transition at work. There *is* a way to control the rapid growth of populations in developing countries. It is to help them develop — and more rapidly achieve the level of welfare that everywhere in the world is the real motivation for a balanced population.

Enough to go Around

Against this success, the proponents of the "lifeboat ethic" would argue that it is too slow, and they would take steps to *force* developing nations to reduce their birthrate even though the incentive for reduced fertility — the standard of living and its most meaningful index, infant mortality — is still far inferior to the levels which have motivated the demographic transition in the western countries. And where, in their view, it is too late to save a poor, overpopulated country the proponents of this so-called "ethic" would withdraw support (in the manner of the hopelessly wounded in military "triage") and allow it to perish.

This argument is based (at least in the realm of logic) on the view, to quote Hardin, that "It is literally beyond our ability to save them all". Hardin's assertion, if not the resulting "ethic," reflects a commonly held view that there is simply insufficient food and other resources in the world to support the present world population at the standard of living required to motivate the demographic transition. It is commonly pointed out, for example, that the U.S. consumes about one-third of the world's resources to support only six percent of the world's population, the inference being that there are simply not enough resources in the world to permit the rest of the world to achieve the standard of living and low birthrate characteristic of the U.S.

The fault in this reasoning is readily apparent if one examines the actual relationship between the birthrates and living standards of different countries. The only available comparative measure of standard of living is GNP per capita. Neglecting for a moment the faults inherent in GNP as a measure of the quality of life, a plot of birthrate against GNP per capita is very revealing. The poorest countries (GNP per capita less than $500 per year*) have the highest birthrates, 40-50 per 1,000 population per year. When GNP per capita per year exceeds $500 the birthrate drops sharply, reaching about 20/1,000 at $750-1,000. Most of the nations in North America, Oceania, Europe and the USSR have about the same low birthrates —15-18/1,000 — but their GNP's per capita per year range all the way from Greece ($941 per capita per year; birthrate 17/1,000) through Japan ($1,626 per capita per year; birthrate 18/1,000) to the richest country of all, the U.S.

---

* These and subsequent values are computed as U.S. 1969 dollars. The data relate to the 1969-70 period.

($4,538 per capita per year; birthrate 18/1,000). What this means is that in order to bring the birthrates of the poor countries down to the low levels characteristic of the rich ones, the poor countries do not need to become as affluent (at least as measured, poorly, by GNP per capita) as the U.S. Achieving a per capita GNP only, let us say, one-fifth of that of the U.S. — $900 per capita per year — these countries could, according to the above relationship, reach birthrates almost as low as that of the European and North American countries.

The world average value for birthrate is 34/1,000, which is indicative of the overall rate of growth of the world population (the world average crude death rate is about 13/1,000). However, the world average per capita GNP is about $803 per year — a level of affluence which is characteristic of a number of nations with birthrates of 20/1,000. What this discrepancy tells us is that if the wealth of the world (at least as measured by GNP) were in fact evenly distributed among the people of the world, the entire world population should have a low birthrate — about 20/1,000 — which would approach that characteristic of most European and North American countries (15-18/1,000).

Simply stated, the world has enough wealth to support the entire world population at a level that appears to convince most people that they need not have excessive numbers of children. The trouble is that the world's wealth is *not* evenly distributed, but sharply divided among moderately well-off and rich countries on the one hand and a much larger number of people that are very poor. The poor countries have high birthrates because they are extremely poor, and they are extremely poor because other countries are extremely rich.

The Roots of Hunger

In a sense the demographic transition is a means of translating the availability of a decent level of resources, especially food, into a voluntary reduction in birthrate. It is a striking fact that the efficiency with which such resources can be converted into a reduced birthrate is much higher in the developing countries than in the advanced ones. Thus an improvement in GNP per capita per year from let us say $682 (as in Uruguay) to $4,538 (U.S.) reduces birthrate from 22/1,000 to 18/1,000. In contrast, according to the above relationships if the GNP per capita per year characteristic of India (about $88) were increased to only about $750, the Indian birthrate should fall from its actual value of about 42/1,000 to about 20/1,000. To put the matter more simply, the per capita cost of bringing the standard of living of poor countries with rapidly growing populations to the level which — based on the behavior of peoples all over the world — would motivate voluntary reduction of fertility is very small, compared to the per capita wealth of developed countries.

Food plays a critical role in these relationships. Hunger is widespread in the world and those who believe that the world's resources are already insufficient to support the world population cite this fact as the most powerful evidence that the world is overpopulated. Conversely, those who are concerned with relieving hunger and preventing future famines often assert that the basic solution to that problem is to control the growth of the world population.

Once more it is revealing to examine actual data regarding the incidence of malnutrition. From a detailed study of nutritional levels among various populations in India by Revell & Frisch (Vol. III, "The World Food Problem", A Report of the President's Science Advisory Committee, Washington, 1967) we learn, for example, that in Madras State more than one-half the population consumes significantly less than the physiologically required number of calories and of protein in their diet. However, the *average* values for all residents of the state represents 99 percent of the calorie requirement and 98 percent of the protein requirement. What this means, of course, is that a significant part of the population receives *more* than the required dietary intake. About one third of the population receives 106 percent of the required calories and 104 percent of the required protein; about 8 percent of the population receives 122 percent or more of the calorie requirement and 117 percent or more of the protein requirement. These dietary differences are determined by income. The more than one-half of the population that is significantly below the physiologically required diet earn less than $21 per capita per year, as compared with the state-wide average of $33.40.

What these data indicate is that hunger in Madras State, defined simply in terms of a significantly inadequate intake of calories and protein, is not the result of a biological factor — the inadequate production of food. Rather, in the strict sense, it results from the *social* factors that govern the *distribution* of available food among the population.

In the last year, newspaper stories of actual famines in various parts of the world have also supported the view that starvation is usually not caused by the insufficient production of food in the world, but by social factors that prevent the required distribution of food. Thus, in Ethiopia many people suffered from starvation because government officials failed to mobilize readily available supplies of foreign grain. In India, according to a recent *New York Times* report, inadequate food supplies were due in part from a government policy which "resulted in a booming black market, angry resentment among farmers and traders, and a breakdown in supplies." The report asserts further that "The central problem of India—rooted poverty—remains unchecked and seems to be getting worse. For the third year out of four per capita income is expected to drop. Nearly 80 percent of the children are malnourished ... The economic torpor seems symptomatic of deeper problems. Cynicism is rampant: the Government's socialist slogans and calls for austerity are mocked in view of bribes and corruption, luxury construction and virtually open illegal contributions by businessmen to the Congress party." (*New York Times*, Apr. 17, 1974)

Given these observations and the overall fact that the amount of food crop produced in the world at present is sufficient to provide an adequate diet to about eight billion people—more than twice the world population—it appears to me that the present, tragically widespread hunger in the world cannot be regarded as evidence that the size of the world population has outrun the world's capacity to produce food. I have already pointed out that we can regard the rapid growth of population in developing countries and the grinding poverty which engenders it as the distant outcome of colonial exploitation—a policy imposed on the antecedents of the developing countries by the more advanced ones. This policy has forcefully determined both the distribution of the world's wealth and of its different populations, accumulating most of the wealth in the western countries and most of the people in the remaining, largely tropical, ones.

Thus there is a grave imbalance between the world's wealth and the world's people. But the imbalance is not the supposed disparity between the world's *total* wealth and *total* population. Rather, it is due to the gross *distributive* imbalance among the nations of the world. What the problem calls for, I believe, is a process that now figures strongly in the thinking of the peoples of the Third World: a return of some of the world's wealth to the countries whose resources and peoples have borne so much of the burden of producing it—the developing nations.

Wealth Among Nations

There is no denying that this proposal would involve exceedingly difficult economic, social and political problems, especially for the rich countries. But the alternative solutions thus far advanced are at least as difficult and socially stressful.

A major source of confusion is that these diverse proposed solutions to the population problem, which differ so sharply in their moral postulates and their political effects, appear to have a common base in scientific fact. It is, after all, equally true, scientifically, that the birthrate can be reduced by promulgating contraceptive practices (providing they are used), by elevating living standards, or by withholding food from starving nations.

But what I find particularly disturbing is that behind this screen of confusion between scientific fact and political intent there has developed an escalating series of what can be only regarded, in my opinion, as inhumane, abhorrent political schemes put forward in the guise of science. First we had Paddock's "triage" proposal, which would condemn whole nations to death through some species of global "benign neglect". Then we have schemes for coercing people to curtail their fertility, by physical and legal means which are ominously left unspecified. Now we are told (for example, in the statement of "The Environmental Fund") that we must curtail rather than extend our efforts to feed the hungry peoples of the world. Where will it end? Is it conceivable that the proponents of coercive population control will be guided by one of Garrett Hardin's earlier, astonishing proposals:

How can we help a foreign country to escape over-population? Clearly the worst thing we can do is send food ... Atomic bombs would be kinder. For a few moments the misery would be acute, but it would soon come to an end for most of the people, leaving a very few survivors to suffer thereafter ("The Immorality of Being Softhearted", Stanford Alumni Almanac, *Jan., 1969).*

There has been a long-standing alliance between pseudo-science and political repression; the Nazis' genetic theories, it will be recalled, were to be tested in the ovens at Dachau. This evil alliance feeds on confusion.

The present confusion can be removed by recognizing *all* of the current population proposals for what they are — not scientific observations but value judgments that reflect sharply differing ethical views and political intentions. The family planning approach, if applied as the exclusive solution to the problem, would put the burden of remedying a fault created by a social and political evil — colonialism — voluntarily on the individual victims of the evil. The so-called "lifeboat ethic" would compound the original evil of colonialism by forcing its victims to forego the humane course toward a balanced population, improvement of living standards, or if they refuse, to abandon them to destruction, or even to thrust them toward it.

My own purely personal conclusion is, like all of these, not scientific but political: that the world population crisis, which is the ultimate outcome of the exploitation of poor nations by rich ones, ought to be remedied by returning to the poor countries enough of the wealth taken from them to give their peoples both the reason and the resources voluntarily to limit their own fertility.

In sum, I believe that if the root cause of the world population crisis is poverty, then to end it we must abolish poverty. And if the cause of poverty is the grossly unequal distribution of world's wealth, then to end poverty, and with it the population crisis, we must redistribute that wealth, among nations and within them.

The Reproduction Function

The Economist, January 8, 1977

The world's population is about 4 billion, twice what it was in 1926, four times what it was in 1866, half what it will probably be in 2011. This alarming and apparently inexorable increase disguises the one hopeful sign among the statistics: the beginning of a slowdown in the rate of growth of world population.

This can be seen most clearly in the developed countries. Austria, Belgium, Britain, Luxembourg, Sweden and the two Germanies now have stable or declining populations. Together these account for only 160m people, about 4% of world population. But, according to a recent study, they could be joined in the next few years by another 360m people living in other developed countries, bringing population stability to an eighth of the world's people. And by 1985 all the industrialised countries, including those of eastern Europe and Japan, could have brought their birth and death rates into balance.

But most of the 200,000 extra people that swell the world's numbers daily are born in less-developed countries (ldcs). Even so, in only one area, Africa, did the annual rate rise between 1970 and 1975 (see table 1); in other areas it dropped slightly, except in east Asia where the decline (from an increase of 1.85% to 1.18% a year) could fairly be called dramatic. Since east Asia includes the world's most populous country, China, its result is significant. It has helped to reduce the world's annual rate of natural increase from 1.90% in 1970 to 1.64% in 1975.

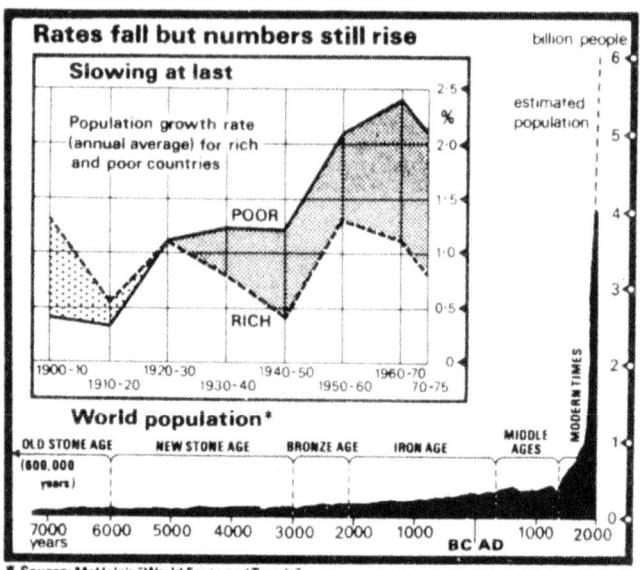

What has brought about this change? In the **developed world** the slowing has been entirely due to a drop in the birth rate. None of the countries with zero growth of population has policies designed to achieve that end; rather it has come about fortuitously, thanks to:
(1) *The desire for fewer children.*
Surveys show a growing preference for small families in the rich world.

In the United States, 74% of wives aged 18-24 questioned in 1975 said they wanted only one or two children; eight years earlier the figure had been 45%.
(2) *Contraception.*
A third of West German women now use the pill; most of the rest use another contraceptive device. In Britain the number of women using family planning services doubled between 1971

and 1975. Vasectomies for men are also on the increase in these and other industrialised countries. Improved contraceptive techniques and a growing belief that the Roman Catholic church's teaching on birth control means merely rhythm and blues have combined to allow couples to limit the size of their families.

(3) *Abortion.*

Many developed countries have recently liberalised their abortion laws. In Britain the number of abortions rose from 82,000 in 1970 to 116,000 in 1975; in Poland and the Soviet Union abortion is available on demand (although if you prefer to grin and bear children you may get a medal for doing so).

(4) *More potential mothers at work.*

In many developed countries an increasing number of women are going out to work (women now comprise more than two fifths of both the American and British labour force) and, though they may be married, they tend to postpone or limit child-bearing.

Together, these trends have been big enough to offset the expected effects of the western postwar baby bulge. It was thought, for instance, that in the United States the many children conceived after the second war would swell the population growth rate when they came of child-bearing age. Not so; the American rate dropped by a third between 1970 and 1975. The prospect is that as the baby-bulge group grows older, the child-bearing group will diminish in size and the population growth rate will fall still faster.

Some developed countries are worried about this. In France, where the birth rate also fell between 1964 and 1975, President Giscard d'Estaing (who sees a link between population and national grandeur) was "happy" to announce that there had probably been 80,000 more French babies born in 1976 than in 1975. In West Germany, the government is less worried than the toy-making industry, whose home market is expected to shrink by 3.6m children in the next 10 years. But everywhere there is concern that the fastest-growing sector of the population will be the elderly, while the numbers coming of working age (15-19) in 1985-90 will be the same in most European countries as in 1970. Thus towards the end of the century there will be a much higher ratio of retired to working people in most of the developed world; in such countries as France and Britain where the national pensions scheme is financed by the productive sector of the population, not by past contributions, the implications are serious.

Table 1. South is growing faster than north

Region	Birth rate (per thousand)	Death rate (per thousand)	Natural increase (%)	Population (m)	Natural increase (m)
North America					
1970	18.2	9.2	0.90	226	2.04
1975	14.8	8.8	0.60	236	1.42
Western Europe					
1970	16.2	10.6	0.56	333	1.89
1975	13.7	10.5	0.32	343	1.12
Eastern Europe					
1970	17.4	9.1	0.84	368	3.14
1975	18.0	9.4	0.86	384	3.31
East Asia					
1970	30.6	12.1	1.85	941	17.43
1975	19.6	7.8	1.18	1,005	11.91
South-east Asia					
1970	42.1	15.5	2.66	278	7.40
1975	38.6	15.3	2.33	317	7.37
South Asia					
1970	40.8	15.9	2.48	709	17.57
1975	37.1	15.8	2.13	791	16.89
Middle East					
1970	44.3	15.5	2.88	136	3.91
1975	41.7	14.5	2.72	155	4.22
Africa					
1970	47.1	21.0	2.61	312	8.16
1975	47.1	20.0	2.71	355	9.65
Latin America					
1970	37.4	9.7	2.77	276	7.64
1975	35.5	9.0	2.65	317	8.39
Oceania					
1970	20.9	9.0	1.19	15	0.18
1975	17.4	8.1	0.93	17	0.16
World					
1970	32.2	13.2	1.90	3,594	69.36
1975	28.3	11.9	1.64	3,920	64.44

Source: Worldwatch Institute

But the rich world's worries are less grave than those of the poor. For in the **less-developed world** the causes of the falling increase have not all been welcome. They are:

(1) *A rise in death rates.*

Improved health care and greater food supplies have combined this century greatly to lower death rates; this in turn has boosted the rate of growth of population. But in the 1970s some ldcs, notably those of the Indian subcontinent, have experienced fiercely heightened death rates. The evidence is as yet patchy, but Indian health ministry statistics show the death rate (per thousand population) in the state of Bihar rising between 1971 and 1972 from 14.2 to 18.3, in Orissa from 15.5 to 20.0, in Uttar Pradesh from 20.1 to 25.6. In Bangladesh, a typical district saw the death rate jump from around 15 in the late 1960s to 21, 16, 14, and 20 respectively in the four years 1972-75. Similar rises have been recorded in Sri Lanka and they probably would be in Ethiopia and the Sahel countries of Africa if better statistics existed.

These increases (and their concomitant effects on the rate of growth of population) may be temporary. They are related almost entirely to food shortages caused by a combination of (a) bad harvests, both in the poor world and the rich (notably the Soviet Union); (b) lack of world food stocks (the Indian harvest failures of 1966 and 1967 had a minimal effect on the death rate because the United States shipped a fifth of its wheat crop to India in those two years; but since 1970 world — ie, North American — grain reserves have been run right down); (c) price rises (the world price of wheat, which had been pretty steady from 1960-71, more than doubled in the early 1970s); (d) overfishing (which has caused a drop in fish consumption per head of 11% between 1970 and 1974); (e) rising oil prices (which pushed up the cost of fertilisers and so contributed to poorer yields - India has roughly as much land under cultivation as America, but average Indian yields are similar to America's in the 1920s). Together, these factors have reversed the trend of improving nutrition and food consumption per head that was a feature of the 1950s and 1960s. But world harvests were generally good in 1976.

(2) *Contraception.*

There has been a striking turnaround in many ldcs' official attitudes to increasing population. A few (eg, Cameroon, where birth control is illegal and family allowances are designed to push up the birth rate) are still pronatalist. Most are now anti-natalist. Among the poor, these pressures have been most effective in China, where the birth rate dropped from 32 per thousand population to 19 in the five years to 1975.

Some governments are now going further than just supporting family planning campaigns. The Indian state of Maharashtra has passed a law (as yet unratified by the Indian president) to sterilise compulsorily one parent in every family with three or more children. Other states in India are applying sanctions on large families.

(3) *Abortion.*
Legal abortion is less common in the poor world than in the rich, with the exception of China, where it has been legal since 1957. Illegal abortion, however, is common; in, eg, Mexico there are probably 1m abortions a year.

But acting against the three factors above are:

(i) *The age structure of the poor countries.*
In Europe and North America about 27% of the population is under the age of 15; in Asia and Latin America the figure is about 40%, in Africa 45%. So vast numbers will soon be coming of age to bear children.

(ii) *Marital status.*
Early and almost universal marriage - common in the third world, but less so in the rich - means lots of babies.

(iii) *No slowdown with urbanisation.*
In developed countries, towndwellers generally have a lower rate of natural increase (11% in 1960) than countrydwellers (14% in 1960); but this is not always true in ldcs (where both rates were 22.5% in 1960).

So what can be done to stop the population boom? Short answer: make the poor richer. By how much? Countries with gnp per head above $800 have an average birth rate of half the 39 per thousand for those with gnp below $600 (the few exceptions are mostly oil-producing states). Most countries have a birth rate that is either above 40 or below 25; few are in the intermediate range. It seems that when the birth rate falls to about 35 it gathers pace until it drops below 25 (see table 2).

Table 2 : Life, death and incomes

Countries with gnp per head (in $) of	Average income per head ($)	Birth rate (per thousand)	Death rate (per thousand)	Natural increase (%)	Share of world populn (%)
0-299	136	39	16	2.3	59
300-599	374	41	13	2.8	9
600-899	695	33	11	2.2	4
900+	2,561	17	9	0.8	28
All incomes	873	33	14	1.9	100

1973 figures. Source: Population Reference Bureau

Influences on the death rate: the higher costs of living

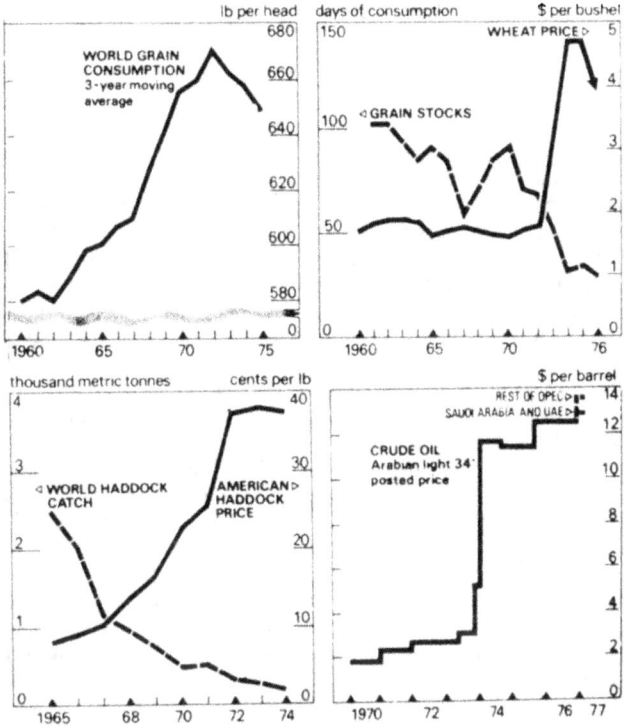

Sources: US Department of Agriculture, IMF and FAO

Statistically, the fertility rate (ie, the number of births per 1,000 women in the child-bearing age-range 15-49) has been found to go down with any rise in income per head, life expectancy at birth, population density, literacy and equality of income distribution.

At any rate, that was found to be so in a study of 64 developed and less-developed countries. But in certain parts of the world other variables play a part. For example, income and urbanisation were more important in Asia than they were in Latin America.

Income distribution within countries is of surprisingly high statistical significance, helping to explain large variations in fertility. The unequal spread of incomes in Latin America apparently accounts for higher-than-might-be-expected birth rates; relatively equal spreads in eastern Europe go with lower-than-might-be-expected birth rates there. One study has found that each additional percentage point of total income received by the poorest 40% of the population is associated with a drop of 2.9 points in the fertility rate. Each additional year of life expectancy at birth is associated with a drop of 1.9% (in India it is reckoned that you need to bear six children to insure for your old age).

Such considerations may be more important than raising gross national product in helping to slow population growth. Kerala has the lowest income per head of any state in India (partly because it has so many children), yet its birth rate dropped in 10 years from 37 to 27. Why? Because Kerala has India's highest literacy rate, highest consumption per head of nutritional foods, lowest infant mortality rate, highest life expectancy and it is the only state where most of the women are educated. China's experience tells a similar story.

It all adds up to the need for a familiar combination: improved education, health, birth control, income and income distribution schemes. It is the only way to defuse the population explosion.

Era of Agricultural Scarcity Looms as Probable Result of Extensive Changes in the World Food Economy, with Profound Ramifications for Mankind

Survey of International Development

The Green Revolution provided an opportunity to buy time, perhaps 15-20 years, in which to stop population growth — "half of that time has now passed" with no perceptible global population decline in sight. Agriculture can no longer rely upon the technological quick fix to ensure continuing improvement in food production. A most disturbing trend in the 1970's has been the decline in grain output per hectare. North America today has an "almost monopolistic control" of the world's supply of exportable grain.[1]

"The world food situation has deteriorated dramatically during the seventies. As it now enters the fourth year of precariously balanced food supplies, the world must at least prepare for the possibility that the current situation may not be a temporary one. The slack appears to have gone out of the system, leaving the entire world in a highly vulnerable situation," stated Lester R. Brown, President of Worldwatch Institute, when he addressed the "Limits to Growth '75" Conference held in Woodlands, Texas, in the third week of October 1975. He added that the "conditions under which the world's farmers and fishermen will attempt to expand food output during the final quarter of this century will be far more difficult than those prevailing during most of the quarter century just ending."

While only a number of years ago the world had available surplus food stocks as well as excess production capacity — and "it appeared that both would be around for a long time to come" — within a few years these have suddenly largely disappeared. The margin of food safety has evaporated, for "today the entire world is living hand to mouth, trying to make it from one harvest to the next. Global food insecurity is greater now than at any time since the years immediately following World War II."[2]

A number of developments have brought about basic changes in the world food economy — the decline of world grain reserves; the Soviet Union's becoming a large food importer; ecological deterioration of food systems; limitations of plant technology, which are beginning to be recognized; downturn in grain yield per hectare; escalating costs of agricultural production — caused mainly by higher prices for energy and fertilizer — and steeper food prices; decline in the global fish catch; unabated and accelerating global population growth; the fact that all of the idled United States' cropland has been placed in production; the overwhelming dependence on North American — United States and Canada — exportable grain supplies and the world's growing food interdependence.

Because of the increasingly severe condition of the world food economy and the corresponding need for urgent ameliorative action, Mr. Brown recommends that a North American food policy be adopted and a Joint United States-Canadian Commission on Food Policy be established.

The Decline of World Grain Reserves — Though it seemed likely as recently as 1972 that "surplus stocks and cropland idled under farm programs would be part of the landscape for the foreseeable future," circumstances suddenly began to change. For the first time since World War II global agricultural production began to fall slightly. Fueled by the relentless growth of population and the rising tide of affluence, the global demand for food "began to outstrip the productive capacity of the world's farmers and fishermen." While the combination of reserve stocks of grain in exporting countries and idle cropland in the United States amounted to the equivalent of 105 days of world grain consumption in 1961 and 69 days in 1972, the following two years grain reserves dropped abruptly — to 55 days in 1973 and 33 in 1974. Though reserves rose to 35 days in 1975, it is estimated that they will decline to 31 days in 1976 — (see Table I). Thus the hoped for expectations for rebuilding the 1975 carry-over stocks "to safe levels have vanished with the poor 1975 Soviet harvest."

The Soviet Union was also mainly responsible for reducing world grain stocks by the middle of 1973 to their lowest level in two decades. Because the Soviet harvest was so poor in 1972 massive purchases had to be made on the world market — particularly in the United States.

Table I

INDEX OF WORLD FOOD SECURITY, 1961-76

Year	Reserve Stocks of Grain[1]	Grain Equivalent of Idled U.S. Cropland	Total Reserves	Reserves as Days of Annual Grain Consumption
	(Million Metric Tons)			
1961	163	68	231	105
1962	176	81	257	105
1963	149	70	219	95
1964	153	70	223	87
1965	147	71	218	91
1966	151	78	229	84
1967	115	51	166	59
1968	144	61	205	71
1969	159	73	232	85
1970	188	71	259	89
1971	168	41	209	71
1972	130	78	208	69
1973	148	24	172	55
1974	108	0	108	33
1975	111	0	111	35
1976[2]	100	0	100	31

Source: Based on U.S. Department of Agriculture data and author's estimates.
[1] Based on carry-over stocks of grain at beginning of crop year in individual countries for year shown. The USDA has recently expanded the coverage of reserve stocks to include importing as well as exporting countries; thus the reserve levels are slightly higher than those heretofore published.
[2] Preliminary estimates by USDA.

It should also be pointed out here that the world could no longer fall back on idle cropland in the United States. "During the sixties and early seventies some 50 million acres out of a total U.S. cropland base of 350 million acres were held out of production to support prices" and provide "security for all mankind." Yet in 1974 all the cropland was brought back into production, "but still food reserves were not rebuilt."

The International Development Strategy of the United Nations Second Development Decade called for the developing countries to reach an average annual increase of four per cent in the production of agriculture. In the first four years of the decade, however, production in the developing countries has increased by only 1.8 per cent a year. Moreover, the increase in agricultural production has not kept pace with their annual population growth of 2.4 per cent.

Though the World Food Conference focused attention on the worsening state of the world's agriculture and demonstrated an inclination to tackle aspects of the food problem, the concept of world food security — to build up and maintain world foodgrain reserves — has hardly made any significant progress. The out-going Director General of the Food and Agriculture Organization (FAO), Dr. A. H. Boerma, said in reference to the International Undertaking on the World Food Security that "progress has been totally inadequate when compared with the urgent practical realities of the world's food needs. Even the rudiments of a policy framework within which an internationally coordinated food reserve system can be put into effect are not yet visible."

Ecological Deterioration of Food Systems; Resource Constraints; and, the Green Revolution Overwhelmed — *Ecological Deterioration of Food Systems* — Because of mounting population pressures the production of food is being extended onto marginal land which is already causing "overgrazing, deforestation, desert expansion, soil erosion, silting of irrigation reservoirs and increased flooding," notes Mr. Brown. "In some developing countries, these negative forces may soon override the drive to step up food output through additional capital investment and technological innovation." In fact, some of the developing countries with rapid population growth may be the first nations to experience absolute declines in national food production due to ecological stresses. "This backsliding will be without precedent in the modern world and . . . our success in anticipating such a reversal may not be any greater than our success in predicting the declining catch in oceanic fisheries."

Resource Constraints — When the future food situation is being analyzed, there must at least be an earnest attempt to examine the state of some of the key inputs required — such as land, water, energy and fertilizer. From the available evidence and information at hand, it is becoming clear that in most respects it will be more difficult to increase food production because the "most poignant aspect of the current agricultural situation is that all the basic resources needed to expand food production are in short supply." This development "contrasts sharply with most of the postwar period, during which energy was cheap, and there was more land than was needed to satisfy commercial demand for food."

While from prehistoric times until about 1950 growth in food output occurred largely through bringing new land under cultivation, production increases since then have been mainly attributable to intensive cultivation — particularly through the introduction of new seed varieties and the application of fertilizers. However, today "most of the good farm land is already under the plow . . . and some parts of the world are actually losing existing cropland, either because of the claims of the population growth and modernization — homes, schools, factories, roads, airports, and golf courses[3] — or because land is being lost to soil erosion and desertification. The fact is, there is very little good land that can quickly and cheaply be brought into cultivation." There seem to be only few fertile new lands left: parts of the interior of Latin America, the Republic of Sudan and the tsetse fly belt in sub-Saharan Africa — that is, if the tsetse fly can be eradicated.

Though the shortage of land will by itself pose severe problems, the "lack of water may be the principal constraint on future efforts to expand world food output." While "between 1950 and 1970 the world irrigated area expanded by nearly 3 per cent annually, a virtual explosion by historical standards," during the last quarter of this century the growth in irrigation "is expected to drop to scarcely one per cent per year." Furthermore, not only are there no short-cuts to continue increasing supplies of fresh water, but "with few exceptions, those sites remaining will be far more complex and costly to develop."

Energy plays a crucial role in the overall food production system. Energy inputs have increased enormously in a country such as the United States which has an industrialized food system. As can be seen from looking at Table II — the United States had to increase its energy input substantially between 1940 and 1970 in order to sustain and increase its huge mechanized and fertilizer-intensive agricultural system. In 1970 12.8 per cent of total U.S. energy was used by the capital-intensive food

Table II
ENERGY USE IN THE UNITED STATES FOOD SYSTEM
(All values are multiplied by 10^{12} kcal.)

Component	1940	1960	1970
On Farm			
Fuel (direct use)	70.0	188.0	232.0
Electricity	0.7	46.1	63.8
Fertilizer	12.4	41.0	94.0
Agricultural Steel	1.6	1.7	2.0
Farm machinery	9.0	52.0	80.0
Tractors	12.8	11.8	19.3
Irrigation	18.0	33.3	35.0
Subtotal	124.5	373.9	526.1
Processing Industry			
Food processing industry	147.0	224.0	308.0
Food processing machinery	0.7	5.0	6.0
Paper packaging	8.5	28.0	38.0
Glass containers	14.0	31.0	47.0
Steel cans and aluminium	38.0	86.0	122.0
Transport (fuel)	49.6	153.3	246.9
Trucks and trailers (manufacture)	28.0	44.2	74.0
Subtotal	285.8	571.5	841.9
Commercial and Home			
Commercial refrigeration and cooking	121.0	186.2	263.0
Refrigeration machinery (home and commercial)	10.0	32.0	61.0
Home refrigeration and cooking	144.2	276.6	480.0
Subtotal	275.2	494.8	804.0
Grand total	685.5	1440.2	2172.0

Source: Steinhart and Steinhart (See Footnote 4.)

system. The United States is by far the world's largest producer and exporter of grain. But to achieve this there has had to be an unabated resort to and reliance upon the application of technology and energy.

What are the implications for other countries — particularly of course most of the developing countries? Will they find that they can only increase food production substantially by relying upon increased energy usage and mechanization? John and Carol Steinhart pose the question whether a piece of the United States industrialized food system can be exported to help developing nations, or whether it is necessary for these nations to first become as industrialized as, for example, the United States in order to operate an industrialized food system.[4] To another question whether or not to export energy-intensive agricultural methods, the Steinharts reply that it is, in their opinion, "quite clear that the U.S. food system cannot be exported intact at present . . . To feed the people of India [which has a population exceeding 550 million] at the U.S. level of about 3000 food calories per day (instead of their present 2000) would require more energy than India now uses for all purposes." Moreover, in order to "feed the entire world with a U.S.-type food system, almost 80 per cent of the world's annual energy expenditure would be required just for the food system." From which sources is the world going to reap sufficient energy to feed the nearly three billion additional people which are expected to be born during the last 25 years of the 20th century?

While the escalating cost of petroleum has had an impact upon nearly all countries, this impact has been especially severe for the non-oil producing developing countries. Many of these countries have to rely upon food imports — which have increased in cost — as well as on an ever-increasing application of fertilizers which, because of their petroleum component, have also become much more expensive. As a consequence, these countries are experiencing a continued deterioration in their balance of payments. It looks, however, as if the price of food will become even more costly and promises to remain so in the foreseeable future — especially because there does not seem any prospect of energy prices declining.

The world will now also need to ask itself the irrevocable question as to what will happen after fossil fuels begin to be depleted. Oil is a non-renewable natural resource and at the volume it is being consumed it is variously estimated that the world will run out of oil within 25 to 30 years — perhaps even sooner if the consumption rate is not significantly curtailed and alternative energy means utilized.

The Green Revolution Overwhelmed — A great deal of hope has been placed in the Green Revolution — the high-yielding varieties of wheats and rices which have enabled so many countries to increase their food production. Though such countries as Mexico, Pakistan, India, and the Philippines managed to increase grain production significantly, the relentless growth in population is nullifying the remarkable efforts of the Green Revolution. Many persons, including Norman Borlaug — the originator of the miracle seeds and Nobel Laureate - and Lester Brown, have warned against looking at the Green Revolution as solving the food problem. For as Mr. Brown has noted, the "only ultimate solution to the food problem in these countries was and is to put the brakes on population growth." He added that the "new seeds were simply buying time, perhaps another 15 to 20 years, to get population growth under control. Half of that time has now passed."

Another aspect of the Green Revolution is often overlooked — that the adoption of these new seed varieties requires a great deal of energy. Not only do many of the new varieties depend upon irrigation where traditional crops did not, but almost all of the new crops also require extensive use of fertilizers. A successful application of the Green Revolution thus necessitates dependence on an energy-intensive food system. But as we have inquired earlier — from where is all the energy supposed to come — especially in the near future — and at what cost?;

The Decline of the World's Fish Catch — The viewpoint has long been held that the oceans of the Planet — in so far as edible fish species are concerned — were synonymous with infinity. The harsh and realistic truth is that the oceans are just as finite as — and ecologically perhaps even more vulnerable than — terrestrial farmland. While technological innovations were instrumental in helping to more than triple the world fish catch between 1950 and 1970 — from 22 million tons to 70 million — these sophisticated innovations have also led to overfishing and a depletion of fish stocks. In 1971 and 1972 the fish catch declined, and in 1973 it was 8 per cent less than in 1970. For example, the cod catch in the North Atlantic was about 2 million tons in 1968 and declined to around a million tons in the mid-seventies, while the Peruvian anchovy fishery reached nearly 13 million tons in 1970 to drop to an average of about 5 million tons in the last number of years. Though some marine biologists are of the opinon that the "world catch of table grade fish may be approaching its maximum sustainable limit" and "others envision brighter prospects . . . not even the most hopeful foresee future gains even remotely approaching those of the past 25 years."

Global Downturn in the Grain Yield per Hectare — Evidence seems to be mounting that certain limitations are beginning to be reached on the manipulations of food-related ecological systems. A most disturbing trend in the world food economy "during the seventies has been the downturn in grain yield per hectare." Mr. Brown found that "if the average world grain yield during the period from 1960 to 1975 is plotted as a three-year sliding average in order to smooth out the fluctuations associated with weather," it will be observed that "from 1960 to 1972 this three-year average increased each year." However, "in 1973 it turned downward, dropping further in 1974 and still further in 1975. At its peak in 1972, the average grain yield per hectare was 1.91 metric tons, but over the next three years it dropped to 1.84 metric tons."

Various possible reasons for this downturn have been suggested: 1) because the 50 million acres of idled cropland placed into production in the United States is below-average fertility, the land's productivity is of lower yield, thereby lowering the average global yield; 2) the high cost factor and tight supply of energy and fertilizer have been inhibiting factors; 3) due to population pressures — in large areas of West and East Africa, Central America, the Andean countries in South America, and Southeast Asia — the fallow cycles are being reduced to the point that they are too short to allow the soil fertility to regenerate fully; and 4) because of the growing shortage of firewood in the developing countries animal dung is being increasingly used as a substitute for fuel — thereby diverting animal manure, an essential source of soil nutrients, from fertilizer to fuel use, causing loss of soil productivity and declining yields.

In the industrialized countries further applications of energy and fertilizer are likely to yield little or no increase in levels of productivity. Consequently severe constraints will be placed on endeavors to rapidly expand food output. Moreover, there are deleterious side effects to concentrating on improving yields because "at times the cost of the increased yield has been the loss of desirable characteristics — hardiness, resistance to disease and adverse weather, and the like."[5] In connection with the use of fertilizer, in the United States the "nationwide curve relating fertilizer consumption to yield . . . is clearly flattening. The curve shows the classic pattern of 'diminishing returns'" and the "use of fertilizer is showing signs of a Limit to Growth." [6] While in the early fifties the application of each additional pound of fertilizer in the United States' corn belt raised corn yields by 15 to 20 pounds, "today an additional pound of fertilizer applied to the same corn field may yield only an additional five pounds." In some industrial countries the use of chemical fertilizer may be simply approaching the point of saturation.

In regard to the production of meat, have the technologists been able, for example, to improve the efficiency of feed use? Data suggest that the "feeding efficiency has been falling, not rising." In the case of beef 11 pounds of beef per 100 pounds of feed could be produced in 1950, "but only 9½ pounds in 1970. For hogs, the ratio fell from nearly 20 to about 16." Though new farm technologies made it possible to breed cows producing 50 quarts of milk daily, the fact is that beef cows are still only able to give birth to one calf per year.

As it is becoming more difficult to raise the productivity of land through the further use of fertilizer, so is the further reliance upon improving farm mechanization becoming counterproductive. "Studies already show that more energy is expended planting and harvesting crops than is yielded in food energy." Furthermore, the "diminishing returns on these key inputs also indicate that additional capital invested in agriculture to increase output will yield steadily diminishing returns." For example, the "returns on the heavy investment in Soviet agriculture over the past decade have been much lower" than the leadership had hoped for.

Though technological advances have led to quantum jumps in the world production of food, it must be realized that there are simply limitations of the plant and animal material with which man must work. "Agriculture can no longer look to the technological quick fix to ensure continued progress in food production." As in everything else, the law of diminishing returns must eventually be confronted. Looking into the future, it is therefore "difficult to see any technological advances on the drawing board which will lead to comparable quantum leaps in world food output." Moreover, with previous quantum jumps, the input of and reliance upon energy have had to be increased commensurately. As the Steinharts indicated, the "farther we get from characteristics of the original plant and animal strains, the more care and energy is required."

Though new commerciable foods are being experimented with — for example such seafoods as seaweed, krill (crustaceans and larvae on which whales feed) and petroleum-based edible substances — these will hardly suffice to meet the dietry needs of billions of people.

Unabated and Accelerating Global Population Growth — That population growth is like a stranglehold on the affairs of man should really need no further elaboration. Yet despite all that has been said about the need to curtail global population expansion, about 80 million people are added to the world each year. This number is equivalent to adding annually a West and East Germany to the family of nations. The continual population increase is having a particularly overwhelming effect on the world food economy. "If one were to select the single dominant factor transforming world trade patterns in recent decades, it would be varying rates of population growth," in the view of Lester Brown. "Certainly the conversion of Asia, Africa and Latin America to deficit status was population related."

Comparing North America and Latin America "illustrates the devastating effect of rapid population growth." While both regions had as recently as 1950 about equal populations — 163 and 168 respectively — in 1974 North America's population had reached 236 million to Latin America's 315 million. The effect on Latin America's agricultural trade has been telling. While the region was able to export grain in 1970, the trend has since been one of having to resort to imports. Population increases have had similar conributory effects on the changing pattern of the world's grain trade — (see Table III).

Table III
THE CHANGING PATTERN OF WORLD GRAIN TRADE [1]

Region	1934-38	1948-52	1960	1970	1976[2]
	(Million Metric Tons)				
North America	+ 5	+23	+39	+56	+94
Latin America	+ 9	+ 1	0	+ 4	- 3
Western Europe	-24	-22	-25	-30	-17
E. Europe & USSR	+ 5	—	0	0	-27
Africa	+ 1	0	- 2	- 5	-10
Asia	+ 2	- 6	-17	-37	-47
Australia & N.Z.	+ 3	+ 3	+ 6	+12	+ 8

Source: Derived from FAO and USDA data and author's estimates.
[1] Plus sign indicates net exports; minus sign, net imports.
[2] Preliminary estimates of fiscal year data.

A number of countries have population growth rates of about 3 per cent or more a year. If these countries — for example Mexico, Venezuela, Peru, Brazil, Nigeria and Algeria — should continue having such high growth rates, then it will lead in every example to a *nineteenfold population increase within a century.*" Brazil's current population of approximately 108 million would in a century thus reach over 2 billion — a population larger than that of China, India, North America, the Soviet Union and Japan combined. In terms of Brazil's agricultural performance, while it was once thought the country would become a major supplier of food for the world, without a strong commitment to family planning such a prospect "is a myth and not a harmless one."

What would the consequences be for the world if North America's population would be increasing annually at a 3 per cent rate? Rather than the current 236 million, the region would instead be inhabited by about 341 million people. "At current per capita consumption levels, those additional 105 million people would absorb virtually all exportable supplies and North America would be struggling to maintain self-sufficiency."

With the world living now from hand to mouth each year and ecological systems beginning to be irreversibly undermined, the continued spectre of relentless population growth is posing an ever greater threat to the welfare of humanity. As the Steinharts indicated, "food is basically a net product of an ecosystem, however simplified. Food production starts with a natural material, however modified later. Injections of energy (and even brains) will carry us only so far. If the population cannot adjust its wants to the world in which it lives, there is little hope of solving the food problem for mankind. In that case," they add, "the food shortage will solve our population problem."

North America's Predominance in the World Grain Trade — While prior to World War II North America was only one of the many regions exporting grain — and not even the largest — after the War North America was on its way to becoming the predominant grain exporter (see Table III). Dependence on North America has increased steadily over the years, and this development promises to continue. "The worldwide movement of countries outside of North America from export to import status is a one way street," according to Brown. The reasons may vary, "but the tide is strong: *no country has gone against this trend over the past quarter century.*"

Though the Green Revolution helped such countries as India, Pakistan, Turkey, Mexico and the Philippines to increase their respective food production — and some even became modest grain exporters — unyielding population growth has compelled these nations to rely upon ever-increasing imports. Except for Australia, New Zealand and North America, the other regions have all become food-deficit. This deficit is especially pronounced for Asia — which must now import nearly 50 million metric tons of grain annually.

Instead of countries becoming less reliant on food imports, the opposite is occurring. Furthermore, "more and more countries, both industrial and developing, are actually importing more food than they produce. Among the countries which now import over half of their grain supply are Japan, Belgium, Senegal, Libya, Saudi Arabia, Venezuela, Lebanon, Switzerland and Algeria. Other countries rapidly approaching primary dependence on imported foodstuffs include Portugal, Costa Rica, Sri Lanka, South Korea and Egypt."

With every passing year, North America's role as the world's granary becomes more pivotal. The region's grain exports have increased from 39 million metric tons in 1960 to an estimated 94 million metric tons in 1976 — "enough grain to feed the 600 million people of India" during the current fiscal year alone. Though North America doubled its grain exports during the past ten years, for reasons already alluded to in this article a repeat performance should not be expected during the next decade. The facts help explain the increased and urgent advocacy, especially to the developing countries, to implement measures spurring on agricultural self-reliance, and the proposal at the World Food Conference to establish the International Fund for Agricultural Development to help improve prospects for agricultural development in developing countries.

An ever-growing dependency on North America by the rest of the world means also greater vulnerability. That North America has had to invoke export restrictive measures is a warning sign of what could lie in store. While the Canadian Wheat Board in mid-July "banned further exports of wheat until the size of the 1975 harvest could be ascertained . . . political pressures forced the United States to limit exports of grain to the Soviet Union and Poland in the late summer and early fall of 1975." That the United States should have to resort to restrictive practices — even after 50 million acres of idle cropland have been returned to production — engenders deep foreboding indeed.

Growing Food Interdependence — In shaping an alternative world economic order, food takes on increasing importance. As we have seen, the "character of the world food economy has been profoundly altered in recent years." National food economies have now become highly integrated and interdependent. Relying upon common sources of energy, fertilizer, raw materials, transportation systems and the oceans, the actions of one particular country "may send shock waves through the entire food system." For example, OPEC's decision to raise prices of petroleum substantially and the quadrupling of phosphate rock prices by Morocco — the world's leading source for that critically important raw material for making fertilizer — have affected farmers around the world. Likewise, "Brazil's failure to curtail population growth makes it a net grain importer rather than an exporter and a drain on the world food economy." As Mr. Brown underscored, "in a world of deepening interdependence, the sum of national food policies may not add up to anything approaching a rational global policy." While over-fishing might satisfy the protein requirements of one country in the short run, in the long run such a short-sighted policy could "completely destroy that source of protein for everyone." In addition, the ecological deterioration of a major food system in one part of the world can have very serious consequences in another part.

The Need for a Cooperative Global Food Strategy and North America's Supportive Role in the form of a Joint United States — Canadian Commission on Food Policy — Because of the deepening interdependencies of the world's separate and pretty much un-coordinated food systems, and also because the state of the world's agriculture is so precarious, there is pressing need for evolving a global food strategy. The broad goals of such a strategy would be to "restore some measure of stability and security to the world food economy, to control food price inflation and to improve the nutrition and health of the overnourished and undernourished alike." In Mr. Brown's opinion, the "backbone of a global strategy should be a worldwide effort to slow the growth in food demand." Without such a slowdown, it is doubtful whether "grants on the supply side of the food equation will be sufficient to prevent recurring and increasingly unmanageable food crises."

To restrain demand an "all-out effort" should be made to slow down population growth as well as "to reduce overconsumption among all the world's more affluent people." In regard to production, "the most important component of a global strategy" is to bring about agricultural reform in countries where output is lagging. The "principal weakness of countries with poorly performing agricultural sectors" is the tenuous or non-existent relationship between effort and reward for those persons actually working on the land. This uncertainty of reward destroys incentive, "weakens effort and discourages the innovation that is the lifeblood of agricultural progress." Soviet-type state collective farms or feudal land distribution patterns as in Latin America likewise "deaden initiative and retard progress."

The price structure of food should also be carefully monitored. Rather than attempting to maintain lower food prices so as not to provoke the consumer, more attention should be placed on farmers receiving adequate payment for their food productions. If there is an incentive to produce more food, the long-term result should be a lessening of further pressure on North American food supplies. Moreover, a more equitable price structure — one which adequately reimburses the farmer — should also help to dampen inflation, which has had a severe effect upon the world economy.

At a time when industrial countries are experiencing diminishing returns on expanded use of agricultural inputs such as fertilizer, and developing countries are compelled to rely on less fertile and less productive land, there is a need to increase the allocation of capital and technical manpower accordingly. However, because "capital is scarce and capital formation increasingly stymied, mankind faces a Herculean challenge." Another pillar of a global food strategy must be the creation of an international system of food reserves. Such a system — like the World Food Security plan referred to earlier in this summary — would not only help "prevent wide fluctuations in food and feed prices," but the built-up stocks would also provide food aid to help meet crop failures or natural disasters. Food assistance should also become a major component of an operational food strategy, for it "can contribute visibly to a workable world order." The United States played a predominant role when food assistance was a major factor in international food trade. However, "U.S. aid levels have dropped from some 15 million tons annually during the late Sixties, to 4 million tons in fiscal year 1975". For fiscal 1976 the U.S. is planning an increase to 6 million tons. The World Food Conference in Rome called for a minimum food aid target, to reach 10 million tons of food grains for the 1975-1976 season.

Joint United States-Canadian Commission on Food Policy —
Because a cooperative approach under strong leadership will be required to help reverse the unfavorable agricultural trends of

the last number of years, Lester Brown recommends the formation of a Joint United States-Canadian Commission on Food Policy, together with the formulation and adoption of a North American food policy specifically designed to render support to the global food strategy previously outlined. As OPEC-induced price hikes "served to focus global attention on the prospective exhaustion of oil reserves within the next few decades and on the consequent urgent need both to conserve petroleum and to devise alternative energy sources," so the proposed Joint Commission could focus the world's attention on the undoubted deteriorating food situation and the need for immediate implementation of constructive food policies.

For example, "if the United States and Canada were to announce jointly the ground rules for assured access to North American food supplies, the announcement itself would have a salutary effect. It would alert and educate governments around the world, forcing them to confront" the worsening food problem "during the Seventies and the grave risks of permitting these recent trends to continue." Governments supporting the internationally accepted strategies — such as those endorsed at the World Food and World Population Conferences — can have free access to North America's food. But "those that refuse will receive no such assurance." Thus countries not following the World Plan of Action agreed upon at the World Population Conference and "not contributing to the stabilization of world population should not count on access to North American food supplies." It is thus envisaged to use access to North American food supplies "as an incentive to encourage and assist countries to do their share in solving the food problem, and thereby to help avoid an unmanageable food crisis."

Though many persons will find Mr. Brown's proposal a "blatant encroachment of national sovereignty," today no country is sovereign since "every country is coming to depend on the resources and cooperation of other countries. In the process, all countries are acquiring obligations to the international or global community." Faced by emerging shortages of basic raw materials, declining fish catch, diminishing returns on the use of energy and fertilizer in the industrial countries, shrinking fertile cropland, unpredictable weather conditions and a turbulent world economy, the agricultural prospects confronting mankind in the last quarter of the century are going to be quite different from those existing after World War II. Now that the margin of safety has vanished from the world food economy, there is a greater need than ever for nations to cooperate. The world's agriculture should no longer be looked at from the perspective of the interests and priorities of individual countries, because "food policy can no longer be treated as an isolated agricultural issue independent of the overall world food situation." Since the "independent pursuit of narrow national objectives in the production and trade of food has led to an obvious deterioration in the global food situation," a concerted, cooperative effort must now be launched. Without such a global effort the food situation would deteriorate futher, inflation would be exacerbated and even greater stress would be placed on the already buffeted national and international political and economic systems.

Within the context of a highly integrated world food economy, the time has therefore come "for Canada and the United States to join forces to attack head-one one of the most complex and intractable problems the world will face during the final quarter of this century."

FOOTNOTES

[1] This article is predominantly based on two papers by Lester R. Brown, noted authority on world agriculture and President and Senior Researcher with Worldwatch Institute. The two papers are entitled: "The Politics and Responsibility of the North American Breadbasket" — Worldwatch Paper 2; and "The World Food Prospect" — presented to the Limits to Growth '75 Conference in Woodlands, Texas on October 21, 1975.

[2] Except where identified by footnote, all quotations are by Lester Brown and are principally based on his Worldwatch Paper 2, which is also the source of Tables I and III. Information for this article has also been drawn from press releases issued by the Food and Agriculture Organization of the United Nations.

[3] James G. Horsfall and Charles R. Frink, in their paper entitled "Perspective on Agriculture's Future: Rising Costs — Rising Doubts" prsented to the "Limits to Growth '75" symposium, made an interesting and pertinent observation. They said that "city people have created the term 'developed land.' When land is removed from agriculture, they say it is 'developed'. One wonders about the mores of a society that 'develops' its land so that it can no longer get food from it."

[4] Drs. John S. Steinhart and Carol E. Steinhart, "Energy Use in the U.S. Food System" — *Science*, April 19, 1974.

[5] Steinhart, *op. cit.*

[6] Horsfall and Frink, *op. cit.*

Patriarchy is Alive and Well

E. Skjønsberg

So far the patriarchal view has been predominant in development aid. What has been exported to the developing countries is not only capital and technology, but also plenty of ideology. The patriarchal ideology considers the world populated with males. Women are their auxiliaries. It is the males who matter and what is good for the male is supposed to be good for his family. At the receiving end, the males have been quite pleased with this ideology to the point of opposing the few attempts made at including women in their own right in the modernization process.

It isn't that women haven't got their development projects. They do. But "the relative unimportant role attributed to women's participation is reflected in the make-up of the budgets of development projects. Women's programmes generally receive a low proportion of overall budgets; and in many instances, when funds run out, the first to suffer from budget cuts are those related to women's programmes."[1]

There are two main types of aid where women are directly concerned. One type aims at the improvement of living conditions through the increase of social services. It is usually small scale, cheap and unproblematic, as health projects and training in the field of home economics challenge no power structures. On the contrary, through such projects, women's role as homemakers is strengthened, but whether sex role patterns confining them increasingly to the home is good for society and for the women themselves is rarely debated.

The other type of aid aims at introducing new and often very different modes of production and the goal is to change existing economic structures. Industrialization, mechanization and modernization in agriculture and fishing are typical areas of investment.

The target population for the second type of aid is mainly men. Women get their share, it is thought, by virtue of being wives, daughters and perhaps also mothers. Jobs and increased incomes raise status and power — male status and male power. Men's lives are modernized, but women, who are not target groups, continue carrying out their traditional tasks as their mothers and often grandmothers did before them.

What then are women's traditional tasks? Unfortunately, the answer is, among other things, food production. In Africa, even today, about 70 per cent of all peasants are women. On a world basis, estimates indicate that women make up about half of the agricultural labour force. Yet, virtually all aid in the field of agriculture has been and still is aimed at men.

The Real Target Group

Agricultural extension services have been offered to men, who have been defined as target groups both for formal and informal training programmes; cooperative schemes have been formed by and for men; men have been encouraged and helped to adopt improved seeds, fertilizers, insecticides and improved tools. Credit facilities have been made available almost only to men, and they have been encouraged, and at times forced, to take up cash-crop cultivation. But when Ugandan women started growing cotton on their own initiative, they were forbidden to do so.

As cash crops bring money, the male is in the position to consolidate his new economic role through investing his income in better equipment and more seed. But increased family income doesn't necessarily mean improved status for all.

In many instances, modernization has added new burdens to women's traditional work but without concomitant rewards. The use of modern machinery made available to men has resulted in an increase in the acreage under cultivation. It is the woman's job to weed the fields, but the profit goes to the man. The introduction of livestock and poultry schemes, without supplying water, means that women have to carry more water than before.

When men give priority to cash crops, women have had to shift subsistence cultivation to less fertile fields requiring more labour input for the same output. Increased schooling for the young of the family means that the women in particular have to do without the help of their offspring in providing water and in looking after the smaller children.

One might ask, aren't the women fortunate *not* to have to be the earner of the family? But such a question overlooks the fact that increased cash economy based mainly on income provided through male labour makes women more dependent economically. And this development is not only contrary to women's productive role, but also to the responsibility women in many parts of the world have toward the maintenance of themselves and their children. The men claim a larger part of the family income as theirs, and spend money on prestige objects and recreation, whereas women would first consider the needs of the family. This is partly the reason that cash crops and wage employment lead to a deterioration of the family's nutritional standard.

Increased financial dependence on male earners has also caused a substantial male migration. In 1969, every third rural household in Kenya was headed by a woman. It is the priority given male employment that has caused this major breakup of families. In industry, as in agriculture, women are given few opportunities. For the women who remain in the countryside without a male partner, the work burden and family responsibility increase. Those who accompany their men to town find that neither in the traditional nor in the modern sector of productivity is there any work for them. Industrialization and modernization do not only leave little room for women, but even threaten them in their traditional fields of activity. In Ghana 80 per cent of the traders were women, but traditional trade is losing ground to modern commercial enterprises where they only make up 24 per cent of the labour force.[2] Women in traditional production are unable to compete with supermarkets and power looms.

The reason that modernization is still aimed at only one sex must be sought in the monopoly men have in virtually all areas of decision making pertaining to aid, both on the donor side and on the receiving side. But the sectorial thinking, so frequently present in the planning and the implementation of aid, is also to be blamed. The failure to look upon society as a whole, made up of innumerable but closely interrelated parts, has been unfortunate not only for women but for development itself. The mobilization of men all over the world has not been able to bridge the growing gap between food production and the population increase. Probably, it will not do so in the future because it is women's role in production and in reproduction that is pivotal.

Sectorial thinking

What has production in common with reproduction? The connecting link between these two vital areas of human activity lies in the concept of status. What development aid and concomitant modernization have meant for women particularly, is first a relative decrease in productivity in comparison to men, and decrease in relative productivity equals loss in status. Here we must make an allowance. In societies characterized by extreme exploitation of women, any new resources made available to women will improve their condition as well as their status. But as politics, religion and bravery are areas of activities normally closed to them, they usually get status only through their role in production and in reproduction. All over the world, mothers of many childdren can claim respect and prestige. The reasons behind this are real enough. Though a burden, fertility is also an important asset for women. With increasing dependency on a male wage earner, children guarantee the durability of the husband's economic responsibility toward the family. Later in life, the children themselves are potential economic assets. At least some of them might get education, jobs, adequate income. As long as women continue being engaged in labour-intensive and time-consuming types of production yielding little reward, children are the only means available to them to raise their status.

From this perspective, it is not suprising that the tremendous efforts put into family planning have had little overall impact. Sectorial thinking has prevented the incorporation of the close relationship between modes of production, number of children and female status. So far women are offered few alternatives to their much rewarded roles as mothers. But, if women's productivity were to increase, childbearing would no longer be their main or only means of obtaining security and prestige. Status also relates to attitudes, and women's traditionalism is closely connected to their low status.

How then, can women's marginal role in development be altered? The answer seems to lie in a holistic approach to development aid. Important elements like women's status, fertility, attitudes and productivity must be recognized as interrelated parts influencing one another in a reciprocal relationship of causes and effects. The maintenance of life through productive work, however, must be given priority and taken as a point of departure, also because a strategy for growing more food cannot overlook women's traditional and potential role in food production. Planners and economists tend not to take this immense contribution to production into account. If suitable substitutes for traditional labour methods were supplied, women's time and energy would be freed for more rewarding types of production. But increased female productivity in agriculture also warrants that women are given access to the same tools of development that hitherto have been made available mainly to men.

The patterns of male superiority and female subordination are being created and maintained all the time. So also in aid. The important contribution women do make in both production and reproduction and can make in the future — provided opportunities are made available — calls for renewed and increased attention. A balanced development presupposes active participation both by men and women.

FOOTNOTES

[1] Participation of Women in Rural Development Programmes, FAO, WS/E5494, 1973.
[2] E. Boserup, Women's Role in Economic Development. George Allen & Unwin, London, 1970.

Section VIII: The Chinese Approach To Development

China's Developmental Approach

Introduction

During the past decade, development theorists in the West have become increasingly interested in the Chinese approach to deveopment; and, as Dennis Woodward argues in the first paper in this section, China's development strategies, while not without problems, have been extraordinarily successful. In the nearly thirty years since the revolutionary victory of 1949, the material conditions of the Chinese people have improved almost beyond recognition. The spectre of famine is no longer present, diseases which once killed thousands have been eradicated or strictly controlled, life expectancy has increased and is likely to continue to do so.

However, it is not China's successes *per se* which have fascinated foreign observers, but the unique way in which they have been achieved. In a textbook capitalist economy, 'the market' decides what is, and what is not, produced. The 'market' is the shorthand term for the totality of purchasing decisions made by thousands of consumers. In the market place, those producers whose goods are widely rejected go to the wall. Successful production, according to the textbooks, depends on consumption—the decision to purchase; hence the notion of 'consumer sovereignty'. The problems which afflict market economies are now admitted by all but their most fanatical defenders. These economies are prone to grave crises; they generate 'public squalor and private affluence', and, most important of all, they are largely immune to rational social planning. In the USA, 'market rationality' sometimes means using chemical fertilisers instead of manure from animal 'feed lots', because it is 'cheaper'. The manure is pumped into rivers where it increases pollution. 'Market rationality' in other words, ignores 'social costs' and makes rational social planning impossible. The textbook planned economy by contrast is unaffected by market pressures. Precious energy resources can be economised; atmospheric and other forms of pollution can be controlled; resources can be channelled into areas of greatest need.

Under the pure capitalist market system, resources flow to areas of greatest 'demand', and demand reflects not just people's wants but their ability to pay for them; without the ability to pay, there is no 'demand', no matter how great the wants. In a planned economy, bureaucratic planners, who often have no way of knowing (or don't care) what consumers want, make production decisions. Lacking consumer feedback mechanisms (which the market system with all its faults does provide), the planned economy often fails to produce goods people do want, while overproducing goods they don't. The ponderous and over-bureaucratised Soviet economy under Stalin was notorious for such failings, but in many ways these failings are trivial compared with some of the other deficiencies of the Soviet-type planned system. Thus, in concentrating economic as well as political power in the hands of a few bureaucrats, the system tends to generate a 'new class'. Accumulating privilege and growing increasingly remote from the mass of the population, the 'new class' perverts the revolutionary socialist principles in the name of which it rules.

The Chinese revolutionary leadership has been acutely aware of the need to prevent such a 'new class' developing in China: hence, as Dennis Woodward points out in his paper, the Chinese emphasis on decentralisation, local initiative, self-reliance, self-criticism and the pursuit of equality. Certainly, a 'Cultural Revolution' such as took place in China in 1966 would be inconceivable in the Soviet Union. The Chinese idea that the 'party in power might initiate mass criticism of the abuse of that power' would be anathema to the Soviet Communists. But, while China has sought to avoid the inequalities and bureaucratic rigidities of the Soviet system, the Chinese Communist party has also constantly struggled against any reversion to the 'capitalist road'. (Current Chinese policy on this crucial issue is far from clear).

China's developmental successes and unique approach to achieving them have excited attention among Western development theorists—especially since the hysteria of the Cold War has largely subsided. The key question among these theorists is whether or not the 'Chinese model' of development can be exported. Bill Brugger's essay addresses this question.

Brugger points out that, pre-revolutionary China was, in some ways, better off than many of today's Third World countries. Imperialist economic penetration had not distorted the Chinese as it had other Third World economies, and the war against imperialism created a dedicated and strong political leadership. The national solidarity generated in the struggle against imperialism, plus the consequent Cold War hostilities, helped create and maintain a degree of national unity rarely found in other Third World countries. Furthermore, the self-reliant development approach adopted by the Chinese was greatly facilitated by China's vast size and the richness of her human and material resources. Self-reliant development is probably not an option for small developing countries.

Finally, Brugger argues that the belief that various Chinese developmental techniques can be exported piecemeal and succeed in a non-revolutionary environment is almost certainly a mistake. China's lessons cannot be mechanically applied elsewhere.

The Chinese Approach to Development

Dennis Woodward[*]

1. Introduction

The most distinctive feature of the Chinese approach to development is the strong emphasis on creating a socialist and ultimately a communist society rather than on economic development (as measured by Gross National Product growth rates, etc.) *per se*. China's development strategy has therefore, to be compatible with this long term goal. This has meant in practice that output maximization has been linked to the *qualitative* character of the processes of production and economic growth. It is this emphasis on man rather than material things which many western economists have labelled as 'irrational', particularly when mass political involvement in campaigns such as the Cultural Revolution causes temporary disruptions to production.[1]

This article attempts to outline and trace the origins of the major features of China's developmental approach. It will highlight the fact that there has been, and still is, a downplaying of the importance of individual material incentives in favour of reliance on collective material and moral incentives. China is striving to create a 'new socialist man' who will be selfless, politically conscious and active, and devoted to serving the

[*] Thanks to Dr. W. Brugger and Graham Young for their helpful advice on earlier drafts of this article.

people. In pursuing this goal the Chinese have attempted to break down the capitalist division of labour and to foster non-specialization — to eliminate the difference between mental and manual labour.[2] It will also argue that political consciousness and technical expertise in China are equally prized ("experts" must also be "red"); that managers must participate in production while workers participate in management, and that the importance of independence and self-reliance is insistently stressed.

In contemporary China the means of production are collectively or state owned, following the most massive and perhaps the most successful land reform programme in the world, and parallel changes in the industrial field. Initial land reform was followed by collectivization so that today private ownership of land is minimal. Furthermore while the productive relations in China are distinctive, the distribution of wealth and income is unique. China rates as one of the most (if not the most) egalitarian societies in the world. Although there are wage differentials and disparities of wealth and income — notably between the urban and rural areas, and between workers and peasants, these differences are very small when compared with those in other underdeveloped countries. Moreover, the residual inequalities are constantly alluded to, and the narrowing of the gap is continually stressed.

The Chinese pattern of development did not emerge fully grown overnight, but rather has evolved in response to changing circumstances. It is derived from a synthesis of traditional Chinese models of production, from the Yenan heritage (that is, the experience gained in Yenan, particularly in the years 1941-43), from the Soviet model of development (during China's First Five Year Plan), and from the continual interaction between Chinese practice and the development of the economic thought of Mao Tsetung and other leaders. The contemporary development approach also synthesises successive struggles within the Chinese Communist Party (CCP) leadership, between those favouring rapid economic development at all costs and those mindful that the socialist end might be forsaken if non-socialist means are used to stimulate economic progress. The tension between these groups has produced a succession of cycles wherein a period of mass political activity is followed by a period of consolidation — ideally at a higher level of economic and social development. Mao has summed up this process of 'creative imbalance' as the normal path for socialist economic development:

Economic construction does not always proceed in a straight

line without regression. Construction, moreover, may be slightly more or slightly less . . . *Economic construction proceeds in wave-like fashion with its ups and downs, with one wave chasing another. That is to say there is balance and disruption with a new balance restored following that disruption.* Of course, wave-like advances cannot be too big. There may be alternatively incidence of recklessness and conservatism. Nevertheless it is inevitable that development will proceed according to laws of wave-like motion.[3]

This non-linear view of development is central to Mao's theory of 'uninterrupted revolution'. It is an approach which seeks to prevent the revolution from stagnating, rather than progressing, within the stage of socialist transition. The theory of 'uninterrupted revolution' (like the later theory of 'continuous revolution') is a much misunderstood but key feature of the Chinese approach to development.[4]

Background to 1949 Position

When the Chinese Peoples Republic was proclaimed on October 1, 1949, China's social, political and economic institutions were in a state of near total collapse. Throughout the previous 100 years China had suffered at the hands of imperialist powers. In the 19th and early 20th century China's leaders had been repeatedly forced to sign away territory and make other concessions in a series of 'unequal treaties'. And this lack of sovereignty had not simply been restricted to foreign concessions along the seaboard, but also included foreign control over domestic customs and taxation and other humiliating impositions. The consequent pattern of Chinese 'development' in the 20th century was similar to that in many imperialist dominated Third World countries. There was very little modern industry and what industrial development had taken place was concentrated in the large foreign controlled treaty ports (for example, Shanghai) and the North-East of China (Manchuria, which was detached from the rest of China by the Japanese in the early 1930's). The rural hinterland remained stagnant and singularly backward. Foreign control was particularly prevalent in key industries such as transport and mining, and the industries which were established were geared to the needs of foreign economies rather than those of the Chinese people.

The Chinese economy in 1949 was shattered from these imperialist depredations and the disruptions of nearly fifty years of continual warfare. In the nineteenth century there had been wars against the British, French, Russians and Japanese. At the turn of the century the *Yi he tuan* ('Boxer') uprising was directed against a combined army of imperialist powers. In the mid-nineteenth century the massive Taiping Rebellion had engulfed much of China in civil war for some fifteen years. After the overthrow of the dynasty in 1911, few provinces in China experienced sustained peace until the 1950's. The country was ravaged by the incessant fighting between warlords (primarily during the years 1916-1928); by the civil war between the Chinese Communist Party (CCP) and the Kuomintang (Nationalists) 1927-1936; by the war against the Japanese from the mid-1930's to 1945 (in which the key areas of China were occupied), and by the renewed civil war in which the communists finally triumphed over the nationalists (1945-9). The disruption of the country's agriculture through warfare and the extortionate levels of taxation exacted to support the warring armies had caused frequent mass famines during which literally millions perished. Dikes and ancient irrigation systems were destroyed or fell into disrepair, accentuating the severity of both droughts and floods. Smallpox, typhoid, and cholera were endemic. Much of China's industrial capacity was destroyed or severely damaged as a result of the anti-Japanese and civil wars. The Anshan Iron and Steel Complex, for example, did not exceed 10% of its pre-war production for the first two years after it recommenced production in 1949.[5] When the Soviet army withdrew from Manchuria at the end of the Second World War, the Russians dismantled and took with them much of the machinery from one of China's major industrial centres. Nationalist forces retreating to Taiwan (Formosa) attempted to sabotage what they couldn't transport with them. Bridges and transportation networks were seldom left intact, and by late 1949 only 11,000 kilometres of railway line (roughly half) were left in operation.[6]

Intensifying the economic problems generated by the material disruption of warfare, the Chinese economy was also suffering from hyper-inflation and vast amounts of capital were taken by the retreating nationalists to Taiwan. Thus, while still occupied with the tasks of consolidating its rule over the entire country, mopping up pockets of Kuomintang resistance, and preparing for the final onslaught against the nationalists, the CCP also faced the monumental tasks of social and economic reconstruction. In other words, the China of 1949 was a backward country, lacking adequate transport and communications, with a war-torn economy and its major industrial capacity destroyed or damaged. It is against this background that the achievements of the Chinese approach to development must be evaluated.

The Yenan Heritage

When the CCP came to control the whole of China in 1949, it was not completely devoid of experience in administering a sizeable economy, as it had controlled base areas (areas from which guerrilla warfare was launched against the Japanese) for quite some time.[7] The largest and most famous base area was that centred around Yenan in China's northwest. The peculiar problems encountered in maintaining these base areas gave rise to a distinctly 'Maoist' strategy for economic development — the Yenan Model.[8] These problems sprang from the economic blockade of the border region instigated by the Japanese (during World War II) and by the Kuomintang. Survival necessitated that the border region's poor and stagnant agrarian economy had to be transformed by self-reliant means into a self-sufficient region capable of supporting both its own population and the Red Army[9] while still maintaining a war footing.[10] As Mao wrote at the time:

> If our party and the government do not pay attention to mobilizing the people and helping the people develop agriculture, industry and commerce, then the livelihood of the people cannot be improved.[11]

Furthermore, without an improvement in the people's livelihood and increases in production, the very existence of the base area would have been gravely threatened. In response to these demands a coherent, integrated economic and social policy was adopted which emphasized increasing production, especially in agriculture. The importance of the Yenan model, however, lies in the *means* devised for achieving these production increases. The means had to be compatible with long-term ends, which in practice meant maintaining peasant support. Hence the heavy emphasis on the creativity of the people which was implicit in the 'mass line'.[12] Party and government officials, troops, and students were integrated with the masses to assist in production tasks — especially at peak periods during harvesting. Great stress was laid on the need for popular participation and mass mobilization to increase production. Labour intensive methods were used to compensate for the lack of capital.

Along with ideological 'rectification' of the leadership, the Yenan period encompassed the creation of a new type of party/government official charged with implementing the 'mass line' — the cadre.[13] The cadre's crucial significance lay in his *participating* in tasks as well as directing them. He was not only closely integrated with the masses, but he led by personal example. This marked a radical break with the behaviour of the aloof traditional Chinese official. The implementation of the 'mass line' entailed as its natural corollary the rejection of domination by an administrative or technical elite operating through a centralized bureaucracy.[14] In other words, the Yenan model was explicitly anti-bureaucratic. There was a streamlining of administration, emphasised by the campaign for 'crack troops and simple administration', and many officials were sent to the countryside to participate in production.

The rejection of bureaucratic methods required of necessity a policy of decentralization. Local initiative was fostered and decisions were made at the grass roots level, but within a general framework determined by the central leadership. This was the policy of 'centralized leadership and divided operations'. Concomitant with the decentralization policy and the increase in community power, was a corresponding increase in Party control at the local level. Another aspect of the decentralization policy was the introduction of 'dual rule', which replaced the previous 'vertical rule', which had been characterized by strict hierarchical chains of command. This meant that enterprises in the same area which under 'vertical rule' were solely responsible to higher authorities, also became responsible to the local government (that is, the local Party branch). This 'dual rule' facilitated the lateral or horizontal co-ordination of enterprises which was previously absent.

Self-reliance was a fundamental tenet of the Yenan model. Local handicrafts (for example, spinning and weaving) were fostered, small indigenous industries were established, and locally financed co-operatives were all encouraged in a concerted drive to increase the self-sufficiency of the border region. Mao also emphasized the importance of mutual aid teams and other forms of collective labour in creating increases in production. Rent reduction and partial land reform were carried out, but while a firm egalitarian principle was followed, absolute equality was not sought since, in the absence of a fully developed revolutionary consciousness, such a policy would have removed much of the incentive for increasing production. The introduction of *minban* education gave communities control over their schools and enabled the type of schooling to correspond with the needs and wishes of their members. This provided yet another example of decentralization and the attempt to prevent the re-emergence of elites — in this case the traditional Chinese scholarly elite. In sum, the 'Yenan model' evolved in response to an externally determined imperative for self-sufficiency which was consistent with revolutionary socialist principles. It involved the 'mass line' and the launching of extensive mass campaigns to increase production, a rejection of bureaucratic methods and a policy of decentralization, the stressing of self-reliance and arduous struggle, and the encouragement of collectivization, within an egalitarian framework. These same elements form the central theoretical core of Mao's economic policies and were to become manifest in later stages of China's post-revolutionary approach to development.

Reconstruction and Land Reform

After the foundation of the People's Republic, the period 1949-52 was devoted to the rehabilitation of China's war ravaged economy, the completion of land reform[15] and the laying of the basic foundations for the future socialist transformation of the economy. By 1952, nearly all sectors of the economy had reached, if not surpassed, pre-1949 levels. The country had been brought under uniform central control, banditry had been suppressed, and much of the railroad system had been restored to operation, as had the flood control and irrigation systems. A new stable currency had been created ending years of hyper-inflation and stimulating the growth of private business. A non-extortionate nation-wide taxation system had been introduced and the previously corrupt bureaucracy largely replaced by honest and dedicated cadres. Public health and sanitation programs were launched and a policy providing a more equitable distribution of food and clothing had been instigated.

Although basic land reform had been initiated in the liberated areas before 1949, the programme was extended nation-wide following the CCP's victory —albeit in a more moderate form. (This moderate policy was later to be denounced as the 'rich peasant line'). The estates of landlords were confiscated and distributed amongst the poor and lower-middle peasants. In some cases, the land reform was carried out without adequate Party control and excesses occurred — reviled landlords who had not already fled, were subjected to struggle meetings and often murdered by vengeful mobs. However, in the light of previous exploitation, landlords as a whole were treated with moderation. They were denied civic rights but were generally allowed to retain sufficient land to support themselves.

By 1952, when land reform had been completed, some 300 million peasants had benefited from the redistribution. However, this period of land reform did not entail a complete equalization of land holdings. Many rich peasants were treated relatively lightly and middle peasants were won over to the revolution by allowing them to share in the redistribution (to have alienated the middle peasants by a completely egalitarian land distribution would have caused massive disruption to grain production). The result was that China had become a country of small owner-cultivators with considerable disparities in the size of land holdings, in the quality of land owned, and in the ownership of animals and implements needed to work the land. The ultimate aim of full socialization of agriculture was not sought at this time since the material and political conditions for its implementation did not exist. Rather, the establishment of mutual aid teams was encouraged and the establishment of lower stage co-operatives was undertaken in advanced areas.

Concurrent with the initial land reform programme, economic control had been secured over such key sectors of the economy as banking, trade, railways, and steel. However, no large scale nationalization of industry took place except for those enterprises which were owned by the 'comprador bourgeoisie' and the 'bureaucrat bourgeoisie' (i.e., those capitalist supporters of the Kuomintang who were also closely allied to foreign interests.) Foreign owned enterprises had failed to recover from war damage and were generally 'squeezed out by various forms of pressure' within a few years of the CCP's nationwide victory.[16]

Many industrial enterprises had been previously state owned under the nationalists and were easily absorbed by the new state. But in contrast to the treatment of the 'comprador bourgeoisie' private ownership of industry by 'national capitalists' (Chinese businessmen without Kuomintang or foreign connections who were sympathetic to the new regime) was not only tolerated but actively encouraged. Between 1949-53 a large number of such new undertakings emerged.[17] Many of these firms took on state contracts and were encouraged to become joint state-private enterprises which fitted in with the government's policy of integrating private concerns to the socialist sector. After the complete socialization of industry in 1956 (when all private enterprises were transformed into state controlled enterprises), national capitalists continued to receive interest payments on their investments.

The First Five Year Plan

Following the post-revolutionary phase of reconstruction came the First Five Year Plan (1953-57) which aimed to lay the basis for a comprehensive industrial structure as swiftly as possible.

Although it was announced that the plan would come into operation in 1953, it was not until February 1955 that it was finalised.[18] The delay resulted from problems in obtaining the adequate statistical information necessary for effective planning and in the uncertainty surrounding the Korean War and Russian aid projects. Despite the experience gained in the Yenan period, the First Five Year Plan did not follow Yenan precepts but was closely modelled on the very different Soviet approach to development. The 'Soviet model' with its emphasis on heavy industrialization, high rates of saving and investment was assumed during this period to be the appropriate approach for Socialist economic development. As a result there was a very high rate of savings and investment during the implementation of the plan, (5.5% of GNP in 1950 went to gross fixed investment and this rose to 17.9% by 1957),[19] and overwhelming priority was given to heavy industry — particularly machine building. Thus some 89% of investment funds during the First Five Year Plan went to industrial construction.[20] Agriculture was to be subordinated to industry, providing it with raw materials (for example, cotton) and investment surpluses. As only 6.2% of the state budget was invested in agriculture,[21] the agricultural sector failed to develop at a pace sufficient to provide adequate surpluses for investment in industry without placing a heavy burden on the peasantry. Other features of the Soviet model which were (in the main) adopted included the emphasis on capital intensive, large-scale, specialized plants; a hierarchical organization of labour (with a vertical chain of command featuring 'one man' factory management); and a reliance on technical expertise with *individual* material incentives used to spur production. The education system was also structured along Soviet lines and was designed to produce elite technicians and engineers.

In many respects the First Five Year Plan was remarkably successful. The growth in GNP for the 1950's was greater than 10% per year in real terms and industrial production rose at the spectacular average annual rate of 20%.[22] Crude steel output had increased from 1.35 million tonnes to 5.35 million tonnes and similarly huge gains were attained in coal and cement production and electric power output.[23]. However, by the end of the First Plan period its weaknesses (and those of the Soviet model) had become glaringly apparent. The relative neglect of agriculture was reflected in its average annual growth rate of about 4%,[24] which barely kept ahead of population growth. Since agricultural output was failing to grow at a sufficient rate, the imbalance in the economy was beginning to retard industrial growth because the necessary raw materials and agricultural surpluses were becoming progressively harder to obtain without 'squeezing' the peasants. The seeds of elitism inherent in the Soviet model's reliance on hierarchical command structures and material incentives were also having damaging consequences for the long term social goals. Wage differentials were increasing rather than decreasing, and the urban-centred emphasis of the Soviet model benefited city dwellers while leaving the overwhelming majority of the population in the countryside with a second rate education, health and welfare system. As a result, there was a drift of population into the cities where sheer size was beginning to present increasing problems. Finally, the revolutionary objective of an egalitarian socialist society was being threatened by the spectre of a new elite of managers and technicians ruling over the workers and peasants, with political and social status differences between elite and mass being underscored by attendant and growing disparities in wealth and income.

In fact, the drawbacks of the Soviet model were apparent long before the First Five Year Plan had run its course. The Soviet system of 'one man management', for example, in which a single factory manager was responsible for the profit or loss of his enterprise was so antithetical to the Yenan heritage that it was not uniformly accepted throughout the country and had been completely abandoned by late 1956.[25] And in April the same year, Mao had addressed himself to some of the crucial economic and social problems which had emerged in China during this period. In contrast to the strategy adopted in the First Plan, he argued (in his speech "On the Ten Great Relationships") that increasing the proportion of investment which light industry and agriculture received would in turn accelerate the development of heavy industry.[26] He said,

> Our conclusion is as follows: one way of developing heavy industry is to develop light industry and agriculture somewhat less. There is another way which consists in developing light industry and agriculture somewhat more. The result of the first method, that is of one-sidedly developing heavy industry without paying attention to the people's livelihood, will be to make people dissatisfied, so that as a result even heavy industry cannot really be well run ... The second method, that is of developing heavy industry

on a foundation of satisfying the needs of the people's livelihood, will provide a more solid foundation for the development of heavy industry, and the result will be to develop it more and better.[27]

Mao also indicated his concern for regionally balanced development, for limiting military expenditure and spending more on economic construction, and for ensuring that the welfare of workers and peasants was given due consideration.[28] These themes were again repeated in a later speech in February 1957, entitled "On the Correct Handling of Contradictions Among the People". Mao again emphasized that:

Accumulation is essential both for the state and for the co-operative, but in neither case should it be excessive. We should do everything possible to enable the peasants to raise their personal incomes year by year in normal years on the basis of increased production.[29]

While Mao saw the importance of building a large number of large scale modern enterprises to serve as the 'mainstay' of industry, he argued that the majority of enterprises should be small and medium scale (using indigenous means) in order to make the best use of the existing industrial base.[30] It was this departure from reliance on large scale capital intensive heavy industry (financed by accumulation forced from the peasants) in favour of simultaneously developing agriculture and light industry (using labour intensive indigenous technology) which was to form the core of the uniquely Chinese approach to development. Since the agricultural and light industrial sectors served as markets *and* sources of raw materials, *and* sources of accumulation for heavy industry it made no sense at all to neglect them in favour of heavy industry. In the marked shift of emphasis which followed the First Five Year Plan, the expansion of heavy industry was no longer an end in itself but rather its role was to provide the machinery needed for the expansion of agriculture and light industry. The expansion of the latter sectors would in turn help to expand heavy industry. (As we shall see the policies associated with the Great Leap Forward attempted to expand the agricultural and light industrial sectors by an even greater emphasis on local inputs of both people and raw materials.)

While agriculture had been relatively neglected in terms of state investment during the First Five Year Plan, it had been transformed from the system of individual peasant proprietors into co-operatives. Although the first campaign for co-operativization of Chinese agriculture was launched in December 1951,[31] the process of co-operativization was not one of a gradual and smooth transition. Rather, it was marked by periods in which co-operatives were dissolved and more moderate and more gradualist policies were pursued. These periods were interspersed by successive campaigns for co-operativization of differing pace and intensity. The gradualist approach envisaged the slow transformation of basic mutual aid teams (which shared labour on privately owned land), into elementary co-operatives (in which the land was collectively owned but co-op members were primarily remunerated according to the amount of land and materials they contributed to the co-operative), and eventually into higher-level co-operatives (which would be much larger and in which land would be collectively owned and members rewarded according to the amount of labour they contributed). However, the gradualist approach threatened to negate the goals of collectivization and even to undermine the gains of land reform. By delaying the process of collectivization, agriculture was not progressing beyond the level of individual peasant ownership of land and this situation was already beginning to degenerate into traditional patterns. Land was becoming concentrated in the hands of rich peasants while poor peasants fell into debt and reverted to the state of landless tenants.[32]

While collectivization was the long term goal for a *socialist* agriculture, it was also seen as a means for breaking out of the subsistence impasse. Collectivization would enable more economically sized plots to be worked, facilitate the construction of capital works (such as irrigation works, land reclamation), provide a social security system, and eventually enable the mechanization of agriculture. Thus the socialist goal of collectivization was seen as being necessary to prevent the re-emergence of a feudal system of agriculture. It was also the most rational method for increasing agricultural production both in the short and long terms. It was for these reasons that, in mid-1955, Mao advocated an acceleration of the movement to establish co-operatives.[33] In so doing he was again departing from the Soviet model (of the early 1950's) because he advocated that agricultural collectivization should *precede* agricultural mechanization rather than vice versa.[34] Despite opposition to this policy from certain sections of the CCP's leadership, the co-operativization of Chinese agriculture was basically completed by the end of 1957 — earlier than Mao had forecast.[35] This remarkably rapid transformation through mass campaigns instigated from above, undoubtedly involved an element of compulsion — even if the coercion was moral rather than physical. However, although there was a serious decline in livestock holdings after collectivization (owing to slaughter by the peasants and inadequate attention by the collective to breeding), there was no marked decline in the harvest and the whole process occurred without the massive disruption which had taken place in the Soviet Union when Stalin had imposed collectivization on a reluctant Soviet peasantry.[36]

The Great Leap Forward

As already noted above, despite the achievements of the First Five Year Plan, the Chinese economy was facing something of a crisis as the plan neared its end. Sectoral imbalances were becoming acute and collectivization had not in itself proved to be a complete solution for lagging agricultural production. There was considerable under-utilization of capacity in light industries due to a lack of agricultural raw material inputs. The relative lack of light industrial consumer goods meant that the peasants had little incentive to increase their marketable surplus and therefore tended to consume any production increases themselves. Without steadily increasing agricultural surpluses, accumulation for investment was impossible and the spectre of urban food shortages arose. Furthermore, China lacked sufficient producer goods to supply the necessary modern inputs (for example, fertilizers and tractors) to accelerate investment in the agricultural sector.[37] Faced with this apparent impasse, a bold plan was adopted (based largely on Mao's economic analyses and the Yenan model discussed in the previous sections). The new plan attempted to increase production simultaneously in all sectors by mobilizing labour as a substitute for capital. This was the rationale for the Great Leap Forward and the formation of communes.

The Leap featured the policy of 'walking on two legs' — the simultaneous development of industry and agriculture, of heavy and light industry, of national and local industries, of large and small enterprises and of modern and indigenous methods of production. It emphasised extensive mass mobilization to increase production and an attempt to decentralize decision-making.[38] It aimed at narrowing the elite-mass and urban-rural gaps in their social and economic dimensions within a framework of expanding productivity. Rather than limiting production to maintain balance, advanced sectors were urged to push production to the limit. The resulting bottlenecks would then be tackled as they arose to push the production limits still further. Mao saw this 'creative imbalance' as part of an 'uninterrupted revolution' which would act as a spur to economic and social progress. That is, instead of following the Soviet model of ordered and balanced development, Mao sought continual advances in all sectors which would bring about a succession of leaps from one level to another — forming an 'uninterrupted revolution'. As he argued in May 1958,

> ... The destruction of balance constitutes leaping forward, and such destruction is better than balance. Imbalance and headache are good things. The First Ministry of Machine Building, the Ministry of Metallurgy, and the Ministry of Geology, for example, are experiencing a hard time and receiving pressure from all sides. *Therefore, they must develop extensively, which is a good thing. Balance, quantitative change, and unity are temporary and relative. Imbalance, sudden changes, and disunity are absolute and permanent.* Many disunities have been overcome and changed to unity. Unification is proposed because of disunity.[39]

The policy of 'walking on two legs' which accorded equal importance to traditional and small scale enterprises as to modern large scale industries marked a severe break with both Soviet and Western approaches to development. There were sound reasons for the promotion of small scale industries. Given the availability of local and regional raw materials and markets, a wide distribution of enterprises was possible. This in turn meant that regional self-sufficiency could be fostered and the strain on China's inadequate transportation networks could be lessened. The advantages of 'centralized policy and divided operations' could be maximized. The location of small scale industries near their source of raw materials, helped in the development of backward areas. Smaller enterprises were less demanding on quality of construction and could utilize raw materials which were poorer and in quantities which would have been uneconomical for large scale use. Small scale enterprises also had the advantage of lower capital-output ratios and shorter gestation periods.[40] These small and less technologically advanced plants were also able to undertake repairing, maintenance and processing activities which could in turn free large capacity enterprises for production tasks which only the modern sector could achieve. It must be remembered that the resort to small scale and labour intensive methods of production (especially of the indigenous type) was largely a temporary measure within a framework of long term priority for large scale and capital intensive techniques.[41]

Thus, small scale local industries formed an ideal pattern for the mobilization of the masses and for their developing technical skills. It could utilize underemployed labour and unused resources, and could provide the gradual accumulation of capital which would enable the expansion and modernization of local industries.

An intrinsic part of decentralization policy and of the policy of fostering local industries was to be played by the establishment of communes. The first communes appear to have been established on an experimental basis in the model province of Honan in early 1958,[42] and initially to have been the result of initiatives taken by local and provincial leaders without any specific directives from Peking. (The need for larger units to undertake water conservancy works played a significant part in this movement.) However, communes soon gained official endorsement,[43] and were to act as production and administrative units, and be responsible for their own education, health and defence programmes. In short, the communes were to form the locus for self-sufficient economic and social development. They were composed of a number of higher-stage co-operatives (or brigades which approximated a natural village), and varied in size from between 5,000 to 100,000 members.[44]

In the early euphoria of the Leap, the communes were seen as a shortcut to obtaining communism and many excesses took place. Attempts at communal living and the free distribution of food were certainly ahead of both peasant consciousness and material conditions, and proved costly failures. Similarly, the collectivization of private plots which peasants had retained after joining the co-operatives was not popularly received. Many of these excesses were corrected as early as December 1958,[45] although the general restoration of private plots did not take place until the summer of 1960, and was not officially endorsed until the Ninth Plenum in 1961.[46]

The Great Leap Forward witnessed some impressive successes in its first two years. The grain harvest of 1958 was the highest recorded, although initial claims that it had doubled the output of 1957 were greatly exaggerated (owing to poor statistical information and cadres inflating figures to impress higher authorities) and an increase of around 30% appears to be more accurate.[47] There was a large rise in industrial production in 1958 and 1959,[48] and great increases in the development of large scale construction works such as canals, reservoirs and railways.[49] Many of these achievements (such as large scale construction works) did not add to immediate production and hence their utility was not indicated in production figures for the years of the Leap.

However, by 1961 the Leap had collapsed. Following three successive bad harvests, the grain shortage was acute and malnutrition widespread. The Chinese economy was in dire straits and the scourge of mass famine loomed threatingly. Without any agricultural surplus, light and heavy industry could not sustain their high levels of production and output slackened off. To exacerbate the problem, the growing Sino-Soviet dispute[50] had led to the withdrawal of Soviet aid and technicians from the three hundred modern industrial plants which the USSR promised to build.[51] The necessity of repaying Soviet loans (from the Korean War as well as construction projects) further heightened the crisis. Conservative economists have attributed the successive bad harvests as the inevitable outcome of the policies adopted during the Leap.[52] They point to hastily planned irrigation works which increased soil alkalinity; to the introduction of close planting and deep ploughing techniques which failed; to reductions in the sown acreage which arose from the planners' (believing inflated statistics) notion that sufficient grain could be produced by more intensive cultivation of smaller areas;[53] and finally to labour being used on construction rather than agricultural tasks. To such economists the failure of 'backyard furnaces' to produce high quality steel symbolizes the ill-conceived nature of the Leap. Yet, while these mistakes did occur, they merely aggravated an already bad situation, the primary cause of which was extremely adverse weather conditions throughout a great part of China.[54] It was thus not primarily the strategy of the Leap which caused the crisis but the harsh weather. (Certainly the policies of the Leap had not noticeably hindered an extremely good harvest in 1958 when weather conditions had been favourable.) However the economic crisis which ended the Leap, also led to the eclipse of Mao's economic strategy.

The Post-Leap Reversals

In the aftermath of the Great Leap Forward, control of the leadership of the CCP was in the hands of 'conservatives' who severely cut back or rejected the radical policies which had been pursued during the Leap. Small local industries were dismantled in many cases, private plots were restored and *expanded,* and the basic accounting unit in the countryside was shifted from the brigade to the team level. The communes were reorganized into smaller units and lost many of their key administrative functions — especially over production. Except for large scale irrigation, terracing or reafforestation projects, the communes were virtually eclipsed. The desire for rapid increases in production (especially in agriculture) led to the reversion to methods which were in contradiction to long term socialist goals. If the criticisms of Liu Shao-chi[55] are correct, he advocated the policies of *'san zi yi bao'*,[56] 'four freedoms',[57] work points in command', 'money in command' and the mechanization of agriculture by means of state controlled tractor stations.[58] In this climate, 'unhealthy tendencies' reappeared. These included peasants going it alone and concentrating on their private plots and individual sidelines rather than collective undertakings (a 'spontaneous tendency towards capitalism'), the re-emergence of 'feudal' customs and practices, the emergence of black markets, the decline in cadre morale and actual corruption among some cadres.

In the industrial sector, markets and profitability were becoming a motive force in the economy, with the accompanying re-emergence of managerial and technical elitism. Managers, professional staff and technocrats ('experts') were restored to their positions of primacy above trade union and party committees ('reds') in the control of factories. [59] Once the economy had recovered, Mao (whose venerated position masked his lack of power) was anxious to prevent the continuation of these policies which were again leading China away from the goal of a future egalitarian socialist society. His attempts to do so during the Socialist Education Movement (a campaign to raise political consciousness and rectify work styles in the period 1962-6) were largely frustrated by conservatives within the Party leadership who were becoming a new elite. It was against this group and their policies that the Cultural Revolution was aimed.

The Cultural Revolution
The Cultural Revolution was a mass movement in the Yenan and Great Leap tradition. It was marked by mass participation in political debates and struggles, by large scale disruption (primarily in the cities) and considerable violence. As many leading Party members were criticized and dismissed, the army took over the political and administrative role of the Party to maintain order and ensure that the economy was kept working. Those economic policies which were deemed to be leading China down the "capitalist road" were criticized. Thus, the renewed

emphasis on individual material incentives was attacked and downgraded. Wage differentials were criticized. Bonuses and other features of "economism" were generally eliminated as moral incentives were stressed. Elitist factory control by managers and technicians was replaced by revolutionary committees which were composed of Party members and workers as well as managers and technicians. To prevent industrial management from becoming divorced from the masses of workers, greater participation in management by the basic levels of workers was encouraged and management personnel participated in production. This implementation of the "mass line" in industrial management not only helped to close the gap between mental and manual labour, but also promoted production by both giving workers greater identification with their work, and by achieving greater co-ordination of production as a result of the planners becoming familiar with the practical problems of production.[60]

The profit motive was rejected as the driving force in industry. Enterprise funds [61] were restricted, and output quotas were decided by consultation between the factory committee and the next highest authority. Most profits of factories are now transferred to the state, and enterprises also pay certain taxes. The revenues from the profits of state enterprises, were centrally used to finance further investment.

During the Cultural Revolution, the Chinese media similarly criticized the "capitalist line" in agriculture (symbolized by *'san zi yi bao'* and the 'four freedoms') and reasserted Mao's principles. However, it would be wrong to accept exhortations in the Chinese media as an accurate reflection of the actual state of conditions generally prevailing in the countryside during this period. The Cultural Revolution was initially primarily an urban phenomenon,[62] with the countryside generally (that is, except for these communes on the outskirts of major cities) not affected by the major upheavals and factionalism which occurred in the cities. Only in the latter half of 1968, with the intensification of the "struggle-criticism-transformation" campaign in the rural areas, was the Cultural Revolution universally brought to the countryside.[63] And it was at this time, with the assistance of PLA propaganda teams, that concrete changes were sought in the communes. These changes encompassed firstly the rejection of policies previously pursued which were criticized as part of Liu's "revisionist line" (for example, *'san zi yi bao'*), secondly the implementation of Mao's policies, and thirdly the reorganization of commune administration necessary to achieve these goals. The fostering of small commune run industries was sought, there were attempts to amalgamate teams, brigades and communes, and the decentralization of rural education, medical, public health, supply and marketing services was sought. The campaign to learn from Tachai (the model of self-reliant agricultural development)[64] was also greatly intensified. Similarly, the farm machinery and tractors which had belonged to state stations under the Liuist scheme for agricultural development, were to be transferred down to individual communes. However, the implementation of these policies was far from uniform and the problems thus created have continued to be part of an on-going policy debate up to the present.

Since the Cultural Revolution

In the period since the Cultural Revolution, radical policies have been continued in some sectors, consolidated in others and partially reversed in still others. Excesses which occurred during and shortly after the Cultural Revolution have been rectified. For example, confiscated private plots have been restored. (Although their size has been restricted). Similarly, excessive accumulation of collective funds and the introduction of absolute egalitarianism which dampened mass enthusiasm has been criticized. In industry "ultra-democracy" and "anarchism" have been attacked and new rules for labour discipline have been introduced. The rehabilitation of many Party cadres who had been criticized during the Cultural Revolution has also taken place. In the field of education, which took much of the brunt of Red Guard dissatisfaction, there have similarly been instances of the reintroduction of policies (for example, entrance examinations to universities) which were eliminated during the Cultural Revolution.

The dismissal of Teng Hsiao-p'ing in 1976 and the campaign to criticize the "attempt to reverse correct verdicts" marked an attempt by radicals to check a new conservative trend and to push the revolution further. Similarly, the dismissal of the "gang of four"[65] in late 1976 can be seen as a continuation of the struggle between conservative and radical forces in the CCP. Tension remains and the future direction of the Chinese revolution is yet to be decided.

However in the economic field, Mao's basic strategy has been largely adhered to. In particular, renewed emphasis on small scale local industries has seen them flourishing throughout the country.[66] These small scale plants, moreover, have rapidly gained significance in terms of total national output. Thus small chemical fertilizer plants and small cement plants produced more than a third of the total national output in 1970.[67] In 1971, more than 40% of China's cement output came from small cement works,[68] while small plants accounted for 60% of chemical fertilizer output.[59] It was also claimed in 1971 that the output of iron ore, pig iron and steel of medium and small iron and steel enterprises, had increased by 70% over the previous year while more than 90% of *xian* (districts) had their own small agricultural machinery manufacture and repair plants.[70] Small coal pits were responsible for 30% of one province's coal output in 1972,[71] and 48% of national cement output for the same year came from small plants.[72] The capacity of small hydro-electric stations run by districts and communes trebled in the 1970-3 period[73] and small chemical fertilizer plants continued to increase production at an average of 3.4 million tons per year.[74]

The Chinese claim of 240 million tonnes for total grain output in 1970[75] which ended a decade long dearth of official statistics, was substantially higher than most analysts had predicted. Subsequent good harvests have demonstrated that China has established her basic agricultural base. That is, the benefits of farmland reclamation and farmland construction, of massive capital construction works (especially in the field of irrigation), of the development of the fertilizer industry, of multiple cropping, of collectivization and gradual mechanization, and of the development and gradual popularization of new improved seed strains,[77] are now finally being realized to the extent that high stable yields can be guaranteed irrespective of weather conditions.

The agricultural growth rate has been estimated at 1.2% during 1957-65 and 3.4% during 1965-71[78] or roughly 2% for the period 1953-73.[79] While there is still some debate over these figures, there is general consensus over the main trends. The People's Republic has managed to increase agricultural output slightly ahead of population growth and more importantly recent growth rates are substantially above (almost double) the population growth rate. While the overall growth rate for agriculture is not outstanding, it is never-the-less significant in comparison with other Third World countries and — certainly in comparison with these countries — the future seems bright. To have banished the perennial threat of famine and to feed and clothe a quarter of the world's population with less than 8% of the world's cultivated area is no mean feat.

Industrial growth has similarly been steady and substantial, although not as spectacularly high as during the First Five Year Plan period. Since 1957, China's average industrial growth rate has been approximately 9-10% per year. Moreover, the quality of output has increased in recent decades to offset the decline in the rate of increase of sheer output which was attained during the 1950's. China is now 95% self-sufficient in machinery of all kinds,[80] and has rapidly developed her crude oil production to the extent that she already exports substantial quantities.

Conclusion

China's achievements in the economic field have been substantial for an undeveloped country of her size. From being a recipient of foreign aid (from the Soviet Union) China has become a net foreign aid donor and lender herself. Her policies of self-reliance and self-sufficiency have made her percentage of foreign trade to GNP exceptionally small — less than 5% by 1971.[81] However, it is in areas that are not measured by production statistics in which China's development has been outstanding. In terms of providing education, health[82] and welfare services for the *entire* population, China's progress is almost without parallel in the Third World. And unlike most Third World countries, these services are not restricted to urban areas but have been extended to the most remote regions. The usual industrialization pattern with its high urban concentrations and social costs has been reversed as interior development through the decentralized commune structure has taken place.

Although the Chinese approach to development has undergone many changes, certain themes remain fairly constant. These can be traced back to the Yenan heritage and to Mao's post-First Five Year Plan economic strategy. They are: reliance on mass initiative and mass mobilization; rejection of bureaucratism and a policy of decentralization; emphasis on self-reliance and self-sufficiency; reliance on collective effort; stress on non-material incentives or group incentives rather than individual material incentives; the simultaneous development of agriculture, light industry and heavy industry; the use of small scale local industries as well as large scale industries; the use of indigenous as well as modern technology; a firm egalitarian policy; attention to the people's livelihood; and constant attempts to narrow the differences between mental and manual labour, between town and countryside, and between workers and peasants. It is these policies which have enabled China to break free from grinding poverty and to illuminate the vista of a future prosperity in which the benefits of development are shared by all.

FOOTNOTES

1. For a good summary of some of the major differences between the Chinese model of development and that advocated by western economists, see, J. Gurley, "Capitalist and Maoist Economic Development" in E. Friedman and M. Selden (eds.) *America's Asia: Dissenting Essays on Asian — American Relations* (New York, 1971)
2. One of the 'three major differences'. The other two are the difference between workers and peasants, and the difference between town and country. The Chinese model of development is aimed at eliminating these differences.
3. Mao Tsetung 1959(?) in *Mao Zedong Sixiang Wansui*, 1967, pp. 149-50 (emphasis added). Another translation in *Miscellany of Mao Tse-tung Thought (1949-1968)* Part 1 (Arlington, 1974) p. 224
4. For discussion on this point, see G. Young and D. Woodward, "From Contradictions Among the People to Class Struggle: The Theories of Uninterrupted Revolution and Continuous Revolution", *Asian Survey*, Vol. XVIII, No. 9, (September, 1978).

5. W. Brugger, *Democracy and Organization in the Chinese Industrial Enterprise (1948-53)* (Cambridge, 1976) p. 69
6. I. Davies, "Economic Geography" in C. Mackerras (ed.) *China. The Impact of Revolution* (Hawthorne, 1976) p. 139.
7. See J. Gurley, "The Formation of Mao's Economic Strategy, 1927-1949" *Monthly Review*, Vol. 27, No. 3 (July August 1975)
8. See, Mao Tsetung, "Economic and Financial Problems", December 1942 (Draft translated by A. Watson) (Original first published by Xinminzhu Publishing Co., Hong Kong 1949) part of which is included in *Selected Works of Mao Tsetung* (hereafter *SW*) Vol. III (Peking 1967) under the title of "Economic and Financial Problems in the Anti-Japanese War". See also Mao Tsetung "Spread the Campaigns to Reduce Rent, Increase Production and 'Support the Government and Cherish the People' in the Base Areas", and "Get Organized!" *SW*, Vol. III
9. Designated the 8th Route Army during the Anti-Japanese War, and later the People's Liberation Army (PLA).
10. See M. Selden, *The Yenan Way* (Cambridge, 1971) p. 209 et.seq.
11. "Economic and Financial Problems", *op.cit.* (draft trans.) p.2
12. See Mao Tsetung, "Some Questions Concerning Methods of Leadership" *SW*, Vol. III
13. For good discussion on this and other aspects of the Yenan model, see B. Brugger, *Contemporary China* (London, 1977) pp. 31-40
14. Selden, *op.cit.*, pp. 274-6
15. For an eyewitness account of land reform in practice, see, W. Hinton, *Fanshen. A Documentary of Revolution in a Chinese Village* (Harmondsworth, 1972)
16. A. Donnithorne, *China's Economic System* (London, 1967) p. 145
17. *ibid*, p. 146
18. Kang Chao, "Policies and Performance in Industry" in A. Eckstein, et.al. *Economic Trends in Communist China* (Edinburgh, 1968) p. 549
19. E. Wheelwright and B. McFarlane, *The Chinese Road to Socialism* (New York, 1970) p. 36
20. Kang Chao, *loc.cit.*, p. 555
21. Wheelwright and McFarlane, *op.cit.* p. 35
22. B. McFarlane, "The Economy of the Chinese People's Republic" in C. Mackerras (ed.), *op.cit.* p. 97 (This is a rather generous estimate, other estimates range between 14-19%.)
23. Wheelwright and McFarlane, *op.cit.* p. 36
24. McFarlane, *loc.cit.* p. 97 (Again this estimate is considered high by more conservative economists who consider 2% average annual growth rate more accurate.)
25. See F. Schurmann, *Ideology and Organization in Communist China* (Berkeley, 1968) p. 284 et.seq.
26. See S. Schram (ed.) *Mao Tsetung Unrehearsed: Talks and Letters 1956-71* (Harmondsworth, 1974) pp. 61-83
27. *ibid*, pp 64-5
28. *ibid*, passim
29. "On the Correct Handling of Contradictions Among the People" in Mao Tsetung, *Four Essays on Philosophy* (Peking, 1966) p. 103
30. *ibid*, p. 128
31. See J. Gray, "The High Tide of Socialism in the Chinese Countryside" in J. Ch'en and N. Tarling (eds.) *Studies in the Social History of China and South-East Asia: Essays in Memory of Victor Purcell* (Cambridge, 1970) p. 87
32. This pattern resulted from poorer peasants needing to borrow money from those with surplus capital during hard times. Successive bad harvests often

meant that poor peasants who were unable to repay their loans (plus interest) had to sell their land to pay their debts. Thus land became concentrated into the hands of the wealthier peasants (traditionally landlords).

33. See Mao Tsetung, "On the Question of Agricultural Co-operation" and "Selections From the Introductory Notes in the Socialist Upsurge in China's Countryside" in *Selected Readings From the Works of Mao Tsetung* (Peking, 1967) p. 316 et.seq.
34. See T. Bernstein, "Leadership and Mass Mobilization in the Soviet and Chinese Collectivization Campaigns of 1929-30 and 1955-56. A Comparison" *The China Quarterly*, No. 31 (July September 1967) for comparisons with the Soviet model of the 1930's.
35. See "Summing-up Speech of Sixth Expanded Plenum of Seventh CCP Central Committee" (September, 1955) in *Miscellany op.cit.*p. 19
36. See Donnithorne, *op.cit.* pp. 40-41 (Wheelwright and McFarlane, *op.cit.* p. 39 argue that per capita agricultural output probably increased after collectivization.)
37. For an analysis of the economic and social rationale behind the Leap, see V. Lippit, "The Great Leap Forward Reconsidered" *Modern China* vol. I, no. 1 (January, 1975)
38. On the manner of decentralization, see, Schurmann, *op.cit.*, p. 175 et.seq.
39. "Speeches at the Second Session of the Eighth Party Congress" (8-23 May 1958) in *Miscellany, op.cit.* p. 112 (emphasis added)
40. Wheelwright and McFarlane, *op.cit.* p. 43 et.seq.
41. C. Riskin, "Small Industry and the Chinese Model of Development" *The China Quarterly*, no. 46 (April June 1971) p. 262
42. Schurmann, *op.cit.* p. 474 et.seq.
43. At the Peitaho Politburo Conference in August 1958. See "Resolution of the CCP Central Committee on the Establishment of People's Communes in Rural Areas" in *Documents of Chinese Communist Party Central Committee, September 1956 to April 1969*, Vol. 1 (Hong Kong, 1971) pp. 299-304.
44. Wheelwright and McFarlane, *op.cit.* p. 49
45. See, "Resolution on Some Questions Concerning the People's Communes" in *Documents of Chinese Communist Party, op.cit.* pp. 123-148
46. See Brugger, *Contemporary China op.cit.*, pp. 212-3 and p. 219; K. Walker, *Planning in Chinese Agriculture; Socialization and the Private Sector 1956-62* (London, 1965) pp. 75-92 for a somewhat different treatment on the role of the private plot in this period.
47. Wheelwright and McFarlane, *op.cit.*, p. 52
48. See F. Snow, *Red China Today* (Harmondsworth, 1970) p. 198 et.seq.
49. For example, Han Suyin, *China in the Year 2001* (Harmondsworth, 1970) pp. 80-1 claims that railways had their construction doubled during the Leap.
50. The Sino-Soviet dispute, although involving elements of differences due to clashes of national interests, was fundamentally an ideological dispute arising from the differing Chinese and Soviet approaches to socialist development.
51. One hundred and fifty-four plants had been finished by the time they withdrew. Wheelwright and McFarlane, *op.cit.* p. 35
52. See, for example, Kang Chao, "The Great Leap" in F. Schurmann and O. Schell (eds.) *Communist China* (Harmondsworth, 1971)
53. A classic example of this argument is presented by K. Walker, "Organization of Agricultural Production" in Eckstein, et.al. *op.cit.*
54. See, for example, Lippit, *op.cit.* pp. 93-4; Brugger, *Contemporary China. op.cit.* p. 212.
55. Former President of the People's Republic of China who was the main target of criticism during the Cultural Revolution.

56. Three Freedoms and One Contract. That is, the three freedoms:— 1) *extension* of plots of land for private production; 2) free markets; 3) *increase* of private enterprise. The one contract: — The allowing of each *household* to assume a contracted obligation toward the state for producing a fixed quantity of grain.
57. That is, the freedom to engage in usury; to hire labour; to sell land; and to run private enterprise.
58. See, *The Struggle Between the Two Roads in China's Countryside* (Peking, 1968) passim
59. B. Richman, *Industrial Society in Communist China* (New York, 1969) p. 230 noted that by 1964-5 "experts" had regained much of the prestige and pay differentials which they had held before the Leap.
60. *ibid*, p. 256
61. That is, profits made by an enterprise and retained by it to cover depreciation costs, and to finance its further investment.
62. Little has been written on the countryside during the Cultural Revolution. Virtually the only study to date is that of R. Baum, "The Cultural Revolution in the Countryside Anatomy of a Limited Rebellion" in T. Robinson (ed.) *The Cultural Revolution in China* (Berkeley, 1971) which is still very much based on attempting to transpose what was happening in urban areas onto the rural scene.
63. See Baum, *op.cit*. and C. MacDougall, "Collision in the Countryside" *Far Eastern Economic Review*, Vol. 63, No. 7 (February 13, 1969)
64. See, *Tachai — Standard Bearer in China's Agriculture* (Peking, 1972)
65. Chiang Ching; Chang Ch'un-ch'iao; Yao Wen-yuan; and Wang Hung-wen (the so-called "Shanghai radicals")
66. See J. Sigurdson, "Rural Industry — A Traveller's View" *The China Quarterly* no. 50 (April June 1972)
67. "Simultaneous Development of Large Size and Medium and Small Size Enterprises" *People's Daily*, August 24, 1970 in *Survey of China Mainland Press (SCMP)* no 4731 (September 2, 1970)
68. "1,800-odd Small Cement Works Set Up in the Whole Country" *People's Daily* November 29, 1971 in *SCMP* no 5032 (December 13, 1971)
69. *SCMP*, no 5089 (March 9, 1972)
70. *ibid*
71. "Hunan Province Develops Small Coal Pits" *Union Research Service*, vol. 69, no. 2 (October 6, 1972)
72. "China Builds More Small Cement Works", *SCMP* no 5291 (January 9, 1973)
73. "Rapid Increase of Small Hydro-electric Stations in China", *SCMP* no 5313 (February 13, 1973)
74. "China's Small Chemical Fertilizer Plants Increase Output" *SCMP* no 5372 (May 11, 1973)
75. First reported by Chou En-lai to Edgar Snow in January 1971. E. Snow, *The Long Revolution* (New York, 1971) p. 49
76. See, Kang Chao, "The Production and Application of Chemical Fertilizers in China" *The China Quarterly*, no. 64 (December, 1975)
77. See, B. Stavis, "China's Green Revolution" *Monthly Review*, vol. 26, no. 5 (October 1974)
78. T. Rawski, "Recent Trends in the Chinese Economy" *The China Quarterly* no 53 (January/March, 1973) p. 8
79. Stavis, *op.cit*. p. 21
80. I. Davies, *op.cit*. p. 133
81. D. Perkins, "Looking Inside China: An Economic Reappraisal" *Problems of Communism* (May/June 1973) p. 10 (China has since somewhat expanded her foreign trade but it still remains a small fraction of GNP.)
82. See, J. Horn, *Away with all Pests* (London, 1969) passim.

China's Relevance for Third World Development[1]

Bill Brugger

Western images of China have constantly changed. In the eighteenth century the French *philosophes*, protesting about European despotism, sought to emulate what appeared to them an ideal, rational, well ordered bureaucracy.[2] In the nineteenth century—during the heyday of imperalism, China appeared not as an object of envy but as a challenge to Western entrepreneurs, or to missionaries wishing to save the "Niagara of souls crashing down to perdition". In the early twentieth century China became the object of American paternalism and then, in the Cold War, the epitome of "totalitarian" evil. When it became clear that this last image was ridiculous, there was a swing in the other direction. China became a source of hope for those disillusioned by the failure of Third World development programmes. In the late 1970s a new image is emerging in which China is pictured— quite absurdly—as a confidence trick perpetrated by China International Travel Service. Yet throughout all those periods a body of quite sound scholarship existed which reveals a more balanced picture. The aspiring student is urged to be cautious.

THE HISTORICAL LEGACY

To assess the transferability of the Chinese developmental experiences we must first ask whether Chinese history before 1949 is at all comparable with the recent history of other Third

World states. Are the problems which confronted China before 1949 essentially the same as those which have confronted Third World states in more recent times? Was China trapped in a "vicious circle of poverty"? Was Chinese agriculture stagnating at a low level of productivity? Was society dominated by an ideology and characterised by a social structure inimical to economic development? Was the economy drastically distorted by Western and Japanese imperialism and totally paralysed by war? If the answer to these questions is affirmative, we may then proceed to a second stage in the examination—that of comparing the world situation of the 1940s with that of later periods. If, however, the answer is negative then using China as a yardstick will not be of much use. All we will be left with is an eclectic abstraction of policies about which we can only speculate.

The Size of the Surplus

When we begin to enquire about the nature of Chinese underdevelopment in the early twentieth century, we find that there is no consensus on the statistics, on the causes of underdevelopment or even the methodology with which to determine the causes. Perhaps the first thing we want to know is whether there existed in China a substantial surplus above subsistence, since without such a surplus there can be no internally generated investment and no self-sustaining growth.[3] If China had been in such a situation it would be possible to speak of a "vicious circle of poverty". What is this "vicious circle"? First, with regard to investment, it is argued that because people's incomes are low and total purchasing power thus limited, the size of the market is restricted. This makes investment unattractive and there is not much demand for capital to invest. Limited capital formation, in turn, limits productivity and thus helps keep incomes low. Secondly, with regard to the supply of savings, it is argued that low incomes limit people's capacity to save and this restricts the amount of capital available for investment. Because of low capital invested per worker, productivity remains low and so do incomes.[4] It is probably true that all countries have an untapped savings potential and there are always markets capable of sustaining some industrial development, but in some Third World countries the notion of a "vicious circle of poverty" does have some applicability. Did it in China?

Some economic historians claim that it is illegitimate to talk about the size of the surplus because it cannot be quantified.

This is so because the notion of subsistence is not absolute and the size of the surplus varies according to the degree of exploitation.[5] Other economic historians have dared to offer a tentative estimation of the size of the Chinese surplus in the 1930s and their data suggest it was quite large. According to one scholar the surplus constituted almost 30 per cent of net domestic product.[6] Given that some 30-40 per cent of agricultural output was marketed, it is apparent that one cannot talk about a "vicious circle of poverty", and in this respect China in the 1930s was in a position more fortunate than some Third World countries today.

The "High Equilibrium Trap"

Academic rigour might lead one to reject all "surplus" theories of economic history and to focus on technology. This is the position of those scholars who speak of China experiencing a "high equilibrium trap".[7] The "high equilibrium trap" theory holds that "traditional" technology had almost exhausted its potentialities. Agriculture, in particular, had stagnated (reached "equilibrium") at a very high level of sophistication. It was thus impossible significantly to raise yields per hectare without the importation of a complete package of modern technology. In this situation people were willing to invest in land for reasons of social prestige but there was little point in investing in the existing technology since so doing could not improve its productivity and thus would not yield a good return. The alleged exhaustion of possibilities for improving the efficiency of traditional technology combined with a dramatic population increase to reduce output to the level of subsistence. Whatever surplus there was had begun to disappear.

Like the "vicious circle of poverty" the notion of a "high equilibrium trap" has been challenged by scholars who want empirical evidence rather than the theoretical plausibility that the surplus was in fact disappearing. They claim that one cannot make a radical distinction between "traditional" and "modern" technology and there is no necessary correlation between any level of technology and the possibilities for improving it.[8] Thus, whatever "trap" there might have been must be explained by factors other than the technological. In my opinion such a challenge is convincing, but even if one were to accept the notion of a "high equilibrium trap", China was still more fortunate than some countries where the adjective "high" would be most inappropriate. There have been few Third World countries, outside Asia, in recent times where yields per hectare were as high as would be possible using 'traditional technology', i.e. without the use of selected seeds, chemical fertilisers, pesticides, electricity and power driven equipment.[9]

Ideological Factors

One argument against the theory of a "high equilibrium trap" is that when foreign technology first became available in China, it did not bring about any major change in investment priorities as the theory would predict. It is sometimes argued that this was because of the anti-technological bias of Confucian ideology which focussed on traditional harmony and gave a very low priority to industry and commerce.[10]

One cannot, of course, deny the importance of ideology. But Confucianism did not prevent China during the Sung dynasty (960-1280) from becoming economically the most advanced country on earth,[11] nor possibly from developing "the sprouts of capitalism" during the Ming dynasty (1368-1644). The most cogent argument against this ideological determinism, however, is that in Japan's early Tokugawa period (17th century), that country shared an ideology with China which was similarly hostile to economic development yet, by the end of the nineteenth century, that ideology was transformed into one which facilitated the development of a strange but vigorous capitalism.

Indeed it is possible to turn the argument on its head. Confucian ideology was anti-technological but it reflected ideal social relationships which were conducive to developing the trust and reliability necessary for business practice. These social relationships, exemplified by the secret societies, were based on simulated kinship (where people behaved towards other members of a group as they would towards their own kin).[12] This simulated kinship has proved to be very important in the development of capitalism amongst Overseas Chinese communities as well as in opposition to capitalism amongst labour movements in many countries. Thus, at the point where real kinship ties are displaced by simulated kinship, a framework may be created for economic development. It is perhaps for this reason that ideologies of simulated kinship (like the Tanzanian *ujamaa* [brotherhood]) are promoted in countries still bound by the restricted ties of real kinship.

The State and Social Structure

Another barrier to economic development in China was said to be the state structure. The nineteenth century Chinese state was a rigid bureaucratic hierarchy organised by, and in the interests of, an elite of scholar officials. This elite had its roots in a "gentry" stratum (which also included aspirant officials and their families). This stratum, in turn, was rooted in the landowning class. It has been argued that the gentry was unwilling to promote economic development because this might give rise to new entrepreneurial strata which could challenge its hegemony.[13] Thus, that part of the surplus which accrued to the gentry (largely through systemic corruption) was hoarded or spent on conspicuous consumption and could not be used for productive investment. We have noted that, for reasons of status, there was some investment in land, though this yielded only some 5-10 per cent per annum, which was about half the return on alternative investments.[14] By the late nineteenth century, however, the picture began to change. As a result of foreign pressure, the state began to promote a number of industries which were to be sold off to private entrepreneurs. Not surprisingly there were few takers with the result that these industries either fell under foreign control or were sold to officials who continued to maintain their state posts.[15] This was to give rise to the phenomenon of "bureaucratic capitalism" which remained a major feature of the Chinese economy throughout the early twentieth century.

The early state-run industries in China were extremely inefficient since they were not run according to the norms of capitalist business practice, but according to those of a disintegrating state bureaucracy. This was in marked contrast to Japan where the initiation of industry was also undertaken by the state. There, control was eventually transferred to very powerful families (*zaibatsu*) which maintained close ties with officialdom and the military, but efficiency was achieved through centralised fiscal policies and, most important, by the entrepreneurial orientation of a proto-middle class. In Japan blocked upward mobility during the earlier Tokugawa regime had produced an assertive grouping of *samurai* (traditional warriors) and merchants. These groups combined to develop an ideology compatible with both capitalism and militarism and assumed a leading role in one of the most spectacular economic revolutions in modern times. In China, on the other hand, a middle class was late in developing because easy upward mobility for commercial strata tended to cause ambitious merchants to invest in land and in official titles and degrees; there was thus no need for them to challenge the existing cultural orthodoxy.

This point is crucial. I suspect that it is almost always the case that the indigenous development of capitalism depends upon the existence of a pre-industrial middle class. This was the case in Japan and may also have some relevance to countries as diverse as Malaysia and Kenya. Most Third World countries were like China in that a discrete native middle class did not precede the appearance of a Western-oriented *bourgeoisie* (which is not the same thing).[16] China was different from most Third World countries in that it had a native élite of "bureaucratic capitalists". The existence of this élite in China south of the Great Wall, and in the Japanese dominated North East (from 1931 to 1945 the nominally independent state of Manchukuo), allowed for the relatively smooth take-over of much of the modern sector of the economy after 1949. This was achieved by the simple expedient of appropriating the Nationalist state and with it the property of a relatively few families with official ties. The existence of this élite also facilitated a policy pursued by the Communist Party of mobilising some of the smaller capitalists to oppose "bureaucratic capitalism" under the Party's banner. Perhaps in other Third World states, where control over the modern sector of the economy is more dispersed, the process of expropriation by a socialist regime may not be such a simple operation.

The Impact of Imperialism

It is probably true, however, that control over the modern sector in many Third World economies is anything but diffuse. It is concentrated in the hands of a few multinational corporations which have managed to distort the economy in their own interests. We must consider, therefore, the extent to which the Chinese economy was similarly distorted by foreign economic interests in the early twentieth century. Here we find another polemic, more intense even than that on the size of the Chinese surplus. The debate concerns the magnitude of the impact of imperialism. As in all such arguments, what is quantifiable is capable of different interpretations, and what seems crucial often cannot be quantified.

One thing which can be quantified is the relative flow of funds in and out of the country. We might, therefore, be in a position to apply the theory of A. G. Frank.[17] This holds that investment and other cash flows into a Third World country may serve a priming function whereby a far greater amount of money may be repatriated to the metropolitan countries than was originally invested, thus removing part of the surplus needed for development. In China in the years 1902-1913 for every dollar which flowed into China, $1.40 left the country. This outflow reached the quite serious figures of $5.26 per dollar in 1931, $3.85 in 1933 and $3.33 in 1936.[18] But how significant was this? If we take Magdoff's point that what is significant is not the annual flow of funds but the impact of the total foreign capital stock in a Third World country,[19] then these figures do not mean very much since in China, as in most Third World countries, new foreign investment was financed by retained profits. What we need to assess is the blocking effect of foreign capital stock, and this is very difficult to quantify. If we take Frank's own point that these figures have meaning only in terms of the proportion of the surplus which is siphoned off, then we are back to the earlier argument about whether it is possible to quantify the surplus. V. Lippit, who was cited earlier with regard to his calculations of the Chinese surplus in 1933, has concluded that the outflow for that year was only just over 1 per cent of that surplus and thus capital drain could not be a major factor in the "development of underdevelopment".[20] C. Riskin, however, a founder of the "surplus" school, is not too impressed by figures showing the flow of funds and suggests we look at the blocking function of foreign imperialism. After all, even if it could be established beyond reasonable doubt that China's underdevelopment was overwhelmingly due to internal problems, one could still offer the hypothesis that it only required a limited foreign penetration to block any remedial measures which might have been taken.[21]

Any comprehensive discussion of the impact of imperialism on the Chinese economy would have to go much further than a discussion of capital flow. It would need to take into account the inflation and the social costs of insurrection consequent upon many of the foreign wars as well as the indemnities which the Chinese government had to pay. Such a discussion would have to determine the extent to which warlordism might have been prolonged by foreign support. To do all this, however, one would have to weigh the relative importance of domestic and foreign factors, and this is well nigh impossible. The spin-off effects of foreign domination of key sectors of the economy such as mining and modern transport (a typical feature of early imperialist penetration) are also important but these defy quantification.[22] Suffice it to say here that the fact that Chinese-owned industry developed by leaps and bounds during the First World War when foreign powers were distracted elsewhere is *prima facie* evidence of a considerable blocking effect.

However great the impact of foreign imperialism may have been, it is clear that no structure of dependence was built up. This is evident when one looks at trade. In the second half of the nineteenth century, tea and silk, the main exports, were very adversely affected by Japanese competition, and this led to peasant privation. But, in general, exports were a very small percentage of GDP and such effects were not widespread. China cannot be compared with those countries in which the effects of foreign competition on the principal exports may wreck the economy. Imports of opium did have an effect far beyond their share of GDP, and later imports of cotton yarn and kerosene seriously disrupted domestic handicraft production, but again the share of imports in GDP was too small to cause the degree of disruption that has occurred in some Third World states in more recent times.[23] The treaty port structure which was set up along the coast did produce something like a "dual economy", but there was nothing like the distorting effect that the "modern sector" has elsewhere in Third World economies. Thus, one may conclude that whatever the magnitude of the impact of imperialism may have been, the effect was not one of gross economic distortion. The Chinese economy was in no way comparable with those of many contemporary Third World states which are skewed towards the export of one or two primary products. Imperialist penetration did promote a vigorous nationalist movement but it was not powerful enough to force the leaders of that movement to participate in a new state structure which could lead only to neo-colonial subservience.

The nationalist movement in China, as in so many Third World states, developed as a response to Western and Japanese imperialism. Yet in China this movement was more successful than in most in welding together diverse regional loyalties. This is perhaps because it built upon symbols of a long cultural tradition. I do not know how successful President Nyerere will be in developing a "Tanzanian tradition", and I do not envisage success for those who seek to create a nationalism in countries whose boundaries consist of lines arbitrarily drawn in the nineteenth century by European colonial powers.

The Impact of War

It is extremely difficult to determine the relative importance of foreign and internal war in inhibiting the development of the Chinese economy, but there can be no doubt that war generally caused severe privation—especially after the 1920s. Peasant standards of living experienced a sharp decline and the problem of landlessness became serious. These wars produced runaway inflation, the destruction of plant and equipment, the looting of much of industry in the former state of Manchukuo and the deliberate flooding of millions of hectares of land. Yet despite the devastation, the wars helped to produce a number of policies conducive to development which could not so easily be initiated in peacetime.

The Yenan "model", for example, had its origins in guerilla war in the Shen Kan Ning border region in 1942 and was dictated by the exigencies of the anti-Japanese campaign and the Nationalist blockade.[24] The policy of mobilising a broadly based "united front" (which even included some landlords) to oppose the principal enemy was a product of the Japanese invasion and was facilitated by the brutality of Japanese "mopping up operations". The "united front" strategy made possible a programme of rent reduction (rather than outright class struggle) out of which the typical "campaign style of politics" was to emerge. The idea of the "cadre", whose commitment to general Party policy was reinforced by "rectification" but who was allowed considerable operational independence, developed out of the requirements of a fragmented system of revolutionary bases. Similarly, the policy of centralising industrial policy whilst productive activities were dispersed was adopted not only out of a desire to diffuse industrial techniques amongst the peasants, but because dispersed operations provided protection against Japanese air attack. Other features of the "model" such as "the mass line", the transformation of existing structures from within, and "people-run" education had great intrinsic value, but such value was only fully discovered after these policies had been initiated for largely instrumental reasons. These derived from the exigencies of mobilising people for war. Significantly other countries which have developed the Chinese style of mobilisation (Vietnam, Laos and Guinea Bissau) have done so in similar kinds of war.

The peculiar nature of Chinese land reform might also be explained by the fact that it was initiated in times of very acute Civil War (1946-49). It was no light matter for peasants to participate in this process since battles along fluid and shifting fronts meant that peasants had to be prepared to face reprisals if ground was temporarily surrendered to the enemy. The consequences were twofold. First, it was extremely difficult to mobilise peasants to take part in land reform and the Yenan leadership style was stretched to the limits. Secondly, when peasants were persuaded to take the initiative, they sometimes took the law into their own hands and tried to eliminate any landlords who might cause them trouble if the Nationalist armies returned. By 1948, it was clear that the Communist Party was having considerable difficulty controlling the "hurricane" they had brought about, and hundreds of thousands of people were killed in violation of Party directives. Despite the chaos, however, the tense atmosphere of 1947-48 brought about a commitment to the whole process of revolution. It was not possible for the peasant just to work his newly acquired land. He had participated in an act of violence which involved an identification with the cause of the Communist Party.[25] Rarely has peacetime land reform brought about such a situation.

The above should not be taken as a celebration of war. It is possible that in some countries mass mobilisation and radical land reform might be brought about in peacetime conditions. I suspect, however, that such policies will benefit little from China's peacetime experiences in this respect since the very nature of those peacetime experiences were determined by leadership strategies and patterns of commitment fostered in war.

Summary

The argument so far demonstrates that the pre-1949 Chinese situation was unique among Third World nations, and that the war-torn economy of 1949 possessed a number of features which facilitated a successful development strategy given the continuation of the right kind of leadership. While traditional ideology had certainly inhibited economic development in the past, it contained features which, if successfully modified, might actually stimulate a certain form of development in the future. The nineteenth century state structure had broken down, yet its legacy had facilitated the nationalisation of much of the modern sector of the economy. The toll taken by imperialism had indeed been severe, but the economy had not been distorted to the point that neo-colonialism was inevitable. Finally it was clear that, although war had set the economy back some years, it had given rise to a pattern of leadership and a mood of commitment among the masses which could do much to remedy all but purely technological problems. Whether there is such a thing as a "purely" technological problem depends, in this context, on whether one accepts the arguments about the "high equilibrium trap".

THE LIMITS OF SELF RELIANCE

The Significance of the Cold War

If China's pre-1949 history contained elements which were conducive to economic development so did the impact of the Cold War. Those who support the notion of a "high equilibrium trap" would, of course, deny this. According to their view, the Cold War could only be a disadvantage since it cut China off from the capitalist world and prevented the importation of technology necessary for the country to break out of the "trap". This view is supported by evidence that agricultural yields per hectare were not significantly raised during the height of the Cold War in the 1950s[26] and it was not until the 1960s that better technology and better seed strains brought about some improvement. The technology which was imported into China during the first decade of the People's Republic was devoted to a "Soviet-style" heavy industry and this was to give rise to organisational problems and an acute investment crisis. Even in the 1960s, however, the technology which China imported to aid agriculture was insufficient for the country to escape from the alleged trap and it is probable that the post-Mao Tsetung leadership perceives this.

In 1973, M. Elvin, the leading exponent of this school, prophesied:

> "Chinese agriculture... can only grow fast by using a vast and ever increasing quantity of industrial inputs, and can therefore never be a leading sector. If industry is to advance rapidly enough to let agriculture, and the economy as a whole, break out once and for all from the old high-level trap, it almost certainly needs to enter the international market to a far greater extent than hitherto. It is capable of doing this with an effectiveness that will come as a shock, if the decision to do so is taken. The consequence, however, will be a disruption of the control over information and thought which is essential to the survival of the Chinese Communist regime."[27]

I suspect that such a decision has been taken in the last two years (1976-78) and the consequences concern not just control but the socialist nature of China's development. I am not at all sure what Elvin means by control over thought, though information in China is certainly controlled. I do not, however, see any correlation between control over information and participation in the international capitalist economy. What is more to the point is that, although greater participation in the international capitalist economy might in the short run raise crop yields, it might also give rise to some quite serious economic problems. Inflation, endemic in the capitalist world, might be imported into China. The purchase of complete plants from overseas might disrupt the Chinese strategy of "walking on two legs" (integrating the old and the new, the large and the small and the agricultural and industrial sectors). China might incur a huge burden of debt in its desire to modernise and might be tempted to set up "export processing zones" (capitalist enclaves in which foreign firms derive considerable profits from cheap native labour). Can socialism survive in such a situation? Unlike Elvin I can envisage the survival of the present Chinese regime long after socialist strategies have disappeared. But unlike many pessimists on the Left, I am not convinced that, now the Cold War is over, China has in fact embarked upon a strategy which will lead to dependence upon the capitalist world. To deny such a danger exists, however, would be an act of blindness.

If, on the other hand, one accepts the arguments of the "surplus" theorists, then China's autarchic pattern of development may have been quite sensible. Before the advent of the Korean War in 1950, China could possibly have developed strong economic ties with the West, which could have produced a relationship of dependence. But it was the West which cut itself off from China and this helped bolster the feelings of national solidarity engendered over many years in the fight against the Japanese. Utilising these feelings of national solidarity, the new regime was able to mobilise the quite substantial surplus and channel it into productive investment.

With the recurrence of class polarisation following land reform in the early 1950s, it was this national solidarity which, augmenting revolutionary commitment and cadre leadership, helped bring about rapid rural co-operativisation. The same solidarity helped develop a strong state structure necessary for cleaning up corruption, reorganising urban ghettos and providing for the unification of *policy* without which there could be no successful decentralisation of *operations*. This "backs to the wall" mentality enabled some of the well-to-do to give up their privileges, and some of the less well-to-do to put up with temporary inequalities for the sake of national defence. The same mentality allowed the state initially to assign high accumulation targets in the rural sector, confident that there would be no great resistance,[28] and which later made possible the ambitious schemes of the Great Leap Forward. The latter, despite all its failures, laid the basis for much that is distinctive about the (pre-1976) Chinese path to development. Thus, though technology was important, it was the institutional changes of the middle and late 1950s which brought about a structure in which that technology could most effectively be used. It was, moreover, the Cold War which facilitated these changes. Now that the Cold War is over, it is possible for China to continue to pursue a relatively autarchic policy and to avoid an excessive reliance on the capitalist world.

Thus, if one accepts the arguments of the "high equilibrium trap" theorists, China's experiences developed during the Cold War are not worth emulating. According to this theory, any future developmental success which China might enjoy will be the result of the impact of technological imports on a very sophisticated traditional technology. If China enters the international economy with "an effectiveness which will come as a shock", no other countries would be able to emulate such a policy. This is because countries in which a similar "high equilibrium trap" may once have existed have long since entered the international economy. If, on the other hand, one accepts the argument based on "surplus" theory, then the Chinese experiences may only be emulated by those countries which have a similar high surplus—and one doubts whether there are many of those. In any case, countries hoping to emulate the Chinese approach will have to contend with a situation where there is no Cold War to create a feeling of national solidarity which may help channel that surplus into productive investment.

The Size Factor

There is no consensus as to the relative importance of social change and technology in raising crop yields in the 1960s and 1970s or whether China's autarchy was an unqualified good thing. I have argued that in the absence of a Cold War it is difficult for anyone to contemplate the recurrence of Chinese-style autarchy but, even under Cold War conditions, it is doubtful whether any type of autarchy might be embarked upon on by most small Third World countries and succeed. The question of size is, after all, very important. As we have seen, China's internal market is huge and its resources rich. China is thus able to profit from economies of scale which, though overstressed in much of the economic literature, cannot be disregarded. "Small" may be "beautiful" but "big" is sometimes necessary.

To illustrate this point let us compare China and Cuba. Both of these countries were cut off by the West, both made the mistake of devoting too much attention to industry in the early developmental phase, and both switched their focus to agriculture.[29] The effects of this mistake were, however, quite different. In China, once the mix of agriculture and industry was adjusted, industry still continued to grow at a rate faster than agriculture.[30] In Cuba, it became obvious that any policy of "walking on two legs" must depend upon foreign support for the industrial sector and this support could only come from the Soviet Union and Eastern Europe; a new structure of dependency was thus established. Certainly many countries may emulate the Chinese policy of "walking on two legs" but it should always be remembered that the sheer size of the Chinese economy has made its legs longer than most.

The size of the Chinese economy also meant that China was able to embark much earlier than most Third World countries on a policy of industrial diversification (though an inherited economic infrastructure was very important in this regard). This is not to claim that industrial diversification is ruled out in most Third World countries. It is merely to say that small ex-colonies will have to diversify much later and according to a different model. There is much argument about what that model should be. One solution which the Chinese themselves seem to support in other parts of the world is the development of regional common markets. These, however, whilst enlarging markets, often fail to deploy resources rationally and often perpetuate regional underdevelopment. One only needs to ask a Scottish nationalist or a Southern Italian to dispel doubts about this. Another solution is to work out plans for tying together the state sectors of a number of adjacent countries so that resources are deployed rationally. To prevent regional underdevelopment, these plans would have to be based on socialist principles of mutual benefit. This is what the East European Common Market (CMEA) tried to do but I doubt whether the complaints of a Rumanian nationalist would differ much from those of the Scottish nationalist. Refinements of planning based on socialist mutual benefit have been proposed for parts of the Third World[31] but I suspect that ethnic factors, local nationalism and the structure of the world capitalist economy are stacked against the success of such proposals. It is probably only in large countries like India, where the basis for political unity exists, that a policy of self reliance might successfully be pursued. But, should its leaders seek to implement such a policy, size seems to be almost the only asset which India has.

The discussion here has focussed on the relationship between size and autarchy. A much more important question is the relationship between size and any kind of economic development. This is a relatively unexplored field of political economy.[32] What is the relative importance of crucial resources at various times in history? What is the importance of geographical location? How important are fortuitous political changes and technological innovation? No general theory has as yet been worked out which can begin to answer these questions and perhaps there never will be. But only a very one-eyed political economist may claim that it is not worth the effort.

THE NEW DIFFUSIONISM[33]

In much of the Third World it seems that the Chinese style of revolution might be a necessary condition for the Chinese style of development. Yet that revolution was a product of historical circumstances which are not likely to occur again. There is, however, a growing body of literature which talks about emulating the Chinese experiences in the world as it is now. Many types of regime, it is claimed, could adopt an "open door" programme of education (see below) and integrate modern and intermediate technology. Quite a few regimes, could learn from China's relatively egalitarian social programmes. An earlier generation of developmentalists naively believed that Western technique might be diffused into the Third World and result in development. The same mistake is now being made with respect to Chinese technique. It would be dogmatic to condemn all diffusionism out of hand but the same kind of objections which constituted the left wing critique of the 1960s may be applied in this context too.[34]

Education

The "open door" system of education aimed at closing the gap between schools and society by involving the general public in school management, emphasising practical skills and testing them outside the formal institutions. It involved employing workers and peasants as teachers and shortening courses to produce a lot of semi-skilled people rather than a few highly skilled technocrats. In general it aimed at creating the conditions for mass fulfillment rather than selecting an elite. In the long run it was believed that this would contribute more to economic development than the orthodox policy. In the short run, however, standards might well suffer and there would be some discrimination against the able. The same logic underpinned the schemes to extend medical services over the whole country using "barefoot doctors", and to raise the literacy level of the masses by calling upon the services of educated youth sent down to the countryside.

In a less controlled and less revolutionary society, however, the involvement of the public in school management might easily result in teaching policies more antiquated than those wished for by even the most conservative teacher. A stress on testing practical skills outside the formal institutions might become a way of exploiting cheap labour. The employment of workers and peasants to teach students might result in mutual contempt. Short courses might frustrate the wishes of ambitious parents and alienate the fully trained professionals who might protect their position by trade union action. Once standards were felt to decline, students might migrate overses in search of more highly valued academic qualifications. Even in China, the "open door" scheme was not without problems and since 1976 it has been severely modified.[35] Being in a hurry to modernise by the year 2000, China could not waste time by not making the full use of trained labour. Critics noted that it might be satisfying to have everyone experimenting with technology, but it was wasteful to have people inventing things which had already been invented elsewhere. The critics, however, seem to have forgotten the long term benefits of developing mass creativity. Since 1976, China, one of the most far-sighted nations on earth, has narrowed its horizons to the year 2000. This experience does not augur well for countries without such a deep sense of history.

Agro-Industrial Integration

The policy of "walking on two legs" would appear to be of great value in any developing country.[36] The fusion of units of administration, residence and production in China helped to solve the problem of seasonal underemployment, to make local education systems relevant to the needs of production and to increase the technological awareness of the peasants. As Mao saw it, socialism would mean very little so long as the gap between town and country, so typical of underdeveloped countries, remained. The same might be argued for capitalist modernisation since growth depends on enlarging the rural market. This may only be done by increasing the purchasing power of the peasants and the best way to do this is to diversify the rural economy. Since technology "trickles down" to the rural areas very slowly, the state must create organisations in which the industrial and financial sectors assume responsibility for technological diffusion.

I have already mentioned a number of factors which might

affect the success of agro-industrial integration. These include the size of the economy, the strength of the state apparatus, and the dedication of its officials. Even if all these factors were favourable, such a policy would depend upon the security of tenure enjoyed by government, since agro-industrial integration depends on the effectiveness of long term planning. Few Third world governments enjoy that security of tenure. Where weak elected governments are in power, it is likely that, in the short run, more electoral support will be generated by imports of flashy technology rather than by policies of agro-industrial integration. Where military governments are in power, we might expect a concentration on sophisticated military technology which is very difficult to integrate with anything else. But perhaps most important of all, there is little likelihood that much can be achieved unless the modern sector of the economy is in state hands. Since fiscal measures (taxation etc.) are rarely sufficient to promote agro-industrial integration, outright state control seems to be required. Meanwhile much of the "modern sector" in third World states is under foreign control. To nationalise it whilst it is still oriented towards an international market would be to court trouble (as the case of Chile has shown). To wait until sufficient diversification has already occurred might be to wait for ever.

Egalitarianism and Revolution

Finally we must consider what chances egalitarian policies might have in Third World development. With one or two exceptions (e.g. Taiwan) most underdeveloped countries which have experienced rapid growth have also experienced a widening of income differentials. This, some Western economists say, has to be the case in the first stage of industrialisation, since this is the only way that sufficient savings can be generated to promote investment. Even amongst socialists it is sometimes argued that such inequalities might be necessary for the development of incentive until socialist consciousness becomes sufficiently developed. I tend to doubt this, but the recent policies announced by the Chinese government concerning modernisation have not done much to fortify my position. All that needs be said here is that egalitarian policies are unlikely to be successful in most Third World countries where there is resistance to the payment of taxes. This is due to low political commitment which, in turn, is because poor countries tend to be governed by corrupted elites. We have seen in the case of China that revolutionary morale can do much to rectify this but first there must be a revolution. For reasons already stated, such revolutions in the Third World are unlikely to resemble that of China.

There is perhaps one thing which revolutionary leaders may learn from China and that concerns the definition of revolution itself. Revolution in China came to be seen, not just as an act whereby a revolutionary party seizes power, but as a whole range of policies aimed at restricting the social division of labour and creating an egalitarian society. Socialism was not a state of affairs to be aimed at, nor the right frame of mind to be adopted when drafting policies. It was the process whereby the capitalist system was destroyed. It was, moreover, *reversible*. For socialist policies to be pursued a strong party was needed, yet that party reflected interest groups which might provide a basis for the formation of new social classes, and these could reverse the whole revolutionary enterprise. Such a reversal could not be prevented by introducing safeguards in party rules; it could only be prevented by a mass movement initiated outside the party.

Though the Chinese Cultural Revolution of 1966-69 was only in part informed by the above view of "continuous revolution",[37] it represented one of the few instances where a section of a party in power initiated mass criticism of the abuse of that power. In retrospect, it seems that the abuses the Cultural Revolution sought to remedy are still very much part of the Chinese political system and if, as Mao hoped, there is a second Cultural Revolution, it will be very different from the first. Many of China's present leaders may well prefer to consign the Cultural Revolution to the museums of history, alongside other "glorious", but embarassing memories such as the Paris Commune of 1871. There will, I am sure, be much discussion in China in the next few years, about the excesses and mistakes of the Cultural Revolution—and who can deny that there were many—but the problem with which it sought to deal is a persistent one! In the process of socialist development how might one prevent the means (party control, industrialisation and a focus on science and technology) perverting the ends (a fully human, egalitarian, co-operative society)?

For capitalists, I suspect that there is not much which may be learned from China. But socialists may learn how human beings responded at a particular historical time, in a country with unique characteristics, to the crucial problem of means and ends. This is a problem which all socialists have confronted since the time of Marx. Mao would have argued that there is no Chinese model to "export" for he, at least, took history seriously.

But, in as much as the problems which China faced in the 1950s and 1960s reflected perennial problems of socialist revolution, China's experiences are worth studying. What may be diffused are not so much particular techniques of development, but the theory which made China's development possible. If that theory is diffused in the form of a package of past policies, the result will be much the same kind of dogmatism against which Mao battled for much of his life. If, however, the theory is diffused in such a way that China's experiences may offer us some insight into the limits of human spontaneity and creativity in a changed world, the "impossible" which China achieved in the 1950s and 1960s may be achieved again.

FOOTNOTES

1. Thanks to Naomi Clare, Steve Reglar, Andrew Watson, Dennis Woodward and Graham Young for their helpful comments.
2. On Western views see F. Wakeman Jr., "The Chinese Mirror", in M. Oksenberg (ed.), *China's Developmental Experience* (New York, 1973) pp. 208-19.
3. On different views of what might constitute a "surplus" see C. Riskin "Surplus and Stagnation in Modern China", in D. Perkins (ed.), *China's Modern Economy in Historical Perspective* (Stanford, 1975). pp. 49-84.
4. The classic form of this may be found in R. Nurske, *Problems of Capital Formation in Underdeveloped Countries* (Oxford, 1953), pp. 4-11. See also the discussion in M. Elvin, *The Pattern of the Chinese Past* (Stanford, 1973), pp. 286-89 and V. Lippit, "The Development of Underdevelopment in China", *Modern China* Vol. 4, No. 3, July 1978, pp. 271-73.
5. M. Elvin, "Comment", in *ibid.*, pp. 329-30.
6. Lippit *loc. cit.*, p. 273 and Riskin, *loc. cit.*, p. 74 (Riskin's figure is 27.2 percent). See also Riskin's reply to Elvin, in *Modern China, op. cit.*, pp. 366-70.
7. See Elvin 1973, *op. cit.*, pp. 298-316.
8. Lippit, *loc. cit.*, pp. 287-94.
9. Elvin 1973, *op. cit.*, p. 306.
10. This is the argument of M. Wright, *The Last Stand of Chinese Conservatism* (Stanford, 1957).
11. For an excellent account of "China's medieval economic revolution" see Elvin 1973, *op. cit.*, pp. 111-99.

12. My ideas on simulated kinship and the economy were developed from J. Bennett and Ishino Iwao, *Paternalism in the Japanese Economy* (Minneapolis, 1963). I have speculated on its importance in China (though only concerning labour recruitment) in W. Brugger, *Democracy and Organisation in the Chinese Industrial Enterprise (1948-1953)* (Cambridge, 1976) pp. 42-45.
13. See Lippit *loc. cit.*, pp. 299-323.
14. *Ibid.*, p. 301.
15. See A. Feuerwerker, "China's Nineteenth Century Industrialisation: The Case of the Hanyehping Coal and Iron Company Limited", in C. Cowan (ed.), *The Economic Development of China and Japan* (London, 1964) pp. 79-110, and A. Feuerwerker, *China's Early Industrialisation: Sheng Hsuan-huai (1844-1916) and Mandarin Enterprise* (Cambridge, Mass., 1958).
16. G. D. H. Cole (*Studies in Class Structure* [London, 1955] pp. 90-91) defines a bourgeoisie as "a body of citizens asserting their collective as well as their individual independence of a social system dominated by feudal power based on land holding and the services attached to it, whereas the words 'middle class' call up a quite different image of a body of persons who are placed between two other bodies—or perhaps more than two—in some sort of stratified social order".
17. See Lippit *loc. cit.*, pp. 278-79 and A. Frank's reply, "Development of Under-development or Underdevelopment of Development in China", in *Modern China, op. cit.*, pp. 341-50.
18. Hou Chi-ming, *Foreign Investment and Economic Development in China* (Cambridge, Mass., 1965) pp. 99-100.
19. H. Magdoff, *The Age of Imperialism* (New York, 1969) p. 10.
20. Lippit *loc. cit.*, p. 279.
21. C. Riskin, "The Symposium Papers: Discussion and Comments", in *Modern China, op. cit.*, p. 363.
22. J. Esherick ("Harvard in China: the Apologetics of Imperialism", *Bulletin of Concerned Asian Scholars*, Vol. 4, No. 4, December 1972, pp. 9-16) argues a strong case for the importance of imperialism.
23. Lippit, *loc. cit.*, pp. 275-78.
24. See M. Selden, *The Yenan Way in Revolutionary China* (Cambridge, Mass., 1971).
25. See W. Hinton, *Fanshen: A Documentary of Revolution in a Chinese Village* (New York, 1968).
26. Elvin 1973, *op. cit.*, p. 319.
27. *Ibid.*, p. 308.
28. This is not to say that at times (e.g. 1954) grain exactions were not excessive and that peasants passively accepted them. See T. Bernstein, "Cadre and Peasant Behaviour Under Conditions of Insecurity and Deprivation: The Grain Supply Crisis of the Spring of 1955", in A. Barnett, *Chinese Communist Politics in Action* (Seattle, 1969) pp. 365-99.
29. See L. Huberman and P. Sweezy, *Socialism in Cuba* (New York, 1969) pp. 65-85.
30. Industrial growth rates in China have been estimated at 18-23% p.a. (1952-60), before the switch to agricultural priority and 5-6% (1960-74) after the switch. There has been much debate about grain output. One estimate puts the growth rate at 2.2% (1952-7) followed by a rise in 1958 and then a sharp decline during the years of natural calamities. From 1963-66, the rate was about 6%. There was then a decline to 2%. See A. Eckstein, *China's Economic Revolution* (Cambridge, 1977) pp. 210-11 and 219.
31. See C. Thomas, *Dependence & Transformation: The Economics of the Transition to Socialism* (New York, 1974).

32. See E. Robinson (ed.), *Economic Consequences of the Size of Nations, Proceedings of a Conference held by the International Economic Association*, (London, 1963).
33. See J. Gurley, *China's Economy and the Maoist Strategy* (New York, 1976) pp. 299-325. Oksenberg (ed.), *op. cit.*, consists of a collection of symposium papers evaluating what in fact might be diffused. They are concerned particularly with what the United States might learn.
34. An example of such a critique is S. Bodenheimer, "The Ideology of Developmentalism: American Political Science's Paradigm-surrogate for Latin American Studies", *Berkeley Journal of Sociology*, Vol. 15, 1970, pp. 95-137.
35. See S. Pepper, "Education and Revolution: The 'Chinese Model' Revisited", *Asian Survey*, Vol. XVIII, No. 9, September 1978, pp. 847-90.
36. See J. Sigurdson, "Rural Industry and the Internal Transfer of Technology", in S. Schram (ed.), *Authority Participation and Cultural Change in China* (Cambridge, 1973), pp. 199-232.
37. For a discussion of this concept, see G. Young and D. Woodward, "From Contradictions among the People to Class Struggle: The Theories of Uninterrupted Revolution and Continuous Revolution", *Asian Survey, op. cit.*, pp. 912-33.

For Product Safety Concerns and Information please contact our EU representative GPSR@taylorandfrancis.com
Taylor & Francis Verlag GmbH, Kaufingerstraße 24, 80331 München, Germany

www.ingramcontent.com/pod-product-compliance
Lightning Source LLC
Chambersburg PA
CBHW071237300426
44116CB00008B/1070